Peter Quennell

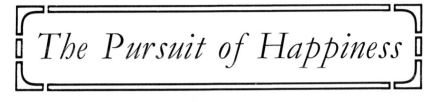

The Pursuit of Happiness

Constable · London

First published in Great Britain 1988
by Constable and Company Limited
10 Orange Street London WC2H 7EG
Copyright © 1988 by Peter Quennell
Set in Monophoto Garamond 12pt by
Servis Filmsetting Ltd, Manchester
Printed in Great Britain by
St Edmundsbury Press, Suffolk

British Library CIP data
Quennell, Peter, *1905*–
The pursuit of happiness
1. Happiness – Philosophical perspectives
I. Title
128'.3

ISBN 0 09 465790 4

To Alexander Quennell

Contents

Illustrations

ILLUSTRATIONS

I

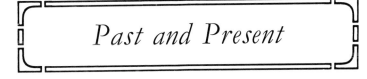

Past and Present

THE origins of almost every book lie hidden somewhere in the writer's past; and my concern with happiness I can certainly trace back to an early period of my childhood. I had then an introspective and vaguely meditative turn that puzzled or annoyed my elders; and I recollect how, many years before I had heard of the great Spanish dramatist Calderon de la Barca, who once chose the haunting sentence '*Life is a dream*' as the title of a play, I was occasionally troubled by the fear that my own pleasant daily routine might prove to be a baseless vision, and that I should presently wake up to find myself in far gloomier surroundings.

I also questioned the real significance of familiar words and phrases. 'Happy', for example. What did 'happiness' mean? Was I happy, and were my parents happy? True, my mother now and then looked sad; she had a nervous disposition. But my father, I long believed, despite all the reverses he had suffered since the outbreak of the First World War, led a cheerfully courageous life, until one day, having just received before breakfast a letter from an admiring female correspondent in which she congratulated him on the splendid work he did, and referred to the happiness he and his wife must enjoy writing and illustrating side by side, he suddenly remarked 'Well, we're *not* happy, are we?' with an expression of profound despair.

The mood soon passed; and, seeing that my mother was both hurt and astonished, he hastened to make affectionate amends. But I never forgot the episode. My father was no Romantic, at least in the accepted literary sense; nor was he a self-tormenting melancholic. He preferred facts to feelings, solid, finely-built objects to ideas or intellectual theories. He fought off doubts that threatened his peace of mind, regarded human happiness, I think, as the legitimate reward of a decent, ordinary career – those two last adjectives, by the way, in his vocabulary were terms of warm approval – and would have refused to admit that the condition called 'being happy' was a rare, mysterious privilege, not necessarily bestowed on virtue, or that its pursuit – frequently a vain pursuit – had perplexed and fascinated imaginative artists for the last two thousand years.

Yet even my father, I remembered, had suffered a momentary pang of doubt; and in later life I have sometimes urged my friends to discuss their personal views of this strange, entrancing state, and asked them how often they could claim that they had unmistakably experienced it. Their answers varied. While some spoke of happiness as a welcome yet always wayward visitor, which unpredictably descended and no less rapidly departed, others told of brief luminous moments, when they had not only been happy but had *known* they were happy and delighted in the knowledge; when, moreover, they had felt so much at peace with themselves, and by extension with the whole universe, that, like Jean-Jacques Rousseau on the Ile Saint-Pierre, they had seemed to soar beyond the reach of Time.

After consulting my friends, I next applied for help to historians and lexicographers. The idea of happiness, I was reminded, had had a very long history; the meaning of the words had slowly changed and each metamorphosis had reflected the changing climate of a different social epoch. In the Middle Ages and the Elizabethan heyday, it signified primarily 'good-hap', otherwise good luck, or the fortunate realisation of some personal design. That was its Shakespearian connotation:

> 'Wish me partaker in thy happiness
> When thou dost meet good hap'

exclaims Proteus, one of the *Two Gentlemen of Verona*, bidding Valentine farewell; and, as the description of a human quality, it was used to mean 'apt', 'appropriate', 'well-suited', or conveyed an air of physical accomplishment. 'He hath indeed a good outward happiness' says Don Pedro in *Much Ado about Nothing* of the highly personable Benedick.

Underlying most early uses of the word we can usually detect the assumption that happiness is a by-product of worldly success, gained either by heroic endeavour or by some brilliant stroke of fortune. Then, during the seventeenth century, it gradually acquired a far subtler and more interesting significance, and began to denote not so much a man's prosperous condition as an harmonious or exalted frame of mind. But it still possessed a double value; and, towards the end of the century, in the grandiose valedictory speech that John Dryden gave to the hero of his blank-verse tragedy *All for Love*, where Mark Antony reviews his squandered life, both shades of meaning are apparently combined:

> 'I was so great, so happy, so belov'd,
> Fate could not ruin me; till I took pains
> And work'd against my fortune, chid her from me . . .
> My careless days and my luxurious nights
> At length have wearied her, and now she's gone,
> Gone, gone, divorced for ever.'

Does Antony, the reader may well ask, most regret the joys of his temporal or those of his emotional existence – the belief that Cleopatra loves him, or the knowledge that he has conquered half the Roman world? Dryden, dictator of literary taste, dramatist and melodious lyricist, died in the first year of the next century; and his throne was rightly occupied by his heir presumptive Alexander Pope, who, between 1733 and 1734, published his ambitious *Essay on Man*, and opened its fourth section with a bold 'address to Happiness', which hails the emotion that it applauds, but cannot precisely define, as a 'seed' that has been dropped from heaven:

> 'Oh Happiness! our being's end and aim!
> Good, Pleasure, Ease, Content! Whate'er thy name:
> That something still which prompts th'eternal sigh,
> For which we bear to live, or dare to die . . .'

Once accepted, and fixed in memorable lines, by an Augustan master-poet, the idea rapidly extended its scope; and this book is an attempt to follow the subsequent pursuit of happiness as it has been recorded by creative artists, and has affected the works and lives of individual men and women. Happiness is clearly multiform. The Greeks coined some six nouns to describe it (of which *eudaimonia* was the word that Aristotle used) and an equal number to denote the supplementary emotion joy, ranging from '*hédoné*', sensuous delight, to '*epicharma*', quietly malicious fun. By comparison, the resources of English and French – 'happiness' and '*bonheur*' developed simultaneously – are a great deal more limited. Yet, in each country, a literature has grown up that depicts every stage of the pursuit, and touches on innumerable aspects of the contemporary human scene. Here an interesting fact emerges. Although a host of strangely different writers have studied the subject, they appear to have reached, now and then, remarkably similar conclusions. Looking back to the past, they tell us, or gazing ahead towards the hopeful future, is always a far happier exercise than looking around us at the present day; and among those who have held that view are a particularly incongruous pair, Samuel Johnson in the Georgian Age and Ivan Turgenev in the nineteenth century.

On English eighteenth-century roads, for a man who did not own a carriage and shunned the discomforts of a public coach, to hire a post-chaise, which usually carried only two passengers, was the most expensive, but also the pleasantest, speediest and most fashionable mode of travelling. In 1776, Johnson, then aged sixty-seven, employed a chaise to carry him home from the North with his favourite disciple James Boswell; and Boswell, who always 'enjoyed the luxury of our approach to London, that metropolis which we both loved so much for the high and intellectual pleasure which it furnishes', and who 'experienced immediate happiness while whirled along with such a companion', referred to a provocative remark that, several months earlier, he had heard his venerable friend throw off, and that had apparently been troubling him. '. . . The present', Johnson had then asserted, 'was never a happy state to any human being', and, 'when he was pressed . . . and asked if he was really of opinion, that though, in general, happiness was very rare in human life, a man was not sometimes happy in the moment that was present, he answered, "Never but when he is drunk." '

Although Johnson was usually displeased to hear his dogmatic assertions questioned, in the ebullient mood their approach to London awoke Boswell was brave enough to risk a snub. 'Sir', he began, 'you observed one day at General Oglethorpe's, that a man is never happy for the present, but when he is drunk. Will you not add, – or when he is driving rapidly in a post-chaise?' 'No, Sir', Johnson replied, 'you are driving *from* something, or *to* something!' For all its outward acerbity, Johnson's character had a sympathetic and good-humoured side; and later he admitted that more than once he had himself felt extremely happy travelling in a post-chaise with a pretty woman. These light-hearted moments, he wished his audience to understand, had been comparatively rare; for, on his way through life, his spiritual and physical infirmities had 'seldom afforded him a single day of ease'. Yet, as a philosopher, he blamed despondency in others. 'The business of the wise man is to be happy', he informed the manic-depressive Boswell; and, on another occasion, having recommended that they should both of them do their best to be happy, he warned him against indulging in what he called the 'hypocrisy of misery' and the 'affectation of distress'.

He would not deny that even his uneasy life had had its memorable compensations. Some time after he had settled down at Streatham among his kindly friends the Thrales – Hester Thrale, his beloved 'mistress', and her dignified, substantial husband – Mr Thrale, always fond of hearing their guests talk, enquired 'which had been the happiest period of his life'; and he answered 'it was that year in which he spent one whole evening with Molly Aston. "That indeed (said he) was not happiness; it was rapture..."' Again at Streatham, discussing *Evelina*, Fanny Burney's recently published novel, he reverted to the theme. Miss Burney's book, he said, 'concludes by leaving her heroine in measureless delight'; and he wondered 'when anybody ever experiences measureless delight', adding that he felt sure that he himself had never done so, since the unforgettable hours he had passed in Molly Aston's company.

Their meeting, of course, had been long ago, about the year 1739, at his humdrum birthplace, Lichfield; and, though to the Thrales he spoke of a 'Teste-a-Teste', he and Molly were certainly not alone; nor could Johnson, the impoverished thirty-year-old son of a bookseller who sometimes set up a stall in Lichfield market, have expected he might win the heart of a rich baronet's unmarried daughter. By that time he had already a middle-aged

[15]

consort, the difficult, exacting Tetty; and he was far too stern a moralist, his early biographer assures us, to cause his wife the smallest chagrin. Miss Aston, incidentally, professed the kind of opinions that in a woman, whatever her appearance and age might be, as a rule he most detested. A sharp-eyed, lively-looking girl with a handsome aquiline profile, she was 'a scholar, and a wit and a Whig' – Johnson, of course, supported the opposite camp – and during their conversation, she 'talked all in praise of liberty!' But his heart had overcome his political prejudices; 'she was the loveliest creature he ever saw!!!' he exclaimed; and Molly's face haunted his imagination so long as he still clung to life.

Boswell's biography is one of those masterpieces which, besides gener-ously enlarging our knowledge of the world, strengthen our respect for human nature. Its hero, perverse, wrong-headed, downright brutal though he may often appear, had a strong attachment to his fellow men; they were his chief 'subject of enquiry', in which he never lost interest; like the Roman playwright, he thought nothing human entirely alien to himself. Another well-known book that provides a yet more extensive, and even more carefully detailed picture of a vanished social epoch, the *Journal* kept by Edmond and Jules de Goncourt, and, long after his brother's death, completed by Edmond in the year 1896, has precisely the opposite effect upon a critic's mind. Only the Goncourts – two unselfishly devoted artists; or so they very often announced – are usually portrayed as '*hommes de bonne volonté*'. Otherwise few of their distinguished colleagues escape some damaging strokes either of private malice or of literary spite. But an exception was Ivan Turgenev, perhaps because he was an interesting newcomer from a romantic foreign land, and also partly, no doubt, because he had an air of natural good breeding – the Goncourts regarded themselves as aristocrats – that George Moore, in his old age at Ebury Street, when he recollected the famous writers he had known, would affectionately describe.

Reopening the Goncourts' *Journal*, I alighted on two passages I had previously half forgotten, that reminded me of Johnson's tribute to the loveliest creature he had even seen, and of the part that Molly Aston had played in his sentimental education. The first entry was dated March 2nd 1872, and recorded a Parisian dinner-party that included Flaubert,

Molly Aston, the handsome young woman, 'a scholar, and a wit and a Whig', in whose company Johnson once experienced 'measureless delight'.

[17]

Théophile Gautier and their friend the Russian novelist – 'a good-natured giant . . . his white hair descending over his eyes', a deep wrinkle, 'deep as a cart-track', crossing his large brow from one temple to another. Flaubert and Edmond de Goncourt having denied that love was supremely important for a writer, Turgenev contradicted them. All he could say, he declared, was that his whole life had been 'saturated with femininity'; that there 'wasn't a book, or anything else, that could replace a woman for him'; and he believed that love produced a certain 'flowering of the personality', or expansion of the spirit, that no other influence could quite achieve.

Then his memory began to dig into the past; and 'a flash of happiness' lit up the giant's eyes. When he was a young man, he said, he had known a girl whom he often visited and made love to if he went out shooting, the child of a miller near St. Petersburg, a delightful being, very pale, with a cast in one eye, which, he explained, was fairly common among Russian women. She had never asked him for a present, until she suddenly admitted that there was indeed something she would like to have. 'Bring me some scented soap', she begged. He had brought it; and she had taken it, vanished, and come back rosy with emotion, holding out her fragrant hands. 'Now kiss them', she exclaimed, 'as you kiss the hands of the ladies in the drawing-rooms at St. Petersburg!' He had thrown himself on to his knees before her. There hadn't been another moment of his life, he concluded, that had given him so deep a joy.

The second passage I found was dated January 28th 1878, and is possibly yet more significant, since it illustrates not only Turgenev's conception of remembered happiness, but the masochistic strain, derived presumably from his painful relationship with his crazily oppressive mother, that may afterwards have dictated his long patient devotion to his one-time mistress Pauline Viardot. At a later dinner-party, he was prompted by his fellow-guests to tell them what had been his keenest amorous sensations; and he replied that, while he was young and innocent, with all the restlessness of a fifteen-year-old boy, and was wandering around the garden of his mother's country house on a damp, dull, rainy day – 'one of those erotic days' – her maid, who had a pretty stupid face, but the type of face that 'stupidity lends a certain grandeur', had walked straight up to him and, although (his companions must bear in mind) he was the master, and she a mere serf, had grasped the locks at the nape of his neck, saying simply 'Come!' That gentle grasp sometimes returned to him; 'and just thinking about it makes me happy!'

The idea of happiness in retrospect clearly fascinated Turgenev; for a somewhat similar incident is recorded by Sergei Tolstoy among his reminiscences of his father's household.* During August 1881 Turgenev visited Yasnaya Polyana; and there a conversation took place that might very well, the younger Tolstoy remarks, have been an episode from one of his own stories. Somebody had 'raised the question as to which were the happiest moments of one's life'; and, while another guest, the high-minded local vice-governor, said that for him such a moment would have occurred had he learned of the ultimate triumph of Good-Will on earth, Turgenev admitted that, in his personal experience, happiness had always reached him through a woman's love, when at last you met the beloved's gaze and knew that she returned your passion, adding, after a brief reflective silence: 'This I experienced once in the course of my life – perhaps twice!' The declaration seemed to warm his heart; and, on the same visit, he amused the juvenile Tolstoys by demonstrating how to dance the French cancan. But he presently slipped and fell, and, although he picked himself up again with the agility of youth, his behaviour did not please Tolstoy, who noted that day on a page of his journal, '*Turgenev – cancan. Very sad.*'

After Turgenev's death, Pauline Viardot remarked that he was the unhappiest man, '*l'homme le plus triste*', she had ever known. Although this odd remark may have included a touch of feminine exaggeration – his fellow writers thought him good company; in his domestic life Madame Viardot's tyrannical treatment of him, once he had ceased to be her lover, probably weighed down his spirits – it is evident that, like Johnson, he had inherited a melancholic strain, from which he sought an emotional relief by looking back towards the past. But a conviction that happiness belongs to the past recurs again and again in literary self-revelations, where Memory selects a single fragment of experience, and then revives and recreates that period as an earthly paradise. Byron, for example, had found such a paradise, he afterwards believed, at his English public school; Harrow had brought him the admiration and the real affection that he had always lacked at home. 'My school friendships', he recorded in 1821 during a

---

* *Tolstoy Remembered*; translated by Moura Budberg, 1961.

latter stage of his Italian exile, 'were with *me passions* . . . that with Lord Clare began one of the earliest and lasted longest . . . I never hear the word *"Clare"* without a beating of the heart even *now* . . .'

In 1809, when Byron was about to set forth on his eastern Grand Tour, there had been a brief estrangement. He had suggested they should spend an hour together; and Clare had excused himself because, he said, he had promised 'his mother and some ladies' to take them out shopping. Yet, long afterwards, Byron had sighted his school-friend's carriage, while they travelled in opposite directions along an Italian high road; and they had dismounted, shaken hands and talked:

> 'This meeting annihilated for a moment all the years between the present time and the days of *Harrow*. It was a new and inexplicable feeling, like rising from the grave to me. Clare, too, was much agitated – *more* in appearance than even myself; for I could feel his heart beat to his fingers' ends, unless, indeed, it was the pulse of my own which made me think so – We were but five minutes together, and in the public road; but I hardly recollect an hour of my existence which could be weighed against them'

Luckily perhaps, we were few of us quite so happy either in our childhood or in our youth that regrets for a lost paradise follow us throughout our adult lives. Such regrets, as the biography of another poet shows, may acquire a dangerous strength. Had Charles Baudelaire's childhood been less idyllic, once the idyll was brutally destroyed by his mother's remarriage he might have escaped many of the miseries and material humiliations that overcast his later years. François Baudelaire, a cultivated survivor of pre-revolutionary France, a great deal older than his young, elegant, attractive wife, had died when their only child was six; and from February 1827 until November 1828 Charles and his mother had inhabited an emotional heaven-on-earth, the 'green paradise of childish loves', to which his imagination constantly returned. Every detail of their life together was precious – Madame Baudelaire's little house near Paris, '*nôtre blanche maison, petite mais tranquille*', with its thin suburban shrubbery that enclosed two plaster statues; their devoted maid-servant Mariette, '*la servante au grand coeur*'; and the 'long and silent' meals he and his mother had shared, while a flood of evening sunshine poured across their table.

Baudelaire had loved his mother as her child, but also, he remembered, as a 'precocious dandy', in whom her feminine appeal, even the scent of her furs, kindled his senses and aroused his taste for elegance. But Madame Baudelaire, though devoted to her son, was still young, and needed, if not love, at least masculine protection; and after less than two years of widowhood she accepted the hand of a dashing and distinguished soldier, Lieutenant-Colonel Aupick, later General and French Ambassador to the Sublime Porte. For her it was a sensible and satisfying match; for her jealous and precocious son, an unrelieved catastrophe. Their green paradise was almost immediately laid waste. His step-father, a well-meaning disciplinarian, found first the difficult, suspicious child, then the ill-behaved boy, lastly the extravagant, self-destructive young man, a problem utterly impossible to solve. Aupick seems not to have been unaware that Charles possessed some genuine gifts, and later proposed to secure him a safe position in the diplomatic service, an offer he vehemently refused. Between the two rivals for Madame Aupick's love a lasting peace was never made; and, during a Parisian insurrection, several years after Baudelaire had escaped from tutelage and begun to lead an independent life, a friend encountered him outside a gunsmith's shop, which the mob had just plundered, carrying a brand-new weapon slung over his shoulder, and heard him announce that shooting General Aupick should be his contribution to the struggle.

Although as a child, he said, he had feared Aupick, and, as an adult, had loathed and despised him, it was on his devoted mother, rather than on the tyrant himself, that he focused his angriest and cruellest feelings. Her he punished by punishing himself; now that they could no longer share happiness, he determined that she should participate at second hand in all his griefs and misadventures. The letters she regularly received from him contain a painful record of his sufferings and disappointments, the anxieties and collapse of his long, ignominious liaison with the half-caste actress Jeanne Duval. Yet he refused to abandon a desperate hope that, since Aupick had left the scene, there was still time for them to resurrect the past – '*Ah! chère mère, est-il encore temps pour que nous serons heureux?*' – despite his age (he was now forty years old), his mountain of debts and, he suspected, the gradual breakdown of his will.

Yet art often defies life by extracting harmony from personal confusion; and, when he was thirty-seven, the poet had already produced his justificatory masterpiece, *Les Fleurs du Mal*, the volume that, according to Marcel Proust, unfolds the spacious 'landscape of his genius', where each poem is only a fragment of the whole, but, once we have read it, links up, as part of a magnificent general scheme, with the poems it follows or precedes. Baudelaire's fellow poets had warmly welcomed his book. Unluckily – Baudelaire was always an unlucky man – at the same time it attracted the attention of the Napoleonic police; and both writer and publisher were prosecuted, and found guilty of an offence against moral and religious standards. Certain poems were suppressed; the poet was fined three hundred francs. But a second edition was issued; and in 1861, undeterred by his recent reverses, he made a courageous, though somewhat half-hearted, attempt to join the Immortals at the French Academy, and began a candidate's customary round of visits. Alfred de Vigny was encouraging; Lamartine seemed 'aimable'. An old family friend, however, whom he had expected to support him, proved peculiarly unhelpful.

Baudelaire was attached to Sainte-Beuve, one of his mother's guests, a man considerably older than himself, and even affected to admire his poems; but the distinguished critic, having an instinctively cautious nature, felt that his championship of Madame Aupick's wayward son must not appear too unreserved; and his mention of the poet in the influential column that he published every Monday was disappointingly evasive. The new candidate, he assured his middle-class readers, was by no means the literary werewolf his enemies would have had them think, but a 'polite' and 'deferential' personage, a pleasant, well-spoken young man, despite the fact that his creative habits were odd, and that, in the literary world, he chose to inhabit a 'singular kiosk', where he sat and smoked his hubble-bubble 'on the furthest point of the romantic Kamtchatka'.

Sainte-Beuve's faint praise was so obviously measured out that it did his subject little harm; and his appearance in the present context may require some explanation. Unlike the other writers from whose pronouncements I have quoted, Sainte-Beuve again and again denied that his memories had ever brought him happiness. 'My evil, nay my crime', he wailed, 'is that I have never been loved as I have wished to be loved. This is the secret of my whole insane existence, a life spent without consistency, without self-discipline, without an aim, without confidence even in the work that remains for me to do'. Later – once more our source is the Goncourts' diary – his confidante was the Emperor's cousin, the generous and warm-hearted Princesse Mathilde. She had no idea, he said, how much it meant to a man, the knowledge that real love had escaped him; which, in his case, was accompanied by a premonition that, now he was so old and ugly, were such a heavenly gift still to come his way, he would no doubt appear ridiculous.

Sainte-Beuve's ugliness has often been described. Short and stout, long-nosed and large-eared, he was said to resemble either a shuffling sacristan or a rather wicked ginger cat. Balzac and Stendhal, of course, both great men whom he frequently abused, were almost equally inelegant; but their personalities had a tremendous backing of unselfconscious energy and romantic zeal that irradiated their awkward looks. Sainte-Beuve's appearance, on the other hand, seems to have reflected something discordant in his private character – a curious streak of spite and envy. 'One of man's most veritable satisfactions', he wrote, 'is when a woman he has passionately desired, and who has obstinately refused to accord him her favours, ceases to be beautiful'. Entirely different was Stendhal's association with his past, which, during his literary life, had taught him so many valuable lessons, and, as an adventurous collector of experiences, he had often thoroughly enjoyed. He had no desire to see its images defaced, and, looking back, still felt a tenderly grateful regard for a woman – indeed, for a succession of women – who had either deserted or rejected him.

Rousseau's Enchanted Isle

S AMUEL JOHNSON had so large and powerfully active a mind that he was seldom ashamed to contradict himself; and, although he often declared that human happiness existed only in the future or the past, where imagination and memory alone seemed capable of grasping it, he told Boswell (his reader may recollect) that to be happy was still the wise man's duty. Here he had already had many strong supporters, particularly beyond the Channel. During the classic period of French literature, even the sternly devout Pascal had admitted that all human beings sought happiness, and had implied that, if they set out in pursuit of it, provided their conception of their goal remained sound, and they did not equate happiness with mundane pleasures, they would not necessarily go astray. 'A reasonable mind aspires to happiness', Bossuet announced in one of his sonorous yet mellifluous sermons; while Voltaire, the giant of the next age, attributed our lifelong pursuit to the effect of a natural law that governed our entire existence – an opinion that, in the early twentieth century, André Gide would boldly reaffirm.

It is not the search, but the quality of happiness sought, that has varied from place to place, and year to year; and dramatic political events have sometimes changed its course by inspiring the seeker with new hopes and problems. Such an event was the French Revolution. Men born under the Old Regime, who had lived on into the Napoleonic era, were always aware of the tremendous gulf they had crossed, a chasm that seemed to separate two different worlds. None had made the crossing more safely and adroitly than Charles-Maurice de Talleyrand-Périgord, arch-turncoat, absentee bishop of Autun, Deputy to the National Assembly in the last years of the Revolution and Minister of Foreign Affairs during the Directory, Consulate and Empire, an office that, after the fall of Napoleon and the restoration of the Bourbons, he almost immediately resumed. Having profited by these diverse experiences, he took a philosophic view of history; and, remembering the vanished world in which he had been brought up, he invented his famous phrase '*la douceur de vivre*' to describe the easy charm of the existence he and his privileged contemporaries had shared.

They, at least, he thought had mastered the art of living – an art that Talleyrand, in his own career, combined with an extraordinary talent for surviving. But he saw the defects of the old world as clearly as he saw its virtues; and his posthumously published memoirs* illustrate both the triumphs of his adult life and the hardships of his childhood. Parental care had not yet come into fashion; '*la mode de soins paternels n'était pas encore arrivée*'; and Talleyrand's parents, who each held a courtly position and could seldom leave Versailles, quickly handed him over to a nurse, at whose cottage near Paris he spent several lonely years. His nurse was a stupid woman; and the boy's fall from a chest-of-drawers on which she had carelessly deposited him left him a demi-cripple for the remainder of his life.

'*Je suis resté boiteux*', he wrote – an humiliating admission for an extremely active man to make. Yet Talleyrand, the cynic and realist, felt no lasting resentment against either his neglectful family or the code of conduct they obeyed. They had their roots in the Périgord; and there, he tells us, 'the manners of the nobility resembled the ancient castles they inhabited'. Little direct light penetrated those solid walls; and such beams as crept through were mercifully subdued. Talleyrand's grandmother, who had retired from the great world and become a rustic Lady Bountiful, had been the first member of his family, indeed almost the first human being, to show him any real love. She was a good Christian of the old school; and he recollected how she would sit ministering to sick peasants in a huge room

---

* *Mémoires du Prince de Talleyrand, publiés . . . par le Duc de Broglie*, 1891.

nicknamed 'the Apothecary's Shop', which was filled with unguents and medicines compounded at home from traditional prescriptions, bottles of syrups and elixirs, and rolls of linen bandages. Madame de Chalais presided, occupying a velvet arm-chair behind an old black lacquer table, wearing a silk- and ribbon- trimmed dress that suited the time of year, a fur stole, a bonnet and a black cap; while a poor relation held the red velvet, gold-braided bag that contained her missal and one or two works of devotion.

During his early days, glimpses of a harmonious domestic life, Talleyrand added, had been comparatively rare; and later, he said, he had been, he supposed, the only young man of his kind – '*d'une naissance distinguée et appartenant à une famille nombreuse et estimée*' – who never for a whole week had had the consolation of finding himself under his paternal roof. Yet, when he was at last permitted to meet his mother, ageing now but still a fashionable woman of the world, she immediately delighted him. In the portrait he drew, he sums up many of the fine qualities that, as ingredients of *la douceur de vivre*, he remembered and regretted. Her conversation had had a charm, an ease, a lightness he had encountered nowhere else:

'She was altogether without pedantic pretensions. She spoke in nuances alone; a *bon mot* never crossed her lips; that would have been far too conspicuous. *Bons mots* are repeated; she wished merely to please, and that what she had said should be then forgotten. A rich stock of phrases, fresh and always delicately appropriate, sufficed to convey the varying turns of her wit'

Both in the French and, at the time, in the English social world, an ability to please, and thus make life more agreeable for one's friends, was accounted a conspicuous virtue. But the well-bred talker shunned excess; 'nothing too much' was still a maxim that 'polite society' respected, and 'enthusiasm' a somewhat terrifying word. If Madame Geoffrin, the rich, dignified middle-class hostess, who entertained French *philosophes* and free-thinkers, as well as Gibbon, Horace Walpole and John Wilkes, thought that the flow of conversation around her table threatened to become violent, she would at once check it by remarking '*Voilà qui est bien*', which quietly hinted 'We've had enough of that!', and re-direct it into safer channels. A regard for *bienséance*, propriety, decorum, fitness, which did not preclude delightful strokes of humour, was evidently one of the characteristics Talleyrand had enjoyed, listening to his parents' conversation; and her example would later disgust him with the loud, dogmatic dialogues he so often heard in Parisian drawing-rooms when the century drew towards its close.

During the reign of Louis XV, he observes, though certain writers and intellectuals – Fontenelle, Montesquieu, Buffon, Voltaire – had already infiltrated aristocratic society, they still respected and, no doubt, admired the manners of the previous epoch, and emulated its careful blend of liberty and licence. But under Louis XVI a roar of talk had arisen, invariably critical and frequently subversive, which sometimes resounded even through Versailles. Social and personal distinctions soon vanished; every barrier went down. The oddest links were formed. The poet Delille, learned translator of Virgil and Milton, dined at Madame de Polignac's house to meet the Queen; the savage aphorist Chamfort, who, after 1789, would coin the revolutionary motto, 'War against the castles; Peace to the cottages!', was observed walking arm-in-arm with a well-known Royalist admiral, the comte de Vaudreuil. Other intellectuals were invited to stay at Marly, the King's country retreat, or supped at the Palace with Madame de Lamballe, Marie-Antoinette's beloved friend. In drawing-rooms and ballrooms, every move the ministers made, and almost every action attributed to the sovereigns, were discussed and usually derided. The young felt particularly sure that, given the opportunity, which would soon come, they were fully capable of governing.

While the Old Regime talked itself to death, the moral and intellectual climate of France underwent a rapid change. 'Sentiments', Talleyrand writes, 'were replaced by philanthropic ideas, passions by the analysis of the human heart; the desire to please by strong opinions; amusements by new plans and projects . . .' These climatic changes, however, although the approach of the Revolution gave them a more definite form, had already begun to appear a good deal earlier in the century. The affection for children, that Talleyrand's parents had lacked, soon became distinctly fashionable; and much-admired artists, notably Greuze and a younger and

Moreau le Jeune's fashionable heroine receives a secret love-letter.

livelier artist, Moreau le Jeune, born in 1741, depicted the beauties of childhood and innocence, and the pleasures of a simple life.

During the seventeenth century La Bruyère had described the French peasants he saw beside the roads as 'certain wild animals, male and female ... black, livid and burned by the sun ... chained, as it were, to the land they are always digging and turning over with an unconquerable stubbornness'. But, he remarks indignantly, they, too, 'have a sort of articulate voice, and when they stand up, they exhibit human features'; one must admit that 'they are men'. It was these little-known beings Greuze had humanised in a series of pictures, some of them commissioned by a Russian grand-duke – 'The Father's Curse', 'The Father's Blessing', 'The Punished Son', 'The Village Betrothed' and others, that illustrate the joys and sorrows, the conflicts and reconciliations, of their harsh, laborious lives. Even Moreau le Jeune, whose most attractive plates are scenes of aristocratic life which show how a privileged young woman spent her pleasant, idle days, was prepared at times to change his subject. His heroine, though she is fond of her children, and at breakfast gives them, as a special treat, a lump of sugar soaked in coffee, is clearly a light-minded worldling; and, when she and her legitimate consort attend the opera, she allows a secret note to be slipped into her hand. But among Moreau le Jeune's charming glimpses of high life we also find a plate he called *Le Vrai Bonheur*, the background of true happiness being a modest rustic cottage, where a sturdy labourer, who has just returned from his work, arrives home to be greeted by his ancient mother, his wife, his handsome, well-grown babes and their amiable shaggy dog.

'*Le Vrai Bonheur*', drawn by Moreau le Jeune but engraved by a different artist, Simonet, was first published in 1776; and, a year later, Jean-Jacques Rousseau, who would die in 1778, was writing the fifth of his *Rêveries du Promeneur Solitaire*, the autobiographical essay that described the climax of his long musings on the theme of human happiness, by which he meant primarily his own happiness; for every line of investigation that Rousseau pursued soon led back towards himself. In his vocabulary, *bonheur* was a key-word; few writers have employed it more often; it represented the ultimate objective of all his dreams and hopes; and, having found and lost it during his own youth, as he grew older he turned his attention to the problems of the world at large, and, much more effectively than any

'True Happiness'; the labourer's home-coming.

drawing-room theorist, would help to undermine the foundations of the established social system.

Born in 1712, the son of a prosperous Genevan watchmaker, Jean-Jacques Rousseau had a naturally impatient and demanding spirit, and enjoyed his first great adult experience at the age of fifteen, when, having decided to become a Catholic, he left his father's house and, at Annecy, encountered Madame de Warens, a well-known patroness of deserving Catholic converts, whom he had expected to find a plain good-doing dowager, but who proved to be a voluptuous twenty-nine-year-old woman, 'radiant with charm', her 'blue eyes filled with sweetness', and who had soon amicably seduced him. His attachment to Madame de Warens, henceforward his adored '*Maman*', protectress, counsellor and bedfellow, provided by far the calmest and happiest chapter of an otherwise distressful life. He was already a vagrant; but not until he and Madame de Warens had parted did his adult wander-years begin – the years when he became a haunted fugitive, constantly in flight, though he had rich and powerful admirers, from real or half-imaginary foes. It is hard to avoid the suspicion that he secretly welcomed his numerous and often humiliating reverses – he had been, his autobiography tells us, a masochist and exhibitionist since childhood – and that failure appealed to him more than any stroke of good fortune.

Even at Court he had once enjoyed a triumph. Among his many gifts were his understanding of music and his skill as a composer;* and in 1752 his pastoral operetta, *Le Devin du Village*,† so delighted Madame de Pompadour and Louis XV, that its first performance at the Palace of Fontainebleau was magnificently successful. Fame and security now seemed close indeed; but Rousseau, learning that next day he was to be presented to the King, who would utter a few words of congratulation, and that he himself must prepare a ceremonious speech, remembered that he had a physical infirmity which sometimes bound him to his chamber-pot, took fright and quickly left the Palace – behaviour that much

---

* Rousseau was a keen admirer of Gluck, for whom he worked as a copyist, until he came to suspect that the great composer was somehow taking sides against him.

† It has been occasionally revived; but, according to Martin Cooper, author of *Gluck*, 1935, it is 'set . . . in a musical idiom simple to the verge of childishness', and may have owed its success to the fact that it persuaded the French world that there was 'still hope for French music.'

displeased the sovereign, who talked of having him arrested and thrown into gaol.

Two years later, Latour painted his portrait; and Diderot, as professional art-critic, found it an absurdly misleading likeness. Rousseau was already a professional writer, author of a *Discourse on the Sciences and the Arts*, where he had attacked contemporary *philosophes* and the whole principle of eighteenth-century Enlightenment; and what Diderot had hoped for, he said, was a work that immortalised 'the Censor of our literature, the Cato, the Brutus of our age'; whereas Latour seemed to have gone out of his way to depict a very different man – 'the composer of *Le Devin du Village*, well-dressed, well-powdered, and ridiculously seated in a cane chair'. When Diderot published his criticism, however, Rousseau had already changed his mask; his likeness to a respectable, even slightly fashionable, citizen was a *persona* that he very soon abandoned. He wished to be regarded as a quiet, hard-working craftsman, no longer the successful composer but a laborious copyist of music, who knew how to 'live in poverty' and hoped, at last, to 'die in independence'.

That was the part he now assumed and, until the end, would resolutely play. Rousseau's 'awareness of living an exemplary life never left him', writes a recent French biographer.* He prized his own virtue above all else. Yet that virtue, as he did not hesitate to admit in his *Confessions*, which he began to read aloud during the last decade of his existence, had a decidedly unstable basis. His detractors presently discovered, and he himself would latterly tell the world, that he and his humble mistress, Thérèse Le Vasseur, had consigned their five bastard infants to the grim Parisian Foundling Hospital, whence it was unlikely they would re-emerge; and this horrid story, which the ever-attentive Voltaire very soon picked up, haunted him throughout his closing years. Madame d'Épinay's assertion that he was 'a moral dwarf on stilts' may reflect the malice of an aggrieved and disappointed friend; but there seems no doubt that his virtues and his vices, his fierce sincerity and his touches of sly humbug, were curiously intermixed, and that the legend of Rousseau the modern Cato or Brutus needs a good deal of critical revision.

* Jean Guéhenno: *Jean-Jacques Rousseau*, 1962.

Jean-Jacques Rousseau, after Latour's portrait; his 'awareness of leading an exemplary life never left him.'

[33]

During his lifetime, though often disputed both by enemies and by friends turned foe, it was still enthusiastically accepted – for example, by James Boswell, then on the Grand Tour, who, preparatory to visiting Rousseau at Môtiers, his secluded Swiss retreat, 'swore solemnly' that, meanwhile, he would neither 'talk as an infidel' nor 'enjoy a woman . . .' The momentous interview that followed, between the young Scottish laird and his 'Dear and Singular Philosopher', took place early in December 1764. Having been welcomed by the forty-three-year-old Mademoiselle Le Vasseur – the romantic tourist, strangely enough, calls her 'a little, lively, neat French girl' – and conducted up a 'darkish stair' and into a room that served as vestibule and kitchen, Boswell, dressed for the occasion in a 'scarlet and gold-laced coat' and 'a great coat of Green Camlet lined with Foxskin Fur', and carrying under his arm 'a hat with sollid gold lace, at least with the air of being sollid', confronted 'a genteel black man in the dress of an Armenian'. Altogether Boswell paid the famous 'Solitary' no less than five prolonged visits; and they found many subjects to discuss – perverse theologians whom the sage ridiculed; Rousseau's health; Boswell's character and aims; his desire to set up a harem of thirty peasant virgins he would impregnate and finally marry off, a suggestion that Rousseau mildly deprecated, though polygamy, he agreed, was a practice of which he did not altogether disapprove; and, yet more important, whether the great man believed that he was still a Christian. 'Each stood steady and watched the other's looks. He struck his breast and replied, "*Oui – je me pique de l'être*" ' – a slightly ambiguous phrase, which might perhaps be translated: 'Yes – I like to think I am'.

On this third visit, besides investigating Rousseau's religious convictions, the searcher for truth made a particularly bold request: 'Will you, Sir, assume direction of me?' he asked. 'I cannot. I can be responsible only for myself', Rousseau answered, adding 'I am in pain. I need a chamber-pot every minute'. Though the sage often spoke of his illness and tiredness, and sometimes begged the young man to cut his visits short, Boswell cheerfully persisted; and the record he kept at the time shows the extraordinary influence Rousseau exercised, despite his own very obvious failings, upon the thoughts and conduct of his fellow men. A wanderer himself, always unsure of his way, he became their special guide. Boswell's strongest and steadiest mentor, of course, indignantly rejected him. He thought Rousseau, Johnson told Boswell, 'one of the worst of men; a rascal who ought to be hunted out of society . . . I would sooner sign a sentence for his transportation, than that of any felon who has gone from the Old Bailey these many years'. Boswell, determined that such an exciting controversy should not subside, then boldly brought in Voltaire's name: 'Sir, do you think him as bad a man as Voltaire?' 'Why, Sir,' Johnson responded, 'it is difficult to settle the proportion of iniquity between them'.

Both in principle and in their private attitude towards mankind Johnson and Rousseau were irreconcilable opponents. Johnson had a voracious appetite for life, and was passionately concerned with the welfare of individual men and women; while Rousseau, although he was persuaded that he loved the human race, or would have loved it if he could, followed a solitary, self-centred course and, among a host of associates, protectors, disciples, made comparatively few friends whose opinions and support he valued. Here one remembers another literary dispute, held some hundred-and-fifty years later, when Henry James, writing to the youthful H.G. Wells, described their fundamental difference. 'You', he explained, 'don't care for humanity but think they are to be improved. I love humanity but know they are not!' Johnson, too, despite his capacity for deep affection, was a life-long pessimist; Rousseau, the suspicious and resentful exile, was an inveterate reformer, and launched the doctrine of 'human perfectibility' that made so strong, and often so confusing, an appeal to English nineteenth-century Romantic poets. He was a teacher; but his chief aim was primarily to teach himself; if he desired to learn, he confessed, it was primarily in order to understand his own character.

Happiness was also a subject on which Rousseau and Johnson inevitably disagreed. For Johnson, a transitory boon; for Rousseau, it was a natural human right. Though he always looked back on the years he had spent with Madame de Warens as his 'land of lost content' – he would have liked, he said, to erect a golden railing around the place where they had first met* – and, two years before he encountered Boswell, declared that his whole adult life had been a mere tissue of 'trouble, anguish and pain', he had never abandoned the pursuit of happiness, and at length, in 1765, when his sufferings seem to have grown most acute, on a little island amid the Swiss

* Such a railing was erected in the nineteenth century, but unfortunately somewhat misplaced.

mountains he felt that he had definitely reached his goal. He did not begin to describe his memorable achievement, however, until some eleven years had passed; and by then he had retired to Paris, where his last disciple, Bernardin de Saint-Pierre, future author of that strange tropical romance *Paul et Virginie*, who at the moment was planning to depict 'a society that owed its happiness only to the laws of nature and virtue', paid him many long visits.

In 1772, Rousseau's rooms above the Rue Plâtrière certainly suited a philosopher. They were on the fourth floor; and the bedroom, which was also his workroom, contained only two small beds, covered with blue-and-white-striped cotton cloth, a chest-of-drawers, a table and a few chairs. On the walls hung a map of the Forest of Montmorency, where he had once lived, and of which he had happy recollections, and an engraved portrait of King George III, who, during Rousseau's disastrous expedition to England under David Hume's wing, had offered him a pension of £100 a year, and whom, though he had then elaborately refused it, he still regarded as his benefactor. Mademoiselle Le Vasseur, now styled 'Madame Rousseau' after an unorthodox ceremony he had organised, sat near him quietly mending linen; a canary sang in its cage; sparrows picked up crumbs from the window-sills; and Bernardin noticed a multitude of pots and boxes that he had filled with plants and wild flowers. Close to Rousseau – then sixty-four years old, a bright-eyed elderly man, his expression sometimes deeply sad, sometimes gay and sharply animated – stood a spinet, symbol of his musical interests, on which he occasionally tried out an air.

Rousseau changed his lodgings for the last time in the early summer of 1778. The Rue Plâtrière was growing too expensive; and the marquis de Girardin, a keen admirer of *La Nouvelle Héloïse*, proposed to build him a thatched cottage at Ermenonville near Senlis, and meanwhile offered him a small pavilion opposite his own château. There he died on July 4th, 1778, clasping Thérèse's hand, without, she told his disciples, 'uttering a single word';* and it was there he wrote the closing sections of *Les Rêveries du*

---

* Afterwards she frequently changed her story, and informed Moreau le Jeune, who painted a portrait of the dying sage seated at his open window, that he had exclaimed 'Be comforted; you can see how pure and serene the heavens are. Well, I am on my way there'.

Promeneur Solitaire, begun at his Parisian rooms, the extraordinary work in which he both looks back to his early youth, when he was Madame de Warens' pupil, and describes and analyses the moment of supreme happiness beside the Lac de Bienne he had enjoyed twelve years ago. His major works already lay years behind him – *Julie, ou la Nouvelle Héloise*, published in 1761, his romantic epistolary novel, which even Boswell conceded 'might do harm', but immediately became a guide-book to the realms of sensation and emotion carried around by eighteenth-century lovers;* *Emile*, his treatise on educational methods; and *Le Contrat Social*, a study of the proper relationship between the individual and society, which, like *Emile*, had appeared and been officially banned in 1762.

These works had given Rousseau the place he deserved beside his ancient adversary Voltaire, who had long watched him from a cautious distance, as a revolutionary liberator of the European mind. But, during his old age, he was less concerned with the general state of humanity, and how it might shed its chains, than with the problem of his own existence. Happiness was a subject that still absorbed him; and he had come to believe that it could only be achieved through a kind of sublimated self-regard.† '*Le moi est haïssable*', Pascal had declared; but Rousseau contradicts that gloomy sentence. Far from abandoning and detesting the Self, one must cultivate an exalted self-love. '*Il faut être soi.*' Nature was the ultimate pattern of Virtue; and, as Natural Man does, one must rely for happiness on the simple sense of living.

Twice, he thought, he had definitely achieved happiness; and of the first occasion he was reminded in April 1788, when the sound of bells announcing Palm Sunday reminded him that it was now 'exactly fifty years since I first made the acquaintance of Madame de Warens . . . This first encounter determined the course of my whole life.' Never a day went by, he wrote in his last manuscript, 'but I remember with tender delight that unique and brief space of time when I was able to be myself to the full,

---

* Among these enthusiasts were Georgiana, Duchess of Devonshire, her beloved friend Lady Elizabeth Foster, and Queen Victoria's father, the Duke of Kent. All three included *La Nouvelle Héloise* in their travelling libraries.
† For an admirable discussion of Rousseau's views, see Marcel Raymond's introduction to *Les Rêveries du Promeneur Solitaire*, 1948.

without adulteration or impediment, and during which I can truly say I lived . . .' The second, a much more transitory experience, is recorded in the *Rêveries*; but it produced no permanently rewarding sequel, and had had a troubled and disturbing prelude.

In 1765 his public persecutors, both French and Swiss, seemed to outnumber his devoted allies; and Rousseau's paranoiac strain, which dramatised evey mishap and detected 'conspiracies' where none existed, became alarmingly apparent. But, now and then, his hardships were real enough. On Swiss soil he had expected freedom and peace; that autumn, however, the rustic inhabitants of Môtiers unexpectedly sided with the enemy. The local pastor, who had once been an admiring acquaintance, but had recently developed, Rousseau thought he noticed, a 'sinister' and 'sombre' look, chose to denounce him from the pulpit. He was insulted as he walked the streets; and, at home, he suffered 'lapidation'; mysterious assailants stoned his lodgings.

From these ugly scenes he sought a new refuge, on the little Ile Saint-Pierre, surrounded by the neighbouring Lac de Bienne, where the custodian of the island's only decent house had good-naturedly agreed to shelter him provided that he gave no trouble. Rousseau, like Shelley, loved water; and he was always especially fond of islands, which he associated with his favourite novel, *The Life and Strange Surprising Adventures of Robinson Crusoe*. Both he and his last friend Bernardin were ardent 'Robinsonians'; and the Ile Saint-Pierre was an almost perfect island of its kind, nearly as well-stocked as the miniature commonwealth Defoe had created for his industrious castaway. Part wild, part carefully cultivated, it contained hills and valleys, fields, vineyards, woodlands, orchards and shady meadows; and Rousseau suggested to his host that, on a much smaller neighbouring island, they should set up a colony of rabbits. The installation of the colony, which would no doubt have prospered and multiplied had its founders recollected that Swiss winters are often very harsh, was celebrated with rustic merriment. 'The pilot of the Argonauts', he wrote, 'could not have been prouder than I was' as he conducted the rabbit-colonists across the water to their new home.

The Ile Saint-Pierre was also a botanical heaven; and botany, since he had acquired a copy of Linnaeus' *Systema naturala*, was now among the

Solitary's strongest passions. Nothing, he recorded, could have given him so much pleasure, such ecstasy indeed, as every discovery he made about the structure and organisation of the vegetable world, and the part played by its generative organs in the fructification of a species. Every detail pleased his eye, and added fresh colour to his vision of a universe beautifully and harmoniously planned. He had always enjoyed walking, if possible walking alone; and the proximity of the Lac de Bienne made his solitary excursions around the island doubly soothing and delightful. Sometimes he would remain on shore; but, if the weather were calm, he would row out towards the centre of the lake and, his gaze turned to the sky, let his boat drift calmly and aimlessly along, directed by some gentle current.

Thus, during this brief holiday, from September to October 1765, passed on or near the Lac de Bienne, Rousseau achieved his second experience of almost undiluted happiness; and, whereas the first had originated in a moving personal relationship, the second was a solitary rapture. When he opened the *Première Promenade*, his spirits were still at the lowest level; and he had subsided yet again into paranoiac self-pity. 'So here I am,' he announced, 'alone on the earth, now lacking brother, neighbour, friend, or any company except my own. The most sociable and the most affectionate of men has been unanimously proscribed. In the refinement of their hatred, they have sought to discover the torture that my sensitive soul would find most cruel; and they have violently broken the links that attached me to them. I should have loved my fellow men despite themselves.'

Then gradually, from the sorrows of his present position that recalled an evil dream, his memory shifted back to his beloved island, on which, many years earlier, he had enjoyed a momentary peace. Above all else, it had been the sound of the waters that had relieved his inward misery. As the evening approached, he would walk down towards the lake; and there the rhythmic flux and reflux of wavelets that constantly broke against the shore would chase away his agitation and, without obliging him to think, make him vividly and delightfully aware of his own separate existence. Wild pleasures and keen affections, he had already often noticed, were those he remembered least distinctly. Far more durable were the rare moments when the soul discovered a firm enough resting-place – '*une assiette assez solide*' – to give it the support that it demanded; when Past and Future

[39]

appeared equally unreal; when the idea of Time completely lost its power; and one enjoyed a complete and perfect happiness – '*un bonheur, parfait et plein*' – that left no inward need unsatisfied. So long as this state of mind endured, '*on se suffit à soi-même comme Dieu*' – the happy man, like his Creator, was sufficient to himself.

Rousseau's discovery of true happiness as an ecstatic recognition and realisation of the Self marks the point at which, he says, 'I bade goodbye to my century and my contemporaries', and, we now see, had begun to foreshadow the Romantic Movement. Earlier, having taught his fellow men that they must love and reverence Nature, and especially adore the Alps, he had explained that he could never have spent so many days 'regarding these magnificent landscapes, had I not found still greater pleasure in the conversation of the inhabitants'. But, since he had turned his back on an unkind world, which, he felt, had finally rejected him, untroubled solitude was all that he asked from life. Real happiness was only to be found within the magic circle of the ego.

3

'A New Idea in Europe'

Rousseau had said that not until some revolution transformed society would mankind be prepared to do him justice; and, in fact, when just eleven years and ten days after his death at Ermenonville, the expected storm broke, although, since Diderot had styled him the Cato or Brutus of the age he had never wanted admirers, it immediately enlarged his fame; he was canonised as a revolutionary saint; and his busts and portraits were sold throughout France, or employed to decorate every kind of domestic object from snuffboxes to pieces of household crockery.* He had been well aware, however, that violent social changes, if they occurred might perhaps prove cruel and destructive; for there was always a danger, he prophesied, that new laws, under the malign influence of human passions, might be used to serve the old nefarious ends; and certainly the French Revolution, in its blood-thirsty later period, would have astonished and appalled him.

Yet, during the first savage years of the Republic, two of his disciples led the way, and preached and organised the Terror – a ferocious bureaucrat, Maximilien Robespierre, who shared the prophet's cult of 'sensibility', and an impassioned orator, Robespierre's devoted lieutenant Saint-Just, whose contribution to the study of happiness is among the strangest yet made, so little does it accord with what we know of his character or of his

* Jean Guéhenno, op. cit. Napoleon himself had a walking-stick with Rousseau's portrait embedded in the handle.

own extraordinary life. Once their savage regime had suddenly collapsed, they would die both on the same day – July 28th, 1794 – and on the same scaffold. Antoine Louis Léon de Richebourg de Saint-Just was then twenty-six, a tall, dark-haired young man, *'d'une belle et imposante physiognomie'*, austere, calm, dignified, elegantly dressed. Despite his patrician air and lofty-sounding name, his origins were fairly modest. The only son of an old soldier, with his two sisters he had been brought up by their widowed mother at a Picard country-town called Blérancourt; and there, during his early manhood, almost for the last time, Saint-Just seems to have exhibited some of the usual human weaknesses. Thus, when he was nineteen, his mother accused him of having stolen and carried off to Paris certain valuable pieces of family plate, a pair of gold-mounted pistols and a precious ring, and had had him temporarily imprisoned; while, about the same period, he was said also to have run away with a youthful married woman. The story remains obscure; but he wrote some romantic verses, in which he told his readers that life was a dream,* advised them to close their eyes and, eyelids lowered, cull its transitory joys, and declared that, at least in imagination, he himself was now 'a King on Earth', punishing the wicked and rewarding virtue.

No sooner, during July 1789, had news of the Revolution reached Blérancourt than such adolescent velleities were forever left behind. He plunged into local politics, spoke at republican clubs, where his orations were greatly admired, and enlisted as an officer of the republican National Guard. Saint-Just would always impress his contemporaries not only by his compulsive eloquence but by the dramatic poses he assumed. In 1790, for example, while he was still at Blérancourt, he conducted a deputation of peasants to the château of a local nobleman; and, hearing that the Count had gone out, he employed the stick he held to decapitate a tall flowering plant underneath the grandee's windows, then, having executed that sternly significant gesture, turned and led his fellow patriots away.

Meanwhile, besides carrying a petition on behalf of the citizens of Blérancourt to the National Assembly, he addressed an eulogistic letter to his hero Robespierre – 'I do not know you', he wrote, 'but you are a great

---

* *'Tout nous le dit: Oui, la vie est un songe. Les yeux fermés, rêvons tranquillement . . .'*

man'; and, at an early meeting, that 'Messiah of the People' quickly recognised the bold young stranger as his predestined John the Baptist. Saint-Just was already well aware of what the situation offered him – the means of rising to the surface of his age; '*je me sens* (he declared) *de quoi surnager dans le siècle*'. His new allies included Camille Desmoulins, an unsuccessful barrister but a naturally accomplished demagogue, whose wild impromptu harangue, delivered on July 11th 1789, from a café table-top to the Sunday crowd that filled the Palais Royal's gardens, had sent his fellow patriots pouring out through the streets and, two days later, once they had gathered arms, inspired the siege and capture of the Bastille.

Supported by Robespierre and Desmoulins, Saint-Just began to establish his position; but Desmoulins, as he watched his protégé's rise, eventually became a critic. He had noticed Saint-Just's arrogance and look of indomitable self-esteem. 'One sees', he wrote, 'both from his carriage and from his attitude, that he regards his head as the corner-stone of the Republic, and that he carries it on his shoulders with respect, like a holy sacrament'; to which Saint-Just replied that, if Desmoulins were not careful, he might presently have to carry his own head under his arm in the style of the legendary St. Denis. It was a prophetic retort; at the end of March 1794, less than five months before his death, and fifteen months after the execution of the King (which he had strongly advocated), Saint-Just headed the prosecution of nine previous colleagues, among them Desmoulins and the mighty Danton, and seven of their younger assistants, and framed an eloquent speech demanding the death-penalty. When he wrote his memoirs, the future Director, the odious opportunist Paul Barras, described the young prosecutor's solemn approach to the tribune, and, as he spoke, the incisive downward gesture of his right hand, with which he repeatedly cut the air, and seemed horribly to imitate the guillotine's descending blade.

Desmoulins, though his early revolutionary record was savage enough, and he had adopted the ferocious nickname '*Procureur Général de la Lanterne*', or '*Minister of the Street-lamp*' – the usual gibbet of aristocrats and suspected Royalists – had recently suggested that a 'committee of mercy' should be set up. But both Saint-Just and Robespierre prided themselves on their conscientious lack of pity. Terrorism, they had decided, must remain the order of the day; their avowed intention was to keep it busily at work – '*maintenir partout à l'ordre du jour la terreur*'; and they continued to anticipate, admittedly on a far less extensive scale, the hideous achievements of twentieth-century dictators, until, during the explosive 'days of Thermidor', July 1794, Robespierre was received in the rebellious Convention with loud cries of '*A bas le tyran!*'

The two arch-terrorists, however, had had some redeeming human traits. No one could question the younger man's courage or loyalty. When Robespierre was shouted down, Saint-Just, obliged to desert the tribune and occupy a slightly lower place, still confronted the vociferous opposition in his customary defiant pose, '*immobile, impassible, inébranlable*'; and, when he mounted the scaffold, where Robespierre lay helpless and speechless, a bloody bandage wrapped around a shattered jaw, Saint-Just awaited death '*avec le calme stoïque et l'impassibilité froide*' that he had already displayed facing German guns on an official expedition to the battle-front. Robespierre was the more prosaic character; he had many of the attributes, some of the good qualities even, of a conscientious civil servant. Nor did he entirely lack feeling; with his exigent cult of republican 'virtue', to which every other consideration must be sacrificed, he combined the personal idealism that he had learned from Rousseau. Like Jean-Jacques he lived quietly and simply; and Barras remembered how he and a fellow politician had visited him at his small, uncomfortable Parisian rooms. His barber had just attended him; as always, Robespierre was carefully arrayed. 'But a film of powder masked his pallid face; and amid the powder one saw a pair of eyes, whose dimness the heavy spectacles he wore usually concealed in public'. He now turned them on Barras, staring fixedly and silently; and, throughout the entire interview, while Barras's colleague made him a lengthy speech, describing their ungrateful treatment by the National Convention, he uttered not a single word.

On the eve of their death, although they were determined that the Terror must continue, Robespierre and Saint-Just were meditating a minor domestic reform, designed to civilise the Revolution and smooth the roughness of proletarian manners. They set their *sansculotte* followers a good example – Robespierre with his expensively dressed hair; Saint-Just with his ear-rings and his high stock. The moment had come, they

[44]

believed, when the people must begin to enjoy their triumphs; '*la révolution*', said Saint-Just, '*est l'ouvrage du peuple; il est temps qu'il en jouisse*'. Enjoyment need no longer be exiled from the revolutionary world, provided, of course, that it was allied to virtue, and never besmirched by aristocratic excesses. He now offered the liberated French people a modest share of human pleasures – 'the satisfaction of detesting tyranny', and 'of inhabiting a humble cottage, beside a fertile field that your own hands have tilled'. Such, he thought, was the spirit of the modern age. On the *8 Ventôse l'an II* (otherwise February 26th 1794), when he delivered a report to the Convention, 'Happiness', he announced, 'is a new idea in Europe.'

To the question that Saint-Just's strange statement must immediately provoke – why the arch terrorist, having once recognised the value of happiness, should then have asserted that among his own countrymen it was a completely new idea – we can find, no doubt, a simple answer: the idea's birthplace, he evidently assumed, had been far away across the Atlantic Ocean, where in 1776 the valiant young American Colonists had proclaimed their independence. Since that day America had replaced England as the modern Promised Land. When Voltaire, during the early summer of 1726, having just emerged from the Bastille, first set foot on British soil, nearly everything he saw and heard delighted him – the grace of English equestriennes managing their spirited horses, the prosperity and dignity of London merchants, the homage writers and scientists received, and the liberal opinions that great noblemen and members of the government themselves were not afraid to voice. Thus he had begun his revolutionary career; he now felt that his mission was to combat all the prejudices and superstitions that victimised his own country; and, after his return, he published a French edition of the book he entitled *Lettres philosophiques*, in which, though he abused England's greatest poet – Shakespeare puzzled and revolted him* – he applauded the whole English social system; with the result that his rooms were searched, his private papers seized, and the book was condemned to be burned by the public executioner.

As the century went on and political unrest grew, what particularly roused the impatience of the middle and upper classes, wrote a French

---

* '*C'est une pièce grossière et barbare*', he wrote of *Hamlet*, '*qui ne serait pas supportée par la plus vile populace de la France et d'Italie*'.

nobleman, the comte de Ségur, was the contrast between their present situation and that of their immediate neighbours. Visiting Englishmen enjoyed an unprecedented popularity. The 1760s were the age of Anglo-mania, when, recorded Edward Gibbon, 'our opinions, our fashions, even our games, were adopted in France . . . and every Englishman was supposed to be born a patriot and a philosopher'. English writers received a particularly warm welcome; and their works were read and discussed in Paris almost as soon as they appeared.

A special hero, both of fashionable society and of the French intelligentsia, was David Hume, private secretary to the British Ambassador since 1763, whose massive *History of England* – his great enquiry into the nature of the Human Understanding was still comparatively little known – had gained him innumerable French admirers. He never outlived his welcome. Until, at last, he reluctantly left Paris, he had eaten 'nothing but Ambrosia', he said, drunk 'nothing but Nectar', breathed 'nothing but Incense', and trodden on 'nothing but Flowers'. Such were the rewards of enlighten-ment. The Scottish historian was a man who appreciated pleasure and had always aimed at happiness. Yet, despite his middle-aged contentment, Hume was a reformed depressive. His youth had been overcast by the type of deep melancholy that his contemporaries labelled 'hypochondria'; from which he had only escaped by recognising its physical origins and taking strenuous counter-measures that included regular exercise, 'Anti-hysteric Pills' and a pint of claret every day.

Unlike Boswell, he had gradually conquered his affliction; and it was his air of cheerfulness and unselfconscious equanimity that most delighted his Parisian friends, among them the fascinating Madame de Boufflers (nicknamed 'Madam Blewflower' by the crowd on her visit to London, during which she paid Samuel Johnson a rapid visit) with whom he very nearly fell in love. Hume's vogue at a time, Madame d'Épinay relates, when, thanks to his personal charm and his literary reputation, 'all the prettiest women were devoted to him and he attended all the smartest supper-parties', lasted from 1763 to January 1766. But the French are a volatile race; and ten years later they responded just as readily to a second foreign hero. The septuagenarian Benjamin Franklin, intermediary between France and the New World, had arrived upon a crucial diplomatic mission.

His task was to organise the shipment of arms and supplies to the embattled Colonists; and before he sailed, he had worked with the committee that produced the Declaration of Independence, signed on August 2nd, 1776.* Never has the joint production of a committee, which took its basic material from a number of different sources, had a more tremendous effect or been more eloquently, yet more simply and more directly, worded. Its object, long afterwards declared Thomas Jefferson, one of its chief authors, 'was not to find out new principles, or new arguments . . . but to place before mankind the common sense of the subject, in terms so plain and firm as to command their assent . . . It was intended to be an expression of the American mind . . . All its authority rests . . . on the harmonizing sentiments of the day.'

Hence the famous lines that soon resounded through France:

'We hold these truths to be self-evident: that all men are created equal; that they were endowed by their Creator with certain inalienable rights; that among these are life, liberty, and the pursuit of happiness'.

Both the constitutions of the new Thirteen States and the Declaration itself were quickly translated into French by the high-minded young duc de la Rochefoucauld, whose mother, Franklin's close friend, would, in 1792, watch him being stoned to death by a revolutionary mob; and the Declaration caused so much excitement that the authorities hastened to suppress it. Yet Franklin escaped reproof; and, after some fifteen months' delay, caused by the protests of the British Ambassador, he was graciously received at Versailles. The costume he assumed on this momentous occasion – a russet velvet coat and white stockings: his hair loose and his spectacles on his nose, a white hat (which the aged Madame du Deffand, writing to Horace Walpole, conjectured might be a symbol of liberty) carried underneath his arm – suggested a diplomatic combination of European correctitude and American *sans gêne*. Louis XVI's response was no less diplomatic. He had been praying in his chapel; his hair was undressed; no preparations, it seemed, had been made to receive the

---

* Independence was neither declared on July 4th (as popular historians have assumed) nor was the Declaration fully signed until August 2nd. See James Truslow Adams: *The Living Jefferson*, 1936.

David Hume; print after a portrait by Allan Ramsay, which shows his resemblance to a 'turtle-eating English alderman'.

envoys. But, as soon as they were introduced, the King assumed 'a noble posture'. He spoke first, 'with more care and graciousness', remembered a veteran courtier, than he had ever heard the sovereign display before. 'He said: "Firmly assure Congress of my friendship . . ." M. Franklin, very nobly, thanked him in the name of America, and said: "Your Majesty may count on the gratitude of Congress and its faithful observance of the pledges it now takes." '*

By this time, Franklin had become the cynosure of Parisian society, though his physical appearance, like that of the 'plump and large and rosy' Hume, said by critics to have resembled a 'turtle-eating' London alderman, was not immediately attractive. Yet he, too, had uncommon personal charm; and his benevolently wrinkled face, bald cranium and thin, grey, unpowdered locks, certainly increased his fascination. Before long a series of brilliant French ladies addressed him as their '*cher Papa*'. These devotees included Madame d'Houdetot, formerly Rousseau's beloved; the beautiful Madame Brillon, who occasionally sat on Papa's knee, though she allowed him 'only some kisses'; and Madame Helvétius, widow of the distinguished *philosophe*, to whom he once proposed marriage.

Franklin, even during his last years, was always much concerned with love; and, if many of his Parisian love-affairs remained platonic, that was evidently against his will. But, whether he succeeded or failed, seen through the eyes of his French admirers his liaisons did him no discredit. Indeed, they enhanced his reputation as a blend of sage and *homme du monde* – a man, moreover, who displayed extraordinary skill in the conduct of his own existence. His 'most original trait', decided an early nineteenth-century enthusiast, was 'his art of living in the best fashion for himself and for others, making the most effective use of all the tools nature has placed at the disposal of man . . . He would eat, sleep, work whenever he saw fit . . . so that there never was a more leisurely man, though he certainly handled a tremendous amount of business.'†

Franklin's ability to combine leisure and business, and the realistic management of life with its imaginative enjoyment, clearly distinguished

* The duc de Croy: *Journal inédit*; quoted by Claude-Anne Lopez: *Mon Cher Papa*, 1966.
† Pierre J-G. Cabanis, quoted by Claude-Anne Lopez, op. cit.

him from most of his contemporaries, either in America or in France. He understood and appreciated '*la douceur de vivre*'; yet he was at the same time sternly practical. Anything he did, he did thoroughly; and, during his American youth, when he had gained his livelihood as bookseller, newspaper-publisher, printer and stationer, he also sold across the counter of his shop iron stoves and cakes of soap, Dutch quills and Aleppo ink, Rhode Island cheese, goose feathers, tea, coffee, Bibles, account books and parchment sheets for legal use. As a modern publisher, he was remarkably adventurous; and among the products of his printing-press were the earliest American medical treatise and the first novel, printed at home, that the Colonists had yet seen – Samuel Richardson's *Pamela*, which he brought out in 1794. It was Franklin's inventive genius, however, that had earned him European fame. Once he discovered that lightning was not a divine visitation but a simple form of electricity, he produced a lightning-conductor so neat and effective that it sent a shock of amazement through the scientific world.

Another characteristic Franklin and Jefferson shared, and that made them well-qualified emissaries of the New World, was their deeply-rooted affection for Europe. True, Jefferson had a puritanical strain, and was sometimes shocked by the artificiality and insincerity that he thought he detected in Parisian life; but he considered the French an exceptionally gifted people; and 'were I to proceed to tell you', he assured a friend at home, 'how much I enjoy their architecture, sculpture, painting, music, I should want words.' It was he who commissioned Jean-Antoine Houdon to execute a famous bust of Washington; and he delighted in the remains of Roman architecture he saw on his travels around Southern France. At the *Maison Carrée*, Nismes' almost perfectly preserved Roman temple, he had gazed 'like a lover at his mistress'; while Orange's splendid arch and the 'sublime antiquity' of the Pont du Gard had astonished and enchanted him.

Franklin was less interested in works of aesthetic genius than, usually, in human beings; and for the English – he had always been happy among them, however, much he detested the 'stupid brutal Opposition' the Colonists had met with from the obscurantist British government and their misguided sovereign – he had never ceased to feel a high regard:

'Of all the enviable things England has [he once told his London landlady] I envy it most its People. Why should a petty Island, which, compared to America, is but like a stepping Stone in a Brook, scarce enough of it above Water to keep one's Shoes dry; why, I say, should that little Island, enjoy in almost every Neighbourhood more sensible, virtuous and elegant Minds than we can collect in ranging 100 leagues of our vast Forests?'

Although Franklin and Jefferson did not originate the 'new idea' that Saint-Just acclaimed in 1794, they and the other authors of the Declaration gave it a fresh and stimulating turn. Since happiness was an 'inalienable right', those who pursued it were merely claiming a privilege that belonged to all mankind. Government, Jefferson believed, was 'a necessary evil* . . . a practical arrangement for securing at any time . . . the greatest happiness possible for the individual citizen.' With this view the cold-blooded visionary Saint-Just would have at least pretended to agree. While he did his ferocious work, he seems never to have lost hope that, by ridding the world of its 'tyrants', he laid the foundations of a modern terrestrial paradise, where the men and women he had released from servitude, and who could now be trusted to obey their own virtuous instincts, might live both happily and freely.

Having completed his mission, Franklin bade France a reluctant goodbye in the summer of 1785; and his departure was triumphal. As a parting gift, he was granted a mark of favour customarily reserved for ministers plenipotentiary if they had signed a treaty with the French government – a miniature of Louis XVI encircled by more than four hundred diamonds; and, on his way to Le Havre, he occupied one of Marie-Antoinette's luxurious curtained litters. Home at last in Philadelphia, he quietly settled down to a philosophic old age. The imminence of death seemed not to trouble him greatly:

'Being now in my 83rd year [he told Madame Brillon] I do not expect to continue much longer a Sojourner in this World, and begin to promise

---

* Karl Marx, of course, also looked forward to the supersession of the state which, although unavoidable in present conditions, would begin to wither away once class differences had been abolished by the proletarian revolution; until, during the 'final phase of communism', it had completely disappeared.

myself much Gratification of my Curiosity in soon visiting some other. Where-ever I may hereafter travel, be assured, my dear Friend, that . . . the Remembrance of your Friendship will be retained, as having made too deep an impression to be obliterated, and will ever, as it always has done, afford me infinite Pleasure. Adieu. Adieu.'

Although he believed in the immortality of the soul, Franklin's religious views were never wholly orthodox; and he admitted, not long before his death on August 13th, 1790, that he respected the moral teaching of Christianity, but was still inclined to question the divinity of Christ. During his last twelve months on earth, as he calmly awaited the end, he was only seriously disturbed by what he heard and read of 'the Misunderstandings and Troubles that have arisen in the Government of that dear Country, in which I pass'd nine of the happiest Years of my Life'; and he felt a deep sympathy for the beloved friends he had left behind there. The news that reached him from France had been 'very affecting'; but, luckily, he did not live to observe, even at a distance, the terrible progress of the Revolution and the advent of the Terror.

Jefferson, who died in 1826, and whose links with France had been far less personal, though he deplored the crimes committed in the Republic's name maintained that its cause was still the cause of freedom, and accepted Washington's view that, during the struggle between Great Britain and revolutionary France, the attitude of the United States must be strictly neutral. Then, early in 1794, he announced that he was resigning from public life and retired temporarily to the classic country house* that, after a careful study of Palladio, he had built on a Virginian hill-top. His decision was accompanied by a letter he addressed to James Madison, where he both explained his motives and gave a definition of the spiritual benefits he now expected to enjoy.

In the history of our subject his letter deserves to take its place beside the Declaration that he had helped to frame. 'Age, experience & reflection', he wrote, had induced him to set a higher value on tranquillity, now that 'the motion of my blood no longer keeps time with the tumult of the world', and had led him 'to seek for happiness in the lap and love of my family, in the society of my neighbours & my books, in the wholesome occupations

---

* 'Monticello' had been built in 1770.

of my farm and my affairs.' As a public personage, he added, he was obliged to give up everything he loved for everything that he detested; and he now felt confident – here, it seems, he was echoing Rousseau's *Promeneur Solitaire* – that he would find the tranquillity he sought in his garden and his fields, 'in an interest or affection in every bud that opens, in every breath that blows around me, in an entire freedom of rest or motion, of thought or incognitancy, owing account to myself alone of my hours and actions'. Jefferson, however, unlike Rousseau, could not finally resist his age; he preferred public usefulness to private happiness and, having re-entered politics, became the third President of the United States on March 4th, 1801.

4

'The Courage to be Happy'

URING the early nineteenth century, two distinguished French-men, having weathered the Revolutionary storm found the problem of human happiness particularly absorbing. Joseph Joubert had been born in 1754, his friend François René de Chateaubriand in 1768; and, although their lives were often closely linked, and each studied the other's character with appreciative attention, both of them very soon recognised how considerably they differed. Joubert, who lived until 1824, belonged to the eighteenth century and had inherited its respect for restraint and moderation, whereas Chateaubriand, who died nearly half-way through the nineteenth, witnessed first the rise and then the slow decline of the great Romantic Age that, in his heyday, he had once led. Joubert was an Epicurean philosopher, who set out to define and conquer happiness; Chateaubriand believed that Man's unhappiness was a proof of his spiritual distinction. 'Man,' he declared, 'you exist merely through suffering; you are nothing except for the sadness of your spirit and the eternal melancholy of your thought'.

Very different, too, were the attitudes they adopted towards the problem of the Self. Like Rousseau, Joubert was convinced that peace and self-regard – '*son repos et l'estime de soi-même*' – should be the individual's chief support, which one might achieve by 'living much with oneself, consulting oneself, listening to oneself'; while his friend, he wrote, soon after Chateaubriand published his immensely popular *Génie du Christianisme*, had, 'so to speak, all his faculties turned outwards . . . He does not speak, with himself . . . never questions himself'; it was his readers' approval, rather than his own, he sought. 'Thus it follows that his talent will never make him happy . . .' As to his life, that was a different matter. There he remained the adventurous philanderer and Romantic egoist.* While he wrote for the benefit of others, and had his eye fixed upon his admiring literary audience, it was for himself alone he lived.

The contrast between the two writers became doubly apparent when they found they loved the same woman, and Chateaubriand's love was passionately returned, but Joubert had to be content with a tender *amitié amoureuse*, a gentle sisterly affection. Pauline de Beaumont belonged to an aristocratic family, the Montmorins, which the Revolution had cruelly broken up. Both her mother and her brother were guillotined; her father died during the hideous September Massacres. But the revolutionary commissioners, who threw Madame de Montmorin into the cart that carried her away towards her death, announced that Pauline was too weak to travel; and, although she tried in vain to run beside the wheels, she was eventually left behind. Her neighbour, Joubert, having heard her story, resolved that he would seek her out, and discovered her sitting before a cottage where she had taken refuge with a pair of kindly peasants.

Pauline was then twenty-six, Joubert already forty years old, a philosophic recluse, sensibly married to a modest, undemanding woman; and for Pauline he conceived a deep attachment that had some of the strength of a passion, but very little of a passion's turbulence and greed. His chief desire, since her worst sufferings had now passed, was to help restore her nearly broken spirit, and give her back the calm she needed. That, he suggested, was the only reward he sought. But, meanwhile, he must tell her, he wrote in 1795, he could not admire and respect her as much as he wished to do until she had shown the most beautiful form of courage, '*le plus beau de tous les courages*', the courage to be happy. She often despaired of life, and had told him that she would like to die quite alone at a village-inn on some casual expedition. A morbid fantasy, Joubert replied; to reach happiness,

* In his *Mémoires d'outre Tombe*, written many years after Joubert's death, Chateaubriand describes his old friend's preoccupation with himself, adding, however, that '*c'était un égoiste qui ne s'occupait que des autres*'.

she needed a determination to care for herself and a firm resolution that she would grow well. Pauline de Beaumont, however, whose health had always been frail, was at once a hypochondriac and a natural melancholic. Even before the Revolution destroyed her family, she had gone through an unhappy marriage. Now she proved a recalcitrant pupil; and, in the autumn of 1803, he was still affectionately scolding her.

Life, he asserted, was a duty of which we must do our best to make a pleasure, or, should it prove impossible, at least, '*un demi-plaisir*'. If that were the sole duty we had received from Heaven, we must discharge it calmly and gaily, and with as much grace as we could summon up, tending the sacred flame of existence and doing all we could to appreciate its warmth. When, at the start of the new century, Pauline fell wildly in love with the author of *Atala*—Chateaubriand's novel, she confessed, played on her nerves, like a hand playing on a clavecin – Joubert was alarmed and pained, yet sympathetic. The novelist, whom his circle nicknamed '*le Chat*', though already married, short, pock-marked and rather awkwardly built – '*un bossu sans bosse*', Madame de Lieven would presently observe – was known to exert a magnetic power over sensitive, impressionable women; and Joubert, being a perfectionist both in life and in literature, soon decided that sexual jealousy was the kind of vulgar emotion that a wise man carefully repressed. Once, invited with Madame Joubert to visit a house in the country that the lovers at the time were sharing, he took a volume of Kant, a philosopher he particularly disliked, to occupy his mind and strengthen his reserve, while he walked the garden paths beneath their windows.

Neither Joubert nor Chateaubriand could hope to save Pauline; but, during their efforts, each of them adopted a completely different method of approach. Joubert had demanded that she should strive against her unhappiness; Chateaubriand, who had ennobled the idea of suffering, tacitly accepted it. Pauline's spiritual woes reflected the human condition; and her physical fragility moved his heart. Her lack of any obvious appeal seems to have particularly attracted him; Madame de Beaumont, he wrote in his autobiography, was plain rather than beautiful – '*plutôt mal que bien de figure*'. Her face was thin and pale; and her almond-shaped eyes might perhaps have been too brilliant, had an air of extraordinary gentleness not tempered the effect they made, just as a sunbeam is refracted and softened slanting through a glass of water.

During the early summer of 1803, Chateaubriand left for Rome, Napoleon, a great admirer of *Le Génie du Christianisme*, having, on Talleyrand's advice, appointed him First Secretary at the French Embassy; and Pauline, much to Chateaubriand's embarrassment and Joubert's dismay, insisted she would join him there. She arrived, totally exhausted after a long and difficult journey, and, on November 4th, died in her lover's arms. Chateaubriand's description of her last days, and particularly of her last attempt to enjoy the outer world, is one of his most moving literary flights. From the villa he had taken for her near the Spanish Steps, which she was rarely able to leave, they had visited the Colosseum. It had been a luminous autumn day; step by step, he tells us, she descended to the amphitheatre's lowest level, and there rested on a stone opposite a Christian altar. Naturally, the imaginative possibilities of the scene did not escape the great Romantic artist, as he watched her raise her eyes and let them stray round the gigantic cirque of ruins – stones that 'long had seen so much of death', now overgrown with brambles and saffron-yellow wild flowers – until they reached the altar and its marble cross, and she said, 'Let us go! I am feeling tired.'

Mourning became the author of *Atala*. 'Sorrow is my element', he had already informed Joubert. 'I only discover myself when I am unhappy'; and, although his friend's grief was equally poignant, it took a somewhat less dramatic shape. Soon after she had gained Rome, he wrote Pauline his last letter, dated October 12th, 1803:

'You bid me love you always [he reminded her]. Alas, can I do anything else, whatever you are, and whatever you may wish? Between us there was a sympathy, to which you have sometimes opposed many obstacles and contradictions . . . No one has ever inspired in me a more solid and faithful affection . . . Farewell, then, cause of such pain, who for me have been the source of so much good. Protect yourself; spare yourself; and come back into our midst one day, if only to give me, for a single moment, the indescribable pleasure of seeing you again'

Joubert shunned slavish displays of feeling; and, after Pauline's death, he assured the poet Chênedollé, a slightly more sympathetic figure than

Chateaubriand, that his sorrow was 'not extravagant', but, none the less, would be 'eternal'. Chateaubriand might 'regret her as keenly as I do', he said: 'but he will not miss her so long'. Then the passionate and the platonic lover each resumed his own career; Chateaubriand went on from triumph to triumph; Joubert continued to cultivate happiness, and presently built up another image that represented for him truth and beauty. Compared with his previous love, Louise de Vintmille was a bold, flamboyant personage – a thirty-nine-year-old *femme du monde*, partly Viennese by birth, who shone in fashionable Parisian society, was fond of fine clothes, silks and bright colours, and whose elderly husband wrote verses, which Joubert regularly took care to praise. She herself, though never a blue-stocking, had cultivated literary tastes. She was devoted to seventeenth-century literature, and claimed that she invariably went into mourning on the anniversary of Madame de Sévigné's death. Since she enjoyed excellent health, Madame de Vintmille, like her favourite authoress, could afford to temper wit with good nature. If a friend squinted, she once explained, she always looked at him or her in profile.

It was on July 22nd, 1802, that Joubert, who had originally met her among Pauline de Beaumont's friends, first began to feel her charm. He and Chateaubriand had walked at her side through the Gardens of the Tuileries; and he had halted to purchase her a huge bouquet of strongly-scented tuberoses – a flower that from that day would occupy as dominant a place in his sentimental recollections as cattleyas would long afterwards hold in the love-story of Odette and Swann. But the relationship that afterwards gradually developed, and was to last until his end, remained solely romantic and platonic, and derived its continued strength both from the delightful memories she evoked and that the fragrance of tuberoses unfailingly summoned up, and from the admiration he had always felt for her gay, untroubled spirit. His penultimate letter, written on the twentieth anniversary of their walk through the Gardens, when he knew that his end was drawing near and he could seldom venture out, refers to her equable nature, her perfectly sound judgement and, wherever she might be, the effect her 'laughing presence' made. She symbolised happiness, and the courage that happiness demands in a world of strife and discord.

During his lifetime, Joubert published nothing – he had luckily a small inherited fortune; and he wished, he wrote, to express no ideas 'unworthy of being inscribed either on silk or on bronze'. But his widow faithfully collected his manuscripts; and, fourteen years later, Chateaubriand edited and introduced them. It was a somewhat belated tribute, to which he added a characteristically melodious and lugubrious phrase; as he worked, he said, he had heard behind him the ebb and flow of memories that recalled the sound of a wave sweeping a faraway beach: '*J'écoute derrière moi les souvenirs, comme le bruissement de la vague sur une plage lointaine*' – an image probably inspired by the famous line of a Latin elegiac poet.* Chateaubriand had the misfortune to live too long, and thus witnessed the Revolution of 1848, which bewildered and appalled him. With the help of his servant, he still punctually climbed the stairs to the little salon kept by his last love, the septuagenarian beauty Madame Récamier, where he heard his memoirs read aloud. But he yearned, he said, to escape from a tormented world he could neither endure nor understand.

Chateaubriand's cult of sorrow was adopted by a succession of Romantic followers. Byron, oddly enough, mentions him only once – in a letter written soon after Waterloo, in which he refers to some anonymous verses on Napoleon's fall that he had sent to the editor of a London daily newspaper, and suggested they might perhaps appear '*as a translation* from some recent *French poetry* . . . It would not be bad fun to call it Chateaubriand's'; for 'the dog deserves no quarter . . .' Byron's animosity, of course, had a largely political origin; despite his much-advertised hatred of tyrants and tyranny, he continued to reverence the fallen Emperor; and the rival poet, having served under Napoleon, had issued, on the very day the victorious Allies entered Paris, a pamphlet welcoming home the Bourbons and defending the principles they represented. Yet the Englishman's literary self-esteem may also have played its part; Byron must surely have been well aware that between their two poetic heroes, Childe Harold and the Childe's predecessor René (who had fascinated Europe seven years earlier) there was an uncomfortably close relationship.

* Propertius: '*Litore sic tacito sonitus rarescit harenae*': 'So on the quiet shore does the sound of wave-swept sand grow fainter'.

Indeed, a shrewd biographer, Harold Nicolson, once told me that Byron, he believed, had never set foot in France because he was reluctant to enter his rival's territory, and preferred to dominate the literary stage alone.

Both Childe Harold and René are the enemies of happiness and have long abandoned its pursuit. Byron was the first Anglo-Saxon poet whose works had a strong, immediate, sometimes disruptive effect upon the existence of a whole generation, and not on critics and literati alone, but on an astonishing diversity of readers, who ranged from Madame de Lieven, the aristocratic Russian ambassadress, to a celebrated English courtesan, and, among the obscure, to 'a poor country girl' who begged for a lock of his hair, and a forlorn bankrupt, named Thomas Mulock, living in exile at Boulogne, who signed himself 'your Lordship's real Christian friend' and asserted that he was 'one of the few beings on earth who can understand the breadth and depth, and length and height, of your intellectual woes – one who has mourned and maddened where you now weep and writhe . . .'.*

The impression that *Childe Harold* made on Madame de Lieven, a woman much courted by George IV and a dazzling member of the clique that ruled Almack's Club, seems far stranger and more unexpected. In 1822, when, two years after the Regent's accession to the throne, she and husband were staying at the Brighton Pavilion – then a scene of profligate luxury, unparalleled, she thought, 'since the days of Heliogabalus' – she wrote to her faraway lover Prince Metternich, recalling a previous sojourn at the same resort. This had been in the summer of 1818; the third canto of *Childe Harold* had just appeared, and, as she was feeling dispirited and listless, she decided she would occupy her mind by attempting a translation:

'. . . I always took the poem with me when I went to sit on a certain rocky point, which is quite dry at low tide, but completely submerged at high. Lord Byron says terrible and sublime things about death by drowning, and I had always thought that passage particularly fine. I was reading it one day on the rocks; and I felt that nothing could be simpler than to stay on the point until the sea had covered it. I conceived the idea quite

---

* These, and many similar extracts from letters written by the poet's obscure admirers, are quoted in *To Lord Byron*, George Paston and Peter Quennell, 1939.

dispassionately. I cannot help believing . . . that we all have a certain tendency to madness . . . Evidently, my hour of madness had come. I experienced . . . nothing but a great unconcern in my heart and in my head. I waited on the rock a good half-hour . . . but the tide did not rise. When at last it did, my madness ebbed as the water advanced.'*

She had not even, she cheerfully assured Metternich, allowed the tide to wet her shoes; and she had burst out laughing on her way home; 'for, at that moment, nothing seemed so delightful as the small details of life, and nothing so stupid as the desire to die'. Madame de Lieven's suicidal impulse had lasted only half an hour; but there were other women – for instance, Caroline Lamb, Claire Clairmont and no doubt many less notorious votaries – who were made of feebler stuff, and whom their infatuation with Byron's 'demonic' genius would permanently bemuse and sometimes nearly destroy. To make his influence still more captivating, the sorrows of Childe Harold, and of Byron's other gloomy heroes, have almost always a mysterious origin. They arise from some unknown depth, and are part of a dark secret that the poet never quite divulges, and that his characters, he seems inclined to suggest, cannot completely understand themselves, though it visibly affects their conduct, and provokes the 'strange pangs' that, in the midst of his wildest dissipations, often 'flash along Childe Harold's brow'.

Not until Byron had reached Venice, and, free at last from the pall of gloom – 'the nightmare of my own delinquencies' – that had enveloped him since he left London, decided he would write a new poem, in which, he said, he meant 'to be a little quietly facetious upon everything', did his magnetic spell begin to wane. His closest friends, among them Hobhouse and Tom Moore, once they had seen the manuscript of *Don Juan*, were 'unanimous in advising its suppression'; they were shocked by his 'sarcasms upon his wife' (whom he caricatured as Juan's mother, Donna Inez), 'the indecency of parts . . . the attacks on religion . . . the abuse of other writers', and, above all perhaps, by the cheerful flippancy of the poet's tone, which replaced Childe Harold's brooding melancholy. After

* See *The Private Letters of Princess Lieven to Prince Metternich*, edited and translated by Quennell and Powell, 1937.

Don Juan's publication, many of his readers were astonished and disgusted; and his moral critics included the famous demi-mondaine Harriette Wilson. Since meeting him at a masked ball, she had long, she admitted, been 'sentimentally in love' with him, and had offered him her devoted friendship – which he had prudently declined, though, when she also begged his financial help, he had sent her fifty guineas. But now, having read *Don Juan*, she dashed off an indignant reprimand:

> 'Dear *Adorable* Lord Byron, *don't* make a mere *coarse* old libertine of yourself . . . I would not, even to *you* . . . lie under the imputation of such bad taste as to admire what in your cool moments, I am sure, you must feel to be *vulgar* at least . . .'

René's melancholy, like that of Childe Harold, was the attribute his admirers considered most attractive; and, again, its source remains mysterious, so long as the tragic secret that eventually drives him abroad, to live in the American forests amid the virtuous Indians, has not yet been laid bare. Until then, he suffers merely from an indefinable disquietude – a sense of loneliness, of ardent, unsatisfied yearnings, of the emptiness of mortal life, that has constantly pursued him. The only human being he truly loves is his sister Amélie; but she grows more and more evasive, and at last retires into a convent. There she sickens and dies, having, on her death-bed, uttered the few dreadful words that explain their joint tragedy – she has conceived a 'criminal passion' for the brother by whom she was innocently loved; and René then leaves Europe and takes refuge in the wilds of Louisiana, where, despite the comfort he has received from a venerable French priest and his good-hearted neighbours, he presently gives up the ghost.

René (which for Byron would one day have a special significance) appeared in 1805; the two opening cantos of *Childe Harold*, in 1812; and together they helped to launch the tide of melancholy feeling that rolls through nineteenth-century verse and prose. Romantic gloom was a very different emotion from many earlier forms of human sadness; it was more pervasive and had fewer obvious causes. In England during the sixteenth and seventeenth centuries, melancholy was often regarded either as spiritual sickness that might have a largely physical origin, or as a deliberate manifestation of the sufferer's sense of wrong and of his private grievances against the world. Such social rebels, whom their happier contemporaries entitled 'malcontents', were easily recognisable when they stalked around the London streets, or skulked through the noisy crowd that filled St. Paul's, their arms folded, their hats pulled down towards their eyes, their hose, like Hamlet's, usually ungartered, wearing black cloaks, their rapiers reversed with the point thrust forward, and their right hands fingering their daggers.

Hamlet himself, superficially considered, is the type of malcontent; for the drama, as it now exists, is thought to have been based upon an old revenge-play popular about 1589, which Shakespeare adapted and, of course, wonderfully enlarged and subtilised. In the original play, the dispossessed Prince must also have adopted what Shakespeare's hero calls 'an antic disposition' and the gloomy trappings of a malcontent, mainly to disarm the suspicions of his wicked uncle's courtiers and guards; and John Marston's play *The Malcontent*, produced in 1604, shows the protagonist, Malevole, the ousted Duke of Genoa, who lives in disguise at the usurper's court, employing more or less the same stratagem. He performs his curious part well; he has become a surly exhibitionist. 'This Malevole', exclaims the reigning Duke, 'is one of the most prodigious affections that ever conversed with nature . . . his appetite is unsatiable as the grave; as far from any content as from heaven: his highest delight is to procure others vexation . . . the elements struggle within him; his own soul is at variance with itself . . .'

The Elizabethans and their immediate successors were fond of assuming a symbolic costume that revealed their inward feelings;* and although we know little else of the remarkable dramatist John Ford, whose master-piece, *'Tis Pity She's a Whore*, unfolds the tragic development of an incestuous passion, a single couplet dashed off by an unknown friend

---

* In *Twelfth Night*, Malvolio's yellow stockings indicate his passion for his mistress; while the Elizabethan diarist Thomas Wythorne, who also loved his employer, wore a russet suit, a colour that signified hope, and a garland of hops, which had the same significance, wreathed around his hat-brim.

> 'Deep in a dump John Forde was alone got
> With folded arms and melancholy hat'

— vividly suggests his character. An imaginary personage wearing the same kind of hat, his arms similarly folded, appears on the frontispiece of Richard Burton's *Anatomy of Melancholy*, the huge encyclopedic work that, after long research and some private experience of his subject, he published in 1621. Here he treats melancholy as a mental illness, of which love-melancholy is probably among the deadliest manifestations – even 'Fishes pine away for love' – and notes the various remedies that may perhaps effect a cure. They include the use of scents and regular scrubbings of the scalp. 'Odoraments to smell to, of rose water, violet flowers, bawme, rosecakes, vineger, &c. do much recreate the brains and spirits'; while irrigations of the shaven head, *'of the flowers of water lilies, lettuce, violets, camomile, wild mallows, wethers head,* &c, must be used many mornings together'.

Burton's learned advice shows that he thought of the dreaded disease as frequently remediable. Its name itself was derived from the Elizabethan theory that a man's character was determined not only by the mysterious influence of the stars, but by the results of the 'cardinal humour'* most effective in his constitution, melancholy's source being the 'Black Bile', which had subdued the livelier, more genial elements, but, given the right medicines, might presently be overcome. Melancholy, regarded as almost a virtue, as an interesting, even an appealing trait, was the conception of a later period. La Fontaine, during the second half of the seventeenth century, includes 'the sombre pleasure of a melancholy heart' among the assets of a civilised existence;† and, in English literature, Pope mentioned the 'not unpleasing melancholy' to which a sensitive poet now and then gave way. Once the first signs of the Romantic dawn had begun to appear on the horizon, it accompanied a passion for Gothic ruins and the more desolate aspects of Nature, and, entitled 'the Spleen', a variation of the

---

* The other humours, or 'chief fluids', were Blood, Phlegm and Choler. Black Bile was first thought to be the origin of 'sullenness and propensity to causeless and violent rages'; later, of 'mental gloom and sadness'.

† From La Fontaine's *Invocation* to the Spirit of Pleasure: *J'aime le jeu, l'amour, les livres, la musique, La ville et la campagne, enfin tout; il n'est rien Qui ne me soit souverain bien, Jusqu'au sombre plaisir d'un coeur mélancolique.*

disease that particularly attacked women, had a somewhat ludicrous and comic side.*

True, the Georgians, were also familiar with genuine melancholy at its ghastliest and darkest. Two distinguished poets William Cowper and William Collins were known to have gone melancholy mad; and, later, Collins' sighs and groans were daily heard resounding through the ancient cloisters of Chichester Cathedral; while Johnson and Boswell, we are often reminded, were racked by atrocious fits of gloom. But both the great man and his pupil deliberately sought for happiness – they were closer to Joubert than to Chateaubriand; and neither would have agreed that suffering was a badge of moral worth. They suffered despite themselves, and in their own lives accepted the human condition and its inescapable sorrows with all the fortitude that they could muster.

* See Pope's description in *The Rape of the Lock*, Canto IV, of Umbriel's descent into the
   Cave of Spleen, and of the Spirit who presides there:
                          'Hail wayward Queen!
                  Who rule the Sex to Fifty from Fifteen,
                  Parent of Vapors and of Female Wit,
                  Who give th'*Hysteric* or *Poetic* Fit . . .'

'An Indissoluble Bond'

NEITHER happiness nor goodness is an attribute that novelists have found it easy to describe. Dickens' most praiseworthy characters are usually the least memorable; and the 'happy endings', with which he and his fellow Victorians frequently rounded off a story, when deserving personages are summoned back on to the stage, and each receives his or her appropriate reward, seldom satisfy a modern critic. One of the few convincing portraits of a really happy man has an unexpected origin; it comes from *Anna Karenina*, the book that Tolstoy, a far more determined moralist than Dickens – for whose genius, 'tinged with humour and melancholy', he had always felt a deep regard – wrote and published, first as an immensely popular serial, between 1873 and 1877. The heroine's brother, Stefan Arkadyevitch Oblonsky, has no obvious claim to approbation. He is happy because the happiness he enjoys, and very often spreads around him, is as much a part of his natural constitution as his height, the length of his arms, or the colour of his eyes. It is a quality that, despite occasional brief misgivings, he finds it almost impossible to overcome.

Yet *Anna Karenina*, in its dramatic entirety, has a strongly moral, indeed a profoundly pessimistic, theme. Under the grim epigraph, '*Vengeance is mine, and I will repay*', Tolstoy illustrates the disastrous effects of a consuming sexual passion. Desire gratified fails to bring happiness. When Vronsky first achieves his conquest of Anna, both are dreadfully transfigured. Tolstoy likens the lover to a frenzied assassin, who falls on his victim's body, and 'drags it and hacks at it'. He covers her face and shoulders with kisses:

> 'All is over,' she said; 'I have nothing but you. Remember that.'
> 'I can never forget what is my whole life. For one instant of this happiness . . .'
> 'Happiness!' she said with horror and loathing, and her horror unconsciously infected him. 'For pity's sake, not a word, not a word more.'

Meanwhile Levin, the novelist's alter ego, takes a very different path. He loves a good, delightful girl, Kitty, Oblonsky's sister-in-law, whom, after a long and arduous courtship, he weds and carries off to his estate, where he hopes to reorganise his large neglected property and improve the condition of his backward peasant labourers. Levin is naturally serious and public-spirited. Yet the daily problems he encounters and, far worse, his spiritual anxieties and metaphysical doubts, soon undermine his peace of spirit; and, throughout his productive and apparently well-ordered marriage, there occur secret crises when, as Tolstoy had done, he feels so close to suicide that he hides the rope with which he might otherwise hang himself and, if he goes out into the fields and woods, prefers to leave his gun behind.

Against this turbulent background, Stefan Arkadyevitch goes his blithe, untroubled way. Critics have at times dismissed him as a mildly ridiculous *bon vivant*, who performs an amusing but unimportant rôle in this dark and complex story.* He is much more than that. Whenever he reappears, he changes the tempo of the narrative, for a while suspends its tragic course, and breathes an atmosphere of life and freedom. A trifler he may be, an Osric at the Russian Court. But he is not a fraud, still less a hypocrite – a fact that the novelist, though he detests every social standard his personage represents, sometimes readily acknowledges. 'Stefan

---

* A notable exception was Matthew Arnold, whose essay on Tolstoy, published in the second series of *Essays in Criticism*, 1888, contains a splendid tribute to Oblonsky. 'No, never, certainly,' writes Arnold, 'shall we come to forget Stiva'. Lionel Trilling, however, in *The Opposing Self*, 1955, mentions his name only once, and then does not discuss his personality.

Arkadyevitch', he admits, 'was a truthful man in his relations with himself', thus reminding us of the splendid advice that Polonius gives his son:

> 'This above all: to thine own self be true
> Thou canst not then be false to any man.'

Being true to himself, Stefan Arkadyevitch is false to no one, except, now and then, to his ageing wife Dolly; and, in that relationship, given their circumstances – his continued youth and Dolly's physical decline – the domestic fibs he is often obliged to tell her strike him as perhaps regrettable, yet also, he assumes, sadly unavoidable.

Anton Tchehov was a story-teller Tolstoy admired; and, in a criticism he published of *The Darling*, he suggested that its author, having first meant to 'knock down' his subject – a wonderfully affectionate but uncommonly stupid woman – at length had glorified and 'raised her up'. Tolstoy does not exalt Oblonsky – he cannot pretend that he approves of him; yet he credits the impenitent man of pleasure with a pervasive sheen or glow. Entering a fashionable restaurant beside this pleasant old friend, Levin notices 'a certain peculiarity of expression, as it were a restrained radiance, about the face and whole figure of Stefan Arkadyevitch. Oblonsky took off his greatcoat and, his hat over one ear, walked into the dining-room, giving directions to the Tatar waiters . . . Bowing to right and left . . . and here as everywhere joyously greeting acquaintances, he went up to the sideboard . . .'

Oblonsky's voice is one of his main assets; it is 'as soft and soothing as almond oil'; and his smile has a distinctive charm. When Levin begins gloomily discoursing on the imminence of death, Stefan Arkadyevitch gives a 'subtle and affectionate smile', which shows that, although he may not necessarily agree, he understands the other's feelings. An egoist by birth and education, he is neither insensitive nor hard-hearted. But deep misery and a sense of moral guilt, since he has never suffered from them himself, are quite beyond his comprehension; and, facing his wretched brother-in-law, Anna's cuckolded husband, he is utterly bewildered:

'"Alexey Alexandrovitch, believe me, she appreciates your generosity", he said. "But it seems it was the will of God," he added, and as he said it he felt how foolish a remark it was, and with difficulty repressed a smile at his own foolishness.'

Anna he has already tried to cheer. She is ill and overwrought, he assures her, and he hints, 'exaggerating dreadfully'. No one else in Stefan Arkadyevitch's place, having to do with such despair, 'would have ventured to smile . . . but in his smile there was so much of sweetness and almost feminine tenderness that his smile did not wound'.

Among the dramatis personae of *Anna Karenina* Oblonsky occupies a privileged position. His vices are implied; they need no underlining, and are never harshly singled out as are the faults of other characters. Tolstoy had an exceedingly close link with the men and women he created – with Levin, especially, who embodied both his ideals and aspirations and many of his own doubts and fears; with Vronsky, the military rake; and with Anna herself, who, when he began work, was to have been an ugly but attractive woman – she would have 'a narrow, low forehead' and 'a short, turned-up nose', and only much later became a famous beauty – his biographer tells us that he fell passionately in love. Stefan Arkadyevitch, on the other hand, was his direct antithesis, a happy man, completely unaware of the incessant spiritual problems that darkened his creator's days.

While he wrote *Anna Karenina*, Tolstoy's own state of mind had been particularly restless. There seemed, he announced during those years, 'nothing else to do in life but die . . . I am writing, I'm working very hard, the children are healthy, but there is no happiness for me in any of it'. He hated his chosen profession – 'writing corrupts the soul'; and he pretended to condemn his book. 'What's so difficult', he enquired, 'about describing how an officer gets entangled with a woman?' Such a description demanded little skill, and served no kind of honest purpose. Yet Tolstoy's portrait of Stefan Arkadyevitch is an imaginative masterpiece, where the artist's gift of sympathising and understanding has surmounted every obstacle that his moral prejudices raised. Although the novelist cannot excuse his heroine, whose worst crime was that she had obeyed the dictates of a rebellious heart, but on whom the vengeance of Heaven must necessarily fall, her kinsman, an unfaithful husband and selfish spendthrift, never faces the divine tribunal; his hat over his ear, 'joyously greeting acquaintances' and giving directions to respectful waiters, he quietly circumvents his judges. Having lost one good official sinecure, he almost immediately finds a second; and we bid him a cheerful goodbye in the concluding chapter. 'There's my son-in-law,' remarks the old Prince, 'Stefan Arkadyevitch, you know him. He's got a place now on the committee of a commission and something or other . . . Only there's nothing to do in it . . . and a salary of eight thousand.'

Tolstoy's personage has clearly a comic side. In his portrait there is something of a patrician Micawber, another resolutely pleasure-seeking man, and, now and then, a touch of Falstaff. The moralist would later revile Shakespeare – Hamlet's 'affectations', for instance, repelled him; but Stefan Arkadyevitch has a true Shakespearian quality; and Hazlitt's eloquent description of Falstaff might almost equally well be a summing-up of Tolstoy's delightful anti-hero. 'His body', wrote the critic (an artist who hungered after happiness, but, alas, very seldom experienced it) 'is like a good estate to his mind, from which he receives rents and revenues of profit and pleasure'; and it is through the equable relationship he has established between mind and body that Falstaff derives 'an absolute self-possession, which nothing can disturb. His repartees are involuntary suggestions of his self-love; instinctive evasions of everything that threatens to interrupt the career of his triumphant jollity and self-complacency.'

Each character has taken his own measure. Surrounded by idealists, romantics, planners, political intriguers and militant 'iron men', he is perfectly content with the human happiness he finds in his day-to-day existence. Falstaff, however, has also a keen imagination and a retentive memory – 'We have heard the chimes at midnight, Master Shallow', he reminds his prosy old acquaintance – and, for all his rampant egotism, an unquestionably warm heart. He loves his callous young patron, as Shakespeare perhaps had loved his golden youth; and Falstaff's victorious career is only cut short when Henry, having just ascended the throne, cruelly compares him to an unclean figment of his own imagination:

'I know thee not, old man. Fall to thy prayers . . .
I have long dream'd of such a kind of man,
So surfeit-swelled, so old, and so profane;
But, being awak'd, I do despise my dream.'

Falstaff rallies, but soon dies. 'The King has killed his heart' laments the ever-loyal Mistress Quickly.

Euphoric characters like Falstaff and Stefan Arkadyevitch are not prone to self-analysis – their greatest strength is that they take happiness as it comes, and accept it almost as a birthright. Thus they have rarely attempted to portray themselves. But there is one magnificent exception. The diary of Samuel Pepys contains the self-portrait of a man who shared some of their tastes and many of their psychological advantages, and avoided most of the lasting conflicts by which other personalities have been undermined. Not that he escaped anxieties and afflictions, or lacked at times a sense of sin; but, throughout the whole *Diary*, although he remained persistently introspective, and never minimised his faults and failures, records of happiness predominate. Here the knowledge that he had succeeded in life evidently assisted him. The son of a London tailor, but luckily a cousin of Lord Sandwich, he had soon developed into an ambitious and efficient civil servant, determined, while he did his duty, to get on in the world and improve his social and financial status, until, at last, he found himself walking and talking familiarly with the rulers of the kingdom.

We still admire the splendid variety of Pepys' lifelong tastes and interests; and, when he left the world in 1703, his old friend and fellow diarist John Evelyn paid him the tribute he deserved: 'This day dyed Mr. Sam: Pepys, a very worthy, Industrious and curious person, none in England exceeding him in the Knowledge of the Navy . . . universaly beloved, Hospitable, Generous, Learned on many things, skill'd in Musick, a very great cherisher of Learned man . . .'. By 'curious', of course, Evelyn meant that Pepys' desire for knowledge about any subject that he undertook, from ship-building to the arts and sciences – he would one day be elected President of the newly-founded Royal Society – was extraordinarily wide-ranging. But, at the same time, unlike many scientifically-minded men, he was devoted to the spectacle of life as it passed beneath his eyes. Every observation he could make, whether it was of his own frequently ill-advised and, now and then, discreditable behaviour, or of the traits of famous public personages, invariably delighted him. During the early summer of 1660, for example, when he accompanied Charles II back to England, he had watched the King on deck:

'. . . We weighed Ancre, and with a fresh gale . . . we set sail . . . all the afternoon the King walking here and there, up and down (quite contrary to what I thought he had been) very active and stirring'.

Later, as the royal procession landed:

'I went, and Mr Mansell and one of the King's footmen, with a dog that the King loved (and which shit in the boat, which made us laugh and me think that a King and all that belong to him are but just as others are) . . .'

Although Pepys is usually most likeable if he conveys the satisfaction he derived from living, even in his darkest private crises, a reader may sometimes assume, he half enjoyed the drama of the scene, as when his wife, distracted by jealousy because she had caught him fondling her maid, threatened him in bed with a pair of red-hot tongs; 'at which I rose up, and with a few words she laid them down and little by little, very sillily, let all the discourse fall; and about 2 . . . came to bed and there [we] lay well all night . . . talking together with much pleasure . . .' Pepys was a deeply attached, but regularly unfaithful, husband; and he, too, having conceived a wild suspicion that Mrs Pepys had become enamoured of her new dancing-master, Mr Pembleton, 'a pretty neat black man', grew 'so deeply full of jealousy . . . that I could not do any business; for which', he wrote a day later, 'I deserve to be beaten, if not really served as I am fearful of being; especially since, God knows, that I do not find enough honesty in my own mind but that upon a small temptation I could be false to her, and therefore ought not to expect more from her – but God pardon both my sin and my folly therein.'

Women and music, he had discovered at an early stage of his life, were his most deeply rooted passions. The first he did not hesitate to satisfy, though often in circumstances that did him little credit; and if he could combine the two, and enjoy the proximity of women while he listened to good music, or sang and played it himself, his satisfaction was unlimited. 'Pleasure' is a word that occurs repeatedly in his account of how he had passed the previous day. Thus, on April 8th, 1667, he and his wife, having begun the evening with a dinner party of twelve and a visit to the King's playhouse, and thence to see the Italian puppets, where they had 'three times more sport than at the play', they returned to their own garden, 'the first night we have been this year'; and the four of them – besides the Pepyses, Mercer, Elizabeth Pepys' companion, in whom her employer took an amorous interest, and her successor, 'our Barker' – all sat up late 'singing very well', and then supper and so to bed. He was 'mightily pleased with this day's pleasure', the happy diarist concludes.

We read of many such earlier and later feasts. In March 1669, to take a single occasion, once 'our music came' and candles had been lit, Pepys, his wife, a group of friends and two strange gentlemen he had casually invited, 'fell to dancing and continued only with intermission for a good supper, till two in the morning', accompanied by a 'most excellent violin and theorbo, the best in town; and so, with mighty mirth and pleased with their dancing of Jiggs', of which the last performers were 'W. Batelier's* blackmore and blackmore maid; and then to a country-dance again; and so broke up with extraordinary pleasure, as being one of the days and nights of my life spent with the greatest content, and that which I can but hope to repeat . . . a few times in my whole life.'

Pepys' most memorable account of a happy day, however, is surely his description of a jaunt to Epsom in July, 1667. Not only is it a vivid piece of simple descriptive writing; but it illustrates some of the characteristics on which his happiness was based – his affection for, and sympathy with, his fellow men, his gift of observation, his love of beautiful things and his imaginative interest in the past. Although earlier that day he had sprained his right foot by leaping a little bank, it had very soon recovered; and he led

* William Batelier was a prosperous London wine-merchant.

his companions, Elizabeth Pepys, a Mr and Mrs Turner and Will Hewer, his devoted clerk, on a walk across the downs:

'... where a flock of sheep was, and the most pleasant and innocent sight that ever I saw in my life; we find a shepheard and his little boy reading ... the Bible to him. So I made the boy read to me, which he did with the forced tone that children do usually read, that was mighty pretty; and then I did give him something and went to the father and talked with him ... He did content himself mightily in my liking the boy's reading and did bless God for him, the most like one of the old Patriarchs that ever I saw in my life, and it brought those thoughts of the old age of the world in my mind for two or three days after. We took notice of his woolen knit stockings of two colours mixed, and of his shoes shod with Iron ... with great nails in the soles ... "Why", says the poor man, "the Downes you see, are full of stones ... and these ... will make the stones fly till they sing before me" ... He values his dog mightily, that would turn a sheep any way ... [He] told me there was about 18 score sheep in his flock, and that he hath 4s a week the year round for keeping of them.'

It is typical of Pepys that the happiness this episode gave him should have been derived from a host of different details – not only from the 'forced tone' in which the shepherd-boy read aloud and the vision of the shepherd as a relic of the ancient world that haunted him, he tells us, for several days, but from the structure of the old man's shoes and the exact amount of a trusted servant's wages, the latter being the kind of solid information he always carefully recorded. Here he much resembled Samuel Johnson, to whom no scrap of knowledge came amiss if it increased his understanding of the world. Like Johnson, too, he needed company, and was usually happiest among his friends. Both men loved the stimulus of social life and had little taste for solitude, a condition the Romantics would deliberately seek. Even a cat, Johnson pointed out to Hester Thrale, never purrs when it is quite alone; and, during the seventeenth and eighteenth centuries, civilised men and women were evidently a great deal more gregarious, more addicted to amusements they could share, than they have become today.

Hence their love of parties. The entertainments they arranged and attended took extremely various forms. Now they might join a simple domestic gathering such as the Vicar of Wakefield and his family enjoyed in a newly-reaped meadow: 'we sat, or rather reclined, round a temperate repast, our cloth spread upon the hay . . . To heighten our satisfaction, two blackbirds answered each other from opposite hedges . . .' Now, if they belonged to the 'polite world', they would appear at one of the fashionable routs, blue-stocking assemblies, balls, concerts and bohemian masquerades that diversified the London season. Here another self-portraitist throws a brilliant light upon the social habits of his age; William Hickey's *Memoirs*, which he began to write about 1808 or 1809, depict the progress of a particularly gregarious man, who, although beside Pepys he may seem a somewhat undistinguished character, was equally energetic, no less fond of life and just as determined to squeeze out of existence every drop of interest and enjoyment that it could be made to yield.

Not until he had abandoned an active career did he finally turn to remembering and writing; and then it was forced upon him by lack of suitable companionship. Once he left India, where he had long practised the law and had earned a fortune that, if not very large by Anglo-Indian standards, was quite sufficient for his purpose, he had settled in a small but comfortable house in the little Buckinghamshire town of Beaconsfield, whence he visited nearby friends and, every six weeks or so, 'ran up to London', the scene of his adventurous childhood and boisterous, undisciplined youth. After a time, however, this prosaic routine lost its charm. Beaconsfield, he decided, was a sadly 'trifling place' and, worse still, had a 'very limited society'. He suffered from dreadful headaches, and presently, from 'my old disagreeable nervous sensations' that even an 'affectionate' and attentive doctor could not wholly cure.

Meanwhile, reliving the past helped him 'fill a painful vacuum' on days when the English climate or some minor malady made it impossible for him to leave the house; and the huge self-portrait he drew – the original manuscript of his memoirs runs to seven hundred and forty-four pages* – enlarged its scope year after year. Son of a prosperous Irish lawyer, who

---

* It has never been published in full; but between 1913 and 1925 the late Alfred Spencer edited a four-volume selection of the text, while I was responsible for the single-volume edition that came out, with less material but fewer expurgations, in 1950.

had belonged to Samuel Johnson's circle, Hickey was very much a man of his age, and, in his opinion at least, essentially an *homme du monde*. He had also been, even during his boyhood, a keen frequenter of the *demi-monde*; for his raffish elder brother Henry had introduced him to 'many of the gay adventurers of London, men who lived by their wits; that is nobody knew how . . . with all of whom I . . . was in high favour, and many a bumper of champagne and claret have I drank in the society of this set, at taverns and brothels, accompanied by the most lovely women of the metropolis, and this before I had completed my fourteenth year'.

Hickey's outlook, it soon becomes apparent, was far narrower and more philistine than that of Pepys; he had little of Pepys' learning and good taste, never mentions a book he has read or a work of art that he has seen. What he admired, and sought to achieve in his surroundings, was an air of smartness, neatness, ship-shapeness and general luxury and elegance. His favourite laudatory adjectives were 'rich', 'capital', 'magnificent', 'choice' and 'fine'. He purchased gaudy clothes – so gaudy that they were sometimes laughed at when he exhibited them in public – and was always fond of bright colours. When he and seven like-minded friends bought and fitted out a cutter for expeditions on the Thames, 'she was painted', we learn, 'a bright azure blue, with gold mouldings and ornaments . . . richly embellished with aquatic devices. The awning was of the same colour, in silk, as were the dresses of the eight rowers, their jackets and trousers being trimmed with an uncommonly neat spangle and foil lace . . . We wore black round hats with very broad gold bands and small bright blue cockades . . . Under the awning we had capital French horns and clarinets . . .'

To a robust appetite for the transitory pleasures of life Hickey added strong nerves and an extremely vigorous constitution – so many children then died in infancy that the survivors were usually made of very solid stuff, or possessed a mysterious inward strength that enabled them to develop, like Horace Walpole, into Herculean invalids. Tolstoy's admirable portrait of Stefan Arkadyevitch Oblonsky and Pepys' and Hickey's vivid self-portraits lead us gradually towards the same conclusion: a gift for happiness may often be an attribute, closely bound up, no doubt, with certain physical traits, that Nature bestows on some human beings, and unaccountably denies to others; and, when George Washington, delivering his Inaugural Address in 1789, announced that there was 'an indissoluble bond between virtue and happiness', and Aristotle, during the fourth century before Christ, proclaimed that happiness resulted from 'the active exercise' of virtue, they seem both of them, although with the noblest intentions, to have grievously misled their hearers.

6

Seeing and Recording

I N 1845, at the age of twenty-six, John Ruskin was allowed for the first
time to visit Switzerland, the country where he had always felt
happiest, as an independent traveller. Yet, although on this occasion
neither his mother nor his father accompanied him, he was still attended by
a Swiss courier named Couttet and George, his faithful English valet; and
one day, while he climbed a mountain-slope, he heard his guardians, who
had fallen a little behind, talking of their young employer. '*Le pauvre enfant,
il ne sait pas vivre!*' remarked the courier to the valet – a not unjust criticism,
with which Ruskin would probably have agreed. He was then suffering
from the after-effects of an unhappy love affair; and in all the relationships
that followed he was to show the same distressful lack of worldly
knowledge. His emotions persistently overcame his reason; the ability to
live happily as a man among men was an art he never wholly mastered.

Yet he survived until the opening of the next century; and before he
reached middle age, despite the frustrations and miseries he endured, he
had already realised his genius and fulfilled his early promise. This he
accomplished through the use that he made of his eyes. Seeing, he often
assured his readers, was the 'greatest thing' a human soul could do.* We
must be constantly *looking* – at alder-stems, 'covered with the white
branchy moss' that so much resembled twigs of coral; the 'intense scarletty

---

* This belief is echoed by Thomas Carlyle, who is seldom regarded as an aesthete: 'No
  most gifted eye can exhaust the significance of any object'.

purple' of shattered larch-boughs; the polished boulders in an Alpine torrent; or, above our heads, the 'long, continuous and delicate formation' of a swelling cloud. Only Chateaubriand has so brilliantly described clouds; and *Modern Painters*, the book of which Volume I had appeared in 1843, contains a memorable paragraph where he distinguishes between the varying shapes that they assume, from the 'colossal mountain of grey cumulus', and the 'quiet multitudes of the white, soft, silent cirrus', to the rain-cloud with its 'veily transparency' and its 'ragged and spray-like edge'.

As an art-critic, Ruskin frequently became a moralist, who asserted that part of a picture's value might depend on the moving story the painter illustrates or the salutary message he expounds. None the less, particularly during his middle years, the critic was simultaneously an imaginative hedonist; and the observation of beauty, pursued for its own sake, provided nearly all the satisfactions that life had otherwise refused him. The chief purpose of any true work of art, he perceived, was primarily to cause pleasure by conveying the creative delight that the artist had himself enjoyed; and, with the passage of time, Ruskin grew more and more reluctant to reject a work simply because he disapproved of its social or its moral background. Thus, he detested the age to which Paolo Veronese had belonged, and the 'corrupt' and 'decadent' architecture of sixteenth-century Venice, yet loved Veronese's sensuous warmth and ebullient humanity – 'Paolo', he said, 'is as full of mischief as an egg is full of meat'; and he believed, he assured a friend, that 'after all, you'll find the subtlest and grandest *expression* . . . hidden under the gold and purple of those vagabonds of Venetians'.

Unselfishness was a virtue that had constituted the basis of his education. But he now discovered that it did not always make for happiness or, indeed, for health and calm. If he worked selfishly, observed and drew and bought the pictures he admired, he was 'happy and well; but when I deny myself . . . and work at what seems useful, I get miserable and unwell . . . Everything that has turned out well I've done merely to please myself, and it upsets all one's moral principles. Mine are going I don't know where.' In fact, the hedonist would never vanquish the moralist; as Ruskin grew older, he became increasingly concerned with the betterment of mankind.

But, meanwhile, his health deteriorated and his grasp on sanity weakened, until, at the end of his life, even Turner's luminous sketches that covered his walls and the landscape that lay beyond his windows had lost their power to raise his spirits. Both had faded; for, he admitted, quoting sadly from *The Tempest*, 'all the best of this sort are but shadows'.

Although Ruskin cannot himself be regarded as an example of the happy man – at some moments, no doubt, he was unusually wretched – he acquired and practised one of the noblest gifts that have ever contributed to happiness, the gift of seeing, and sometimes recording, the beauty and wonderful variety of the universe into which we have been born. A modern writer, the late Norman Douglas, announced that he would rather have been blind than deaf; but, if we except musicians and musicologists – and some of the latter I have heard admit that they derived just as much enjoyment from *reading* a score as from listening to a piece of music played – surely no intelligent man today could hold the same eccentric view. For every good painter and almost every imaginative writer, close and accurate observation has been throughout their lives a ruling passion, which, unlike so many passions, has had the happiest results.

Diaries left by famous artists are full of the verbal sketches they have jotted down. Both Eugène Delacroix and John Constable – a fellow-artist Delacroix greatly admired – enliven their pages with such detailed notes. The French painter, though naturally drawn towards huge and grandiose subjects, studied a garden slug with as keen and appreciative an eye as elsewhere he turned on an imprisoned lion. Of the lions, watched during a heat-wave at the Jardin des Plantes, 'I managed to observe [he records] that . . . the light tone visible beneath the stomach, under the paws, etc., is merged more softly into the rest than I usually make it . . . the colour of the ears is brown, but only on the outside.' Of the slug's colouration, he was equally observant; it was 'spotted like a jaguar, with broad rings upon its back and sides, turning into single spots on the head and near the stomach, where it was lighter in tone, as in quadrupeds'.

Constable, too, made an intense preliminary study of every landscape or object that he painted; and, before he began work, 'the first thing I try to do', he said, 'is *to forget that I have ever seen a picture*'. Having thus cleared his mind of preconceptions, he became completely self-absorbed; and his biographer Charles Leslie reports, as 'a curious proof of the stillness with which he sat', that, one day while he was working in the open air, a field mouse was found to have crept into his coat-pocket. But, besides observations, Memory played a part. Sights and sounds that had once fascinated his boyhood – 'the sound of water escaping from mill-dams . . . willows, old rotten planks, slimy posts and brickwork' – still excited his imagination. The technical expert who, when he was about to hang a picture, might be seen at the last moment, with the help of a palette-knife and a mysterious liquid he had himself compounded, putting on what he called its 'dewy freshness', was above all else a visionary artist.

'Painting is with me,' he announced to a friendly correspondent, 'but another word for feeling'; and that feeling, from what we know of his work and table-talk, must have brought him, so long as his beloved wife still lived and he preserved his aesthetic self-confidence, deep and well-deserved joy. He shunned melancholy, detested Byron's verse, and seems to have enjoyed romantic exaltation, yet escaped the influence of Romantic gloom. His earlier pictures reflect his own contemplative serenity. But then, after all, there is no major work of art, however grim or tragic its theme,* that does not transmit something of the artist's pleasure in his work to even the least curious and most casual observer.

Many years ago, at a Japanese university,† I caused a good deal of consternation among my students and colleagues by suggesting that the enjoyment we derived from a book or a picture was the true basis of critical appreciation, and that, having first enjoyed, we should next, like Baudelaire discussing Wagner's music, 'investigate the *why*', and seek 'to turn our pleasure into knowledge'. Most Western critics today would admit the importance of the pleasure principle, and have discarded the early-twentieth-century belief that 'significant form', 'rhythmic unity', 'plastic sensibility', and sometimes 'inner tension', are necessarily the hallmarks of a painting's value. In his admirable book *Looking at Pictures*, Kenneth Clark, a pupil of Roger Fry, who, he declared, had originally taught him 'how to look', dwells both on the merits of a picture's

* For example, Géricault's *Raft of the Medusa* or Goya's *The Third of May*.
† *The Marble Foot*, 1976.

[81]

composition and on the subject the artist has chosen and the experience of human life it unmistakably reveals.

Our ability to share and re-live that experience is one of the delights of seeing – for example, when, at London's Kenwood House, we confront Rembrandt's splendid self-portrait. Our first thought, Kenneth Clark writes, 'is of the soul imprisoned in that life-battered face . . . it is primarily the record of an individual soul', and, we immediately note, a tragic record. Rembrandt's head is very far from handsome; the nose is bulbous and red-blotched; the cheeks are rugged and sagging; heavy wrinkles score the forehead. Nor is the expression calm; it betokens determination and immense creative strength, a kind of fierce pride, but not the smallest hint either of personal equanimity or of professional self-satisfaction.

It is by no means a 'pretty picture'; and in its neighbourhood hangs one of the prettiest and most vivacious portraits that Thomas Gainsborough ever painted – the likeness of a dashing, elegantly dressed young woman who trips across a pastoral landscape. The hurried visitor immediately succumbs to her charm. Rembrandt attracts a less enthusiastic crowd. Yet it is the self-portrait – the ugly scarred face with its severe background, which consists of two half-circles apparently traced on the wall – that always draws us back again. Rembrandt's record of his vexed, tormented soul is far more deeply and enjoyably moving than Gainsborough's vision of carefree youth and fashionable grace.

The state of mind that a masterpiece helps us enjoy no doubt has many different causes. Among them is the pleasure of recognition; the work that confronts us somehow satisfies our sense of *rightness*; we find there the strange quality, indefinable yet inescapable, that distinguishes a work of art from a mere commercial counterfeit. It is an exposition of truth as an artist himself sees it; and in his self-portrait Rembrandt tells us the whole truth about his individual knowledge of the world, about the sorrows of age, the woes of poverty and failure. The marvellous frankness with which he lays his soul bare simultaneously warms the beholder's heart and quickens his intelligence. '*Il y a de l'oraison en toute grande oeuvre*' – there is a hymn of praise in every great work – believed the French religious thinker Alain; and, though Rembrandt's picture has no devotional message, it seems to voice an artist's gratitude for life, for the gifts that, despite the

Rembrandt's self-portrait 'tells us the whole truth about his individual knowledge of the world'.

hardships he has undergone, have enabled him to remain so very much himself. When he painted it, during the early 1660s, he was near the conclusion of his fifth decade – he would die in five or six years' time – a lonely figure, who had long outgrown his earlier wealth and popularity, but never lost touch with the satisfaction of working or a spontaneous zest for living.

Although Rembrandt was an extraordinarily individual artist, he paid close attention to the works of other men, studied the techniques employed by previous painters, sketched Roman busts and collected and copied Indian miniatures. Any discovery we make, if it provides some new insight into art or life, is usually stirring and refreshing; and to discover the connection between different artists, which emphasises the recurrent patterns of life and the continuous growth of art itself, as it has developed since the Neolithic Age, almost invariably gives us pleasure. Not long ago, for example, by a 'happy chance' – to use the adjective's original meaning – I opened a fine new picture book* – where I found a photograph of Mantegna's *Presentation of Christ* that reminded me of a 'Florentine painted terracotta relief, attributed to Donatello', then being exhibited at a London saleroom.

Mantegna, I next learned, had met Donatello during a visit to Padua, and later, in 1485, 'was to paint a *Virgin and Child* (Brera, Milan) surely dependent' on one of Donatello's works. Between Mantegna's *Presentation* and Donatello's terracotta relief there is a curious resemblance. Mantegna's handling of his subject is peculiarly his own. Each of the six personages represented has a separate attitude towards this memorable occasion. The Child has begun to cry; the High Priest appears to feel its sacredness; but two minor characters, on the left and the right, have a cool, uninterested look;† while the Virgin holds out her swaddled child with an air of suppliant reverence. She has a beautiful face, which, it soon occurred to me, was somehow pleasantly familiar. Had she not a fascinating likeness

* *The Bible and its Painters*, by Bruce Bernard, with an introduction by Laurence Gowing, 1983. Mantegna's picture is now in the Staatliche Museum, West Berlin.
† The figure on the right is a self-portrait; that on the left, gazing into vacancy, his wife, the sister of Giovanni and Gentile Bellini.

to Donatello's pensive Virgin? They have the same narrow downcast eyes, the same poetic line of mouth and chin, even the same slightly tip-tilted nose.* Since the artists, when they met at Padua, no doubt exchanged ideas, may they not have used as their model the same Italian peasant-girl? The knowledge that they had a close and productive relationship certainly adds to our enjoyment of their work.

Meanwhile, I have sometimes wondered if the pleasure of looking at pictures, and studying the relationship of artists, is today really much more general than it was a hundred years ago. The human race might still be roughly divided into two opposing groups – those for whom seeing is a workaday function that helps them guide their steps from hour to hour, and those for whom the visual images they receive are a major source of happiness. '. . . Man has closed himself up', wrote Blake in *The Marriage of Heaven and Hell*, 'till he sees all things thro' the narrow chinks of his cavern'; and one need not be a Blakeian mystic, or believe that, were 'the doors of perception' cleansed, 'every thing would appear . . . as it is, infinite', to agree that, whether we are considering art or nature, or any single object we can examine through a fresh, unclouded eye, the precious gift of seeing, used with imagination, will effectively enlarge the cavern's chinks. A picture we call 'great' is the lasting record of such a visionary enlargement. An artist recreates the world; each painter has his own world; and to enter it, and admire its landscape, is always a memorable experience; so that looking at new pictures, in a gallery or on other people's walls, may from a pastime eventually become a passion. When I open the door of an unfamiliar room, my first impulse is to approach the pictures it encloses. Not only do they arouse my curiosity – in portraits, how extraordinarily compulsive an unknown face may be! – they raise my hopes of stepping across the margin of the frame into a country I have never visited before.

Some pictures seem especially designed to satisfy that aspiration. By popular German critics they are sometimes called 'walk-about-pictures'; and if there is a masterpiece that thoroughly deserves the title, it is Nicolas Poussin's glorious work, *The Body of Phocion carried from Athens*, painted

* In Donatello's bas-relief, I learn, the Virgin's robe has a rich pomegranate pattern that also appears on some of Mantegna's works.

Nicolas Poussin's glorious Athenian landscape is entirely the product of his own creative genius.

half-way through the seventeenth century. A companion-picture, *The Gathering of the Ashes of Phocion*, illustrates the same subject – the undeserved end of a valiant Athenian soldier, who, wrongly suspected of having betrayed his countrymen, was condemned, like Socrates, to drink the hemlock.

Each portrays a wide and airy landscape, supposed to be the neighbourhood of Athens. Poussin himself, born at Andelys on the banks of the Seine, could never have visited what was then the Turkish Empire; and, although he knew Italy well, the marvellous prospects he unfolds are neither Grecian nor Italian, but entirely the products of his own creative genius. Except for the frontage of a temple that overlooks the scene, most

[86]

details of the two landscapes, despite the fact that we observe them from an identical standpoint, are perplexingly dissimilar. In *Gathering the Ashes* behind the temple's façade rises a fantastic rocky peak, which in its companion has been replaced by an impressive circular tower. Even the tall trees on the left and right of the sinuous path that winds away towards Athens are of different forms and species. But, whichever picture we are examining at the time, that sinuous path tempts us to follow it until we have entered the Ideal City.

Should we yield to the temptation, we must expect a long walk; we shall pass more inhabitants of the place, out in the fields for the day, than we can reasonably attempt to count; and those who populate the landscape from which Phocion's corpse is being carried are particularly numerous. A peasant is shepherding his flock; two strange white-shrouded figures occupy a bullock-cart. Across the middle distance gallops a solitary red-cloaked horseman, and far off a long religious procession moves to the sound of music beneath the temple's walls. Though the trees are still in full leaf, the season is late summer or early autumn. The sun has begun to sink; an immense cumulus cloud drifts high overhead; and the city that climbs the hill beyond the temple, where its buff-coloured masonry catches the evening light, has an air of antique peace and splendour.

Many such imaginary cities emerge in the backgrounds of Renaissance pictures; and they, too, persuade us, once we have absorbed the main subject – a Virgin and Child, or Mantegna's vision of *The Agony in the Garden* – to move around and beyond it into a completely separate realm of feeling. A work of art, however, is not an escape-route from life, but provides a purification and vivid intensification of our everyday experi-ence; and 'walk-about-pictures' are merely a single aspect of the search for happiness – if by 'happiness' we mean a sense of celestial harmony that inspires a painter's or a writer's efforts.

Some artists, of course, have been more alive to the search than others and pursued it more deliberately. Renoir, for example, having filled so many canvases with the scenes he liked best – plump, sleek girls sunning their naked bodies, or dancing and drinking with their lovers at a riverside restaurant – once protested that pictures of people whole-heartedly enjoying themselves were not always inferior as works of art to pictures of a more dramatic and heroic kind. Two other great eighteenth-century French artists, Fragonard and Chardin, in their very different ways were almost equally concerned with a certain kind of sensuous bliss. Fragonard, a native of Provence, having won the Prix de Rome, which earned him a visit to Italy, had soon turned against the Old Masters. Michelangelo's energy 'terrified' him. Raphael moved him to tears; but 'the pencil fell from my hands' he wrote; and 'I remained for some months in a state of indolence that I lacked the strength to overcome'. Tiepolo was one of the few Italian artists whom he admired and understood.

It was the air of feminine elegance and underlying gaiety, with which the great Venetian managed to enliven his most ceremonious allegorical frescoes, that, no doubt, attracted Fragonard. Gaiety became the keynote of his genius; few eighteenth-century artists have had so light and elusive a touch, and, simultaneously, so affectionate an attitude towards every subject that they handled. Beside Fragonard, Watteau was a visionary melancholic; about his exquisite pastorals there is always a shade of sorrow; he is haunted by Beauty's evanescence and the fragility of human pleasures –

> '. . . Beauty that must die;
> And Joy, whose hand is ever at his lips
> Bidding adieu . . .'

as a carefree group prepares to embark for Cythera, or a single dancer moves across the lawn.

Fragonard's lyrical series, entitled *Le progrès de l'amour dans les coeurs des jeunes filles*,* which Madame du Barry commissioned for her country house, but, after some disagreement, the artist took away with him to Provence to decorate his own walls, is by comparison a high-spirited tribute to Youth and Love at their most radiantly hopeful. Love, traversing the hearts of young girls, throws them into a dazzling confusion. One is apparently running for her life; yet, as she flees, both virginal arms extended, she glances back over her shoulder at the young man who stretches out his hand, not to grasp her skirts and violate her innocence, but simply to offer her a rose. It is a prearranged flight rather

* Now in the Frick Museum, New York.

than a genuine surprise; and two succeeding pictures, entitled 'The Declaration of Love' and 'The Lover Crowned', show that passion soon reaches its 'right true end' amid the classic urns, venerable garden-statues and huge umbrageous avenues of this long-lost Earthly Paradise.

Chardin, on the other hand, was perfectly content with his everyday domestic surroundings and the splendid discoveries he made there. Born in 1699, son of a successful carpenter who manufactured billiard-tables for the King, Jean-Baptiste-Siméon Chardin had begun his professional career as an assistant to other artists; but when his employer at the time, Noël-Nicolas Coypel, brother of the famous 'history-painter' Antoine Coypel, ordered him to paint a huntsman's gun, this commission, his first chance of painting directly from a homely natural object, had a liberating effect upon his genius. Then, in 1728, his still-life of a fishmonger's skate, *La Raie*, gained him admission to the Academy, where Largillière, after considering his works, assumed that they were excellent products of 'the Flemish School', and was astounded to learn that they were the achievements of a French artist. Chardin had quickly recognised his true vocation; and, ever since he exhibited *La Raie*, his vision of the world has been described and applauded by critics, among the earliest being Denis Diderot, one of the more recent Marcel Proust, who made him the subject of a long and moving early essay.*

The critic, Diderot wrote to Grimm in 1762, needed 'taste of many different kinds, a heart responsive to all delights and a soul capable of an infinity of different enthusiasms; a variety of style corresponding to the variety of artists . . .' Having so many of these qualifications himself, Diderot soon responded to what Bernard Berenson would have called the 'life-enhancing' properties of Chardin's work. While we examine one of the still-lives Diderot praised, the human condition, otherwise often so tedious and burdensome, seems a privilege we feel glad and proud to share. He irradiates every object he sees. 'There is nothing in nature', wrote the Goncourts, 'that his art cannot respect'. He enters the field, Proust would add, as authoritatively 'as does the light, giving its colour to everything, conjuring up from the timeless obscurity where they lay entombed all nature's creatures, animate or inanimate, together with the meaning of her design', a meaning that art alone can momentarily reveal.

* See *Marcel Proust on Art and Literature, 1896–1919*, translated by Sylvia Townsend Warner, 1984.

Like Rembrandt's, Chardin's self-portrait depicts the artist as a magnificent survivor.

Take a single canvas, entitled *Panier de Fraises des Bois*. Beside a glowing pyramid of wild strawberries, symmetrically piled up in a wicker basket, a couple of white carnations lie near the basket's edge, next to a solid tumbler full of white wine. The artist was never a moralist; he is merely representing the objects he has arranged upon his own domestic table-cloth; yet he manages to invest each separate detail of the composition with a deeply pleasurable significance – so long as there are strawberries growing in the woods, and there is wine to accompany a meal, we can hope to keep despair at bay. Chardin remained primarily a well-known painter of still-lives until the year 1753, when he exhibited a full-length portrait; and thenceforward he became more and more preoccupied with the human figure and with the comings and goings of an ordinary Parisian household. He painted children, whom he clearly loved – a little girl playing with a shuttlecock, a boy building a card-castle or talking to his mother on his way to school. He also depicted older members of the family – for example, a handsome servant-girl, *La Pourvoïeuse*, who just visited a local market, and *L'Oeconome*, an aged housekeeper in a frilled cap placidly doing her accounts.

Unlike Greuze, born a quarter of a century later, Chardin does not preach virtue or hint that the ordinary men and women he represents, because they are prosaic and unaffected, have any special claim to be admired. They are merely themselves, the kind of sober middle-class people among whom he had been brought up; and today the society to which Chardin belonged, the *bourgeoisie* of eighteenth-century France, seems to have occupied a peculiarly enviable position. Whatever might happen or be beginning to happen at a higher or a lower level, the skilled craftsman and the industrious tradesman then shared singularly well-ordered lives. They had their own *douceur de vivre*, which depended among other things, as Chardin's pictures of the dinner-table and the kitchen repeatedly show, upon the important art of cookery; and an authoritative manual *La Cuisinière Bourgeoise*, the earliest French recipe-book, appeared in 1746, when Chardin was forty-seven, and the Revolution, which would demolish both the bourgeois and the aristocratic 'sweetness of life', still lay many years ahead.

Chardin's self-portrait, executed during his old age, like Rembrandt's masterpiece at Kenwood House, shows the artist as a magnificent survivor. Since above all else he cherished the gift of seeing, he wears a broad shade to protect his eyes, and balanced across his blunt nose a pair of big spectacles, while a nightcap warmly encompasses his head and a scarf is knotted round his neck. Few more unpretentious self-portraits have been painted by a great master. Chardin neither pretends he is an ordinary man, nor asserts he is a hero. The artist, he had once said, 'who has never felt the difficulty of art', would achieve nothing of any real value; and here he faces a complex yet fascinating task, which, thanks to a lifetime's hard practice, he does not for a moment doubt he will ultimately overcome. He records his physical appearance, and, doing so, his sense of his own identity, with the same imaginative skill that he has already devoted to his usual range of subjects – a basketful of strawberries, a glass of wine, a gleaming black bottle, an old kitchen-knife on a wrinkled sheet of newspaper, or a crumbling loaf of bread.

7

'Happy Living Things'

SAINT-EVREMOND, the elderly French exile whom Charles II had protected and befriended, was an Epicurean philosopher of the gentlest, most persuasive kind. He held many views on the human condition which he imparted with style and wit; and he maintained, for example, that, once a man had reached old age, nothing strengthened and supported life quite so happily as Love. Descartes' proposition, that we know we exist because we think, he considered much 'too cold and languishing'; it is because we retain the ability to fall in love, he said, that we are aware of being still alive. The fact that he himself was almost always enamoured – usually of a famous beauty, often far beyond his reach – 'sometimes bribes my imagination to suppose that I am young'.

He had other original opinions on how we should conduct our later years. 'When we grow old', he wrote, 'and our own spirits decay', to keep a number of living creatures about us 'and be much with them', has a delightfully restorative effect. Once Charles appointed him 'Keeper of the Ducks in the Decoy in St. James's Park', he could put this theory into practice. His London house was full of birds and beasts; and, unless he were at Whitehall, amusing the King or joking and roistering among rakish courtiers, they appear to have been his favourite companions. Saint-Evremond, of course, was not alone in his belief that the proximity of vigorous, attractive animals makes for human health and happiness, and that between animals and civilised man there is a very close connection, which has existed, archaeologists assure us, since the passing of the Ice Age. It was through this relationship that imaginative art first entered Europe. The Palaeolithic artist had learned to depict the beasts he hunted

[93]

long before he could produce equally convincing representations of the other members of his tribe; and, in the newly discovered Lascaux Cave, the only huntsman portrayed, a doomed figure lying near a ferocious bison's hooves, is a coarse and rudimentary sketch.

I was lucky enough to be able to visit the cave before ordinary sight-seers had been shut out; and I found the experience strangely moving, yet often curiously puzzling. Compared with many caves in the same region, it is neither long nor very wide, a passage that runs for some thirty metres into the flank of a small rocky hill; and its roof is both rather low and fantastically irregular. Over that crude surface sprawl the huge images, usually deer, wild oxen and small shaggy horses, black or a rich reddish brown, that the Palaeolithic artist left behind him. They have a wonderful verisimilitude – especially the great cattle that forever rear and gallop just above our heads; but, beside delighting, they also baffle and bewilder us, so difficult is it to understand either the creator's purpose or the technical methods he employed. Clearly he had little sense of order; one image may be superimposed upon the next. It never forms part of a general scene, but was evidently painted for its own sake, while the vivid impression it records was still vivid in the artist's memory.

The Palaeolithic painter seems to have been literally an impressionist. He fixed his immediate recollections of what he saw, and rendered the shape and density and weight of his subject with the help of an embracing outline, that conveys not only an animal's form but its essential character and movement. Although there are a few striking exceptions such as the so-called 'sorcerers', who appear to be masked magicians, and vague erotic female shapes, the human species seldom emerges on a painted cave-wall; and, if it does, like the dying huntsman at Lascaux, it is represented in a series of schematic strokes which embody not the artist's real vision but his childish conception of how a human body ought to be depicted. That primitive sketch (which archaeologists, for obvious reasons, call the 'Phallic Man') sets us a multitude of interesting problems. Why was he painted, between a bison and a rhinoceros, deep in a natural crevice or 'oubliette', his bird-headed staff, conjecturally a staff of office or a spear-thrower, which he seems to have dropped or flung down, lying at his right-hand side? It is thought by students of early cultures that he may perhaps have been a shaman, a prophet and priest, who, among his other gifts, understood the language of the animals. It is even suggested that his antagonist, the ferocious wounded bison, was possibly a rival shaman in disguise.

Modern authorities are now inclined to agree that these prehistoric refuges – more than a hundred caves are known today – were once the scene of secret magic rites, and that their decorations gave huntsmen a mysterious power over the animals they hunted. A modern art-historian, however, the late Kenneth Clark, has advanced a very different view. In cave-paintings, he reminds us, men, compared with their prey, habitually 'cut very poor figures'; for animals, distinguished by their greater strength and speed, were at that time still in the ascendant, and men a wandering predatory species. 'Can we seriously believe', the historian asks, 'that they thought they were gaining power over their magnificent companions? Are they not rather expressing their envy and admiration? . . . Personally I believe that the animals in the cave paintings are records of admiration. "This is what we want to be like", they say, in unmistakable accents; "these are the most admirable of our kinsmen" . . .'*

Although Kenneth Clark, a peculiarly sophisticated writer, was perhaps not very well qualified to grasp the mentality of an unknown semi-savage people, it is an interesting hypothesis; and there seems no doubt that the Palaeolithic artist, to judge from the extraordinary sensitiveness with which he represented their grace and strength and decorative splendour, revered the animals on whom his life depended, and, now and then, felt for them a kind of love. At the same time, as an artist, he must certainly have *enjoyed* his work and, whatever his magic purposes may have been, experienced the special form of happiness that rewards creative effort.

Otherwise, it was a grim and dangerous world. During the Palaeolithic Age, a drab tundra stretched northwards across Europe as far as the glaciers of the ice-cap; and through that dismal landscape men dogged the itinerant herds, sometimes meeting their match in a rhinoceros or a mammoth, whose round baldish head, thick hairy coat and small fierce eyes above enormous curving tusks, often appears among the larger beasts they painted. During their long expeditions, their empty homes were frequently occupied by cave-bears, which have left piles of now fossilised droppings, scattered bones, claw marks, and, if the inner passages of the cave are particularly narrow, the traces of their shoulders on the rocks they

* *Animals and Man*, 1977.

Christ and his disciples at Emmaus by Paolo Veronese. Before them the master's children are playing with a noble dog.

rubbed smooth while they lumbered to and fro; and, once a tribe returned, the intruders, which presumably put up a savage resistance, had to be driven out again.

Into this harsh life came creative art and emotions we recognise and share today. The little museum at Altamira, the famous Spanish cave archaeologists first studied,* is one of the sacred places of European art-history; for there we are shown not only the lamps with which the Palaeolithic artists worked, almost always far from daylight, but the fresh-

---

* It was the Abbé Breuil who, at the beginning of the present century, first made careful drawings of its decorations. At times, however, he was apt to improve on, or over-elaborate, the images he sought to copy.

water shells they used as palettes and small heaps of the primitive substances that they employed as colours.

Once *homo sapiens*, now more and more master of his surroundings, had begun to domesticate and breed animals, a new chapter opened in the relationship of men and beasts, which art again reflected, and which at length found its way into literature, until it presently became a subject that concerned both philosophers and theologians. With Descartes' harsh assertion that an animal was a mere soulless piece of sentient machinery few poets and artists have agreed. In the works of most Renaissance painters, particularly in those of Paolo Veronese, huge handsome dogs sleeping, alertly reclining, being caressed by their master's children, occupy an honoured place; while the European 'Great Horse',* the breed that soldiers and sovereigns rode before the introduction of an Arab line, was admired and lovingly depicted.

At the Emperor's Viennese court, good horsemanship was an especially valued gift; and in 1574 two distinguished English visitors, Edward Wotton and the soldier-poet Sir Philip Sidney, often attended the Imperial riding-school, where they set themselves to learn the latest modes. Their instructor Ion Pietro Pugliano, Sidney writes, not only spoke admiringly of practised horsemen – 'the noblest of soldiers . . . the maisters of war, and ornaments of peace, speedie goers, and strong abiders, triumphers both in Camps and Courts' – but eulogised the horse's nature, 'telling what a peerless beast the horse was . . . the beast of most bewtie, faithfulness, courage and much more, that if I had not been a peece of a Logician. . . . I think he would have persuaded mee to have wished myselfe a horse.'†

Thus the rough little horses that Palaeolithic man had chased and killed, frequently by driving a whole herd over a cliff, at length developed, some enthusiasts maintained, into counterparts of human virtue, just as the minor carnivores that must have slunk and scurried, until they were driven away, around pre-historic camp-fires, gradually established their privi-

* A fine specimen of the Great Horse is to be seen in the equestrian statue of Charles I that looks down London's Whitehall. The King, not every passer-by may have noticed, is mounted on a massive stallion.
† *Defence of Poesie*, Chapter I. For drawing my attention to this passage, I am indebted to my friend Patrick Leigh Fermor, himself an enthusiastic horseman, in his admirable travel-book *A Time of Gifts*, 1977.

leged positions in the households of mankind, and, among the ancient Egyptians, were identified with the powerful goddess Bast, 'the Lady of Life', who had a majestic feline head. Of all the animals that have accompanied the human race down the millennia, cats, thanks to their instinctive genius for survival, their blend of courage and strength and cunning, and to the beauty that, if they are well-loved and well-tended, almost every one of them possesses, have made a particularly strong appeal to the literary imagination; and some, through their portraits in literature and art, have now become historic characters – for instance, Montaigne's cat, of whom he wrote that, should they play together, he was never quite sure if he were playing with her, or she had decided she would play with him; the big black-and-white animal who sits protectively behind Shakespeare's friend Lord Southampton in a contemporary canvas painted at the Tower of London during his imprisonment; Horace Walpole's favourite, 'the pensive Selima', whose narcissistic death, 'Drowned in a Tub of Gold Fishes', was celebrated by Thomas Gray;* and Johnson's no less memorable 'Hodge', whom he fed on oysters he bought in Fleet Street, and Boswell watched scrambling up the great man's breast, 'while my friend smiling and half-whistling, rubbed down his back and pulled him by the tail; and when I observed he was a fine cat, saying, "Oh, yes, Sir, but I have had cats whom I liked better than this", and then as if perceiving Hodge to be out of countenance, adding, "but he is a very fine cat, a very fine cat indeed." '

Since the Cheshire Cat, from the branch of a tree in Wonderland, explained to Alice how little cats resembled dogs, their varying merits and demerits have been endlessly debated. Of dogs Anatole France once said that 'the dog knows reverence and knows shame – the cat knows neither; the dog has the elements of religion in him'; and it is certainly true that, although cats sometimes look furtive and apprehensive, they very seldom look guilty. Whereas we like and esteem dogs because we think they share some

* The beautiful line, in which Gray describes Selima while she gazes admiringly at her own reflection before she notices the goldfish, 'her conscious tail her joy declared', has often reminded me of a sentence of Beatrix Potter's *Tale of Peter Rabbit*: 'A white cat was staring at some gold fish. She sat very, very still, but now and then the tip of her tail twitched as if it were alive.'

of our virtues – and, probably, our sense of sin – for cats, besides admiring their natural grace, we feel an involuntary regard because, staunch amoralists that they are, they seem to have escaped so many of our human foibles. Here the contrasted behaviour of slumbering cats and dogs is particularly significant. Dogs and their masters are often equally anxious; a dog's anxieties pursue him into his dreams, and from his basket he stirs and sighs and growls,* while a cat, tired out by the day's adventures, which may have included hazardous thefts, desperate escapes and sanguinary crimes, appears to drop at once into a bottomless oblivion, the 'rêve sans fin' which Baudelaire admired.†

It is understandable that, in the nineteenth century, cats should have particularly delighted French Romantic painters and poets, and that both Delacroix and his ill-fated friend Géricault were devoted cat-observers. Each artist portrayed his subjects, just as Delacroix depicted lions at the Jardin des Plantes, from an essentially Romantic point of view – not as man's placid fireside-companions, but as patrician individualists. On a page of ten sketches of a single cat by Géricault, in each portrait he has caught a deep yawn or an impatient snarl; and Delacroix, who is said to have resembled a cat himself with his 'tawny feline eyes and thick arched brows', attempted to portray, above all else, his subjects' air of untamed pride. Contemporary poets and prose-writers followed Delacroix's example. Baudelaire, apostle of literary dandyism and arch-opponent of bourgeois standards, suggests in *Fusées*, his posthumously published notebook, that cats are patrician dandies of the animal world; and that it is easy enough to understand why modern democrats detest them: 'the cat is good-looking; he reveals ideas of luxury, cleanliness, physical pleasure'. Three poems concerned with the beauty and pagan hardihood of cats are included in *Les Fleurs du Mal*; while Théophile Gautier, to whom the poet dedicated *Les Fleurs*, had a cat called Éponine.‡ Although she frequently leant against his writing-arm, he would encourage her to share his desk, and, as a further mark of his esteem, allotted her a regular place at his domestic dinner-table.

* 'Like a dog, he hunts in dreams': Tennyson, *Locksley Hall*.
† '*Ils prennent en songeant les nobles attitudes Des grands sphinx allongés au fond des solitudes Qui semblent s'endormir dans un rêve sans fin . . .*'
‡ See *La Nature chez elle, et Ménagerie Intime*. Éponine, after whom Gautier named his cat, was a heroine of Gallo-Roman history.

The head of a cat by Delacroix.

According to Kenneth Clark in a passage I have quoted above, the earliest artists may have felt both admiration and a touch of deep envy for the beasts they and their tribe hunted; and that mixture of feelings still emerges, now and then, in the work of modern writers. It is not so much their relationship with, as their dissimilarity from ourselves, that helps to give most animals their fascination; and for Walt Whitman, at least, it also manifested their considerable superiority. This was the reason, he declared in *Leaves of Grass*, that he sometimes wished to live with them:

[100]

'. . . They are so placid and self-contained . . .
They do not sweat and whine about their condition,
They do not lie awake in the dark and weep for their sins,
They do not make me sick discussing their duty to God . . .
Not one is respectable or industrious over the whole earth.'

Another distinguishing trait that all animals possess, and that constantly excites our envy, is their freedom from the rule of Time. Unaffected by the dreadful procession of Yesterday, Today and Tomorrow, they exist in an Eternal Present. Thoughts of the past bring them no regrets and ideas of the future no alarm. One of the most moving passages in the *Odyssey* relates how the hero, while re-entering his island kingdom heavily disguised, had passed his old hound Argos, whom he himself had bred, but who, neglected and 'full of vermin', lay abandoned on a dung-heap; and how Argos, suddenly aware of his master's presence, 'wagged his tail and dropped both his ears', though nearer to Odysseus 'he lacked the strength to move'. Yet, after all, despite this sudden flash of memory, I doubt if poor Argos really 'remembered' Odysseus or his own vigorous youth in the accepted meaning of the word. Had he been a deserted human servitor, his fate might have been much more poignant; during their long separation he would then have been repeatedly thinking of his loss, and of the carefree days when the huntsmen 'used to lead him out against wild goats and deer and hares'. But for Homer's Argos, despite his vanished happiness and his wretched old age, the past was as vague and insubstantial as a dream. Nor did he suspect that, now he had again caught sight of Odysseus, 'black death' would very soon descend. Man, wrote André Malraux, is the only species of animal that knows it is bound presently to die.

Whether animals possess 'souls' and, if that be true, whether in some form they may conceivably enter Heaven, is a problem that has often troubled Christian thinkers. Marlowe's Dr Faustus, facing the dread result of his compact with the Devil, exclaims in his agony that he would willingly accept a subordinate form of life to escape unending retribution:

A cat in different moods; ten sketches by Géricault.

'. . . all beasts are happy,
For when they die,
Their souls are soon dissolv'd in elements'

They lose, that is to say, their separate identity and vanish into the great flood of terrestrial existence. A modern theologian, on the other hand, C. S. Lewis, author of *The Problem of Pain*, found it 'difficult to suppose that the apes, the elephants and the higher domestic animals, have not, in some degree, a self or soul' which might possibly survive death, and observes that, although the Fathers of the Church held the opposite view, so far as he is concerned a Heaven completely stripped of beasts would be a much less paradisial place.

Today from some regions of the earth, for example, from the cities of modern China, dogs, we learn, have been ruthlessly removed. But such a deprivation even a Communist government would not venture to impose on the citizens of any Western state; our relationship with and affection for animals is now too deeply engrained in our ways of life and thought. When Saint-Evremond recommended that, particularly during our old age, we should surround ourselves with other living creatures, he was already addressing the converted. Robert Herrick kept an intelligent pig, which he had taught to use a tankard; at Whitehall, Charles II shared his bedchamber with the spaniels that bore his name; and the household of a seventeenth-century country gentleman – unlike Saint-Evremond no philosopher, but evidently a shrewd manager of his own existence, since, we are told, he 'lived to a hundred, never lost his eyesight but always writ and read without spectacles and got to horse without help' – is admirably described in an autobiographical fragment written by the first Lord Shaftesbury, 'the false *Achitophel*' of Dryden's satire:

'Mr. Hastings . . . was peradventure an original in our age, or rather the copy of our nobility in ancient times . . . His house was perfectly of the old fashion, in the midst of a large park well stocked with deer . . . The parlour was a large long room . . . On a great hearth paved with brick lay some terriers and the choicest hounds and spaniels; seldom but two of the great chairs had litters of young cats in them, which were not to be disturbed, he having always three or four attending him at dinner, and a little white stick of fourteen inches long lying by his trencher that he might defend such meat as he had no mind to part with to them.'

[103]

During the next century, though cats may no longer have fed from a gentleman's own plate, the presence of animals was held to confer both physical and psychological advantages. Regularly inhaled, the wholesome breath of a cow, it was supposed, might often cure tuberculosis; and a well-known specialist had opened a private hospital where a partition, conveniently placed behind the bed, would every night be drawn up to bring the patient into easy breathing-distance of a milch-cow ruminating in her stall. Her proximity, the physician believed, would effect a natural cure; for, the Romantic Age having then dawned, Nature was regarded as a fount of health and wisdom; and it was a great Romantic poet, Samuel Taylor Coleridge, who described how the sight of happy and beautiful creatures, playing in their native element, had enabled an unhappy, guilt-obsessed man to at last throw off his load.

The original version of *The Rime of the Ancient Mariner* was composed in 1797, a year after Coleridge, 'the rapt One, of the godlike forehead', having leapt over their orchard fence, first appeared upon the Wordworths' threshold, and been quickly recognised by William as the 'only wonderful man' that he had ever known. But Coleridge's senescence began early. Although many years would pass before the young visionary, who dazzled the Wordsworths, became 'the fat, flabby, incurvated personage' whose prophetic voice had 'contracted itself into a plaintive snuffle and singsong', while, pontificating about some philosophic subject, he zigzagged down a garden walk,* his hopes had very soon declined. 'The poet is dead in me', he declared in 1801; and he gradually acquired a load of guilt that an unsuccessful marriage and his frustrated love for Sarah Hutchinson were perpetually increasing. Yet, as sometimes happens, Coleridge's sense of guilt seems to have attacked him before it had a genuine cause. He was twenty-five, and still a poetic enthusiast, when he wrote the *Ancient Mariner*. Yet his theme was already guilt and remorse; they provide the burden that the grim old protagonist carries slung around his shoulders.

Taken as a whole, Coleridge's poetic narrative is an odd, uneven work. The Mariner himself, distinguished by his 'glittering eye' and the clutching hand he employs to buttonhole the unfortunate Wedding Guest, at least until he starts to tell his tremendous tale is the self-centred Neurotic

* Carlyle: *Reminiscences: Edward Irving.*

[104]

and, indeed, the Social Bore personified; and Coleridge, where he blends the 'sublime' and the 'horrid', seems to have borrowed some of the paraphernalia of the late-eighteenth-century 'Gothick' novel. Yet again and again his imaginative genius appears. The peace that he rarely achieved through ratiocination he often reached through observation. He was an exquisite observer; and his notebooks contain numerous vivid records of the natural phenomena that enchanted him – the behaviour of birds, the ascension of sun and moon, the noise of the wind, phosphorescent surges sweeping beside a ship, and, twice affectionately described, a fountain on the sea-shore: 'The spring with the tiny little cone of loose sand ever rising and sinking at the bottom, but its surface without a wrinkle'; and, elsewhere, 'a fountain with unwrinkled surface yet still the living motion at the bottom, that "with soft and even pulse" keeps it full.'

Just as Coleridge's observations of the natural world helped to ease his moral sufferings, and brought him a happiness he could find neither in his philosophic musings nor in his practical experience of life, so the Ancient Mariner, when from his becalmed ship he notices the beauty of the water-snakes, creatures far freer and immeasurably less thought-burdened than himself, circling around its sides, suddenly discards his burden; and the dead albatross, symbol of his own guilt, sinks 'like lead into the sea':

'Beyond the shadow of the ship,
I watch'd the water-snakes:
They moved in tracks of shining white,
And when they rear'd, the elfish light
Fell off in hoary flakes.

Within the shadow of the ship
I watch'd their rich attire:
Blue, glossy green, and velvet black,
They coil'd and swam; and every track
Was a flash of golden fire.

O happy living things! no tongue
Their beauty might declare:
A spring of love gush'd from my heart,
And I bless'd them unaware:

Sure my kind saint took pity on me,
And I bless'd them unaware.'

Thus, although the grace of animals and their presence around us, as Saint-Evremond said, may be a concomitant of happiness, merely because we relate them to our own life, and we sometimes think they share our feelings, their essential difference – few creatures could be more remote from humanity than an oceanic water-snake – is almost equally appealing. 'How do you know,' demanded Blake in his early masterpiece *The Marriage of Heaven and Hell*, 'but ev'ry Bird that cuts the airy way, is an immense world of delight, clos'd by your senses five?' 'Energy', he added, 'is Eternal Delight'; 'every thing that lives is Holy'. Thus the small signs that mark the passage of an unseen animal may themselves acquire a mysterious significance – for example, the strange labyrinth of silvery interwoven tracks left by a predatory snail over a single slab of garden-pavement. Where the snail hides, and why its search for food is so extraordinarily circuitous, are puzzles I have never solved. Yet, morning after morning, it has inscribed a similarly complex design, which resembles the calligraphic scribblings of an accomplished modern draughtsman, before it crawls home into its secret crevice; and each day, when I open the garden-door, I am happy to observe its latest work, and wish that I could follow the designer's plan.

8

'La Chasse au Bonheur'

I T is difficult nowadays to reread the Emperor Napoleon's biography without an occasional pang of horror; in almost every episode, the personality he shows the world seems to become more and more repellent. Thus, during the first furies of the Revolution, we meet him as an ambitious young officer who, at the siege of Toulon, had told Barras that a true patriot could not be 'revolutionary enough', but, watching a Parisian mob invade the Tuileries, quickly drops into coarse Italian slang: '*Che Coglione*', he exclaims, 'they should have swept away four or five hundred with cannon, and the rest would still be running'. Then we move on to one of his greatest campaigns, to Eylau, where in February 1807 he vanquished both the Russian and the Prussian armies, and twenty-nine thousand dead are lying scattered. While he strides across the field, followed by his brilliant troop of Marshals, he pauses to turn over one or two corpses with his boot, remarking dispassionately 'small change!'* The expression was characteristic; Napoleon often spoke of his ability to 'afford' soldiers, and 'replace' them if a temporary reverse occurred. His fellow men were merely an array of ciphers on his prodigious balance-sheet.

Yet, despite the demonic military genius he revealed at the height of his powers, even in those days his private character appears sometimes to have been curiously crude and commonplace. Notwithstanding the air of imperial grandeur that he presently assumed, he had little natural distinction. He retained, said Jean-Antoine Chaptal, Minister of the Interior during the Consulate, 'the manners of an ill-bred young

---

* See Jean Savant: *Napoléon raconté par les témoins de sa vie*, 1954.

[107]

lieutenant', and no one, at a rapid glance, would have thought that he possessed 'the smallest knowledge of society'. As the First Consul, if he were receiving guests, he might 'come out of his study whistling, accost women without breaking off . . . and go back again humming an Italian song'. Towards women, indeed, his behaviour was usually brusque and now and then strangely brutal. Neither in conversation, nor in his random love affairs, did he ever spare their feelings; 'he would have liked', wrote Madame de Rémusat, the Empress Josephine's aristocratic confidante and *dame du palais*, 'to be the sole master of reputations, and make and unmake them at pleasure. He would compromise a man or tarnish a woman for a word . . .'

That a strain of native brutality ran through his character his former school-friend Louis de Bourrienne noted. Should he be opposed or, for any other reason, particularly annoyed, he would sit down behind his desk, tilt his chair back at a dangerous angle, and vent his exasperation on the chair's right arm, mutilating the wood with a penknife that he carried for that special purpose. Napoleon seems very seldom to have regretted the past, or doubted the rightness of his own actions. During his exile, questioned by a devoted follower about the judicial assassination of the gallant young duc d'Enghien, the House of Condé's last heir, he accepted complete responsibility for the crime – it was less a crime than a terrible mistake, Talleyrand subsequently observed – and spoke of the victim's kidnapping and execution as a necessary dynastic *coup*. Why, he asked, had the subject been brought up? 'The Enghien affair? Pooh! What is one man, after all?'

His cynicism, however, was half his political strength. Great fame, such as he possessed, he once explained to Bourrienne, was primarily 'a great noise. The more one makes the further it carries. Laws, institutions, monuments, nations, all have their day. But noise remains, and resounds in other ages'. This was a topic to which he frequently reverted; 'my power derives from my glory', he told his intimates, 'and would collapse if I failed to base it on more glory and fresh victories . . . Conquest alone can maintain me'. Napoleon, Bourrienne believed, was 'not disposed by temperament to think well of mankind'; there were two great levers, he asserted, capable of moving men, 'fear and interest'. Affection he had always discounted; 'friendship is only a word', his old friend heard him say, adding that himself he 'cared for nobody'.

Yet his voice and the echo of his victorious achievements carried wonderfully well, and easily traversed frontiers. In England he soon acquired, and long retained, many enthusiastic advocates, among whom Byron was one of the most eloquent. News of the Emperor's abdication, at Fontainebleau on April 20th, 1814, struck the poet with the force of a personal blow. He had just left his beloved sister in the country, and 'on my return [he wrote] found my poor little pagod, Napoleon, pushed off his pedestal; – the thieves are in Paris', the thieves, of course, being the Bourbon dynasty and their foreign supporters, who championed 'the dull, stupid old system – balance of Europe – poising straws upon kings' noses . . .'. Meanwhile, he had composed 'a very beautiful *Ode to Napoleon Buonaparte*'; and in 1815, at the end of the Hundred Days, when he heard that the Emperor had fought his last battle and was rapidly falling back towards Paris, Byron declared that he felt 'damned sorry for it', adding after a pause, 'I didn't know but I might live to see Lord Castlereagh's head on a pole. But I shan't, now'.

Later, we hear, he had sought the first refusal of Napoleon's Coronation robes, which a London tradesman had acquired and hoped to sell; and, as he prepared to bid England goodbye, he commissioned a magnificent new travelling carriage, 'copied from the celebrated one of Napoleon taken at Genappe'. That the poet to some extent identified himself with the Emperor, at least during his more hubristic moments, is shown by an account of his 'fractious' moods and wild remarks that Augusta Leigh sent in 1816 to the 'unforgiving' wife, who had just deserted him. He regarded himself, he had then proclaimed, as 'the greatest man' alive; and when his cousin, Captain George Byron, who happened also to be present, put in tentatively 'Except Bonaparte?', hoping maybe that he could give his conversation a slightly less vainglorious turn, 'God, I don't know that I do except even him,' Byron immediately replied.

Had a confrontation between the poet and the emperor ever taken place, it would have formed a fascinating addition to the narratives of Napoleon's interviews with Chateaubriand and Goethe, but, like those occasions, perhaps, have had very few results. Napoleon was not at home in the company of writers, and took little genuine interest in books, or in the arts generally, unless they served some political purpose, as Chateaubriand's

Génie du Christianisme had done, or enhanced his own imperial renown. Ossian, the fictitious Gaelic bard, invented by James Macpherson about the middle of the eighteenth century, whose verses celebrated the deeds of heroic antique warriors, remained Napoleon's favourite poet; while, again according to Chaptal, 'having been informed that David was the first painter of the day', he repeated this view, but did not venture into any detailed comparisons with other distinguished modern artists. On the merits of Greek and Roman literature, he held typically strong opinions, revered Homer but mistrusted Virgil, believed that Suetonius, since he had described the crimes committed by the early Roman emperors, was 'the worst historian of antiquity', and that Horace's *Odes* were 'only fit for sybarites'. In seventeenth- and eighteenth-century French literature, he detested Racine, Voltaire and Rousseau, but had a due respect for Corneille, whose tributes to the value of 'duty' and 'honour' struck a much more useful note.

Yet Napoleon's influence, or, rather the influence of his tremendous career, on nineteenth-century Romantic writers, their conception of life and their quest of individual happiness, was extraordinarily far-reaching. Poets and novelists, who might have been expected to revolt against his cruel record, were carried away by his legendary appeal; and a young German poet, Heinrich Heine, in his imaginative discursion *Reisebilder*, would draw a particularly flattering portrait of the victorious dynast at his ease. The background was Dusseldorf's Court Garden:

> 'The Emperor with his attendants rode directly down the avenue . . . He wore his invisible-green uniform and the little world-renowned hat. He rode a white steed . . . Calmly, almost lazily, sat the Emperor, holding his rein with one hand, and with the other good-naturedly patting the horse's neck. It was a sunny marble hand, a mighty hand . . . Even the face had that hue which we find in the marble of Greek and Roman busts; the traits were as nobly cut as in the antique . . . Those lips smiled . . . It was an eye as clear as Heaven . . .'

Later, it is true, still an unknown young man 'of student-like appearance', Heine returned to Dusseldorf and, sitting in the same garden, watched French prisoners of war, captured during the retreat from Moscow, now tattered and miserable, slowly trudging home. Yet his vision of the divinised despot somehow never quite faded; and two great French novelists, Stendhal and Balzac, who also cherished it, continued to revere his memory. Since, under Napoleon's influence, they invented and put into action a new mode of seeking happiness, their readers will certainly ask if the Emperor himself expressed any views upon the subject. But again his opinions appear to have been fairly commonplace. Talking about happiness with an intelligent young woman, Victoire de Chastenay, one day in 1795, 'he said that for a man it must lie in the greatest possible development of his faculties';* and his companion, who did not then know that he had merely quoted the eighteenth-century philosopher Condillac, author of *Traité des sensations*, thought that the remark was 'dazzling'.

At the time, his triumphs had scarcely begun. But, towards the end, on the eve of his abdication, he came to believe, like Saint-Just, that his true aim had been primarily to improve the condition of his fellow citizens. 'I have meant to make France happy', he assured his generals gathered around him at Fontainebleau; 'I have not succeeded. Events have turned against me.' Finally, on St. Helena, he spoke of the dream he had always hoped he might realise. He had looked forward to a happy old age when he would drive around his peaceful Empire, accompanied by the Empress and their son, in an open carriage behind their own horses, visiting every corner of his dominions, 'receiving complaints, redressing wrongs, and scattering public buildings and benefactions wherever we went'.

Far less prosaic were the aspirations of the two novelists on whose life and works he made so strong a mark. They envisaged Napoleon as an irresistible conqueror rather than as a disappointed benefactor. Balzac's guests in 1828, besides admiring his elegant roseate bathroom and his resplendent bedroom (which resembled the 'bridal chamber of a fifteen-year-old duchess') when they examined his magnificent study, saw among red morocco-bound volumes stamped with his fictitious ancestral arms, a plaster statuette of the Emperor and, attached to its scabbard, a grandiloquent inscription that the novelist had signed: '*What he could not achieve by the sword I shall accomplish by the pen*'. Henri Beyle, who, for reasons unknown, adopted the pseudonym Stendhal after an obscure middle-

* Jean Savant, op. cit.

[111]

Honoré de Balzac; a photograph by Félix Nadar. A great
admirer of Napoleon, 'what the Emperor could not achieve
by the sword', he proclaimed, 'he would accomplish by
the pen'.

European town, was equally devoted to the Napoleonic legend; and in 1821 he wrote his own epitaph, where he enumerated his great aesthetic passions – Cimarosa, Shakespeare, Mozart, Coreggio – listed the initials of the women he had passionately loved, four or five of whom, he thought, had loved him – and informed posterity that the Emperor Napoleon was 'the only man he had respected'. Nor did he change his view; at the end of his life he would sit at the fireside of his old Spanish friend the comtesse de Montijo, and recount the glorious exploits of the *Grande Armée* to her appreciative daughters, one of whom, the beautiful Eugénie, would presently become the Empress of the French.

Stendhal's cult seems all the more remarkable since he had himself been engaged in Napoleon's most disastrous campaign, had witnessed the occupation of Moscow and the terrible retreat that followed. From the Emperor's example both he and Balzac had inherited a dominant idea. Happiness, they believed, was not a fortuitous gift – and certainly not the reward of moral virtue – which we should patiently await, but a benefit we must pursue and conquer by the bold exercise of skill and energy. '*La chasse au bonheur*' preoccupied them all their lives; and the pursuit is repeatedly portrayed, under realistic or symbolic forms, in the novels that they wrote. Balzac's version of what constituted real happiness was the more material of the two. As Proust objected in *Contre Sainte-Beuve*, his genius was counterbalanced by a 'vulgarity so massive that a lifetime could not leaven it'. His hero Rastignac, type of the fiercely determined young *arriviste*, sets before us as his goal 'the most grovelling ambitions'; while Balzac himself, having achieved the boldest of his romantic designs, and at last persuaded Madame Hanska, a rich and cultivated Polish noblewoman, to become his wife, wrote reminding his favourite sister Laure that, whatever she might think or say, in Paris it meant a great deal 'to throw open one's house and entertain the cream of society, who will meet a woman there who is polished, stately as a queen . . . related to the grandest families, witty, well-educated and handsome'.* Balzac's vision, once the marriage had taken place, almost immediately dissolved; he was then much too ill and tired to enjoy his matrimonial triumph; but it is clear that, having, with the *Comédie Humaine*, rounded off his gigantic literary campaign and drawn 'a

* *Marcel Proust on Art and Literature*, translated by Sylvia Townsend Warner, introduced by Terence Kilmartin, 1984.

complete picture of society from which nothing had been omitted', he expected to conquer the dominant social position he had always ardently desired.

By comparison, Beyle, although, as Stendhal, he dreamt of literary glory, set no great value on immediate public acclaim or on the social renown that might perhaps accompany it. For him '*La Chasse au Bonheur*' was a wholly private concern; he did not expect that the books in which he described the pursuit would immediately be welcomed, but liked to assume, he said, that his true qualities might be recognised about 1880, or possibly 1935, when he had gathered a sympathetic audience and could 'dine late' among 'the happy few'. Meantime, he coined the magic word '*Beylism*', to describe his own method of organising and executing his lifelong chase. Whether he listened to music, met friends he loved, revisited a city he had once admired, or surveyed a tremendous battle-scene, it consisted in arranging a pattern of recollections, emotions and ideas that gave him a sense of being vigorously and enjoyably alive. At the same time, he must be able to satisfy his insatiable appetite for knowledge.

Happiness, he had decided, was the product of 'love + work'. There is a strange resemblance, it has often struck me, between Henri Beyle and James Boswell. The latter's Swiss servant Jacob complained that 'Monsieur had not the habits of a gentleman'; he was too open-hearted and perpetually asking questions that his unfortunate domestic was obliged to answer; '*il voudrait savoir tout au fond*'. Beyle's interrogative attitude towards life is endlessly reflected by his novels, *Le Rouge et le Noir*, published in 1831, and *La Chartreuse de Parme*, the product of less than two months' work, which appeared in 1839, and Balzac then saluted as a 'masterpiece of the literature of ideas'. With the Romantic spirit, Beyle combined the enquiring scepticism of an eighteenth-century *philosophe*. Few things was he prepared to take for granted; he was perpetually investigating his protagonists' real motives, delving into their minds and seeking to discover the secret '*fond des choses*' beneath any given situation. What always most concered him were the different means his characters adopted during their individual search for happiness; and his chief aim was himself to see and write clearly. 'If I don't see clearly', he confessed, 'my whole world is totally destroyed'.

During at least one or two periods of his life, when *Beylism* brought him rich rewards, he must be regarded as a happy man – in Northern Italy, principally at Milan, a city for which he felt a keen affection,* where he had loved Angela Pietragrua, 'adored music and literary glory', and, being a Napoleonic dragoon, fought a duel and 'greatly esteemed the art of giving a good sabre-stroke'; and, more unexpectedly, over twenty years later, in London, a metropolis he otherwise detested. Between these two epochs he had had several vivid experiences of a less pacific kind as he followed Napoleon's advance across Europe, nearly witnessed the battle of Jena, seen the Emperor ride into Berlin and, on the heights of Bautzen, from the safety of a good open carriage, observed 'all the complex movements of an army of 140,000 men opposing another army of 160,000'.† Despite the tremendous cannonade, which might have distracted any other man, he calmly noted in his journal that it had been 'a splendid day for *Beylism*'.

At Moscow, too, in 1812, the Beylistic method had produced admirable results. 'As we left the city,' he recorded, its buildings were 'lit up by the loveliest conflagration in the world, forming an immense pyramid that was like the prayers of the faithful, the base on the earth and the apex in the heavens'. Although he escaped the worst horrors of the ensuing retreat, it cured him of all his military ambitions; he was glad to take refuge in the humdrum consular service, and at length settled down quietly and resignedly at Civitavecchia, a drab Italian sea-port town. Yet even there his pursuit of knowledge and the hunt for happiness continued; and it would scarcely slacken until his death in 1842. 'My own soul', he explained, 'is a fire that suffers if it does not blaze. I need three or four cubic feet of new ideas a day, as a steam-boat needs coal'; and the fuel he demanded he never ceased to provide, while he moved thoughtfully towards old age.

Of all his lesser-known works, his autobiographical *Souvenirs d'Égotisme*,‡ begun at Rome, during a holiday from Civitavecchia, in June 1832, is

---

* Here, in October 1816, Stendhal met and talked of the Emperor with Byron: '*un joli et charmant jeune homme*', he wrote, '. . . *c'est l'original de Lovelace* . . .'

† At this battle, as at Eylau on February 1807, Napoleon, in May 1813, defeated both the Russian and the Prussian forces.

‡ Long hidden away among Stendhal's unpublished writings, it first appeared in 1892, when it was warmly welcomed by the fashionable novelist, Paul Bourget. The present text, translated as *Memoirs of an Egoist* by T.W. Earp, came out in 1949.

probably the most revealing. Here, for example, he recounted a visit in 1821 to London, whither, 'profoundly disgusted with Parisian life', he had gone 'to find a cure for the spleen'. His quest had 'succeeded well enough'. But, although he much enjoyed watching Edmund Kean on the stage and strolling beside the Thames 'towards *Little Chelsea*', whose small houses 'set off with rose-trees' he 'found truly elegiac' – it was the first time, he adds, that he had been 'affected by the sentimental mode' – London, as a rule, did not encourage his researches. His hotel, which overlooked Covent Garden, seemed a strange and gloomy place; the bedroom he occupied was ridiculously cramped; but he breakfasted off 'an infinity of beefsteaks', in a gigantic dining-room; and every morning, down a broad arcade, he watched 'about thirty good Englishmen, walking gravely, and many of them looking unhappy'. Nor was he always very happy himself until an odd adventure, slight but memorable, occurred to brighten his existence.

In London he had certain French companions; and, while with one of them, a friend named Barot, an intelligent banker from Lunéville, he was discussing the laborious life of the English poor, and remarked that the poor Italian was 'infinitely nearer to happiness' – at least, 'he has time to make love' – Barot's foppish young English valet, who seemed to think that 'his national honour was slighted', broke into their conversation. Beyle having replied that if, as foreigners, they failed to appreciate London, their failure might be due to the fact that they had no pleasant feminine acquaintances, 'I'll manage that for you, sir', the valet helpfully announced; and next day he told them of an assignation he had arranged and a bargain he had struck. He had insisted, he said, that the gentlemen should be given early-morning tea; and the girls in question finally agreed to 'grant their good graces and their tea for twenty-one shillings'. They inhabited, on the other hand, 'a lost quarter', called the Westminster Road; and English acquaintances quickly pointed out that Beyle and Barot would be 'taken miles away from London' and probably fall into an ambush, and be beaten and robbed by a gang of ruffianly sailors.

Nevertheless, after some hesitation, the intrepid tourists decided to set out, summoned a cab and, having twice or thrice been nearly overturned as they passed through 'so-called streets without any pavement', were deposited at the door of a three-storeyed house 'perhaps twenty-five feet high', and received by 'three slender girls of small stature, with beautiful chestnut hair, rather shy, very anxious to please, very pale'. Everything about the house into which Beyle and Barot were led was pathetically diminutive; 'the furniture seemed meant for dolls', and the visitors, being themselves fairly substantial, were afraid to sit down. 'Our little girls noticed our embarrassment; their own increased.' But then Barot, clearly a good-hearted man, thought of mentioning the garden. ' "Oh, we have a garden," they said, not boastfully, but with a kind of joy at having an object of luxury to show us.' The garden, which they explored by candle-light, was just as small as the house, extremely narrow and some twenty-five feet long; but it contained a laundry-tub and even a little vat for brewing beer. Barot laughed, and suggested that it was time to pay and go home. But Beyle objected that they must not hurt the girls' feelings.

Thus an occasion that, in other circumstances, might have been both sad and squalid, for the novelist acquired all the charm of a romantic fairy-tale. It was the girls' essential innocence, so different from the well-advertised virtue of such eighteenth-century heroines as Bernardin de Saint-Pierre's preposterous Virginie,* that at once touched his impressionable heart. Here, he felt, was native human goodness; and 'it seemed as though I was with tender friends whom I was seeing again after being a year away'. Both he and Barot had arrived with numerous defensive weapons; and when they went to bed, he was slightly alarmed by the discovery that none of the doors had either lock or key. But then, after all, he reflected, of what use would a locked door have been? A single blow of a man's fist would have demolished the flimsy brick partitions.

In bed, he was anxious to keep the light burning; but 'the modesty of my new friend, albeit so obedient and so good, would never consent. She made a gesture of obvious fear when I spread my pistols and daggers on the night-table . . . she was charming, small, well-made, pale. Nobody murdered us. The next morning we let them off their tea'; and when their hostesses heard that they proposed to spend the day in London – Barot was anxious to examine 'the brazen young women who then filled the foyer at Covent Garden' – but would very soon return, Beyle's bed-fellow, whose name, we learn, was Miss Appleby, declared that she wouldn't leave the

* In *Paul et Virginie* the heroine prefers death by drowning to making a gesture that would have saved her life, but might perhaps have looked immodest.

house if she could hope that he would certainly return that night. And so he did, having throughout the whole day 'only thought of a good, calm, quiet evening (*so snug!*)* that awaited me . . . What is amusing is that during my stay in England, I was unhappy when I could not finish my evenings at that house.'

Although the happiness Beyle found in the Westminster Road was scarcely a Napoleonic triumph, it was the 'first real and intimate consolation' he had experienced since he left Paris; and, in 1832, he clearly much enjoyed recording it. The story of his Lilliputian adventures, he thought, might serve an important literary purpose: 'If this book is boring, at the end of two years it will be wrapping up butter at the grocer's; if not, it will be seen that egotism, *so long as it is sincere*, is a means of depicting the human heart', in the knowledge of which he and his contemporaries, he thought, had recently 'made giants' strides . . .'.

When he slipped back into Parisian life, he felt stronger and far more self-confident. His memories of the great Emperor continued to inspire his efforts; but by 1832 the climate of the age had changed; for, once Napoleon had fallen, the young, whether, or not they had revered the Emperor themselves, suffered a pervasive sense of loss. France had ceased to be a country where juvenile talents were soon recognised, and might be wonderfully rewarded, where anything seemed possible, and, amid the announcement of victories and a beating of drums, marshals, dukes and princes were created overnight. What Byron had denounced as 'the dull, stupid old system' seemed once again to have descended on the world; and young men, now that they had lost the grand Napoleonic impetus, aspired towards much more spiritual but considerably vaguer goals. 'We were living at that time' wrote Gérard de Nerval in 1853, prefacing his poetic novel *Sylvie*, through 'one of those strange periods which usually follow a revolution or the downfall of some mighty empire . . . composed of activity, diffidence and inertia, splendid utopian dreams, philosophic or religious aspirations, hazy enthusiasms, the whole interpenetrated by certain instincts of renewal . . .'. But the young now lacked a sense of purpose, '*l'ambition n'était . . . pas de nôtre age*'; and, although the hunt for happiness continued, it had begun, during the 1830s, to take a much more visionary turn.

* Here the author, as he was fond of doing, uses an English phrase.

9

'The Valley of the Shadow'

WHEN Byron, in July 1823, embarked on his last voyage, he carried with him a variety of books, Scott's *Life of Swift*, Grimm's *Correspondence*, Colonel Hippesley's account of an expedition to South America, accompanied by the *Maximes* of François de la Rochefoucauld, a classic he already knew well; and, as the *Hercules* began its journey south, he preferred to sit alone and read. He 'looked unusually silent and serious', noted his travelling companion Edward Trelawny. He did not expect he would ever return from Greece, he had told the Blessingtons at Genoa; and in this mood he must have found the cool, sharp seventeenth-century aphorist, who had dismissed almost every pleasing illusion, but bidden his readers eschew humbug, cultivate self-knowledge, learn to understand and endure and see the world just as it is, a particularly sympathetic guide.

During past years, Byron had sometimes quoted from La Rochefoucauld, and once cursed him for 'being always right! In him a lie were virtue – or at least a comfort to his readers'; and, when he reopened the book, his eye would certainly have rested on the hundred-and-thirteenth maxim, where he reminds us that, although some marriages are perfectly tolerable, none is totally delectable – '*il y a de bons mariages, mais il n'y en a point de délicieux*'. Of La Rouchefoucauld's own marriage we know regrettably little, except that, at the age of fifteen, he had become the husband of a suitably well-born girl, Andrée de Vivonne, offspring of the Grand Falconer of France and, like Byron's wife, an heiress, who, before she died in 1670, had borne him numerous sons and daughters. Men of our class don't talk about our wives he had remarked; and we may therefore assume that Madame de la Rochefoucauld customarily stayed at home and was content to do her matrimonial duty and await her husband's dashing visits, while, caught up in the two French civil wars, nicknamed *La Fronde*,* that raged between 1648 and 1653, he and his bellicose mistress, the duchesse de Longueville, galloped valiantly around France. By 1665, however, when his masterpiece first appeared, he was beginning to grow old and gouty, and had long ago settled down to enjoy his memories and reflections. Much of his time was now spent with some of the cleverest women in Paris, particularly with his close and dear friend – she may perhaps have been his last great love – Madame de Lafayette, authoress of *La Princesse de Clèves*. At her house, Madame de Sévigné describes him in April 1671 for her cherished daughter's benefit, as a favourite *ami de la maison*, making slightly unkind fun of another guest's far-too-girlish coiffure, which her hostess had just declared was '*complètement ridicule*', but which he gently affected to applaud: '*Ma mère, ah! par ma foi, mère*, we cannot stand for that. Come a little closer – *Ma mère*, you really look quite good.' Her daughter will 'recognise that tone', Madame de Sévigné comments.

I wish that some admirer could have overheard Byron's remarks on La Rochefoucauld's opinion of the married state. No doubt, they were violent, possibly rather scabrous; to him, even at the end of his career, his wife's 'unforgiving' behaviour was still a very painful subject. Few marriages have ended more suddenly and abruptly, or brought the partners less contentment. It was, indeed, almost the exact reverse of the kind of 'happy marriage' that, except for Thackeray in *Vanity Fair*, so many popular Victorian novelists would sketch upon their closing pages. At the time, viewed through the eyes of an uninstructed spectator, the causes of Byron's matrimonial catastrophe seemed comparatively obvious; Annabella Milbanke, a blue-stocking débutante and an heiress into the bargain, a high-minded, slightly pretentious, maybe rather frigid girl, had determined that she would marry a celebrated poet and reform a well-known rake. Not unexpectedly, her ambitious project had failed; marriage had merely shown Don Juan in his most aggressive colouring; and there was little more that need be said.

* These conflicts took their name from the sling (*fronde*) with which Parisian urchins used to combat the police.

Since 1816, however, a great deal of miscellaneous information has thrown fresh light upon the story. It was far more complex than its early critics supposed; and the state of mind in which Annabella deserted the poet was not so simple and straightforward as some biographers would have us think. Her experience of marriage, we now learn, had not been uniformly wretched, but had included passing joys. Although, both morally and emotionally she often condemned Byron, physically she clung to him, until, having escaped at last from his magnetic presence, she decided she must break the spell. This was an aspect of the problem that bewildered her husband. How could she, he demanded, have persisted in rejecting and abandoning him when – a fact she would surely not deny – they had remained on warmly conjugal terms throughout the gloomiest periods of their married life, and, indeed, until the day they parted? 'Were you then *never* happy with me?' he wrote. '. . . Have no marks of affection, of the warmest and most reciprocal attachment, passed between us? or did . . . hardly a day go down without some such on one side and generally on both?'

During hours of crisis Byron's attitude was seldom consistent; nor was he always strictly disingenuous; but here, it seems, he spoke the truth. Their marriage, catastrophic in some respects, had unquestionably succeeded in another. Annabella's '*passions*', he had informed his elderly confidante, her worldly-wise aunt Lady Melbourne, not very long before his wedding, were a great deal stronger than they had either of them supposed; and, being himself an accomplished amorist, who may occasionally have taken hints from a novel he much admired, Choderlos de Laclos's *Les Liaisons Dangereuses*, clearly he did not hesitate to rouse them. Once aroused, they followed her into later life. During her long years of aggrieved, self-righteous widowhood, she appears often to have struggled against her own passionate impulses, which she did her best to disarm with the help of faith and good works. Leaving Byron, we know, had caused her exquisite anguish. As she passed his bedroom door – he had not risen to bid her or the child goodbye: he was then in what she called a 'fractious' mood – and caught sight of the mat on which his big Newfoundland dog slept, she had felt inclined, she remembered, to throw herself down there and 'wait at all hazards'. But the temptation, she added, had lasted 'only a moment'; and she had then fled towards the waiting carriage.

Annabella Byron, for the remainder of her life, was a deeply restive and unhappy woman, whose treatment of her wayward daughter, her solemn son-in-law and her unlucky grandchildren, though her intentions were always high-minded, did them incalculable harm. Hers could never have been a felicitous, even an enduring marriage; but it seems possible that, had she attached a greater value to the pagan joys of her youth, she might have grown old more benevolently. Here, nevertheless, as in many other married relationships, there are still aspects of the Byrons' situation that we cannot wholly understand. Marriage, says the Anglican prayer-book, is an 'excellent mystery'; and, although the word 'mystery', had, of course, quite another significance for a seventeenth-century bishop, the biographer who has investigated the strange married lives of certain famous married couples must admit that few marriages, ancient or modern, do not, now and then, deserve the epithet.

Below, for example, is a letter from another rakish poet to an injured wife that, unless perhaps they have seen it before, may very well perplex its readers:

> ''Tis not an easy thing to be entirely happy, but to be kind is very easy and that is the greatest measure of happiness. I say not this to put you in mind of being kind to me – you have practised that so long that I have a joyful confidence you will never forget it – but to show that I myself have a sense of what the methods of my life seem so utterly to contradict.'*

It was written, in fact, by John Wilmot, Earl of Rochester, whose methods of life, at that stage of his existence, about 1678 or 1679, were particularly destructive. His marriage, before he was twenty years old, to Elizabeth Malet, a young woman whom Grammont calls 'the melancholy heiress' and Pepys 'the great beauty and fortune of the North', had had a strange, dramatic prelude. On May 28th, 1665, Pepys was able to provide the wife of his cousin and patron, Lord Sandwich, with an interesting piece of London news – the heiress, while she drove home, accompanied by her

* From *The Letters of John Wilmot Earl of Rochester*, edited with an introduction by Jeremy Treglown, 1980.

grandfather, from a supper party at Whitehall, 'was at Charing-cross seized on by both horse and footmen, and forcibly taken from him, and put into a coach with six horses and two women, and carried away'. They were immediately pursued; 'my Lord of Rochester . . . was taken at the bridge; but the lady is not yet heard of, and the King mighty angry and the Lord sent to the Tower'.

Charles quickly forgave a favourite courtier, but commanded that he should now join a naval expedition against the coast of Holland, and, although the plan itself proved a costly failure, and two of his friends were shot down beside him on the quarter-deck, he played his part with great distinction. Later that same year, he was appointed a Gentleman of the Bedchamber, a position supposed to carry the generous fee, though it was seldom regularly paid, of a thousand pounds per annum. Then, in January 1667, the heiress, just why none of their acquaintances could tell, suddenly decided that she might accept his hand. Perhaps the kidnapping was a romantic adventure she had thoroughly enjoyed; and no doubt he was a far more seductive young man than any of her previous suitors, 'my Lord Herbert . . . my Lord Hinchinbroke . . . my Lord John Butler', even Sir Francis Popham, who 'would kiss her breech to have her', she had once self-confidently declared.

Rochester's portraits, the canvas by an unknown artist that represents him, his sword at his belt, leaning negligently on his left elbow, and the fantastic picture that shows him crowning his monkey with a laurel wreath, depict a curiously handsome face, well-suited to the baroque curls of an exuberant Restoration wig. The nose is pointed and long; the eyes are heavily lidded; and the full, sensuous mouth has a slightly feminine look, which reminds us that, according to his poems* and his letters, his sexual inclinations were very often paederastic. Rochester's record as a 'rake-hell', the perpetrator of endless freaks and follies, which ranged from smashing the King's sundial in the Privy Garden, because, he alleged, it had an impertinently phallic shape, to fighting the watch and running naked through Woodstock Park, a royal demesne of which he had just been appointed Ranger, often startled and shocked his contemporaries, whose indignation was not easily aroused. For Pepys, a conscientious civil

---

* See, for example, 'The Disabled Debauchee', in *The Complete Poems of John Wilmot, Earl of Rochester*, edited by David M. Vieth, 1968.

Rochester, poet and rake-hell, proposes to crown his monkey with a laurel-wreath; portrait by J. Huysmans.

servant, Rochester typified everything he found discreditable about the
lazy sovereign's raffish favourites; and, in February, 1669, he heard an
unusually scandalous story: when the King had dined last night at the
Dutch Ambassador's and after dinner they had drunk and 'were pretty
merry', Rochester boxed Tom Killigrew's ears, 'which doth both much
give much offence to the people here at Court, to see how cheap the King
makes himself, and the more for that the King hath not only passed by the
thing and pardoned it to Rochester already, but this very morning the
King did publicly walk up and down, and Rochester I saw with him, as free
as ever, to the King's everlasting shame to have so idle a rogue his
companion'.

Here Pepys, it is true, seems for once to have been somewhat ill-
informed. As a result of this escapade, Rochester, we know, was
temporarily banished from the Court; and his behaviour, a fellow courtier
admitted, was not altogether inexcusable, since Killigrew had abused him
'for keeping his wife in the country'; and his marriage – he had been
wedded only two years – was presumably a topic on which he would have
very much resented drunken dinner-table jokes. At the time, he still hoped
to reconcile the claims of his London life with his domestic obligations,
and possibly thought that he might yet succeed. But his failure soon
became obvious. Rochester was a natural extremist, whose pursuit of new
pleasures and violent sensations, complicated by his avid thirst for
knowledge – always an omnivorous reader, he took a special interest in
works of philosophy and theology – allowed him very little peace; and, at
the age of thirty-three, he was already an exhausted man. Meantime, he
told Bishop Burnet, the ghostly counsellor who attended his death-bed,
'for five years together he was continually Drunk: not all the while under
the visible effect of it', but not cool enough to be perfectly 'Master of
himself'. Once he had quitted the country, he felt his nature change; 'he
was wont to say', wrote the ever-informative John Aubrey, 'that when he
came to Brentford the devill ent'red with him and never left him till he
came into the country again'.

Yet the devil that then possessed him, though it may have hastened his
physical ruin, was also a creative daimon; and during his riotous course he
produced a series of the finest lyrics written by an English poet in the later

seventeenth century. Some, it appears, were addressed to his wife at home; some to Elizabeth Barry,* his unruly mistress; some have an odd devotional colouring. Here fidelity was very often his theme, together with the unaccountable ambivalence of human feelings, and the difficulty of fixing one's emotions upon a single worthy object. If he cannot be constant in his own life, neither does he expect unwavering constancy from the woman he desires:

> 'Tis not that I am weary grown
> Of being yours, and yours alone:
> But with what face can I incline
> To damn you to be only mine?
> You, whom some kinder power did fashion,
> By merit, and by inclination,
> The joy at least of a whole nation.

Yet Rochester's dread of losing the emotional refuge he sought, and sometimes he hoped he might have found, seems to have endlessly tormented him:

> . . . When wearied with a world of woe,
> To thy safe bosom I retire,
> Where love and peace and truth does flow
> May I contented there expire.
>
> Lest once more wandering from that Heaven,
> I fall on some base heart unblest,
> Faithless to thee, false, unforgiven,
> And lose my everlasting rest.

Between Rochester and his wife and their young children, an only son and three daughters, the bond remained unbroken till his death. He was a warmly affectionate parent, who, in the many letters he wrote Lady

---

* One of the stars of the Restoration stage, Mrs Barry was seen at her best in the plays of Thomas Otway, who had desperately loved her, and whose masterpiece *Venice Preserv'd* was first produced in 1682.

Rochester, usually included tender messages to the nursery, and sometimes added 'great and glorious' gifts, among them a puppy from the royal
kennels, intended for his heir, Lord Wilmot, which, to amuse the boy, he
described as 'a dog of the last litter of lap-dogs so much reverenced at
Indostan', where they 'lie on cushions of cloth of gold at the feet of the
Great Mogul'. Yet more significant is an elaborate lyric dialogue,
composed by husband and wife, which shows that Lady Rochester herself,
besides being a sensitive and intelligent woman, was a gifted minor poet;
and in her contribution* she half-apologises for the mask of severity that,
since 'kindness' has again and again failed, she sometimes feels obliged to
wear —

> Though you still possess my heart,
> Scorn and rigor I must feign;
> There remains no other art
> Your love, fond fugitive, to gain.

— while the fugitive replies that it is for kindness he still yearns, and protests
that, come what may, he is inescapably her prisoner:

> Ah! Be kinder, then, for I
> Cannot change, and would not die.

The Rochesters' marriage, in short, was one of those unions it would be
wrong to call 'happy', yet from which happiness was never completely
absent. Like Byron, the poet must have recognised that his character was
fast changing, and that, at least until his physical strength gave way and, on
his death-bed, he took refuge in religious repentance, he had an anarchic,
yet creative spirit that refused to be expelled. Such ill-balanced marriages,
seen through a biographer's eyes, are often particularly absorbing; but
they become most memorable should their story exhibit the conflict of two
gifted, though very different personalities, whom their ignorance, both of
themselves and of one another, dooms to a protracted union where each

* The lines, of which some are quoted here, have been preserved in the authoress's own
  script.

develops, not perhaps into a determined foe, yet certainly into an obstinate antagonist. That, for example, was the destiny of Thomas and Jane Carlyle. After considering the problems of a Restoration poet, to leap across the centuries and review the difficulties of a puritanical Victorian prophet may seem a somewhat hazardous adventure. But marriage, as an institution, has many aspects, good and bad alike, that recur in every age; and, as the Carlyles were both keen observers of the world, and each had a fine descriptive gift, their joint chronicle provides a more elaborately detailed picture of domestic happiness and misery than almost any similar record published during the last three hundred years.

Not only were they remarkably different characters; but they had entered adult life and approached wedlock by completely separate paths. For Carlyle it had been a hard way, so seldom enlivened by happiness that he remembered with a peculiar gratitude the few occasions when the clouds had lifted. This he had known in his early manhood, at an old farmhouse named Hoddam Hill, which had then afforded him a contemplative refuge from the world. The year he passed there, he afterwards wrote, lay in his memory 'like a not ignoble russet-coated Idyll – I lived very silent, diligent, had long solitary rides'. But, during those months, he found 'that I had conquered all my scepticisms, agonising doubtings, fearful wrestlings with the foul and vile and soul-murdering Mud-gods of my Epoch . . . and was emerging, free of spirit, into the eternal blue of ether . . . and, for a number of years, had, in spite of nerves and chagrins, a constant inward happiness that was quite royal and supreme . . .'

At the same period, however, he was already carrying on a lengthy, argumentative, yet affectionate correspondence with a well-educated and well-brought-up girl he hesitantly planned to marry. Jane Baillie Welsh had had an agreeable youth. An 'ex-spoilt' child, a blue-stocking and social belle, said to be equally proud 'of her Latin and her eye-lashes', she admired and respected the rough-edged peasant-scholar, yet remained, for the moment at least, perfectly conscious of the gulf that lay between them. Why she had at last crossed it she would explain, after many years of marriage, to a favourite cousin Jeannie Welsh. Her reasons, she admitted, had not been wholly idealistic. But, merely because he was 'the least

Jane Carlyle, who first described marriage as the 'Valley of the Shadow'.
Portrait by Samuel Laurence.

unlikable man in the place, I let him dance attendance on my young person, till I came to *need* him – all the same as my slippers to go to a ball, or my bonnet to go out to walk. When I finally agreed to marry him, I *cried* excessively and felt excessively shocked – but if I had then said *no* he would have left me.'

Feminine self-absorption, of which Jane Carlyle had her full share, has seldom been so candidly revealed; and she could not have known that Carlyle, too, had had secret doubts, which grew more and more oppressive as he approached his wedding day. Nor did the first night of marriage help to raise his troubled spirits. Next morning, 'sick with sleeplessness, quite nervous . . . splenetic and all the rest of it', he was sufficiently distraught to seek the professional advice of his brother Dr John; for he was still 'in a maze', he reported, 'scarce knowing the right from the left in the path I have to walk'. He begged, nevertheless, that John would reassure their anxious mother, telling her that 'I do believe I shall get *hefted* [adjusted] to my new situations, and then be one of the happiest men alive'.

Whether such an adjustment was ever successfully made is a question that we cannot answer. Since James Froude, his literary executor, first informed Carlyle's readers that their hero had suffered from lifelong impotence, it has been frequently proposed. But, although there is no doubt that Carlyle was a man to whom passionate love meant very little – he might have agreed with a modern poet, the late Philip Larkin, who once declared that he regarded 'sexual recreation as a socially remote thing, like baccarat or clog-dancing' – it is evident that, whatever his physical shortcomings may have been, he did not lack emotional strength, and that, in its later stages, their long, difficult alliance – earlier, they had passed through a devastating storm – would finally come to rest on a solid basis of affection and esteem. Jane was convinced she had married a great writer, whose interests she shared and whose sufferings she understood; while Carlyle listened appreciatively to her brilliant talk, and admired her as not only the most graceful, but the most practically accomplished woman – she alone could defend him against builders, painters, tax-collectors and noisy neighbours – who had ever come his way.

Where they constantly differed was in their attitude towards the outer world. Carlyle detested the society into which he had been born, and abhorred and feared its loathsome 'Mud-gods'. Jane had a keenly social nature; she was fond of her fellow men and women, and all the more attached should they, besides engaging her affections, excite her gift of lively ridicule. A truly absurd personage, for example, the wild Italian artist Spiridione Gambardella, she found immediately sympathetic. Carlyle, on the other hand, though he is said to have once laughed aloud at Emerson delivering a lecture, did not smile easily; of an antagonist he seldom made fun; and to light-hearted derision he preferred stentorian reproof. If he esteemed certain contemporaries, it was because he thought he had detected in them high ambitions, coupled with an intellect and a strength of creative purpose, that he recognised as not unlike his own. Lastly, there was the eternal problem of happiness, to which Jane tentatively and wistfully aspired, and Carlyle, if it were regarded as a serious aim in life, always angrily dismissed. At the age of forty-three, when a philosophic German friend, Plattnauer, nicknamed 'Plato', who had for a while vanished, and then, out of the blue, written to inform Jane that he had now been completely restored and become the 'happiest of human beings', she congratulated him 'on having arrived at happiness by whatsoever inconceivable means', but added that she was apt to receive statements of this kind '*with a superstitious shudder – Happiness if there was such a thing at all seeming to me of the nature of those delicate spirits which vanish when one pronounces their name.*'

Yet it is hard to believe that the elusive spirit did not sometimes visit her at the pleasant Queen Anne house, No. 5 Great Cheyne Row (today No. 24 Cheyne Row), where she had long entertained, and was conscious of having delighted and amused, so many odd and celebrated guests. For Carlyle, a laborious cenobite, the house he inhabited was primarily a cave, in which, from the huge mass of relevant material, written and printed, that always accumulated on his desk, he struggled to weave a single strong thread of historic or prophetic meaning. For Jane, however, who cherished her private background, and did all she could to beautify it, her own house was the stage on which she looked and talked her best, and the setting of endless human dramas. There Mazzini and Godefroi Cavaignac, both distinguished exiles, and each apparently a little in love with her, found their favourite refuge at her feet; while Charles Dickens, also a

Thomas Carlyle produced most of his books, he said, 'in a state seldom enlivened by happiness', but often in a 'period of deep gloom and dubitation'. Crayon portrait by Laurence.

platonic devotee, listened to the strange stories she told them about 'The House of Mysteries' next door, and assured her that, if she decided to employ her literary talents, she would make a gifted novelist. No less interesting and picturesquely varied were the visitors that Carlyle himself attracted, among them Emerson, the homespun Bostonian sage, and Count d'Orsay, the prince of London dandies, who arrived wearing exquisitely skin-tight pantaloons, numerous gold chains, and generally glistening like a diamond beetle.

It was behind the scenes, before the first admirers had arrived or after the last had gone, that 'the Valley of the Shadow of Marriage' – a phrase that Jane employed in a letter to her cousin – when one personality had room to grind against the other, might seem almost unendurable. After her death, looking back with a widower's bitter remorse on the forty years that he and Jane had shared, Carlyle would describe them as a 'sore life-pilgrimage'; and, although a succession of different problems, including his lack of sexual and emotional sympathy, had helped to make their pilgrimage more grievous, the fact that he so seldom derived any real happiness from his labours was possibly the worst of all. Only the enthusiastic reviews that, in 1837, greeted *The French Revolution* had afforded him 'wild gleamings of a strange joy', followed twelve months later by 'a sense of peacable joy', which, he characteristically admitted, did not long remain with him. Otherwise, his major works, *Frederick the Great, The Letters and Speeches of Oliver Cromwell* and his controversial volume *Latter-Day Pamphlets*, the product, he said, of a 'period of deep gloom and dubitation', would appear to have brought him, while he laboured in his sound-proof room, little but daily anguish and despair.

Yet, not until 1842, when Carlyle was nearly fifty, and Jane forty-three, did a violent emotional tempest shake the foundations of their marriage; and this crisis, in various guises, with many lulls and fresh outbursts, dragged on nearly fifteen years. Its origins were unforeseeable. Jane had long believed, and had sometimes assured her friends, that to women *'as women'* Carlyle remained totally indifferent. Yet, in middle age, he developed a disturbing passion for a celebrated London hostess. Lady Harriet Baring (later Lady Ashburton) was herself already thirty-seven; and when they first met, he noted that, although 'full of mirth and spirit', and 'one of the cleverest creatures' he had yet encountered, she was 'not very beautiful to look upon'; for she had an engaging, quickly intelligent face, but a substantial Junoesque figure and a short, square nose that even her admirers said somehow reminded them of Thackeray.

Carlyle's passion for his 'Sovereign Lady', his 'Queen', his 'Daughter of the Harmonies' and 'Daughter of the Sun', seems to have been exalted and imaginative rather than, in the ordinary sense, physical; and thus, confronted with a woman he adored, but to whom he had none of the sexual obligations he knew he could not properly fulfil in marriage, he felt free to revive some of the romantic daydreams he had harboured since his lonely youth. It was the romantic, even phantasmagoric character of his affection that most tormented and perplexed his wife. And then, to increase her woes, she could not refrain from secretly respecting and admiring her rival. An accomplished *femme du monde*, Lady Harriet was so versed in the ways of the world, and so subtle a diplomatist, that, because she enjoyed her 'dear old Prophet's' company and his fascinating table-talk, she refused to give his clever life-companion the smallest excuse for appearing neglected and aggrieved.

Nothing she did or said, however, could permanently ease Jane's heartache or Carlyle's dark nostalgic longings. He would gladly attend a fashionable ball that the Sovereign Lady held; but, once he had returned home, for all the 'divine benevolence' she had shown him there, he was immediately struck down by an overwhelming sense of deprivation:

'You gave us a glorious Ball . . . It is something to have seen such a one, and been seen by her – though only as if from precipice to precipice, with horrid chasms, and roaring cataracts, and black rivers of Acheron flowing between, forever! . . . I will call tomorrow, about four; can stay half an hour . . .'

The story of this strange episode in the Carlyles' relationship has already been sensibly and sympathetically related;* but here its pacific sequel most

* Best of all by Iris Origo in her account of 'A Victorian Friendship', *A Measure of Love*, 1957.

concerns us. Carlyle's feelings lost their dangerous strength; Jane slowly recovered her hold on life; and her confidence that she still kept Carlyle's love was, at length, successfully restored. Then, in 1857, Lady Ashburton died, having shown to the end her usual gaiety and courage; and meanwhile, at overcast Cheyne Row, a reconciliation had begun to dawn. Each of the contestants was prepared to admit some faults. Jane, for example, agreed that she was occasionally a poor companion: 'God knows how gladly I would be sweet-tempered and cheerful-hearted . . . if my temper were not soured and my heart saddened, beyond my own power to mend them'; and Carlyle patiently assured her that she had never lost his love, although she might fail to understand his problems: 'You know nothing about me just now. With all the clearness of vision you have, your lynx-eyes do not reach the inner vision of me, and know now what is in my heart . . . I wish you did; I wish you did.'

By April 1865, peace, so far as they were capable of experiencing it, had settled on the Carlyles' household. Jane had put behind her eighteen months of an exquisitely painful psychosomatic illness,* and Carlyle was offered the Lord Rectorship of Edinburgh University, one of the few public honours he was ready to accept. Both were gratified; but neither, of course, escaped anxiety; and Jane's apprehensions were particularly acute. Carlyle, she knew, was expected to address the assembled university; and, once he had set out, she suffered great alarm not from 'over anxiety', she wrote, 'about the success of the speech when spoken, but from a wild idea that it might never get spoken at all, that what with previous sleeplessness and wild hubbub . . . and the whole unsuitability of the thing, when he rose up to speak he might probably . . . *drop down dead*!' Her fears were groundless; Carlyle's speech, as a telegram from Edinburgh soon informed her, had been unquestionably 'A Perfect Triumph'. Discarding the notes he had made, but afterwards decided that he would not use, Carlyle spoke for an hour-and-a-half – on his youth at this same university, on his later life, his struggles and his doubts, and then advised the listening

---

* It had begun with a painful accident, when she was knocked down in the street; but its after-effects seem to have bewildered her doctors, one of whom declared that he could not contend against 'hysterical' mania.

students how to prosecute their own researches, to read thoroughly and carefully, think calmly and oppose the false gods of the present age. During his speech he made several references to Goethe. Carlyle, as a rule, mistrusted poets; their behaviour was usually loose; their principles were vague and self-destructive. But Goethe was a grand exception, a master-poet who was also a prophet and a teacher, and whose view of the universe was supremely solemn. 'Awe', he had told the world, 'was the highest thing in man'; and if, a man experienced that, he should be content; he could be aware of nothing higher.

Carlyle shared that sense of awe. What had been denied him, however, was Goethe's delight in the natural world and eager wide-ranging curiosity about every manifestation of life that met his eye – a school of dolphins, their colours changing from gold to green, and then from green to gold, as they leapt across the waves; or a Sicilian garden, where he revived his 'old fancy' concerning the origin of species, and hoped perhaps to distinguish the basic forms, the *Urphänomene*, of all the flowers and plants he loved. Carlyle had neither Goethe's capacity for keen sensuous enjoyment nor the breadth of his poetic vision; but both believed that suffering was an important part of human experience, which quickened and enriched the soul; and at Edinburgh in 1886 he quoted not only Goethe's message of hope and comfort; but some lines he had himself translated:

> Who never ate his bread in sorrow,
> Who never spent the midnight hours
> Weeping and waiting for the morrow,
> He knows you not, ye Heavenly Powers

Meanwhile, Jane, having heard of Carlyle's magnificent reception, hastened to express her pride and love; but this letter, headed simply 'Dearest', and one of the most affectionate and least querulous she had written him for many years, also proved to be her valediction; for on April 23rd, John Ruskin, who was about to leave England and had called at Cheyne Row to bid her goodbye, was met by a weeping maid-servant on the threshold with the news that Mrs Carlyle had died a few hours earlier, suddenly and peacefully in her own carriage as she drove round Hyde Park.

10

'The Golden World'

WITH the pursuit of happiness goes the quest for the Heavenly City or the Terrestrial Paradise; and, when Samuel Johnson announced that complete felicity was discoverable only in our recollections or in our expectations, he might have added that the place where a man at present finds himself is seldom altogether to his liking. Visions of 'Somewhere Else' – '*N'importe où hors du monde*': 'Anywhere out of the World'* – have haunted poets since imaginative literature began; and, although a few have written contentedly and gratefully of their own immediate surroundings – Horace often praises his little Sabine farm – others, Baudelaire and Leopardi, for example, have regarded the present-day world as, if not a gaol, at least a penal colony, in which they were condemned to serve. Worldly success and the free enjoyment of power do not necessarily appease a restive spirit. Alexander the Great, we are told, never ceased hankering for new frontiers to cross and fresh kingdoms to invade; and among dynasts Shah Jehan alone, most sympathetic of the Mughal Emperors, seems to have escaped a secret malaise. 'Should there indeed be a paradise one earth,' he exclaimed, looking out over Delhi from his magnificent Red Fort, 'it is this. Oh, it is this! It is surely this!'

As the poetic account of an expedition to a far-off country where happiness and harmony reign, Homer's description of Odysseus's visit to the Land of the Phaeacians is probably the earliest and the best. On his way home after

---

* Baudelaire gives his prose poem both a French and an English title.

capturing and sacking Troy, the hero had suffered grim vicissitudes, exposed to the martial ferocity of the Cicones and the Laestrigonians and the primitive brutality of the cannibalistic giant Polyphemus; and then, once he had reached Ogygia, the island home of the enchantress Calypso, held in amorous captivity for several long unhappy years, until Hermes, messenger of the Olympian Gods, carrying his golden wand of office, had demanded she should set him free.

On the stout raft that Odysseus therefore builds himself, and that Calypso generously provisions with fresh water, wine and corn, he yet again becomes a wanderer; but he has forgotten that he has a divine enemy, the powerful sea-god Poseidon; a huge wave soon destroys his raft; and, naked, exhausted, scurfed with sea-salt, he is cast ashore upon an unknown beach. There a stroke of brilliant good fortune awaits him; he meets the virginal princess Nausicaa, busy at the time with the pile of household laundry she and her maids have brought down in a mule-cart to the river-bank. Nausicaa is one of literature's most delightful and endearing heroines. Brave and free-spoken, she has also the gift of beauty, which Odysseus, exhausted though he is, quickly recognises and eloquently acclaims. She reminds him, he says, of a young tree he had seen in other days growing at Delos beside the altar of Apollo; and he marvels at her, and fears to approach her and touch her knees as a proper suppliant should have done. But Nausicaa calmly reassures him, summons her frightened maids, commands them to bring him food and wine, and provide a tunic and a cloak from the garments they have just laid out to dry. She is the daughter, she explains, of Alcinous, sovereign of the Phaeacians, a people the Olympian Gods especially love, who dwell on the utmost verges of the earth, far beyond contact with ordinary men.

Half a century ago, to rehearse the story of Odysseus's meeting with Nausicaa might very well have seemed impertinent; but now that neither Homer's text nor Pope's vigorous translation (praised by Johnson as 'the noblest version of poetry that the world has ever seen'*) is still an essential part of any good library, this enchanting fairy-tale may perhaps be a little less familiar. Homer does not depict Nausicaa's beauty in detail, giving us

---

* The famous scholar Dr Bentley, on the other hand, once remarked to the translator: 'It's a very pretty poem, Mr Pope, but you mustn't call it Homer.'

her carriage, the line of her youthful cheeks and chin, the colour of her eyes and hair. These the reader himself must recreate; and, although at other periods he would probably have visualised her as a smooth Praxitelean nymph or, later, as a Graeco-Roman demi-goddess, today she recalls a member of the bewitching family of *Korai*, the band of graceful girls, statues of ministrants carrying votive offerings to Athene's shrine,* whom we admire today on the Acropolis. They are slender and straight-limbed; their long locks are invariably braided and curled; and all have the same subtly enigmatic expression, the corners of their mouths slightly turned up, that archaeologists have labelled 'the Archaic smile'.

To Nausicaa's home, the palace of her father Alcinous, its remoteness lends a particular distinction; the Phaeacians admit they are emigrants; harried in their native country by Polyphemus' monstrous kinsmen, they have withdrawn to their present remote land where they are safe against their foes. The Gods moreover have favoured them, and they have developed extraordinary skills; 'their ships are as swift as the flight of a bird or as a thought', so that their seamen have ceased to depend on pilots or rudders; their craft themselves understand the sailor's purpose. Given these blessings, the Phaeacians are a quiet, contented race and lead modestly luxurious lives; 'for we', their ruler assures Odysseus, whom, after some diplomatic questioning, he has accepted as an honoured guest, 'are not skilled boxers or wrestlers, but fast runners and good seamen, and dear to us always are feasting and music, the dance and frequent changes of clothing, and the warm bath and love and sleep.'

I remember how much in my youth, 'doing Greek' at an English public school at which athleticism was highly valued, this evocation of the Phaeacian way of life appealed to me. Homer must certainly have admired it. Whether he was a single poet, or the skilled editor and co-ordinator of a host of ancient legends, he is now believed to have worked during the seventh or eighth century B.C., and to be looking back at a state of society, based perhaps on recollections of the glorious Mycenaean Age, that had no longer any real existence.† Alcinous' palace with its brazen threshold and

* They were probably carved about six centuries before Christ, and desecrated during the Persian invasion.
† See M.I. Finley: *The World of Odysseus*, 1956.

walls, surmounted by a bright blue frieze, its golden statues of youths and hounds, and the orchards and gardens that encompass it, must undoubtedly have borne some resemblance to the ruins of a Mycenaean palace recently excavated at Pylos (the modern Navarino) where Telemachus, in quest of news about Odysseus, discovers the venerable Nestor and his subjects sacrificing black bulls on the sea-shore to the Earth-Shaker Poseidon; for there we find both a noble bathroom and the kind of circular open hearth Alcinous' consort Areté sits beside with her maidservants, spinning skeins of purple wool. Thus, Phaeacia is a romantic Utopia or Never-Never Land, and represents life not as it was when Homer immortalised its ancient splendour, but as a beautifully organised society in which human happiness - Alcinous feels proud of his people's welfare – is among a sovereign's chief concerns.

The whole episode has a lyrical and nostalgic colouring: and, when I read Homer's description of Nausicaa, I have sometimes thought of a far later and less classic heroine. *A Winter's Tale* is not Shakespeare's most expertly balanced comedy; it includes too many ill-assorted elements, for example, a slightly preposterous transformation scene, the unveiling of Hermione, no doubt devised to please the new-fangled Jacobean taste. The play, first seen in 1611 and acted before King James the same year, is a product of Shakespeare's last phase, which also gave us *The Tempest*; and, like that fascinating work, it suggests that the poet's state of mind when he wrote it, was not altogether tranquil; it contains such alarming reflections of jealousy, cruelty and tyranny; and it is from them that the dramatist at last escapes when Prince Florizel approaches the Shepherd's cottage, now the home of Perdita, the lost princess.

This was not the only romantic refuge from the hardships of real life that the poet had presented. In 1599 or 1600 he had written *As You Like It*, where his background is the Forest of Arden, named after his mother's dignified land-owning family, whither the old Duke and his cheerful companions have retired to follow Robin Hood's example, and 'fleet the time carelessly, as they did in the golden world'. That world is an anticipation of the Earthly Paradise; and there a seeker after happiness, temporarily at least, is well protected against the harsher and uglier aspects of ordinary life. Between 1599 and 1611, Shakespeare himself had lived

A Greek girl, wearing the typical 'Archaic smile'; one of the statues of Athene's ministrants, now in the Acropolis Museum.

[141]

through a succession of painful crises, and produced the tremendous tragedies of what critics call his 'Dark Period'. In 1601, Essex and Shakespeare's patron and friend Southampton had staged their abortive revolt, which came to a catastrophic end: and, while Essex had paid with his life on the scaffold, Southampton had suffered close confinement in the Tower, which would last until the old Queen's death. Even worse was the sequel; eager loyalists, anxious both to protest their own devotion and share in the spoils of the favourite's disgrace, had loudly begged for their reward. Human cupidity and falsehood had seldom been so miserably displayed.

In *A Winter's Tale* Shakespeare seems for a moment to cut free from the real world; and his story and treatment of it alike have a deliberately fictitious turn. Bohemia is given a sea-coast; an inexplicable bear suddenly emerges, and chases Antigonus back into the wings. Few details, once we have reached Act IV – Act I contains a realistic and extraordinarily moving picture of Leontes' affection for his son and jealous attachment to his wife – are not playfully fantastic. 'This is fairy gold, boy,' says the Shepherd, 'and 'twill prove so', fairy gold being a stuff that pleases the eye, and very soon afterwards dissolves. But, although the Shepherd's cottage is situated in the land of legends, one of the occupants has an unconquerably vital spirit. Perdita is no mere poetic wraith; and, almost as soon as she emerges, we hear her voice and, like Odysseus confronting Nausicaa, quickly recognise her wit and beauty. Odysseus compared the Phaeacian princess to a young tree; and Perdita in movement, Florizel exclaims, has the grace of an ocean wave:

> '. . . when you do dance, I wish you
> A wave o' the sea that you might do
> Nothing but that; and move still, still so,
> And own no other function . . .'

She has all her period's most engaging traits – its passion for flowers, its appreciation of fine language and its unblushing lack of prudery. She does not conceal the romantic attraction that draws her irresistibly towards Florizel; and, when she delivers the incomparable speech in which she enumerates the flowers, from spring daffodils to 'the flower-de-luce', that she wishes she could strew about him, and Florizel protests 'What, like a corse?', she replies with delightful boldness:

'No, like a bank for love to lie and play on;
Not like a corse . . .
But quick and in mine arms. Come, take your flowers.'

All the inhabitants of Shakespeare's Bohemia are bohemians in the modern meaning of the word – rebels who stubbornly reject convention and obey their own rebellious instincts. Seen through the eyes of a Jacobean magistrate, Autolycus, the thievish pedlar, would have appeared an incorrigible 'rogue and vagabond'; not only does he sell his wares – 'ribands of all the colours i' the rainbow . . . inkles, caddisses,* cambrics, lawns' and 'sings 'em over as they were gods or goddesses' – during his rambles through the country; but he has also found a profitable sideline in pilfering the clean sheets that foolish housewives hang out upon the wayside hedges. Though his is a precarious and perilous existence, he keeps anxiety at bay: 'beating and hanging are terrors to me', he admits; yet for them, as 'for the life to come, I sleep out the thought of it'; and meanwhile he is perfectly content with the pleasures of the present hour:

> The lark that tirra-lirra chants,
> With heigh! with heigh! the thrush and the jay,
> Are summer songs for me and my aunts,
> While we lie tumbling in the hay.

– his 'aunts' being the rustic loves he has picked up on the road.

For Shakespeare and his contemporaries travel-books that reported the wonders of the New World were a constant source of inspiration. *The Tempest*, written about the same time as *A Winter's Tale*, derives both wise old Gonzalo's account of an Ideal Commonwealth and much of its romantic imagery from *A discovery of the Barmudas, otherwise called The Ile of Divels*; and writing both plays, he was also indebted to John Florio's translation of Montaigne's *Essays* that had been published in 1580. Here a chapter entitled 'Of Cannibals' is devoted to a primitive race, inhabitants of a remote Brazilian forest, who are 'wild just as we call wild the fruits that

* 'Inkles' are a kind of tape, 'caddisses' worsted ribbons.

[143]

Nature has produced herself', and barbarians only in so far as 'they have been fashioned very little by the human mind'. There follows a definition of happiness that recurs in varying forms throughout the *Essays*: 'To know how to enjoy our being rightfully, and to accept the terms of our own existence gladly, is the height of human wisdom.' Those are the gifts he imagined the Cannibals possessed; and the fact that his greatest friend, Etienne de la Boétie, had once thought of abandoning corrupt and over-civilised Europe for the natural pleasures of the New World he did not find at all surprising.

Although Montaigne himself was content to remain at home, jogging meditatively around his pleasant estate – it was in the saddle, he believed, that he thought most sensibly and clearly – or reading and writing in his turret room, where he had had painted on the beams the Delphic phrase *'Gnōthi Seauton'*, *'Know Thyself'*, and some forty-nine other admonitory maxims, he shared the restive spirit of his age and its insatiable thirst for knowledge. Like an English poet, he identified this craving with all that is noblest in the human character:

> Nature, that fram'd us of four elements . . .
> Doth teach us all to have aspiring minds:
> Our souls, whose faculties can comprehend
> The wondrous architecture of the world,
> And measure every wand'ring planet's course,
> Still climbing after knowledge infinite,
> And always moving as the restless spheres,
> Will us to wear ourselves, and never rest . . .*

Christopher Marlowe, the Elizabethan *poète maudit*, who put these resounding, though oddly anachronistic lines into the mouth of Timour-Leng, the fourteenth-century Tartar war lord, was such an aspiring mind – so boldly and rashly speculative indeed that, just before his tragic death, he had aroused the suspicions of the Privy Council; while Sir Walter Ralegh, at whose so-called 'School at Night' he is said to have propounded his

* *Tamburlaine the Great*, Part I, Act II.

[144]

atheistic doctrines, was a no less adventurous climber after knowledge. Ralegh's aspirations as he summed them up in one of his own poems –

'To seek new worlds, for gold, for praise, for glory,
To try desire, to try love severed far'

– both determined his career at the Elizabethan Court, where he became a richly rewarded royal favourite, and presently carried him across the ocean to combine his search for the Golden City, the legendary El Dorado, with more romantic but almost equally elusive aims.

In 1595, he had an early glimpse of the unexplored Americas, and sighted not the Golden City, but, as he surveyed the banks of the Orinoco, an Arcadian landscape stranger and more romantic than any that had yet confronted him:

'I never saw a more beautiful country, nor more lively prospects, hills so raised here and there over the valleys, the river winding into divers branches, the plains adjoining without bush or stubble, all fair green grass, the ground of hard sand easy to march on either for horse or foot, the deer crossing in every path, the birds towards the evening singing on every tree with a thousand several tunes, cranes and herons of white, crimson and carnation perching on the river's side, the air fresh with a gentle, easterly wind, and every stone that we stooped to take up promised either silver or gold by his complexion.'*

It is characteristic of Elizabethan travellers that, besides enjoying the beauty of this Arcadian prospect, Ralegh and his companions should also have scrutinised the pebbles they saw at their feet for any trace of gold or silver; the English like the Spanish *conquistadores*, who, in their own search, soon ravished and destroyed the splendid civilisation of the great Mexican cities they had originally so much admired, were always ardently acquisitive; and on his last expedition to the New World Ralegh was still seeking the fabulous South American mine that, if discovered and exploited, would restore his credit with the King. His adventure failed; in

* *The Discoverie of Guiana.*

[145]

1618, an old charge of treason was revived, and he was thereupon condemned to death.

Once the legend of El Dorado had been finally abandoned, however, it was followed by a succession of other dreams; the New World was not the only region that now seemed to offer happiness. Even the Chinese Empire was regarded, temporarily at least, as an ancestral home of wisdom. English architects adopted Eastern modes, until, a critic complained, modern cowsheds and dairies had begun to develop strangely curvaceous roofs; while gardeners adapted the Chinese principle of design,* and skilled exponents of *chinoiserie* covered European walls and ceilings with imaginative representations of Far-Eastern landscapes, where bearded sages sat placidly smoking their pipes under elegant pavilions, amid their favourite disciples.

Thus, although the supposed location of the Earthly Paradise has varied considerably from age to age, when the United States had declared their independence it was the New World that, for the young Romantics, seemed again to offer special promise. Thither Chateaubriand's doomed hero, René, was to escape from the sins and sorrows of the old; and in 1794, the year Saint-Just described happiness as a 'new idea' that all revolutionary patriots were entitled to enjoy, the twenty-year-old Coleridge met Southey at Cambridge, and the two enthusiasts discussed the foundation of a self-governing Pantisocratic society, where every citizen would be free and equal. But such a society required a different political background; and, later that same summer, Coleridge, who then used to spend his nights in a London ale-house entitled the 'Salutation and Cat', drinking 'Porter and *Punch* round a good fire', happened to meet 'a most intelligent young man who has spent the last five years of his life in America – and is lately come from thence as an Agent to sell Land'.

He offered easy terms; two thousand pounds would probably be enough to establish the settlement that they intended:

'. . . For six hundred Dollars a thousand Acres may be cleared, and houses built upon them. He recommends the Susquehannah from its

---

* Known as 'Sharawadgi', it was first introduced by Sir William Temple in his essay *Upon the Gardens of Epicurus* (1685) and denoted the use of elegant irregularity.

excessive Beauty and its security from hostile Indians . . . Literary characters make money there . . . He never saw a Bison in his life, but has heard of them . . . The Mosquitoes are not so bad as our gnats – and after you have been there a little while, they don't trouble you much.'

Yet the enthusiasts would never set sail; by 1795 Coleridge decided, rightly no doubt, that their Pantisocratic Plan had done more credit to their hearts than to their heads. His affectionate association with Southey, however, had one disastrous result. Under its influence, he began to think of marriage, perhaps in the romantic Susquehannah country, and, having broken off an earlier engagement, he proposed to Sarah Fricker, sister of Southey's future wife – a young woman, he said, he had previously courted 'from principle, not feeling' – and met a reward that far exceeded 'the greatness of the effort: I love and am beloved, and I am happy.' Coleridge was by nature a moral theorist, and this discovery seemed to establish a point he had already once made: 'he cannot long be wretched who dares be actively virtuous.' But here he was very soon proved wrong. The Coleridges' marriage, though he begat children, and remained an intermittently domestic husband until 1806, brought them very little joy.

The impulse to leave home and found a new, more liberated and happier society that Coleridge and Southey failed to realise, has been shared by many English writers. In our own days, D.H. Lawrence spent much of his adult life on the same exhausting quest; and almost all his later novels describe the adventures of a different journey – to Tuscany, the Abruzzi, Mexico, New Mexico, Australia; and, whenever he could temporarily settle down, he hoped his best-loved associates might join him and build a spiritual haven, where the old conventional values would be discarded and the 'blood relationship' of man with man restored. Of these books, *The Plumed Serpent*, published thirteen years after his autobiographical masterpiece *Sons and Lovers*, is the strangest and the least appealing; for there, under the leadership of a typical Laurentian hero, Don Cipriano, a perfectly masculine man, 'a little fighting male', he depicts the dethronement of the Christian faith and the restoration of the ancient Aztec gods, Quetzalcoatal and the ferocious war-god Huitzilpochtli, whom Don Cipriano's followers acclaim with a typical Hitlerian salute. But Lawrence the raucous prophet – T.S. Eliot called him a 'tin-chapel' orator – had a many-sided talent, and his love and understanding of the natural world far exceeded his comprehension of mankind. His personages, because they reflect his dogmas, prejudices and deep-rooted private obsessions, are often ill-drawn, even here and there grotesque; it is only when his theme is a landscape, a bird or a beast, and the strong effect they produce on his own imagination, that his genius seems to shine through.

The Spirit of Place, the splendid anthology of Lawrence's descriptive prose-writings made by Richard Aldington in 1944, is an endlessly illuminating work, and shows the pleasure that, like Coleridge, he derived from observation practised as a branch of literary art. It also suggests that, for him as for Rousseau in *Les Rêveries du Promeneur Solitaire*, the mere sense of being alive, which he had developed to so fine a point, and of having an integral link with the whole universe, might itself be happiness enough. Comparatively few modern English writers have had Lawrence's especial gift; but, during the Romantic Age,* both the Wordsworths – Dorothy in her prose-jottings no less apparently than William in his verse – displayed the same aptitude for evoking the spirit, the other-worldliness or mythopoeic aspect, of a scene that they describe.

Here, for example, is Dorothy's description of the evening sky as she had watched it change from the threshold of Dove cottage:

> The vale looked as if it were filled with white light when the moon had climbed up to the middle of the sky; but long before we could see her face, while all the eastern hills were in black shade, those on the opposite side were almost as bright as snow. Mrs. Luff's large white dog lay in the moonshine upon the round knoll under the old yew-tree, a beautiful and romantic image – the dark tree with its dark shadow, and the elegant creature as fair as a spirit.

While she watched, the Terrestrial Paradise must have seemed momentarily very close indeed; and, although Nausicaa, Perdita and the Shepherd's

---

* The idea of Man's correspondence with Nature also fascinated the French Romantics. Thus Gérard de Nerval in *Aurélia*, his account of his own madness, relates how from every natural detail he observed '*Je voyait ressortir des harmonies jusqu'alors inconnues. "Comment" me disais-je "ai-je pu exister si longtemps hors de la nature et sans m'identifier à elle? Tout vit, tout agit, tout se correspond . . ."* '

Cottage, the Forest of Arden, where the old Duke and his companions
fleeted the time away as men 'did in the golden world', even perhaps
Ralegh's poetic vision of a great American river, are now fugitive 'fairy
gold', almost every human being, once or twice in a lifetime, must have
had a glimpse of an ideal universe, made for peace and happiness alone.
Such recollections die hard; and I remember myself standing on a grassy
Dorset cliff and looking down across a ten-mile stretch of brackish water
named the Fleet, that here divides the coastline from a famous pebble
ridge.* Not far off an ancient monastic swannery is still kept up by an
enlightened landlord; and, as the sun was sinking, along the tranquil
surface of the Fleet, which reflected a calm roseate sky, I saw a galaxy of
swans drift past.

* One of the peculiarities of the Chesil Beach, said to be the most extensive in Great
  Britain, is that its pebbles, which vary in size from that of a pea to the dimensions of a
  small plate, are graded by the action of the tides; and we are told that, if a blind man who
  knew the Beach well were set down at any point, he could say exactly where he stood.

II

> # Paradise at a Stroke

I
N the early nineteenth century, London maid-servants, who had just begun their day's work, were very often seen hurrying towards a nearby druggist's shop, where, for a shilling or less, they purchased a large flagon of the clear purplish fluid named 'laudanum', a tincture of opium with an admixture of alcohol, which at the time was as important a part of the household pharmacopoeia as some harmless sedative today. It had a dozen different uses; and Jane Austen records that, on a long and tiring journey, her mother was advised by a local physician to take 'twelve drops . . . before she went to bed'. But, even at that period, its excessive use was considered slightly dangerous; and Lady Byron, besides deploring the poet's addiction to brandy, was also suspicious of the 'black drops' she found in his dressing-room and among his travelling equipment. Her alarm had little real foundation. Byron was excessive in nearly everything he did. Laudanum, however, seems to have had no decisive effect either on his work or on his personal character.

Others were less fortunate; and meanwhile for two of his gifted contemporaries, Coleridge and Thomas De Quincey, the pleasures and pains of opium-taking had developed a terrible significance. Each was a fugitive, in flight not only from the trials of the present day but from a host of oppressive recollections. Since his early youth, Coleridge remembered, he had been 'most, MOST cruelly treated' by his unkind nurse and a sadistic elder brother who acquired a taste for beating him; and at Cambridge he first 'fled to Debauchery', next left his college and, having adopted a grotesque pseudonym, enlisted in a British cavalry regiment, where, unable to manage his charger or keep his equipment clean, he had proved absurdly unsuccessful.

De Quincey, too, had fled from the immediate problems of his life, and, deserting his respectable family, become a homeless wanderer around London; and both, at an early age, were introduced to opium, Coleridge before 1791, De Quincey in 1804 by a 'beatific' London druggist, the 'unconscious minister of celestial pleasures' and, at the same time, of unending miseries. But, like Coleridge, what he had originally sought was not happiness so much as relief from pain, in De Quincey's case 'excruciating rheumatic pains' that he had himself induced, having with a characteristic lack of good sense plunged his head into a basin of cold water and gone to bed without troubling to dry his hair.

The Confessions of an English Opium-Eater, published in 1821, is one of the most maddeningly diffuse and prolix books ever produced by a writer who, at his best, was a master of the language. De Quincey strays from theme to theme; his footnotes threaten to submerge the text; but then some wonderfully illuminating paragraph emerges, such as the poignant account – in my edition we must await it until page 177 – of how his addiction had long ago begun:

> 'It was a Sunday afternoon, wet and cheerless; and a duller spectacle this earth has not to show than a rainy Sunday in London. My way homeward lay through Oxford street; and I saw a druggist's. The druggist . . . looked dull and stupid . . . and when I asked for tincture of opium, he gave it to me . . . and furthermore, out of my shilling returned to me what seemed . . . real copper halfpence taken out of a real wooden drawer . . .'

As soon as he had regained his lodgings, he took the quantity prescribed. 'O heavens! What a revulsion! What a resurrection, from its lowest depths of the inner spirit!' Not only had his pain vanished; but 'this negative effect was swallowed up in the immensity of those positive effects which had opened up before me . . . Here was the secret of happiness, about which philosophers had disputed for so many ages . . . happiness might now be bought for a penny and carried in the waistcoat pocket . . .'

[151]

Although the druggist's shop probably existed – and some students claim they have discovered exactly where it must have stood – the whole story of De Quincey's introduction to opium has a somewhat dreamlike quality. In his world, as in Coleridge's, dreams, 'tumultuous dreams', played an exceedingly important part; and neither could easily decide where visions ended and 'real life' began. Very often they were aware of a closely interwoven pattern. In his sleep De Quincey was haunted by visions of his dear Ann, the 'noble-minded' young prostitute, who had kept him company and protected him in his London wanderings – again the background of the scene is Oxford Street – but, during his brief absence, had for ever disappeared. Coleridge was equally dream-obsessed, and liked to believe that the signs he thought he had received while he slept might sometimes prove to be celestial tokens. 'If a man could pass through Paradise in a dream', he noted on April 19th, 1817, 'and have a flower presented to him as a pledge that his soul had really been there, and if he found that flower in his hand when he awoke – Aye! and what then?'

While drug-addiction heightened the imagery of their dreams, which became beatific on the one hand and strangely terrifying and hideous upon the other, it encouraged and constantly frustrated the writers' search for individual happiness; and both had come close enough to their goal, and had viewed their objective with sufficient clarity to have a lasting sense of failure. It was as historic failures, sad survivors of a memorable past, that Carlyle described them in their later lives – Wordworth's fallen hero, during his last retirement grown stout, flaccid, helplessly irresolute; and De Quincey seen as a talkative ageing man by the sharp-eyed, sharp-tongued pair at Cheyne Row:

'A pretty little creature, full of wire-drawn ingenuities; bankrupt enthusiasms, bankrupt pride; with the finest silver-toned low voice, and most elaborate gently winding courtesies . . . A bright, ready and melodious talker: but in the end an inconclusive and long-winded. One of the smallest man-figures I ever saw . . . When he sat, you would have taken him, in candlelight, for the beautifullest little Child . . . had there not been something too, which said "*Eccovi*, this Child has been in Hell".'

The Hell where Coleridge and De Quincey suffered was a very real inferno that they were condemned to enter almost every night of their latter-day existence. 'Sleep', Coleridge told his friend Tom Wedgwood, 'is my tormenting Angel . . . Dreams with me are no Shadows, but the very substances and foot-thick Calamities of my Life . . .'. As for De Quincey, he saw a close connection between his dreams with their strange scenery – 'the great lights and shadows' – and painful memories of his vagrant youth. But neither pretended that opium alone was the villain of his private drama. Opium, a modern literary historian writes in her excellent survey of *Opium and the Romantic Imagination*,* was 'a symptom, not the cause' of Coleridge's downfall; and this seems equally true of the English Opium-Eater. Like other drugs, for example mescalin whose praises Aldous Huxley sang,† it does no more than accentuate the tendencies, and sometimes perhaps sharpen the vision, of an individual writer. It did not lead Coleridge directly to Xanadu, though if laudanum was the so-called 'anodyne' that, he explained, had plunged him into a profound sleep during which, 'without any sensation or consciousness of effort', he believed he had written the two to three hundred lines he was afterwards unable to transcribe in full, no doubt it started him along the road.

For the benefits he now and then received the penalty Coleridge paid was sometimes hideous. Yet opium, as the example of another writer shows, need not always be disruptive. During the same half-century, the poet George Crabbe, much admired by Wordsworth, Byron and Tennyson, who became an addict in his middle life, despite the nightmares it regularly provoked – he was vexed by a gang of ghostly ruffians he referred to as 'the Leather Lads', no doubt contemporary 'Hell's Angels' – long combined the habit with a highly successful poetic career and a calm domestic life. The only opium-taker I have myself observed at first-hand, an elderly South American diplomatist, seemed singularly well-preserved. Don Antonio shared De Quincey's reverence for the drug, and was delighted to learn that the famous English centenarian 'Old Parr' had habitually smoked or eaten it. He called it his '*bouillon de légumes*' and would leave a

* Alethea Hayter, 1968.
† *The Doors of Perception*, 1954.

party – he was a great party-goer – the moment he began to feel he needed it, but return, contented and sedate, within three quarters of an hour. I remember, when we were staying at the same house, having to walk through his room, where a scent-burner was smoking beside his bed, but I immediately detected the strong, unmistakable odour I had once enjoyed in Peking, a pungent vegetable fragrance, no more sinister or exotic than the smell of a hayfield on an English summer day.

I do not know if Don Antonio had read De Quincey; but Baudelaire's famous essay, *Les Paradis Artificiels*, which *The English Opium-Eater* had inspired, he must certainly have known. It recounts the poet's experiences at a period while, still a rebellious dandy, he occupied an apartment in the antique Hôtel Lauzun on the Ile Saint Louis; and he and his friends, including Théophile Gautier, held nightlong parties there for the sole purpose of experimenting with the hallucinatory effect of drugs, sometimes opium, but apparently more often *cannabis indica* or hashish. The two drugs, they soon learned, had completely different powers – hashish evoked large and grandiose scenes; opium induced a deep, delightful calm.* But Baudelaire and his fellow addicts, '*le Club des Haschisins*', had all very much the same objective; they planned to 'conquer Paradise at a stroke', and break into new realms of the imagination, by means of a mysterious chemical agent that would help them see the world anew. Compared with the extraordinary results they achieved, how simple, Baudelaire pointed out, was the apparatus that the Haschisins required! Itself it was nothing more than 'a green sweetmeat'. Yet there lay the secret of happiness, in something only 'large enough to fill a small spoon'.

Baudelaire, however, made various reservations. 'Hashish', he conceded in *Paradis Artificiels*, 'shows to a man nothing but himself'; and it is not a risk that everyone will take, or, if he takes it, finds he can endure. Among visitors to the Hôtel Lauzun came Balzac and Ernest Meissonier; and, whereas the great novelist, tempted to accept the pernicious sweetmeat, was fascinated, 'and listened and asked questions with an amusing attentiveness and curiosity', he was shocked by the 'notion of

---

* 'Opium is a peaceful seducer; hashish is a disorderly demon'; *Paradis Artificiels*, translated by Norman Cameron, 1950. On Coleridge it had the same effect. He wished, he said, 'like Vishnu to float . . . along an infinite ocean cradled in the flower of the Lotus, and wake once in a million years just to know that I was going to sleep a million years more'.

Baudelaire's caricature of himself under the influence of hashish, 'the drug that shows to a man nothing but himself'.

letting his thoughts pass beyond his own control . . . His inner conflict between his almost childish eagerness for knowledge and his loathing of self-surrender, was revealed on his expressive countenance', until his love of human dignity had won the day and he had decided that he must refuse. The popular artist, on the other hand, agreed to try the drug, which, no doubt, he thought, would bring out his splendid creative gifts, but was sharply disappointed to find himself wandering through a labyrinth of immense geometric parterres. 'I might have been in one of Le Nôtre's gardens!' he disgustedly exclaimed.

So far as we can now judge, none of the adventurous Haschisins did himself inoperable harm. Syphilis then was still the great adversary that carried off so many artists; and one may forget that, until the end of the Second World War, drug-addiction and its commercial exploitation had yet to become a major public problem. At Oxford, in 1924 and 1925, though we practised many other forms of self-indulgence, among my fellow undergraduates I cannot remember encountering an addict; and my few tentative experiments with drugs were reserved for later life. The oddest and the most disturbing was made about 1958, when, at a rather raffish New York evening party, the guests were offered a mixture of heroin and cocaine (picturesquely renamed 'hyacinth' and 'crocus') which we inhaled from little wooden spoons; and, besides completely abolishing my sense of time, it eliminated the smallest trace of boredom or fatigue, so that I spent nearly the whole night engaged in a sensible and decorous conversation with an English woman friend, whom I liked but neither loved nor particularly admired.

During a slightly earlier stage of my life, I had been invited to smoke opium at a pre-war dinner-party in Peking, where my host, a musician and himself an opium-lover, kindly acted as my guide. The procedure had a ceremonious charm. First, the raw opium was cooked, crackling and bubbling over a small flame, to which the pipe's bowl, a circular metal disc, must then be kept carefully applied; and I was told to breathe in constantly and regularly, 'like a child', said my experienced host, 'sucking at its mother's breast'. Clearly this ritual, which necessitated fixing one's eyes on a single brilliant point of light, while gazing down the pipe's long polished stem, had a mild hypnotic influence. I smoked only a few pipes and left the huge Victorian brass bed, on which, overlooked by an array of tin alarm-clocks and other odd apparatus of a Chinese dining-room, I had been invited to recline, feeling calm and content, but no more intoxicated or illuminated than if I had smoked a strong Churchillian cigar. Certainly I felt no worse; the evils of the habit, Chinese acquaintances assured me, were often considerably exaggerated, provided the opium employed was pure, contained no dross scraped out of previous pipes, but came straight from the vast poppy-fields that, in those days, stretched beyond the Great Wall. The habit developed very slowly; and a general carelessness and lassitude, which admittedly might have disastrous results, sometimes accompanied by constipation and even sexual impotence, were frequently among its deadliest symptoms.

My last experience of the effect of drugs was both accidental and ridiculous. Ten or fifteen years ago, when I had attempted to cross a glazed roof on some ill-advised domestic errand, I heard the horrid sound of cracking glass, felt my foothold giving way and, with the sensation of a letter being mailed, shot down into the room below. It was a fairly heavy fall, and, as I lay immobile on the floor, a friendly doctor stood over me and began a good-natured inquisition. He thought, he said, that I might have suffered 'cerebral damage'; and, by way of testing my wits, he suggested that I should now repeat the names of the last five British Prime Ministers – a task, I had to confess, of which, whatever my state of mind, I should have been utterly incapable. After some further brief examinations, he therefore bade me goodbye, but left behind him a few large brown pills that he recommended I should take if I had a painful, restless night.

My night was undisturbed; but I am always interested in unknown pills, and maybe I exceeded the proper dose; for next day I found that my vision of existence had undergone a dazzling change. I believe that the pills' basis may conceivably have been morphine, which my dictionary describes as an 'alkaloid principle of opium . . . popularly called "morphia" '. That morning I entered a new world, or a world with which I was already familiar, but now marvellously transmogrified. Here scenes and objects that had once been commonplace had acquired an extraordinary fascination. I looked forward eagerly to the coming day and all the visual splendours that it promised – in the glorious red of an omnibus and the

Piranesian flight of steps that would lead me down to the station-platform whence an eagle-swift train would waft me to my Fleet Street office.

In fact, I had achieved a degree of euphoria, indistinguishable from true happiness, that, although it slowly faded and declined, had lasted, so far as I can recollect, some two or three delightful hours. Such, no doubt, was the Artificial Paradise Baudelaire and his fellow Haschisins claimed to have conquered at a stroke, but from which the addict, having set foot there, is eventually expelled. I have never entered that paradise again; during my absence, a well-wisher decided to destroy my pills. Nor do I regret their loss; but it was an experience worth having. I am glad to have seen a temporarily transfigured world, and mounted a London omnibus so superbly coloured and majestic that it resembled a 'Chariot of fire' in one of Blake's Prophetic Books.

I 2

```
┌─────────────────────────────────┐
│    Voyages of Discovery         │
└─────────────────────────────────┘
```

I n my early childhood, if my spirits were low, I was often told to 'count my blessings' – advice that, between 1905 and 1914, as the eldest son of a fairly prosperous middle-class English family, I did not find it hard to follow. Since those far-off days it has become increasingly difficult, now that the world itself is threatened with atomic devastation, and so many fields of human happiness are constantly invaded and destroyed. Yet, while some have vanished or are fast vanishing, others have been opened up; and the preliminary steps towards such a discovery were first taken over two hundred years ago by an intrepid Frenchman named Alexandre Charles. He was not the earliest astronaut to leave the surface of the globe; only a month earlier, Pilâtre de Rozier and his friend, the marquis d'Arlandes, had enjoyed the first free flight towards the heavens. But their ascent had lasted less than half-an-hour; and the balloon that carried them was lifted by hot air, and therefore quite unsuited to a lengthy passage. Charles, on the other hand, and his companion Robert, whose immense yellow-and-ochre balloon contained hydrogen, once they had risen from the Gardens of the Tuileries floated off westwards across open country, pursued on horseback at breakneck speed by two enthusiastic noblemen, the duc de Chartres and the duc de FitzJames, and as, some forty kilometres beyond Paris, Charles began his descent, by peasants running through the fields 'like children chasing a butterfly', he wrote.

After a successful landing, the chief astronaut decided on a second venture, abandoned Robert in order to lighten his load, and, having re-entered the gondola that hung beneath the balloon – a rococo *coquillage* embellished with golden wings, a royal crown and *fleurs-de-lis* – rose this time, according to his own eloquent narrative, about two miles above the earth. Nothing, he thought, could ever equal the splendid 'moment of hilarity' he had experienced when his enormous craft again smoothly cleared the ground; and now he had an even deeper and more entrancing satisfaction:

> 'The cold was sharp and dry, but not at all unbearable. I could then examine . . . my sensations in complete tranquillity . . . I stood up in the middle of the gondola, and lost myself in the spectacle offered by the immensity of the horizon.'

He felt, we learn, a sense of almost mystical happiness, of 'inexpressible delight', and 'an ecstasy of contemplation' he had never known before:

> 'No human being, I reflected , has yet penetrated these solitudes; man's voice has never been heard here, and I struck the air with a few sounds as if to stir the silence all around me. The calm, the gathering darkness, that immensity in the midst of which I was floating. All this gripped my soul . . .'*

Charles, in fact, seems to have discovered a totally new form of happiness; and this account of his emotions above the earth may be compared with Rousseau's rediscovery of happiness, in 1765, beside the Lac de Bienne. But, during the present period, a friend, who has passed many years flying American fighter-planes, informs me that Charles's romantic sensations are sometimes shared by modern airmen, and that he himself has felt them more than once, for example, when, having flown seven hundred miles to attend the funeral of a companion killed in a flying accident, he climbed to thirty-five thousand feet, and there the rapture Charles so well conveyed took complete possession of his mind.† Night had fallen; viewed from that altitude, the sky was a deep blue-black, with a huge full moon and a host of stars that looked extraordinarily large and bright. The funeral had

---

* Charles Coulston Gillispie: for a detailed account of Charles's adventures, see *The Montgolfier Brothers and the Invention of Aviation*, 1983.
† At an altitude of more than two miles, this state of mind, which is named *hypoxia*, and involves a heightened sense of one's true identity and a feeling of union with Nature, is said to be the general experience of flyers.

saddened him; it had seemed a dull, unmeaning ceremony. But now that he had reached 'the edge of space' he had a marvellous sense of solitude; and, determined he must pay his dead friend homage, he performed a succession of great looping manoeuvres, called 'barrel-rolls', 'aileron rolls' and 'lazy eights'.

Thus, although modern life frequently destroys happiness, or provides vulgar marketable substitutes, its pursuers need not yet lose hope. New experiences may still await us. I have already quoted Ruskin's announcement that seeing was 'the noblest thing' a soul could do; and during the last hundred years, even the last three or four decades, our range of vision has been extraordinarily enlarged. Sights that would have fascinated, though perhaps alarmed and disturbed, Ruskin are constantly presented to us on the television-screen. We can follow the flight of a humming-bird, peer down into the vividly coloured labyrinth of a Caribbean coral-reef, study the strange inhabitants of an Eastern rain-forest, or, high above the gloomy, sodden forest-floor, visit the huge aerial plateau of sunlit leaves and flowers that stretches far away across the jungle. One night, as the ship on which I was then travelling towards Japan approached a distant, dusky coast-line, a faint but exquisite fragrance crept along the deck, the scent, I was told, of innumerable blossoms that, because they spring only amid the loftiest branches, very few botanists had ever seen.

Today, thanks to modern climbing-equipment and an adventurous use of the camera, those same flowers, like the vast population of beasts and birds and insects who pass their whole lives immediately beneath the sky, have been examined and recorded.* Yet, although our knowledge of the natural world has so remarkably increased, the workings of Nature itself have grown more and more mysterious. Between eighteenth-century poets, William Collins, James Thomson, John Dyer, Thomas Gray, and the natural scenes they described, there was still a strong admiring sympathy; Nature they regarded as 'greatly charming'; he knew of 'no

---

* Rope-climbing techniques were first employed in the jungle not many years ago; and from David Attenborough's richly instructive and rightly popular book *The Living Planet* we learn that an earlier botanist, anxious to catalogue the forest trees of Borneo, was obliged to train a monkey, which, having climbed a tree he pointed out, would pick and throw down its leaves and flowers.

subject', wrote Thomson in his preface to his famous work *The Seasons*, 'more elevating, more amusing; more ready to awake . . . the philosophic reflection, and moral sentiment . . . Where can we meet with such variety, such beauty, such magnificence?' At the same period, connoisseurs of painting would often carry around an ingenious apparatus called a 'Claude Glass' that enabled them, while they contemplated a landscape, to distinguish its resemblance to a classic work of art; and the poet carried in his mind a somewhat similar device that helped him bring out the moral and philosophical aspects of the scene that met his eyes.

Much less comforting is the point of view of the twentieth-century spectator, now that the strangeness and wildness of the natural world seem to increase with every discovery we make. Until Charles Darwin had entered the field, for example, the methods of propagation and self-preservation that certain flowers and insects employ were still unknown to modern scientists. Who could have guessed, for example, that some South-American orchids, in order to attract the fly they need to transfer their pollen, had developed a system of mimicry so fantastically elaborate that it defied even a Darwinian explanation – sometimes representing themselves as female insects to attract a wandering male; sometimes swaying like a swarm of bees which the real bee may be tempted to attack; or, now and then, alluring a victim by means of a female fragrance they exude and, once it has entered the labyrinth, intoxicating it by a liquid they distil,* so that the drunken insect may lose its balance and waywardly brush its wings against a hidden stem where a store of precious pollinea awaits collection?

The argument, dear to eighteenth-century sermonists, that the ingenious design of the universe reveals the existence of a benevolent Creator,† may lead in more than one direction. Might we not also suspect that it was the masterpiece of a sublimely eccentric Intelligence which revelled in its own complexity? Such was Victor Hugo's opinion. His relationship with

---

* The orchid pollinated by drunken bees is named *Stanhopea Wardii*. See Alice Skelsey: *Orchids*, 1979.
† The chief English advocate of the so-called 'Argument from Design' was William Paley (1743–1805), whose *Evidences of Christianity*, published in 1794, Sir Timothy Shelley often recommended to his disbelieving son Percy Bysshe. The 'Argument' was strongly opposed both by Kant and by Hume.

the Creator was always engagingly personal; and on the verge of death he remarked to a young disciple that he would very soon be meeting God; and 'what a magnificent occasion that would be!' He often though of it, and was already preparing his speech. Meanwhile, at an earlier stage of his life, he had gone so far as to reproach the Creator with the bizarre diversity of his creation, in which humming-birds, flowers and rainbows were accompanied by the presence of huge monstrous reptiles; and he occasionally wondered if God, though like himself a great poet, did not, at certain moments, show a curious lack of good taste.* But then, he concluded, some excuses should probably be made for the Universal Genius!

Although we may not share Victor Hugo's views, we must still admit that, the more we know of creation, the more difficult it becomes to reconcile it with any idea, human or divine, of harmony and order. Yet, whatever the effect of a new discovery may be, discovering itself remains a happy exercise. Alexandre Charles, in his balloon 'about two miles above the earth', felt not merely scientific satisfaction but a sense of 'inexpressible delight'; and something of the same delight must be enjoyed by the earth-bound seeker after knowledge when he suddenly reaps his reward – by a botanist, for example, in the old days of famous plant-hunters, while they were still allowed to explore Asiatic terrains that today are prohibited 'military zones', should he happen to cross a Himalayan range and see far below him a whole valley filled with unknown trees and flowers. Archaeologists, too, are, now and then, equally fortunate; and I recollect my old friend Seton Lloyd describing, many years ago, such an especially memorable occasion.† As he excavated a small Sumerian shrine, he noticed that the knife of an elderly workman, told to scrape a clay floor, had inadvertently broken through the surface and opened a large cavity beneath. Having struck a match, Seton gazed down into the gulf, and there confronted the unbroken alabaster votive statue of an ancient Sumerian citizen, his hands folded in prayer on his naked chest, his solemn big-nosed

---

* *'Moi, je n'exige pas que Dieu toujours s'observe,*
  Il faut bien tolérer quelques excès de verve
  Chez un si grand poète, et ne point se fâcher . . .
  C'est son humeur à lui d'être de mauvais goût'
† It is well described in his extremely interesting book, *Mesopotamia: Excavations in Sumerian Sites*, 1936.

countenance framed in black shoulder-length curls and long black densely corrugated beard. But the most impressive feature of the face that looked up at him were its enormous globular eyes, inlaid with lapis lazuli and polished bone, on which the sun now gleamed 'for the first time in five thousand years.'*

My own ambition to become an archaeologist, encouraged by a chance meeting with the renowned Sir Leonard Woolley, the great discoverer of Ur, was presently extinguished both by my sad failure to win an academic degree and by the lack of a small private income that, Sir Leonard said, a young archaeologist usually required. In my youth, however, I had a single modest *trouvaille*, when, walking over the Chilterns, near a prehistoric barrow, I happened to kick down a molehill and unearthed a carefully-pierced wolf's tooth that an expert at the British Museum recognised as having originally hung in a Stone Age hunter's necklace. Otherwise the gift of 'Serendipity' – the word Horace Walpole coined to describe a mysterious aptitude for making unexpected, if sometimes useless, finds – has very seldom come my way. After discovering the wolf's tooth, nevertheless, I had a single stroke of luck that, although itself even more insignificant, caused me momentary delight. Shown a small wooden casket, a beautiful piece of work that had clearly come from an early-nineteenth-century dressing-table and contained many ingenious partitions, I suggested that, if only we could find the right place, it must enclose a secret drawer, and then, fumbling around, happened to alight upon the hidden spring. Behind the minute panel that obediently leapt open lay a store of little three-penny pieces that carried King William IV's head, and were still as delicate and brightly polished as if they had just been issued from the Mint.

Among discoveries, great and small, scientific, imaginative, phantasmago-ric, that have aided the pursuit of happiness, self-discovery must take a place. The maxim 'Know Thyself', which Montaigne had inscribed on his ceiling, has an universal application; and any honest autobiography should give us an account not only of the discoveries a man has made about

---

* Crushed beneath lay another dozen votive statues, male and female, now known collectively as 'the 'Tell Asmara hoard'.

himself but of the circumstances in which he made them. For Montaigne, an unusually well-balanced character, they were always an absorbing subject. Like the learned English physician and master of poetic prose, Sir Thomas Browne, he believed that Man was among the strangest phenomena the natural world could show, and deserved as much study: 'I could never content my contemplation', he wrote in *Religio Medici*, 'with those general pieces of wonder, the Flux and Reflux of the Sea, the increase of Nile, the converse of the Needle to the North . . . We carry with us the wonders we seek without us: there is all Africa and her prodigies in us . . .; since bold and adventurous' Man was a 'great and true Amphibian . . . disposed to live . . . in divided and distinguished worlds', both in the spirit and in ordinary sensuous existence, and in both to flourish and evolve.

Thus introspection, which, if wrongly and self-destructively employed, becomes an unending source of misery, may also, as Montaigne found, once we have explored the Africa we carry around within ourselves, help us to establish a reasonable degree of happiness. Here we are assisted by the discoveries we make; a life from which an ability to discover was absent would indeed be dark and wretched. The process begins at a very early age, usually the moment we have learned that we can read; and I recollect the time, and even the exact place, at which for me this miracle occurred – lying on the tiled floor of my parents' dining room, as I turned the pages of a yellow-clad magazine, and saw the long pageant of a continuous narrative unfolding dramatically beneath my eyes. I cannot date this adventure exactly; but it must, I think, have not been very long after my father had carried me out of the house to observe a luminous blur called Halley's Comet* floating rather low down in the heavens; and just before, through a neighbour's telescope I had been shown the Rings of Saturn and the mysterious Mountains of the Moon, on which, I was told to notice, the dawn was then breaking.

All these were memorable experiences; but the discovery that I could read was evidently the most decisive, for it set me out on a journey of exploration that has continued ever since, and, I hope, will end only with my life. Meanwhile, I am so addicted to the printed word that, if I am

---

* Named after the astronomer Esmond Halley (1656–1742), it reappears, as it did recently, every seventy-eight years.

temporarily deprived of books, I find myself eagerly studying newspaper advertisements or the inscriptions plastered around medicine-bottles. At the same time, to the happiness that reading brought me, I added the joy of enlarging my vision of the world in which I lived, for example, by scrutinising the pictures, often late-Victorian reproductions of the Italian masters, Botticelli, Carpaccio and Gozzoli, that my parents hung upon their walls. These works themselves, and the inexplicable details the artist had sometimes chosen to portray, aroused an avid curiosity. 'Children', observed John Locke, 'are travellers newly arrived in a strange country'; and 'for a child', wrote Baudelaire in his famous essay on the draughtsman Constantin Guys, 'everything is new . . . nothing bears a more striking resemblance to what is called inspiration than the joy with which forms and colours are absorbed by the child'; while Coleridge, whose *Biographia Literaria* Baudelaire seems unlikely to have read, agreed that 'to carry on the feelings of childhood into the power of manhood; to combine the child's sense of wonder and novelty with the appearances which every day had . . . rendered familiar . . . is the character and privilege of genius'.

Still closer was the link that Wordsworth thought he could distinguish between his rapturous experiences as a child and his evolution as a poet; and, if *The Prelude* is much the most moving account of an imaginative childhood yet written in the English language, it is because, to the various strains of youthful feeling that had helped to make him what he was, he added its 'terrors, pains and early miseries' and 'the impressive influence of Fear'. Nature, which delighted, also sometimes terrified him, and a sense of 'visionary dreariness', of 'want and horror'* would temporarily weigh him down. The idea of childhood as the happiest period of man's life, of course, is an adult fiction. Yet there seems no doubt that keen joy and profound wretchedness, eager expectation and crushing disappointment, are then more acutely contrasted than at any other period. But, 'fostered alike by beauty and by fear', it is still, in Wordsworth's term, 'the seed-time of the soul', the point at which our voyage of discovery begins. Not until the poet himself had halted its progress, and set about systematising and moralising his observations, did his genius at last decline.

---

* 'Another time in a lowering and sad evening . . . a certain want and horror fell upon me, beyond imagination' – Thomas Traherne (1637–74); *Centuries of Meditations.*

13

The Philosopher's Garden

EPICURUS, the philosopher once described by La Fontaine as 'the noblest of Greek spirits', and the adjective 'epicurean', which his name presently inspired, seem to have developed a somewhat derogatory significance many years before the birth of Christ. Thus the pleasure-loving poet Horace, whose sybaritic life and growing corpulence amused both his literary patron Maecenas and his sovereign the Emperor Augustus, tells a friend in one of his *Epistles* that he is now becoming sleek and fat – '*Epicuri de grege porcum*', a hog from Epicurus' stye – and advises him to follow the philosopher's example, to take no thought of the morrow, and conduct his personal life as if the next day might prove to be his last.*

Yet Epicurus, who entered the world in 341 BC and left it in 270, was a deeply serious philosopher and attracted no less serious students. A native of Samos, after 306 he had made his home in Athens, where he purchased a large and magnificent garden in which, as he walked, he lectured to his school. The greatest good, he informed them, was happiness; and, whereas the Stoics, whose founder was Zeno of Samos, asserted that virtue should be cultivated for its own sake, Epicurus, a thorough-going Pragmatist, declared that, although to live happily one must also live wisely and well, pleasure itself was 'the beginning and end of the blessed life'; and that 'beauty, virtue and the like' were to be valued only 'if they produced pleasure; and if they did not, we must bid them goodbye'.

---

* Plato had said that the luxurious citizens of Akragas, called by Pindar 'the loveliest city of mortals', built as though they dismissed the thought of death, and dined as if they assumed that their next dinner-party would be the last they might enjoy.

Epicurus' interpretation of pleasure, on the other hand, was by no means primarily physical. What he sought, and advised his followers to seek, was a steadfast quietude of mind, a state he entitled *ataraxia*, which would both protect them against the fear of death and dispel a superstitious terror of the Gods, whose existence he did not deny, but whom he assumed to be completely detached from, and sublimely indifferent to, the affairs of mankind.* A similarly estimable attribute he called *galené*, an ability to remain calm even in the centre of a storm. But there was nothing unduly passive or soporific about the gospel that he preached. It demanded constant effort. 'Friendship and affection dance around the world', he said in one of his rare published dicta, reminding us that, to enjoy happiness, we must deliberately exert ourselves.

For the benefit of his followers, in whom he inspired a keen personal attachment, Epicurus is reputed to have written some three hundred books and a long series of letters, which, it is thought, may perhaps in certain respects have slightly resembled the *Epistles* of St. Paul. Few have been preserved. More fortunate was his predecessor Aristotle, a citizen of Macedonia, born in 384 BC, whose teachings survived to instruct the Middle Ages, and who devoted the whole first volume of his *Nicomachean Ethics* to the theme of 'human welfare or Happiness', which he 'found to consist in the active exercise of . . . the virtues of man's nature'. Based apparently on his lecture-notes, the *Ethics* are not an immediately attractive work; and Thomas Gray complained that Aristotle was 'the hardest author by far I ever meddled with . . . He has a dry conciseness that makes one imagine one is perusing a table of contents rather than a book; it tastes for all the world like chopped hay . . .'

Yet his central message is strongly and consistently maintained. Happiness, Aristotle believed, 'is not a product of action', but itself a form of activity, a mode of life that depends on the employment of pure reason. The happy man is one who 'lives well', or 'does well'; for, whereas the majority of mankind seek enjoyment from confused and conflicting sources, the votary of what is noble naturally finds his pleasure in actions that conform to virtue; and, since such actions are always essentially pleasurable, he requires no other joy. Happiness, therefore, is not a by-

---

* The separateness and indifference of the Gods is also described by two famous poets, Lucretius in *De Rerum Natura* and Tennyson in *The Lotos-Eaters*.

product of mere worldly good fortune. It is in itself 'a thing honoured and perfect . . . the great principle or starting point' from which all that is best in human life derives, and therefore, 'the supreme end and aim of conduct'.

Across the centuries we can distinguish an obvious link between the Macedonian philosopher and the first President of the United States, from whose Inaugural Address I have already quoted; and, since Washington's day, the true nature of happiness and its connection with virtue have provoked unending arguments. On these debates social changes have evidently had some effect. In England, during the second half of the eighteenth century, while France had her Voltairean Enlightenment, Britain's educated citizens believed that they inhabited a continuously changing and improving world. Georgian London was thought to resemble Antonine Rome; never had intellectual standards been so high, or personal habits more refined. The metropolis itself, since Hogarth painted it, had become a far cleaner and quieter place. There was less crime and drunkenness – legislation had reduced gin-drinking; and its streets were better paved and better lighted. 'The present age', Lord Chesterfield informed his contemporaries, 'has . . . the honour and pleasure of being extremely well with me'.

During the mid-nineteenth century, however, although Victorians were rightly pleased with their material progress, a shade of anxiety and doubt, accompanied by fears of some impending revolutionary upheaval, shared by writers otherwise as far apart as Ruskin, Matthew Arnold and Disraeli, often underlay their pride; and such questions as whether a man should expect happiness, or, indeed, deserved to be happy, became particularly numerous. The period's most gifted and argumentative prose-writers were all to some extent concerned with them. Ruskin came near to happiness by the use he made of his eyes and his knowledge of, and devotion to, the visual arts, but despaired of it in his emotional life; Carlyle sternly rejected it as an aim; and his friend John Stuart Mill declared, like Aristotle, that virtue was 'happiness in its highest form' and seems to have found a measure of personal contentment in his long devoted relationship with Mrs Taylor, a learned, high-minded lady, by the Carlyles significantly nicknamed 'Platonica', adding nevertheless: 'Ask yourself whether you are happy and you cease to be so', just as Jane Carlyle had compared happiness with a spirit that, if one mentioned its name, was apt immediately to disappear. Of the later Victorians, Robert Louis Stevenson, a man for whom, both in his personal and in his literary character, Henry James felt a particularly deep affection, seems to have followed Joseph Joubert's lead. He, too, asserted that life was a duty of which we should do all we can to make a pleasure, but a duty, that we consistently neglect and underrate more than we do almost any other obligation.

Today, as guides to the Happy Life, philosophers are rivalled, and have been to some extent replaced, by psychologists and social moralists; while modern journalists, English and French, sometimes produce an enlivening 'middle' on the subject. I have here, for instance, an essay by a thoughtful woman writer, once cut from the pages of the popular press, in which she explains her view of what constitutes happiness, and how it may most simply be achieved. She does not belong to the Aristotelian school, 'because [she reminds us] happiness can't be bought, organised, bequeathed or even earned. You can be worthy, pious, forever . . . giving old crusts to starving birds . . . and remain as sad as sin . . . Happiness you've got to be susceptible to. You've got to like yourself enough to be prepared to indulge in it . . . when it suddenly rears up . . .' It is not a right, but a quality we 'unearth in ourselves' and that depends on our ability to seize, cherish and enjoy the pleasures of the passing moment.*

Today, psychiatrists, Freudian or Jungian, also offer us their advice in print; and among the popular biographies and semi-pornographic romances that crowd a modern bookshop's shelves, one finds numerous admonitory publications, such as a slim best-seller that recently came my way, entitled *How to be your Own Best Friend*, subtitled *A Conversation with two Psychoanalysts*, named Newman and Berkowitz, who, we read, 'have already helped thousands of people to lead more rewarding lives'. In the entourage of the rich and powerful, I have been told, a salaried analyst sometimes occupies much the same position as an alchemist or soothsayer used often to hold in the court of a European sovereign or grandee, and that the great executive may frequently consult him before undertaking some momentous move. The booklet I have mentioned seems to be

* Lynda Lee-Potter, *Daily Mail*, 15 February 1984.

[170]

addressed to a somewhat less exigent section of society, to ordinary people asking the ordinary questions of modern life, but still wanting an adequate reply. Questions of this kind, the two analysts believe, are growing more and more numerous. 'When Thoreau remarked', they write in their prefatory chapter, 'that most men live lives of quiet desperation, he could not have foreseen how noisy that desperation would become . . . Modern man . . . does not suffer in silence. Our malaise is articulate . . . Resignation is not for us; if we are unhappy, we feel cheated, displaced, left out . . .'

The modern world, they observe, offers us an immense variety of diversions; but none seems to provide the escape-route that their patients need. And may not this, they enquire, be due to the fact that 'too many people have just not mastered the art of being happy?' For happiness, they contend, is certainly an art we can learn; and a multitude of sufferers, who 'go to a lot of trouble to learn French or physics or scuba diving', lack the patience or clear-sightedness to set about its acquisition, a feat they can only accomplish by learning to look into, and thus assume a responsible attitude towards, themselves. They should try their hardest to 'operate' their own characters just as they have discovered how to drive a motor-car, and thus at last become their own best friends.

In the advice they give, readers will soon notice, Newman and Berkowitz make few references either to religious faith or to the lasting happiness we find in imaginative art. Nor, although, as analysts, they believe that 'analysis is a great tool of liberation', and when the first patient lay down on the couch, it was a 'truly giant step for mankind', they agree that, once a sufferer has left the couch, there are many problems he may have failed to solve; while Freudian terms are, no doubt deliberately, avoided. I have mentioned the book here because it represents, like some of Epicurus' sayings, a completely pragmatic approach to the problems that it poses. In modern commercial society, the art of happiness can be learned without much more difficulty than the management of an efficient twentieth-century vehicle.

A similarly euphoric little book, clearly addressed to somewhat more simple-minded readers, but also popular on airport bookshelves, is Dr Norman Vincent Peale's *Positive Thoughts for the Day*, an ambitious compilation of '366 upbeat and positive thoughts, one for every day in the year', which he hopes that his converts will keep readily available on a desk or on a bedside table, or in the kitchen, 'or perhaps have a copy in each place'. The author has already published thirteen manuals of the same kind, which include, with two collaborators' assistance, *The Art of Real Happiness*; and each records his own thoughts on a variety of elevating topics. He suggests that we should tear them from the page, inscribe them on a card, and preserve them in a shirt-pocket. 'Putting the cards into the pocket means putting the quotations over the heart, thus emphasizing the emotional factor.' There they may have many daily uses: 'While driving your car, if you become annoyed . . . by another driver, instead of reacting in kind – send up a sincere prayer for him . . . Perhaps your prayer may reach his problem. One thing is sure; it will reach you . . .'

Pocket-moralists will continue to flourish so long as they can find an audience. But, since in 1903 George Edward Moore published his *Principia Ethica*, few genuine philosophers have considered the subject of happiness and its emotional and intellectual value. Bertrand Russell's treatise on *The Conquest of Happiness*, which appeared in 1930, did not attract, as *Principia* had done, a group of enthusiastic sympathisers. It is, even his votaries confess, one of his least stimulating books. On philosophic and mathematical questions, those who themselves can climb to the same heights assure us, he wrote brilliantly lucid prose; but here his style has a kind of dry, angular didacticism that constantly exasperates the reader. His opinions, too, social and political alike, are sometimes curiously perverse. He introduces and dismisses subjects with an air of irritable self-assurance, knocks a contradictory statement down and brusquely pushes it aside. In the early 1930s he was still a staunch supporter of the Russian Revolution;* and, when he discusses happiness and where it may most often be found, he announces that

> the intelligent young at the present day are probably happier . . . in Russia than anywhere else in the world. They have there a new world to create . . . The old have been executed, starved, exiled, or in some way disinfected, so that they cannot, as in every Western country, compel the young to choose between doing harm and doing nothing.

* Lenin, he wrote, was 'the supreme type' of the statesman who has directed his whole life to producing order out of chaos.

There is an unpleasant unction about Russell's use of words 'otherwise disinfected' that recalls a speech by Robespierre, Desmoulins or Saint-Just. Like many protagonists of the French Revolution, Russell had had an aristocratic origin; the Russells, kinsmen of the Duke of Bedford, belonged to a rich and important clan that had played a large progressive part in the history of Great Britain; and he combined a patrician intransigence with all the intellectual arrogance of a highly gifted man. Thus, having been born among the rich, he felt entitled to despise them as a class. Today, he informs us, the rich man 'never reads. If he is creating a picture gallery, he relies upon experts to choose his pictures; the pleasure he derives from them is not the pleasure of looking at them, but the pleasure of depriving some other rich man from having them', though 'in regard to music, if he happens to be a Jew, he may have a genuine appreciation . . .'

Russell's own sensitiveness to Beauty as a source of happiness appears to have been remarkably restricted. He valued love, however, 'because it enhances the best pleasures . . . A man who has never enjoyed beautiful things in the company of a woman whom he loved has not experienced to the full the magic power of which such things are capable'. Otherwise, his instructions for the conquest of happiness are often very largely negative; he gives a long list of the states of mind we should carefully avoid – competitiveness, boredom, fatigue, envy, the sense of sin, persecution mania, fear of public opinion – all weaknesses he castigates at considerable length.

Then, having enumerated the *Causes of Unhappiness*, he devotes the second half of his book to 'considering the happy man' and heads his first chapter with the poignant question 'Is happiness still possible?' to which he answers that, given the right circumstances and some smattering of common sense, it is certainly within our reach. 'The happy life', he echoes Aristotle, is 'to an extraordinary extent' indistinguishable from the good life. It is also a quiet life, as the records of many great men show. 'The happy man', he concludes, 'is the man who lives objectively, who has free affections and wide interests', and is untroubled by the fears of death thanks to his instinctive sense of union with the natural world at large. Russell 'wrote as a hedonist', he said; and the asset he valued most, though I am not sure he ever achieved it himself, was the quality that the Greeks called *ataraxia*, the steadfast quietude of mind Epicurus had once recommended while he walked round his Athenian garden.

[173]

14

A New Athens

THE first thirteen years of the twentieth century were not one of those enlightened epochs in which we sometimes wish that we had lived ourselves; nor do modern social historians give us a very pleasant picture of the age. Yet for those who at the time were already grown-up but still comparatively young, it was a period of hope and promise; and in his autobiography Leonard Woolf has described how, on his return to England from Ceylon, the European scene delighted him. Whereas since the Second World War, he points out, we have learned to live 'more or less contentedly' beneath the shadow of some huge impending disaster, he then felt a general sense of security, accompanied by a 'growing belief that it was a supremely good thing for people to be communally and individually happy'.

Both in London and in Cambridge, Woolf had an extremely kind reception. His old university was full of good friends; and, although that part of the English literary landscape we now call 'Bloomsbury' had not yet definitely taken shape, he again met and admired Virginia and Vanessa Stephen, both beautiful in their strange Pre-Raphaelite way, and both, he saw, extremely talented. They were the feminine stars of a no less gifted society; and around them gathered such rising young intellectuals as Roger Fry, Clive Bell, whom Vanessa married, Lytton Strachey, Desmond Mc-Carthy and Maynard Keynes. Their guide through life was the philosopher George Edward Moore, author of *Principia Ethica*, which they all first read at Cambridge and had become their layman's gospel. Moore's message made an immediate appeal to the young. 'By far the most valuable things, which we know or can imagine', he assured his followers, 'are certain states of consciousness, which may be rightly described as the pleasures of human intercourse and the enjoyment of beautiful objects . . . It is only for the sake of these things . . . that any-one can be justified in performing any public or private duty . . . They are the *raison d'être* of virtue . . .' This message was simple and moving enough; but Moore had also a passion for exactitude; and '*Exactly* what do you mean by that?' he would often demand with a curious sidelong movement of his head.*

The influence of *Principia Ethica* on the citizens of the Bloomsburian world was evidently strong and far-reaching; for not only did it encourage their love of art, but it glorified their cult of friendship. Around Virginia Woolf and her associates a great deal of academic rubbish has recently been piled up. They were not a 'school', a 'movement', a '*cénacle*', so much as a group of close friends, who, except for Roger Fry and the Misses Stephen, had originally met and talked at Cambridge, and in London still found one another's conversation and companionship highly stimulating and enjoyable. Moore had emphasised the importance of the personal affections, which in the scale of human values, his disciple the economist Maynard Keynes declared, should always come 'a long way first'; and, though they might sometimes disagree and, since they were most of them somewhat malicious conversationalists, poke rather acid fun at an old friend's private foibles, friends they remained throughout their adult lives. It was their passion for the truth, natural communicativeness, desire to establish a 'mental intimacy' with those they knew and loved – an idea to be effective *must* be shared, they thought – that gave them their peculiar distinction.

Unluckily the Bloomsburians had no Boswell; but, in her reminiscences,† Frances Partridge, an engaging youthful member of the group, beloved by Ralph Partridge who was himself beloved by Lytton Strachey, recorded the remarkable variety of subjects that they enjoyed discussing, and that, both in bed and at breakfast the next day, might vary from such

* See *The Bloomsbury Group: A study of E.M. Forster, Lytton Strachey, Virginia Woolf, and their Circle*, J.K. Johnstone, 1954.
† *Memories*, 1981.

human problems as the origins of sentimentality and 'modesty about facts' to interesting literary questions – had Lady Ashburton really been Carlyle's mistress? – and, a little later, might lead to 'an interesting argument' on logic, provoked by Bertrand Russell's new book, which Frances at the time was reading. Similarly, Roger Fry would hold up a dinner-party while he read aloud from his renderings of Mallarmé's poems, and – 'with magnificent reverberations', Virginia Woolf said – describe the nature of the Symbolist poet's genius. Yet the tone of these colloquies, however erudite their theme, was always spontaneous and enthusiastic rather than dogmatic. They talked as readily and, indeed, as volubly as their predecessors had done during the great days of the French Enlightenment; and Clive Bell, the group's most vocal member, had acquired the precious gift of persuading his guests, when they dined with him at his flat above Gordon Square, that, thanks to their presence, and the learning and wit they displayed, this was an occasion some of the most distinguished talkers of the past would have been flattered to attend.

'. . . Happiness', wrote Leonard Woolf in 1964, 'is politically now a dirty word'; but the Bloomsburians, inspired by Moore, were certainly devoted to the quest. For only one of them, Virginia Woolf, did it prove almost insuperably difficult. From the threat of madness she would never long escape; and her physical attitude towards the world betrayed the sufferings of her mind. 'She had,' writes Frances Partridge, an 'agonised tautness . . . The way she held herself, turned her head or smoked a cigarette struck one as awkward even while it charmed . . .' In her vicinity one felt an electric current circulating; and few of her younger visitors were always completely at their ease. Vanessa Bell, on the other hand, charmed and reassured while Virginia troubled and perplexed. She seemed a happy woman; and her dearest companions – her husband, the euphoric Clive, her long-devoted lover, Roger Fry, and her fellow painter Duncan Grant with whom she spent her last years – were all prolific and argumentative characters.

Stendhal's definitions of happiness as the offspring of 'love + work' was a maxim that the Bloomsburian group appear to have put successfully into practice. Their personal and their professional lives, their friendships and their love affairs, were very often closely linked; and in some ways the records of their communal life may impress us more than many of the works they left behind them. Roger Fry was a fascinating, highly gifted man, but not, he himself recognised, a very good painter; the furniture and fabrics he designed at the Omega workshops were apt to be strangely hideous; and the decorations with which Vanessa Bell, Duncan Grant and their kin once covered the walls of a little Sussex church* have now a sadly amateurish air, and might very well have been mistaken for the efforts of the clergyman's own 'artistic' family. What really counts today is the contribution they made to the 'science of happiness', as Coleridge had once called it, by establishing a small coherent society that satisfied both their aesthetic sense of order and their ambitious conception of the good life. They were happily self-assured; had Bloomsbury produced Roger alone, it would have been as historically memorable as Athens in its greatest days, Virginia Woolf believed.

Their sense of superiority they did not trouble to conceal; and, as other self-sufficient groups have done, they made an individual use of language, and had a vocabulary and an intonation that were all their own; their voices were usually high-pitched, rising and falling and placing a dramatic emphasis on the most important words. '*Simply-Too-Extraordinary*' was the kind of epithet with which they characterised any theory or dogma, that, like the Christian faith in its more puritanical aspects, entirely passed their comprehension. But this did not preclude an eager appetite for knowledge. Roger Fry, whom the sheer 'extraordinariness' of the Old Testament (which he had not opened since his childhood) reduced to stentorian peals of laughter, on other subjects, wrote his admiring friend Clive Bell, displayed an 'occasionally nefast gullibility', now and then in his aesthetic judgements, but also in the value of certain queer patent medicines he enthusiastically recommended.

Even for a comparative outsider, observing the Bloomsburians, listening to their gossip and hearing their descriptions of one another, was always a memorable experience; they had the same ideals, which, of course, they might interpret variously, and the same conception of happiness, based both on personal and on intellectual relationships, that they preserved

* At Berwick, near Lewes. Cyril Connolly was buried in the churchyard.

until the end. Oddly enough, Leonard Woolf, after he had lost Virginia, though the most ascetic of them all, just as Clive Bell was the worldliest and most frivolous, seems in his last years to have been among the most contented; and I remember a meeting with Clive, not very long before his own death, at which he spoke of Leonard's solitary existence alone in the small country house where he had spent most of his troubled married life. Clive himself evidently much regretted the passing of youth, and, although he never grew openly melancholic, found his gradual attrition by old age, and the disappearance of his youthful pleasures, a more and more disheartening process. But he was warm-hearted, and had once, he told me, sympathetically enquired how Leonard, as a rule, began the day. With a feeling of expectation, Woolf replied; there were so many things to which he could look forward – his bath and his breakfast, the arrival of the postman and the latest *Times*, and then, accompanied by his devoted dog, a leisurely walk around the garden. Clive could not refrain from expressing his astonishment. 'I do believe, you old wretch,' he had commented, 'you're really a *happy* man, aren't you?'

Modern Bloomsbury is now once again a fairly prosaic London neighbourhood; and its inhabitants could hardly compare themselves to the citizens of ancient Athens. The original Bloomsburians have had no legitimate successors. Today the art of good talking, and, indeed, of appreciative listening, which has done so much to found friendships and thus promote happiness, seems to have fallen into a temporary decline. In Samuel Johnson's period, an ability to talk well was so important a part of social life that a somewhat taciturn man attracted unfavourable notice. Mrs Thrale, for instance, had an elderly friend who, besides being fat and slow, would occasionally stammer.

> 'Of Colonel Boden's conversation [she remembered in her *Anecdotes*] I . . . heard Johnson say that it reminded him of the Aloe Tree; that blossoms once in a hundred years & whose Shoot is attended with a cracking Noise resembling an Explosion; when that is over all is quiet till the return of the periodical Effort.'

A famous talker, of course, need not be a professional performer; and I doubt if we should now always enjoy hearing Sydney Smith – 'the loudest wit' to whom Byron said he had ever had to listen — weave his elaborate conversational tapestries, or Macaulay, who, another critic remembered, 'not only overflowed with learning, but stood in the slop', discourse for the benefit of Lady Holland's guests. Table-talk at Holland House, though said to have been brilliant and discursive was, no doubt, a little studied. During the mid-Victorian Age, it was the splendid spontaneity of Tennyson's outbursts that once delighted Jane Carlyle. The time was January 1845; and she was alone, having made up her mind 'for a nice long quiet evening of *looking into the fire*', when a carriage drew up and she heard the sound of men's voices:

'. . . The men proved to be Alfred Tennyson of all people and his friend Mr Moxon . . . Alfred is dreadfully embarrassed with women alone . . . for he entertains at one and the same moment a feeling of almost adoration for them and an ineffable contempt . . . The only chance of my getting any right good of him was to make him forget my womanness — so I did just as Carlyle would have done — get out *pipes* and *tobacco* — and *brandy and water* — with a deluge of *tea* over and above — The effect of these accessories was miraculous — he *professed* to be *ashamed* of polluting my room . . . but he smoked on all the same — for *three* mortal hours! — talking like an angel — only exactly as if were talking with a clever man . . .'

When Tennyson had at last bidden her goodbye, and Carlyle, who had finally returned, found his wife sitting alone 'in an atmosphere of tobacco so thick that you might have cut it with a knife, his astonishment was considerable!' For the poet, despite his imaginative meanderings and chase of will-o'-wisps that would perhaps one day get him into trouble, the historian had always had a deep respect; and, much later, in his correspondence with Emerson, he portrayed both Tennyson's impressive physiognomy and his vigorous conversational style:

'. . . A man solitary and sad . . . dwelling in an element of gloom, — carrying a bit of Chaos about him . . . which he is manufacturing into Cosmos! . . . One of the finest-looking men in the world. A great shock of rough dusty-dark hair; bright-laughing hazel eyes; massive aquiline face, most massive yet most delicate . . . His voice is musical metallic, —

[179]

fit for loud laughter and piercing wail and all that may be in between; speech and speculation free and plenteous . . .'

Tennyson, Carlyle concluded, was indeed 'a true human soul, or some authentic approximation to it'; and I feel sure that, if the sage had lived on to witness the arrival of Oscar Wilde, the most magnetic talker of the late-Victorian Age, he would have found little to applaud either in the quality of the brilliant Irishman's soul or in his peculiar mode of self-expression. For a student of the present subject, however, Wilde's character and the history of his life seem to have a lasting interest. Happiness, his biographer assures us,* was his natural element; and there is no doubt he made his friends happy, and, as a speaker, delighted every audience he faced – whether they were a gang of American miners, whom, it is said, he could also sometimes drink under the table, or the cultivated frequenters of a London drawing room, whom their hostess had attracted by inscribing the words '*to hear Mr Oscar Wilde tell a tale*' at the bottom of her card.

He generously shared his own enjoyment of life. Yet no man with such an abundance of personal resources, to which he added a large share of executive, if not imaginative gifts, could have more deliberately squandered them; and this he did, not merely by ill-chance – his calamitous involvement in a savage family dispute – but through a perverse determination he had already formed at the height of his prosperity and fame. To fulfil his own genius, of which he was firmly convinced, he must at length adopt a tragic rôle. In 1895, when he entered his fourth decade and was travelling around Algeria, he met an enquiring young Frenchman, André Gide. His duty, Gide heard him say, should now be 'to amuse himself terribly'. It was not happiness he sought but pleasure; 'one must always desire what is most tragic'.

Yet, even after he had accomplished his social downfall, survived disgrace and imprisonment, written *De Profundis*, his lamentable apologia, in which he pretended that, as soon as he had emerged from gaol, he would become a solitary wanderer and 'seek clefts in the rocks where I may hide, and secret valleys in whose silence I may weep undisturbed', something at least of all his old 'invincible happiness' helped to support him through the years of exile. His letters at this period, where he describes, for instance, the

* Hesketh Pearson: *The Life of Oscar Wilde*, 1946.

rapacious yet attractive 'little friends' he frequently picked up on the boulevards, are among the most engaging that he ever wrote. His wit had kept its early edge; and, although the wounds inflicted by 'that tiger, Life', were now evidently past healing, he retained his kindliness and good humour. Those were the qualities that his remaining friends – two of whom, Ada Leverson, the golden-hearted 'Sphinx', and the veteran novelist Mrs Belloc Lowndes, I was lucky enough to meet before they died – spoke of with particularly deep affection; and Mrs Belloc Lowndes recollected his delicately understanding treatment of a tedious clergy-man's wife he and Mrs Wilde had once entertained at Tite Street. When she confessed that she was terrified of shipwrecks, he did his ingenious best to amuse and, at the same time, reassure her. On his own travels, he said, he invariably took with him his private hencoop that, used as a life-raft if the vessel sank, would always ensure him a safe passage home.

15

'Happy the Man'

SHOULD one suddenly notice that a picture one admires on a friend's wall hangs perhaps a quarter of an inch askew, the temptation to set its position right grows sometimes almost irresistible. This may well displease its owner; and the habit of meddling with and readjusting objects has, now and then, been diagnosed as a perverse neurotic trait. I remember hearing that, when a young man I knew visited an eminent psychiatrist, and his hand strayed towards some pencils strewn across the desk, his adviser, giving the slight smile of a satisfied expert, murmured 'Yes, yes, definitely *obsessive*!' while he made a rapid note upon his pad.

I prefer to think, however, that this odd tendency may have a much less morbid origin. In our general pursuit of happiness, does it not suggest our longing to give our existence a truly harmonious pattern, and substitute a sense of symmetry and equipoise for one of conflict and disorder? Thus, a poet whose art depends so much on balance and rhythm, but whose personal life, like that of Baudelaire, may be notably disordered, will often find that certain images have an especially deep imaginative appeal. 'The sober and elegant beauty' of a nineteenth-century sailing ship, Baudelaire wrote, was 'derived . . . from its regularity and symmetry which, in the same degree as complication and harmony, are among the primordial requirements of the human spirit . . .'. These splendid vessels, so calmly balanced on the waters, are they not asking us a silent question: '*Quand partons-nous pour le bonheur?*' When shall we set sail for happiness?

Any image that reconciles us both to our discordant selves and to the chaotic world in which we live, may make the expedition less difficult; and a modern Italian dramatist introduces a character who, despite an appalling physical flaw, is still so nearly happy that he clings to life, he tells us, 'like a creeper to an iron railing'. Pirandello's play is entitled *The Man with a Flower in his Mouth*; and the 'flower' that blemishes the chief character's face, a small, perpetual spot, is the symptom of a disease that will, he knows, soon return and kill him. Meanwhile, his chief source of happiness – indeed, his only relaxation – is every evening to watch through a shop-window the girls measuring out lengths of ribbon and men expertly tying up parcels. For hours at a time he follows their operations:

> 'They pick up . . . a large sheet of double-thickness paper . . . Then with the back of the hand . . . they bring up one edge of the paper from underneath. Then they bring the other down – and so deftly, so gracefully, make the narrowest of folds . . . one they don't really need . . . put in, as it were for the sheer love of the art.'

His observation of a commonplace task skilfully performed gives Pirandello's hero as much happiness as, on another plane, he might have experienced from watching the creation of an aesthetic masterpiece, and that, as a picture or a piece of music would have done, quickens his spirit and strengthens his desire to live. But his consolation is transitory; the window will grow dark, the assistants disappear; and writers who describe the effects of happiness and the different forms it takes – which range from a sudden shaft of elation to a longer-lasting glow of pleasure – have also dwelt on its mortal transience and on the regrets its passing leaves behind.

In a song for a Christmas masque called *The Vision of Delight*,* written by Ben Jonson for James I's luxurious court, these nostalgic feelings are memorably recorded:

> 'We see, we heare, we feele, we taste,
> We smell the change in every flowre,
> We only wish that all could last,
> And be as new still as the houre'

Towards the end of the same century, however, a yet greater poet, John Dryden, introduced an equally moving but much less melancholy theme, which he had freely adapted from an ode by Horace.† The Past, both the

* Presented at Whitehall in 1617.
† '*The twenty-ninth Ode of the third Book . . . Paraphras'd in Pindaric Verse . . .*'

Roman and the English poet assert, is a treasure-house over which Memory, Mother of the Muses, should sit perpetually on guard:

> 'Enjoy the present smiling Hour;
> And put it out of Fortune's Pow'r . . .
> Happy the Man, and happy he alone,
> He who can call to-Day his own:
> He who, secure within, can say
> To-Morrow do thy worst, for I have liv'd to-Day,
> Be fair, or foul, or rain, or shine,
> The Joys I have possess'd in spite of Fate are mine.
> Not Heav'n itself upon the past has Pow'r;
> But what has been, has been, and I have had my Hour.'

Every speculative and imaginative human being has his own attitude towards the past, and attaches a different value, in terms of happiness or misery, to the experiences he has gone through. While some, like Byron, cherish romantic regrets, others, like Coleridge's mariner, carry around with them an albatross-load of guilt, and still others, when they grow older, and less and less hopeful, acquire a philosophic detachment that enables them to see the vicissitudes through which they have travelled as details of the same not necessarily harmonious but possibly inescapable pattern. Such a view of life was expressed in the nineteenth century by Scrope Davies, one of Byron's closest early friends, but during his autumnal years a broken-down dandy, whose last refuge was a hayloft perched above a Belgian stable. In 1828, four years after the poet's death, he wrote to Francis Hodgson, another of Byron's old friends, thanking him for a particularly welcome letter:

'Your letter has recalled to my mind scenes the recollection of which now constitutes my only delight. Bacon somewhere observes: "Aristotle saith the young may be happy by hope, so why should not old men and sequestered men by remembrance?" The past and the future are the sole object of man's contemplation. There is no present, or if there is, it is a point on which we cannot stand. While I am now writing the future becomes the past. Happiness then is a pursuit, not an attainment.'*

* *The Life and Times of Scrope Beardmore Davies*, 1981.

[184]

Scrope Davies was by no means a professional writer, though a sensible and well-read man; and one of the functions of an imaginative artist, he would have agreed, is to hold a balance between the present and the past, and from what he has once felt and observed and his quotidian experience of life build up an intelligible scheme. Every writer is to some extent haunted by the memories of his youth; Dickens, for example, was so dominated by his recollections of his unhappy London childhood that there were certain streets, which, although he describes them with extraordinary vividness, as a successful middle-aged novelist he admitted that he could hardly bear to enter. In our own century Proust and Colette gazed back to past times even more keenly and sensitively than they looked around them at the present day. But there was one essential difference between the two great novelists, who made so large a contribution to the modern art of writing, and who, moreover, liked and knew one another well. Each had had a happy childhood – Proust at the little country town he rechristened Combray, which forms the background of *Du Côté de chez Swann*, where stood Tante Léonie's 'old grey house' and the medieval church that 'slipped its belfry into every corner of the sky'; Colette at the Burgundian home of her beloved mother Sido, from whom she inherited both her deep affection for all natural things and some of the basic virtues that were to carry her through a long adventurous bohemian career.

Only in Proust's opening volumes, however, does he portray either lasting happiness or genuine goodness; and the second quality is almost always reserved for the mother he adored but who sometimes disappointed him, or for his grandmother, Madame Amédée, a nineteenth-century disciple of Rousseau, who in their garden is constantly doing her best to restore the air of romantic wildness that their gardener so much dislikes, and who will now and then quietly remove an enclosing stake, so that the roses should look 'a little more natural', just as a mother might run her hand through her boy's hair, after the barber had smoothed it down, to allow it to stick out properly around his head.

Otherwise, except for these loving and lovable figures, while Proust's majestic journey into the past proceeds, illusion after illusion vanishes, and even the traits he had once admired in a character develop a very different and far uglier meaning. Thus, Robert de Saint-Loup, the aristocratic young cavalryman to whom the narrator had once attributed a genuine nobility of heart and mind, undergoes, as he enters middle age, a strange and saddening transformation. He had still 'the grace and ease of a cavalry officer; but his swift-footedness was now generated by the fear of being seen and by the self-dissatisfaction and boredom' that dog him through his clandestine sexual life.

Before Proust had done with his characters only three of them remain permanently admirable – the painter Elstir, the novelist Bergotte and the composer Vinteuil; for all are selflessly devoted to the difficult art they practise; and through art alone, Proust came to believe, could he establish the mystic relationship he sought between the present and the past. Colette, on the other hand, though she might deal harshly with an individual character, had a deep regard for life itself, which extended to the whole creation. It was not enough to say, wrote Maurice Goudeket, her gifted third husband and the devoted guardian of her later years, that Colette loved animals. 'Before every manifestation of life, animal or vegetable, she felt a respect that was akin to a religious fervour.' And, at the same time, she was deeply conscious of the unity of the natural world 'in its infinite variety of shapes'. Hence the peculiar moving effect that her literary images produce: 'one doesn't read Colette', said a contemporary critic; 'one sees what she sees. One breathes in what she breathes; one touches what she touches'; and, since her senses are more delicately attuned than her reader's, 'he finds himself, for a few hours, living an intensified life', as though he were 'an ordinary violin . . . suddenly transformed into a Stradivarius'.*

If an affection for the world, and the ability to convey that affection, be an index of happiness, Colette, though life had often treated her roughly, and she had broken most of its social and moral rules, and suffered some unpleasant consequences, was indeed a happy woman; and her sympathetic attitude towards Nature was often reflected both in her letters and in her conversation. At our only meeting† she spoke of her single visit to England, and of a stream she had noticed wandering through a garden. Her visit must have taken place at least forty or fifty years earlier; but, thanks to

---

* Jean Larnac: *Colette, sa Vie, son oeuvre*, 1927; quoted by Joanna Richardson: *Colette*, 1983.
† See *The Wanton Chase*, 1980.

the tenderness of her phrase - '*une assez aimable petite rivière*' – the brooklet seemed to flow again.*

While writers of talent repeatedly disagree, genius will often respond to genius; and, despite their dissimilarity both as artists and as human beings, Colette had quickly recognised in Proust one of the greatest writers of their age. When the first volume of *A la Recherche du Temps Perdu* arrived, she became 'passionately attached to it'; they began to correspond, and from that day the appearance of a new Proustian volume was an important event in her life that induced her to put aside all other reading. This declaration, during the course of an interview with a literary editor, she made in 1925; and Proust had died on November 18th, 1922, leaving behind him, stacked around his comfortless room, a huge accumulation of proofs and manuscripts, all heavily amended and corrected. The last passage, dictated to his faithful servant, Céleste, he considered 'very good'. But now he must stop, he said: 'I can't do any more.'

Colette herself, crippled with arthritis but, as a rule, very much aware of life, survived him until August 1954. Only after her eightieth birthday did her mental energy show signs of flagging; she appeared slowly to lose touch with the present day; and on the afternoon of August 3rd, after long spells of semi-consciousness, she spoke her memorable last words, which Maurice Goudeket, in his loving tribute to his wife's genius, has recorded for our benefit.† They were accompanied by a wide embracing gesture that drew his attention to all the delightful details that surrounded them – the cases of brilliant Brazilian butterflies that were hung around her bed, her illustrated travel-books and her collection of nineteenth-century glass paper-weights, each with its own fantastic pattern – and simultaneously to a flight of sharp-winged swifts from the gardens of the Palais Royal that swept back and forth across her window. '*Regarde!*' she exclaimed, 'only *look*, Maurice!' It was a command she had issued again and again to her readers in almost everything she wrote.

* From a letter written to the poetess, Anna de Noailles, in 1928, I have copied an even more evocative passage: 'It's raining very gently and feels very good on the face and in the eyes. The entire park is starred with the white behinds of rabbits . . .'
† In *Près de Colette*, 1956.

Epilogue

I F this book has a single recurrent theme (which I may perhaps have over-emphasised) it is that, although happiness has many diverse forms, a particularly precious kind is often to be achieved not so much through a purposeful '*chasse au bonheur*' as through quietly observing and enjoying. 'The only thing in all my experience I cling to', the painter Walter Sickert told his young disciple Nina Hamnett, 'is my coolness and leisurely exhilarated contemplation. . .'. She must adopt the same attitude. 'Let this advice be my perpetual and most solemn legacy to you.'* Sickert's counsels were not intended for painters or poets alone; they apply, in some degree, to all mankind, even to Bertrand Russell's readers, whom he taught to 'feel themselves citizens of the universe, enjoying freely the spectacle it offers and the joys that it affords', thus reaching a 'profound instinctive union with the stream of life . . .' The exhilarated contemplation that Sickert recommended may be applied both to nature and to art; and not long ago I saw its effect on a well-known modern poet, who had a wide knowledge of art, but, apparently for the first time, had just come face to face with a famous work of classic sculpture.

It is one of a group of four statues that many other artists have loved and sometimes represented in a picture. Thus in Carpaccio's delightful vision of Saint Augustine meditating at his desk, while his little dog admires him from below, a medieval astrolabe hangs over the saint's head; but on the shelf that bisects the opposite wall more unexpectedly stand the statuette of a naked Venus and a miniature reproduction of one of San Marco's

---

* Quoted by Cyril Connolly: *The Unquiet Grave*, 1944.

[188]

St Augustine's little dog, from Carpaccio's painting in the *Scuola Dalmata dei S.S. Giorgio e Trifone* at Venice.

glorious Golden Horses. Although these familiar aspects of the Venetian scene have had a long eventful history, their origin is still mysterious; for, whereas some scholars attribute them to the fourth century BC, others believe that they may have been modelled and cast after the second century AD, during the dusk of Roman civilisation – a theory that would make their classic splendour even more remarkable. Rarely have masterpieces been so often stolen. The Emperor Constantine, who had acquired them no one knows how, set them up as ornaments of the Hippodrome at Constantinople; but the Doge Dandolo, leader of the Crusade that in 1204 conquered and plundered the imperial city, carried them away to Venice. There, however, they did not receive an immediately warm welcome; and for fifty years they were stored in the Arsenal until their value – should they

[189]

The Golden Horses of San Marco.

be melted down for cannon? – had been successfully decided; and they were raised on the façade of San Marco to the noble position that they hold today. Napoleon, of course, was the last plunderer. He included them in the loot of his Italian campaigns; and between 1797 and 1815 they framed the principal entrance of the Tuileries.

Since they were restored to San Marco, they have seldom been removed;

[190]

but in 1979 one of them (the second to the left of the team) briefly appeared in London for a Venetian Exhibition. There it was given the separate room it deserved; and among the crowd it drew I caught sight of my old friend John Betjeman. He was growing infirm, half crippled by the paralytic disease that had already confined him to a wheelchair; but from his chair, I saw, he was gazing up at the Horse's burnished beauty, at its proudly arched neck and majestic brazen flanks, in a state of silent rapture, which absorbed him completely, and no doubt had excluded for a while all ideas of age and illness. As the only gifted Poet Laureate since Tennyson, whose poems often sold no less readily than Byron's most romantic eastern Tales, John led an enviable literary life. But even at the height of his career, I remember thinking, he could have had few happier moments.

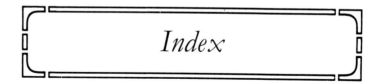

Index

THE ROMAN
WAR MACHINE

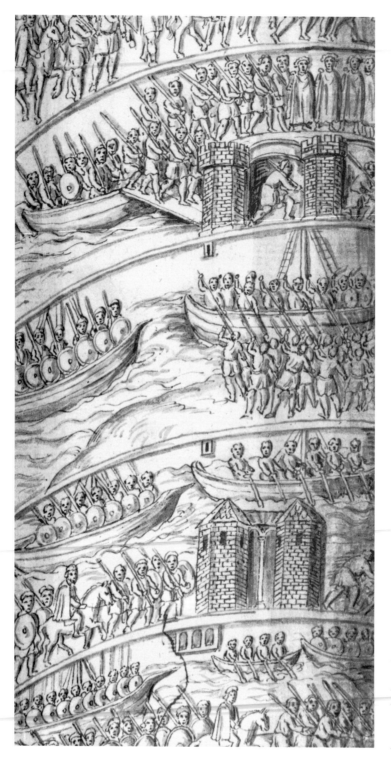

*The east Roman
army and navy
in about
AD 400, from a
sixteenth–
century drawing
of the Column of
Arcadius*

THE ROMAN WAR MACHINE

JOHN PEDDIE

ALAN SUTTON PUBLISHING LIMITED

First published in the United Kingdom in 1994
Alan Sutton Publishing Ltd · Phoenix Mill · Far Thrupp · Stroud
Gloucestershire

Reprinted 1995

British Library Cataloguing in Publication Data

Peddie, John
    Roman War Machine
    I. Title
    355.00937

    ISBN 0-7509-0673-1 (case)
    ISBN 0-7509-1023-2 (paper)

*Endpapers: Details from Trajan's Column, Rome (Frank Lepper and Sheppard
Frere)*

Typeset in 11/12 pt Erhardt.
Typesetting and origination by
Alan Sutton Publishing Limited.
Printed in Great Britain by
Hartnolls, Bodmin, Cornwall.

Contents

They are quick to act as they are slow to give way, and never was there an engagement in which they were worsted by numbers, tactical skill or unfavourable ground – or even by fortune, which is less within their grasp than victory.

Josephus (AD 37–93)

List of Illustrations

The author and publishers gratefully acknowledge the following for their permission to reproduce illustrations: B.T. Batsford/RCHM (46); Bodleian Library (3); The Carson Clark Gallery, Edinburgh (2); Colchester Museums (47); Corbridge Roman Museums (48); Egypt Exploration Society, London (40); Ermin Street Guard (6, 11, 21, 36); Paul Lewis Isemonger (10, 15, 22, 28); Oscar and Peter Johnson Ltd (34); Frank Lepper and Sheppard Frere, authors of *Trajan's Column* (Alan Sutton Publishing, 1988) (8, 19, 20, 26, 29, 35, 42); The Mansell Collection (4, 5, 7, 13, 33, 41, 49, 54, 59); Museo Lapidario Maffeino, Verona (Umberto Tomba) (17); Oxford University Press (39); Rheinisches Landesmuseum Trier (18, 23); Margaret Rylatt (27); Society of Antiquaries/RCHM (38); Trinity College Library, Cambridge (1).

Introduction

Early historians have provided us with a wealth of literature on Roman military matters. Some, of whom perhaps Onasander is the most illuminating, have bequeathed us treatises on the qualities required for Roman generalship. Many, such as Julius Caesar, Josephus, Livy and Ammianus Marcellinus, writing from practical experience, have left us colourful accounts of battles in which military tactics of the day are well described. Frontinus has condensed extracts from these works into a book of *Stratagems*, some bizarre but many remarkable in their similarity to modern-day tactics – 'Go for the high ground!' has long been the cry of the infantry, it appears. The works of other authors, among whom number Aenas and Vegetius, have consolidated contemporary military practice into manuals and textbooks, and have assembled for us technical accounts of ancient battle drills and tactical formations, as well as interesting detail of day-to-day administration and the occasional nugget of strategical thinking; but, almost invariably, much of what we would wish to know about their command techniques, staff planning arrangements and logistical techniques is omitted.

As a consequence, we are frequently left to ponder how Roman generals achieved so much with such seemingly scant resources and we are occasionally tempted to draw wrongful conclusions. 'The truth is', one military historian has written, 'Julius Caesar was not an organiser; careful preparations – adequate supplies, sufficient fighting forces and many other requirements needed to assure the success of a campaign – were either distasteful to him or lost to sight by reliance on his genius to solve all difficulties.'[1] This is an accusation which reads uneasily when set against a list of Caesar's military successes, for it was surely this genius, with the great man's mastery of manoeuvre and his ability to surprise and destabilize his opponents, which enabled Caesar to emerge victorious from his many campaigns, particularly as conqueror of Gaul. Sound administration is a natural prerequisite for the success of any operation. On the other hand, the nice balance between planned administration and operational arrangements, which must inevitably vary according to the military situation, is something which can only be determined by the commanding general; and his degree of success in doing this establishes his reputation.

Nevertheless, if it were true that Julius Caesar placed his supply arrangements at risk in order to achieve his objectives, he would not have been the first general to do so – he was certainly not the last. Indeed, he may be thought to have had much in common with the spirited commander of the German Afrika Korps,

Field Marshal Erwin Rommel, who likewise earned a reputation as an improviser with a tendency to impetuosity. Rommel's dashing leadership, despite his scarce resources and the initial orders he received from his superiors to limit his main activity to the defence of Tripolitania, brought him close to total victory against the British in 1942, when he drove his army headlong along the North African coast in an effort to seize the Nile basin, together with the strategically important Suez Canal.[2] He failed only by the narrowest of margins. In Burma in 1945 Lieutenant General Sir William Slim, commanding the XIVth Army, took a similar chance. He concluded that, if he were to capture Rangoon before the coming of the monsoon, he would have to commit all his supply vehicles to the advance and, as a consequence, impose half-rations on his soldiers. He wrote,

> It was very plain to me – and if it had not been, plenty of people were willing to enlighten me – that this dash for Rangoon by a mechanised force, confined to one road, thrusting against time through superior numbers, was a most hazardous and possibly rather un-British operation. I knew the risks and the penalties of failure but, as I checked over the final plans, I was ready to accept them.[3]

Sometimes, therefore, it is militarily necessary to take calculated risks, the nub being that the commander should be sufficiently competent to recognize when the culminating point has been reached and that the moment has arrived to revert to the defensive in order to rebuild his fighting power. This is a recognized tenet of military philosophy. We may assume that Julius Caesar, a natural fighting soldier, would have been prepared to take such risks as much as any other general of his, or later, generations; but a charge that careful preparations were distasteful to him can surely only be levelled if it can be shown that he had an inadequate back-up organization to support him. There is no clear evidence of this and it is a matter to which we shall return in the chapters which follow.

It is a truism to say that the supply arrangements of an army vary according to the fruitfulness of its theatre of operations. In Gaul (54–51 BC), Caesar was fortunate to be campaigning in a prosperous grain-producing country, with powerful allies nearby, albeit his enemies frequently subjected him to a ruthless 'scorched earth' policy. Four years later, during the opening weeks of his North African campaign, he faced a different situation, for here he was compelled to send a considerable distance, 'to Sardinia and the other neighbouring provinces', for reinforcements, supplies and corn.[4] In the following century, during the 70s, when the emperor Vespasian was on the throne, foodstuffs, *materiel* and men were being despatched to Rome's army on the Armenian front, along a lengthy supply line, reaching from the Danube estuary to the Black Sea port of Trapezus and beyond. Such intricate arrangements could surely not have been contemplated, set in place and carried forward without the existence of an accomplished supply organization briefed with the task of establishing sources of provision, systems of transportation and the means of getting reinforcements and stores forward to the fighting forces in the field.

Such an organization implies the existence of a staff corps, of which Josephus[5] may have been hinting when he penned the words that, in Roman war, nothing is done without plan or on the spur of the moment; careful thought precedes action of any kind, and to the decisions reached all ranks must conform. . . . They regard success due to luck as less desirable than a planned but unsuccessful stroke, because victories that come of themselves tempt men to leave things to chance, but forethought, in spite of occasional failures, is good practice in avoiding the same mistake. . . . Unfortunate accidents that upset calculations have at least this comfort in them, that plans were properly laid.

Likewise, Vegetius,[6] in his remark that the Romans owed the conquest of their world to high standards of military training and discipline and 'the unwearied cultivation of the other arts of war', appears to confirm the presence of such a staff structure, with military schools for its training and education. Time and again, throughout the writings of the ancients, we encounter clues to the existence of such a body. Julius Caesar's briefing of his generals and staff at sea, immediately prior to his landing in Britain (together with their remarkable presence at that moment when they might otherwise have been expected to be with their formations); the huge concentrations of siege artillery at Alesia under Caesar and at Jerusalem under Titus, both of which would have demanded decentralized command if the weapons were to be flexibly employed; and the highly detailed and effective preparations for the Claudian invasion of Britain, with its sophisticated arrangements for the seaborne landing,[7] are just some examples which would have required a planning body of this nature. In effect, in an age when armies numbered scores of thousands of animals and men and their movement and manoeuvring, without the benefits of modern-day transport and communications, would have posed major problems of command and control, the presence of some such supervisory staff structure would have been essential.

Equally, there are other aspects of Roman war, discussed within the pages of this book, about which much information is lacking. The employment of animals, for example, used prolifically by the ancients both for cavalry and transportation, raises a host of questions, mainly logistical. When the huge numbers involved are set alongside the defensive and administrative demands of the marching-camp technique, which required an army on the march to entrench itself behind ramparts at the end of every day, the immediately apparent answers quickly become shrouded in doubt. What did they do with the horses? remains a cry frequently raised and not easily answered, when considered in the light of the competing needs of grazing areas, control and security from ambush.

There are three constant factors upon which military historians may depend when glancing into the distant past. First, armies, like men, cannot survive without essentials such as food and drink. Where forage and provisions have not been carefully provided, wrote Vegetius, whose treatise *Epitoma rei militaris* became the military bible of European leaders well into medieval times, the evil is without remedy. The movement of armies is therefore guided by the whereabouts of these important necessities, or by the lack of them. A second factor is the Earth's relatively rarely changing landscape, the configuration of which constantly dictates the scope of the tactical decisions a commander may adopt, limiting or broadening his choice. The third is the predictable thinking process of man himself, particularly

Conrad Peutinger's (1465–1547) road map of the Roman empire exemplifies the unchanging nature of the military world. In 1948 an Israeli armoured column from Jerusalem captured Eilat by using an old Roman road (see Appendix 1)

when educated within the disciplines of a military environment. There is a further, fourth, consideration, argued by Field Marshal Viscount Montgomery of Alamein,[8] namely that, even though weapons have become more powerful and the problems of the battlefield more complex, the art of war is fundamentally the same today as it was in the ancient world. If we bear these important guidelines in mind when searching for the answers which elude us, we will discover we are erecting signposts which point to areas where they may be hidden.

When thumbing through old reference books, I have repeatedly been reminded of Montgomery's words. In most modern battalion 'Standing Orders for War', for example, it is laid down that every man should have a hot meal before battle. This advice is also sensibly voiced by Onasander in his treatise, *The General*.[9] Here he writes that senior officers 'should not hesitate to order the first meal at sunrise, lest the enemy, by a surprise attack, force his men to fight while still hungry. . . .This matter should not be considered of slight importance nor should a general neglect to pay attention to it, for soldiers who have eaten moderately . . . are more vigorous in battle.' Similarly, any soldier who has experienced the problems of trying to eat while actively engaged in the field, will recognize the drill initiated by Philip of Macedonia in 200 BC, during battle with the Aetolians, when

he ordered the men to fetch water and to have their meal, in succession, the cavalry by squadrons, and the light infantry by companies, while he kept some on guard under arms, as he waited for the column of infantry, which moved more slowly under the weight of their equipment. On arrival they were ordered to plant their standards, pile their arms, and make a hasty meal, not more than two or three at a time being sent from each company to fetch water; meanwhile the cavalry and light infantry stood in formation, on the alert in case the enemy should make a move.[10]

Livy's description of Paulus's systematic withdrawal of his troops from battle with the Macedonians in 168 BC, to take up positions behind the ramparts of his marching-camp, is yet another case in point.[11] It might have been quoted in any good twentieth-century military training manual as an example of the care to be taken under these circumstances:

he first withdrew the *triarii* from the rear of the battle-line; then he brought back the *principes*, while the *hastati* maintained their position in the front of the line, in case the enemy should make a move; lastly, he gradually withdrew the *hastati*, bringing off the soldiers of one maniple at a time, beginning with the right wing. Thus, while the cavalry and light armed remained facing the enemy in the front line of battle, the infantry were withdrawn without commotion.

There is no shortage of such examples, as Vegetius's rhetorical question demonstrates,[12] when he asks whether a man may be reckoned a good soldier 'who through negligence allows his arms to suffer by dirt and rust?'. It arouses memories of those countless nights of war, when weapons were produced, cleaned and lightly oiled in preparation for the morrow.

The basic arts of soldiering have surely changed but little in two thousand years and more.

A page from the Notitia Dignitatum *showing the insignia of the first secretary of the* Chancellery. The Notitia *is an invaluable source for the structure and organization of the Roman army*

CHAPTER ONE

Roman Generalship

'A clock is like an army,' I used to tell them. 'There's a main spring, that's the Army Commander, who makes it all go; then there are other springs, driving the wheels round, those are his generals. The wheels are officers and men. Some are big wheels, very important, they are the chief staff officers and the colonel sahibs. Other wheels are little ones, that do not look at all important. They are like you. Yet stop one of those little wheels and see what happens to the rest of the clock!'

Field Marshal Sir William Slim, *Defeat into Victory*[1]

The fundamental problems that have confronted armies and their commanders over the years – the need for a secure base; the sustenance of the army in the field; the provision of trained manpower and the creation of the right political climate – have always been factors of prime consideration. Nevertheless, the various ways in which they have been resolved differ greatly, and no more so than in the case of ancient Rome as it developed from a city-state.

The highest office in Republican Rome was vested in a pair of magistrates, consuls, who were elected annually by an assembly of the people and held power alternately. They were advised in their duties by the Senate, a body of ex-magistrates. The precise extent of this advice is not clear but, plainly, it could have acted as an inhibiting brake when urgent decision-making was required. The reason for joint command by consuls is obvious: each provided a check on the other and thus reduced the opportunity for either to seize power and retain authority, but it was a watchfulness which verged on impracticality. In time of war, each consul commanded the army (then standardized at a strength of four legions, plus allies), on alternate days. There was another complicating factor, particularly in the Republican era, which might have been thought to dilute efficiency still further, if, strangely, it had not so often proved to the contrary. All important magistracies, governorships and army commands were held by senators, generally without any military ability, their qualifications resting largely on their wealth and their circumstance of birth. Yet the positions to which they aspired were recognized as being of great import to the nation. 'For who can doubt', commented Vegetius, 'that military skill is superior to all other accomplishments, since through it our freedom and authority are preserved, our territory enhanced and our empire safeguarded.'[2]

The frailties of the command structure, and the problems created by this lack of continuity of leadership, were recognized by the Senate in two ways: firstly, on the outbreak of war, by the appointment of a supreme commander, a *dictator*, but, even then, for the restricted period of one campaigning season only; secondly, by the re-appointment of consuls at the completion of their tour of duty or, alternatively, by allowing consuls to retain their military status and carry forward their service in the rank of proconsul. It was a system which produced some extraordinary successes, but more because of its non-observance than because of strict adherence to it. Gaius Marius, to whom are attributed many of the major reforms which moved the Roman army forward to near-professionalism, held an unprecedented series of consulships in the decades at the end of the second and the beginning of the first centuries BC. He was contemptuous of the Senate but popular among the masses, in part because of his declared intention not to force men into military service against their will but largely because, in an age when Italy was under threat of invasion, he was an able commander with a bent for leadership and a proven success record in the field. To the people he was a military hero; to his men, to whose training and welfare he gave unflagging attention, he was 'a soldier's soldier', a hard but fair man, who shared their way of life and understood their needs. In battle, he had a reputation for courage and unhurried thoroughness.

Julius Caesar, nephew of Gaius Marius, one-time governor of Farther Spain (61–60 BC), conqueror of Gaul (58–50 BC), victor in the Civil War (49–46 BC), consul (49 BC) and *dictator* (46–44 BC), was another product of the system. In history as in life, his name provokes controversy. 'Why, man,' eulogized William Shakespeare, through the mouth of Cassius,

> . . . he doth bestride the narrow world
> Like a Colossus, and we petty men
> Walk under his huge legs and peep about
> To find ourselves dishonourable graves.
> *Julius Caesar*, I, ii, 134–7

Eminent historians have opined that 'no commander who ever lived showed greater military genius',[3] and have referred to him variously as 'the entire and perfect man'[4] and 'the greatest man of action who has ever lived',[5] but such views are by no means universal. Professor Hugh Last, writing in the *Cambridge Ancient History*,[6] while acknowledging his leadership qualities, made the controversial declaration that Caesar bequeathed to those who followed him 'no receipt for victory except one beyond their reach – to be Caesar . . . he made no single innovation in the technique of soldiering'. Colonel Theodore Dodge, the distinguished American military historian, held him to be 'the greatest man in antiquity',[7] but also remarked that, if the months were counted, 'more than half of Caesar's campaigns were consumed in extricating himself from the results of his own mistakes'.[8] Major General J.F.C. Fuller extended this criticism by asserting unequivocally that, even though these extrications may have been brilliant, Caesar was guilty of 'incontestably bad generalship':[9]

His defective system of supply frequently compelled him to change his area of operations to his disadvantage; his untrained, barbaric cavalry at times led him

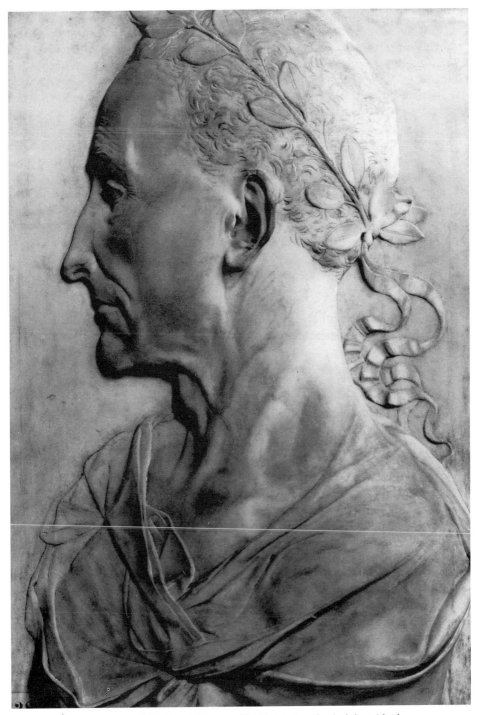

Julius Caesar, conqueror of Gaul and dictator, 48–44 BC: '. . . he doth bestride the narrow world/ Like a Colossus'.

into critical situations; and when his enemy took to guerilla warfare, he could do nothing to respond to him. It is astonishing that a soldier of his outstanding intelligence . . . could have failed to realise how defective was his army organisation.

This is strong meat and, within these pages, we shall be examining this statement further and aspiring to contest the 'incontestable'.

The policy of extending consular service, which applied equally to dictatorships,[10] was one of vital importance for, so far as is known, the Romans had no military training institutions and no formal process of either testing or educating officers in staff duties and the problems of command. In the absence of such establishments, they looked instead to experience and it has been suggested[11] that, until the last years of the second century BC, candidates for office had to serve a minimum number of campaigning seasons in order to be eligible for consideration, a sort of staff attachment, which Pliny,[12] in the reign of Domitian (AD 81–96), described when he wrote that

in olden times there was a custom by which we acquired knowledge not just by listening to our elders but also by watching their conduct. In this way we learnt what we had to do ourselves and what should be passed on to our juniors. So, men were immersed in military service at an early age and learnt how to give orders by obeying them, how to be a commander by following others.

There are, however, two very relevant factors which should not be overlooked when considering the Roman army's needs for officer material; firstly, the core of battlefield veterans to be found among the centurions, a hardy, hand-picked body of men of great dependability and courage, who provided the army with a broad leavening of experience and military wisdom; and, among the staff, the presence of permanent civil servants responsible for military planning, whose availability within the secretariat is rarely recognized but whose office, inevitably, must have provided an invaluable breeding ground for staff officers. Nor is it difficult to visualize that planning teams from this 'ministry for war' would have been deployed at moments of crisis to assist governors of provinces and commanding generals in their work.

The likely staff role of the secretariat in these matters is underlined by the presence at Boulogne, prior to the Roman invasion of Britain in AD 43, of Narcissus, private secretary to the emperor Claudius. He was a former slave, who had risen to being clerk in the civil service and was later to be appointed secretary-general and head of the state department. It was fortunate he was there, for the army, grumbling at being ordered to serve outside 'the inhabited world', had mutinied and refused either to embark or listen to their general, Aulus Plautius. Narcissus, as the personal representative of the emperor, was now called upon to address them and was greeted, good-humouredly, by the cry of '*Io Saturnalia*', a reference to the fact that, at the feast of Saturn, slaves were permitted to appear wearing the clothes of their masters. In my book *Invasion*, I expressed the view that he had arrived at the coast to make arrangements for Claudius's impending arrival and departure to Britain; but this is likely to have been only part of the story. It is equally probable that he was present primarily as the emperor's chief staff officer, with the purpose of coordinating the plans which he, with his team from the secretariat, had outlined in Rome and finalized in Boulogne for the embarkation and departure of the task force and for the implementation of future supply arrangements. With a thousand ships to launch across the Channel, these plans would have been considerable and intricate, calling for a staff empowered to make instant decisions.

In the imperial period, the emperor was commander-in-chief and, nominally at least, led his army on to the field of battle or, in his absence, designated a member of his family to take his place. In the event of a war outside Italy, then it was customary either for a consul or ex-consul of suitable seniority and experience to be nominated to command the campaign or, alternatively, for its conduct to be passed to the governor of the territory or province concerned.

The sequence of the build-up to the invasion of Britain provides an example of this behaviour. The emperor Claudius selected Aulus Plautius, at that moment governor of Pannonia, to lead the expedition. Plautius was a kinsman of his first wife but it is more likely that his choice was influenced by the fact that the general had considerable experience of waterborne operations on the River Danube, working in close cooperation with the Roman navy. The task now confronting him posed similar demands. Plautius at once assumed command of the task force assembling at Boulogne on behalf of his commander-in-chief. When all was ready, he placed himself at the head of the invasion force, crossed the Channel and, when he felt assured that Colchester was ripe to fall into his hands, in accordance with his instructions, he sent for Claudius.[13] Upon the emperor's arrival from Rome, he handed command of the army to him. He re-assumed it once again, sixteen days later, when his master returned to Gaul.

This, then, was broadly the structure of command at the top, but what particular skills might have been sought of their generals by the Roman people? There were a multitude of views, as might be expected. Cicero, soldier and distinguished orator, opined that a good commander had to be a man of proven reputation, courage and good fortune, with a grasp of military science.[14] Onasander, in a treatise on generalship dedicated to Quintus Veranius, consul in AD 53, took a slightly divergent view. He underlined the necessity for common sense and strength of character but saw no great need for a detailed knowledge of technical matters: rather should a general take advice from men of experience. He should at all times lead by personal example but not by 'fighting in battle', a philosophy which would not have been supported by Julius Caesar. It is likely, however, that Onasander was suggesting that a commander should not get caught up in the cut and thrust of the fighting and thus find himself distracted from the duties of command. Scipio was probably indicating something similar when, accused of lacking aggression, he answered 'My mother bore me a general, not a warrior.'[15] Agricola, according to Tacitus,[16] took the field in person as soon as the campaigning season opened:

> He was present everywhere on the march, praising good discipline and keeping stragglers up to the mark. He himself chose sites for camps and reconnoitred estuaries and forests; all the time he gave the enemy no rest and constantly launched plundering raids.

Velleius,[17] writing of his hero Tiberius, stressed the virtue of caution; the safety of the army was paramount. Victory should not be sought through the sacrifice of Roman troops; a general should make his own decisions and never place his own reputation before common sense.

From the above paragraph, two things emerge: first, no one definition exists which can encompass the qualities of a general, particularly if he lies in the class defined by Montgomery as the *grand chef*; and, second, many qualities that today might be considered essential for inclusion have either been underemphasized or omitted – but need not necessarily have been unpractised.

Generals, whatever their generation, are expected to win wars and their reputations are gained almost as much by the extent of their successes as by the character of their campaigns. The basic ingredients that affect the conduct of a campaign are available to every commander; the phases of war, the nature of manoeuvre and the guiding principles (of which surprise, concentration of force, high morale, maintenance of the aim and sound administration number but a few) are unchanging and constant constituents. The greatest single winning factor is the spirit of the warrior himself. Thus to suggest, like Professor Hugh Last, that Caesar bequeathed no recipe for victory to those who followed after him, is to express an exaggerated confidence in the ability of commanders to conjure bright new methods of war from their knapsacks. Success comes from the artful degree to which all the ingredients listed above are, in the first place, appreciated and then handled and brought together.

This is a truism of which Julius Caesar possessed a natural understanding. He was fully conscious of the limitations of his tactical arsenal and squeezed the maximum benefits from it. He was the master of the Roman technique of the marching-camp (see Chapter 3) and of siege warfare, as he proved during his investment of Alesia during the Gallic rebellion. His chief weapon was the element of surprise, coupled with the scale, timing and speed of an attack. 'He joined battle', wrote Suetonius, 'not only after planning his movements in advance but on a sudden opportunity, often immediately at the end of a march, and sometimes in the foulest weather, when one would least expect him to make a move.'[18] There are numerous examples of the manner in which he achieved this: in 55 BC, in a move to discipline the Germans, the speed of his advance threw his enemy 'into sudden panic; they had no time to think what to do or to arm themselves'; in 52 BC, when operating against Vercingetorix in the Loire Valley, 'the shock of [his] appearance unnerved the enemy and the crossing was effected without loss': again, a year later, when dealing with a revolt by the Bituriges,[19]

> Caesar's sudden march found them unprepared and scattered, tilling the fields without any thought of danger, and naturally they were caught by cavalry before they could take refuge in the town. They had not even the usual warning of a hostile invasion – the sight of burned buildings; for Caesar had commanded that nothing should be set on fire in order to avoid giving the alarm, and to save the corn and hay, which he would need if he decided to advance far.

In order to practise this philosophy to its utmost, the ability to strike with lightning suddenness was essential. In an age when the speed of advance was constrained to that of the supply train which moved with the infantry column, he frequently gambled by leaving his heavy baggage behind and travelled light, each man carrying operational rations and the minimum of equipment. Almost invariably, it profited him to do so. Occasionally, as at Ruspina, when he was said to be in a 'ferment of impatient expectancy'[20] awaiting the arrival of reinforcements and supplies, after having landed with a perilously small expeditionary force, he cut matters very fine. As a result of pursuing this policy, which compares with the successful but equally administratively ill-prepared Allied dash for the Meuse in 1944, Caesar has sometimes been accused of having a 'dislike for preparations, due to his eagerness to clinch with his enemy as rapidly as possible'[21] – surely a laudable ambition. But, if the final outcome were victory, which it was, and he carried his soldiers with him, which in the main he did until the divisions of civil war interposed, there can be little justification for such complaint.

Despite the difference in terrain, there are many similarities between the military problems experienced by the Romans in their day, in particular by Caesar in Gaul, and those which confronted Field Marshal Sir William Slim in Burma during the Second World War, when he found himself, in his words, facing three major anxieties – supply, health and morale. There is thus some merit in bearing in mind the difficulties of his XIVth Army, when considering those of earlier Roman commanders.

The strike force, in each case, largely comprised infantry columns, together with lightly equipped local levies. Both were supported, in the main, by the light artillery of their day, frequently pack-borne, and were heavily reliant upon animal transport. Supply was subject to a tenuous system of communication, the bulk being brought forward from the rear, until improved resources, in Slim's case, rendered air supply possible, with some commodities, such as eggs or vegetables, being purchased from local tribes. Rations for as many as seven days were frequently carried by the individual soldier. Scipio's army likewise bore 'several days' rations, under such conditions that they became accustomed to enduring cold and rain, and to the fording of streams'. Quintus Metullus allowed no meat on the hoof, only precooked meat, presumably so as not to slow down the rate of march. In another instance, to quote a much repeated tale, Gaius Marius, in order to reduce the scale of his demand for pack animals, made his soldiers tie their utensils and food up in bundles and carry them on forked poles, over their shoulders.[22] Slim has made it clear to us, in his book *Defeat into Victory*, how he resolved his many problems. Roman generals, with their contemporary biographers, rarely revealed such administrative detail, although it was equally vital to the success of their campaigns.

The health of the soldiers, together with the hospital care and the evacuation of sick and wounded, apart from being morally important, were major concerns of Roman commanders-in-chief, although, obviously, the degree varied according to the personality of the individual. Velleius Paterculus has described how Tiberius looked after the medical welfare of his men during the campaigns of the early first century AD. Throughout the whole period of the German and Pannonian War, he tells us, there was not one of us, of higher or lower rank than ourselves alike, who fell ill without having his welfare and health looked after by Caesar with as much care as though they were the chief occupation of his mind, preoccupied though he was by such heavy responsibilities. There was a carriage ready for those who needed it, his litter was put at the disposal of everyone, and I and others enjoyed the use of this. Now his doctors, now his kitchen, now his bathing equipment, which had been brought for his own exclusive use, relieved the sickness of absolutely everyone.[23]

Others, including such as Hadrian, Trajan and Germanicus were renowned for the attention they gave to the welfare of the sick and wounded, visiting them in hospital and uttering words of encouragement. Indeed, when Germanicus was engaged in fighting, north of the River Rhine, his wife Agrippina, a great-hearted woman according to Tacitus,[24] assumed command of his army's base camp and

Agrippina, wife of Germanicus, 'dispensed clothes to needy soldiers and dressed the wounded'

'dispensed clothes to needy soldiers and dressed the wounded'. The Romans clearly placed more emphasis on medical care than has been chronicled by contemporary military historians, who tend to make more of battles and the dying and the dead, rather than of efforts to succour the wounded. In the days of the Principate, this may have been because of a general awareness that a properly organized military service existed, a consideration well recorded by medical manuals.[25] Frustratingly, they make no mention of its field organization. In the Republican era, it is notable that even Caesar, despite the length of the Gallic War and the many casualties incurred by his army, makes mention neither of his medical arrangements nor of the casualty evacuation system he employed.

Supplies of medical dressing for the wounded were a normal provision in the early first century. All soldiers received some training in first aid, and, within each cohort, the equivalent of a battalion, there was a fully qualified physician with four medical attendants. The importance to morale of providing speedy treatment for the sick and wounded was recognized and, on campaign, tented hospitals were based well forward, deep in the operational area. There is much clear evidence of this, as will be seen in later chapters, in particular in an account by Caesar[26] of an incident in 53 BC, during operations against the Eburones.

Slim considered morale to be a factor of such vital importance that he made it a prime task to tabulate its foundations. Briefly, he considered that, if morale were to be sustained at a proper level, there must be 'some great and noble object' for which a man could strive; that he must have confidence in his leaders and pride in the organization of which he is a member; and that his weapons, working conditions and equipment must be seen to be the best possible. He considered that there was a spiritual as well as a material side to morale, which was a theme also recognized by Montgomery in his *Concise History of Warfare*:[27]

> While operational problems will tend to be the main preoccupation of a general, he must never forget that the raw material of his trade is men and that generalship, basically, is a human problem. . . . The general who looks after his men and cares for their lives, and wins battles with the minimum loss of life, will have their confidence. All soldiers will follow a successful general. A general, therefore, has got to 'get himself over' to his troops. My own technique was to speak to them whenever possible. Sometimes I spoke to large numbers from the bonnet of a jeep, sometimes I spoke to just a few men by the roadside or in a gunpit . . . it is the spoken word above all which counts in the leadership of men.

Both Slim and Montgomery were senior generals, cast in the modern mould and fired in the crucible of the horrendous, mud-filled, blood-stained trenches of Flanders in the First World War. This is where they learnt the principles which were later to guide their actions in North Africa, Normandy and Burma and lead them to the pinnacles of their careers. Their observations on these aspects of leadership therefore demand not only the most careful study but also practice: but it must be said they are not new. Onasander, a Greek military writer of the first century AD, who wrote a treatise on generalship dedicated to Quintus Veranius (who died in AD 59 while in command in Britain), stated his view that a general must be a ready speaker:

> For if a general is drawing up his men before battle, the encouragement of his words makes them despise the danger and covet the honour; and a trumpet-call resounding in the ears does not so effectively awaken the soul to the conflict of the battle as a speech. . . . Should some disaster befall the army, an encouraging speech will give the men's souls new strength; and a not unskilful address by the commander is far more useful in counteracting the despondency of an army in the hour of defeat than the physicians who attend to the wounded.

Onasander also echoed Slim's important message that an army must be motivated by 'some great and noble object':

> The causes of war, I believe, should be marshalled with the greatest care; it should be evident to all that one fights on the side of justice. For then the gods also, kindly disposed, become comrades in arms to the soldiers and men are more likely to take their stand against the foe. For with the knowledge that they are not fighting an aggressive but a defensive war, with consciences free from evil designs, they contribute a courage that is complete; while those who believe an unjust war is displeasing to heaven, because of this very opinion enter a war with fear. . . . For those whose cause is weak when they take up the burden of war, are quickly crushed by it and fail.

Without doubt Caesar practised a similar routine with his generals. It was his habit, dependent upon the operational situation, to address his troops before battle. His accounts of these occasions give the impression that he did this to an assembled gathering but, in view of the large numbers involved and the distances over which they would have been deployed (see Chapter 4), it seems more likely that he rode along the battle line on his favoured war horse, speaking to the cohorts as he came to them, and encouraging the centurions, most of whom he knew personally. He and his generals appreciated the powerful influence of these men and used them as a means of strengthening communication with the troops. In one instance, in the opening stages of the Gallic Wars, and disturbed by signs of disloyalty and a slump in morale among all ranks, Caesar summoned the centurions of every grade to a council, and reprimanded them severely for permitting such a condition to fester. On another occasion, when preparing for operations against the Bellovaci, he summoned his officers and 'communicated to them all the information he had received and told them to encourage the men by passing it on to them'. Likewise his senior general, Labienus,[28] in skirmishing prior to the second crossing of the Rhine, 'summoned the military tribunes and first-grade centurions to explain his plans' to them.

Generally, despite the obvious importance of the subject and with the exception of Onasander, direct considerations of morale, in the modern sense, were rarely uttered by Roman or Greek historians of the day, nor by the ancient military manual writers, such as Vegetius, Frontinus, Arrian and Aenas, who directed much of their work on

The centurions were a hardy, hand-picked body of men of great dependability and courage

the handling of armies in peace and war towards the education of reigning emperors and other senior officers. Truly, Frontinus devoted a chapter to 'restoring morale by firmness',[29] which dealt largely with the lack of leadership by standard-bearers, who were expected to head the advance into battle and sometimes showed reluctance to do so, but this was a narrow approach to a complex subject. Generally, they ignored what Slim called the 'spiritual' factors and stressed, instead, two main components: the essential confidence inspired by training and the need for the strictest discipline, both, of course, highly important. Victory in war does not depend entirely on numbers or mere courage, wrote Vegetius,[30]

only skill and discipline will ensure it. We find that the Romans owed the conquest of the world to no other cause than continual military training, exact observance of discipline in their camps and unwearied cultivation of the other arts of war. Without these, what chance would the Roman armies, with their inconsiderable numbers, have had against the multitude of Gauls? Or with what success, and for the same reasons, could they have opposed the multitude of Germans? The Spaniards surpassed us not only in numbers but in physical strength. We were always inferior to the Africans in wealth and unequal to them in deception and strategem.

He then added the very sage remark that the consequence

Two officer candidates (c. 100 BC) present themselves for recruitment in the Roman army. The clerk on the left is entering the name of one on his ledger. The second candidate appears to be undergoing some form of examination

of engaging an enemy without skill or courage is that part of the army is left on the field of battle, and that those who remain receive such an impression from their defeat that they dare not afterwards look the enemy in the face.

Discipline was ruthlessly, even savagely enforced. Domitius Corbulo who commanded the army in AD 58, during the war with Parthia for the possession of Armenia, was reinforced prior to the campaign by troops from Syria. Tacitus relates that he found the slackness of these troops, demoralized by years of peace-time soldiering, 'a worse trouble than enemy treachery'.[31] Corbulo, a tough and seasoned campaigner, not given to eloquence, determined to provide them with the experience they had missed. He instructed that the whole army would spend the winter under canvas, in weather so severe that ice had to be removed and the ground excavated before tents could be pitched. In the words of the chronicler, frostbite caused the loss of many limbs and sentries were frozen to death. The general was unmoved; thinly dressed and bare-headed, he circulated among the men, encouraging the sick, of whom there must have been many, and praising efficiency. There were, not unreasonably, many deserters: he treated these with unabated severity. Whereas, in other armies, first and second offences were excused, Corbulo executed deserters immediately and without mercy. Tacitus records the remarkable fact that, in the spring, his 'forces were as ready for fighting as for marching'.

On the battlefield, discipline was no less harsh and Frontinus lists numerous examples.[32] When two legions broke in the face of an enemy attack, Fabius Rullus chose men by lot and beheaded them in sight of their comrades. In a similar situation, Aquilius beheaded three men from each of the centuries which had failed to hold their ground. On another occasion, when his defences had been set afire by the enemy, Mark Antony 'decimated the soldiers of two cohorts of those who were on the works, and punished the centurions of each cohort. Besides this, he dismissed the commanding officer in disgrace and ordered the rest of the legion to be put on barley rations.' Human life was cheap and there seems to have been no limit to the numbers of lives taken in punishment. Livy[33] records that, in 279 BC, when Pyrrhus was in southern Italy, the people of Rhegium applied to Rome for protection and were provided with a garrison of a legion which 'criminally took possession' of the city it had been sent to protect. The soldiers plundered the city, killed or expelled the menfolk, and 'took possession of the women and children'. All 4,000 men were condemned to be executed and the Senate declared it a crime to bury any one of them or to indulge in mourning for them.

It is perhaps almost inevitable that, once again, Caesar's approach to discipline, as to so many other matters, should have been different. Perhaps because of his predilection for leading from the front, he understood the chemistry of morale

Trajan addressing his troops before battle

more clearly than most. He judged his men solely by their fighting record. If they failed, he dealt with them all with equal severity. In battle, he kept a careful eye on the ebb and flow of fighting and, if his troops gave ground, he was generally there to rally them. Suetonius relates that he would grasp by the throat any man who fled the ranks and would turn him around to face the enemy.[34] He dealt severely with such behaviour. Discipline in battle was paramount; elsewhere and off-parade, he was inclined to be indulgent. 'My soldiers fight just as well when they are stinking of perfume', he once boasted. As a result, he earned the devotion of his troops to the extent that, at the outbreak of the Civil War, every centurion in every legion volunteered to equip a cavalryman from his savings and the private soldiers unanimously volunteered to serve under him without pay or rations.[35]

Thus, an army must not only be clear in its mind how the complex situations, difficulties and hardships which inevitably arise in war are to be tackled; it must be physically capable of fighting and should be mentally and morally prepared to do so. There is ample evidence to suggest that the Romans were aware of these principles. We may, therefore, also anticipate that running through the entity of the Roman army there was a central doctrine, directing its shape and activities and providing guidelines to be pursued by its general officers. It is thus disappointing, in the various writings provided for us by such as Livy, Tacitus, Josephus, Ammianus Marcellinus and particularly Julius Caesar, including many others, that we are allowed only occasional glimpses of these. Equally, the contributions made to our understanding of Roman military affairs by contemporary Greek and Roman authors of instructional military handbooks have been singularly limited in scope. This is remarkable since much of their work was dedicated to reigning emperors of Rome and, as a consequence, might have been expected to be directed to a more elevated plane than the often simple one it occupies.

Probably the most influential of these writers was Vegetius (fourth century AD), whose work *Epitoma rei militaris*, addressed to Valentinian, was closely studied by European military commanders until as late as the Middle Ages. In presentation and scope, it bears the nearest resemblance, of all its rivals, to a modern training manual. Vegetius had the advantage, of course, of coming on the scene later than most and his work probably benefited from being melded with that of earlier authors. It is said to contain many errors but, nevertheless, this need not necessarily lessen its importance for, without doubt, the work generally points the way to a higher level of military thinking than that of his contemporaries.

Another writer, Frontinus (first century AD), was the author of two valuable military works, namely *The Art of War*, which he followed closely with his handbook, *Stratagems*. This latter volume dealt with military stratagems of Greek and Roman history and won the approval of the emperor Trajan (AD 98–117). Frontinus had been a Roman soldier and, as provincial governor of Britain, had brought about the subjugation of the Silures, a powerful and warlike tribe in south-east Wales. It is thus regrettable, with this professional background – for he could have had much to tell us – that his work, *The Art of War*, should have been lost. It is sometimes suggested that Vegetius may have incorporated much of it in his *Epitoma rei militaris*. Frontinus's *Stratagems* comprises four books, the first concerned with events before the battle, the second with the battle itself and the third with siege warfare. The fourth book is devoted to discipline and there is controversy as to whether or not he compiled it himself. The whole volume contains some nine hundred examples of a variety of 'tactics' employed at different times by commanders in the field and all are selected as being illustrative of various aspects of war.

Some of these exempla are bizarre, one such being an account of an incident during Hannibal's siege of Casilinum, when the Romans scattered nuts on the waters of the Volturnus, as it flowed downstream, so that they might be netted as they arrived in the city and thus beat the food blockade;[36] others are rare nuggets of military practice. Corbulo's dictum, for example, that the pick was the weapon with which to beat the enemy was an expression that might have been voiced by any twentieth-century army commander, even though he was, in this instance, speaking of marching-camp techniques (Chapter 3) and the circumvallation of siegeworks (Chapter 7). Equally, Gaius Caesar's claim that he followed a policy 'of conquering the foe by hunger rather than by steel' has a similarly modern connotation. Vegetius made this latter point even more strongly when he wrote that 'the main and principal point in war is to secure plenty of provisions and to weaken or destroy the enemy by famine'.[37]

The careful attitude of Roman generals to enemy populations, provided they had behaved with reasonable correctness, is also marked by Frontinus. He relates how Augustus, during his war with the Germans, ordered compensation to be paid to local inhabitants for all crops he had included within the fortifications he had erected. In another instance, he tells how a tree laden with fruit, and located inside a marching-camp, 'was found, the day after the withdrawal of the army, with the fruit undisturbed'. And yet again, he writes of a personal experience in Gaul, when the wealthy Lingones people, fearful they were about to be plundered by an approaching Roman army, were so delighted to be left alone that 'they returned to their previous loyalty and handed over to me 70,000 armed men'.[38]

There was a natural wisdom in this exercise in public relations aimed at gaining the friendship of local inhabitants, for Roman armies, compared with the populations of their conquered territories, were small in size, and the numbers of troops required to maintain numerical superiority would have been considerable and wasteful. Thus, as Frontinus indirectly points out, a good relationship with the enemy population was essential. This became progressively more true as the frontiers of conquest advanced and the necessity to return law and order to the occupied homelands became increasingly important. It is possible, here, to make yet another comparison with the war in Burma, where, long before that country's reconquest had been set in hand, Slim had already established a Civil Affairs Organization for this very purpose. As a result, when the relief forces stormed across the Chindwin on their march to Mandalay, teams of civilian officials moved close behind, armed with the essential paraphernalia of administration, and ready immediately to move into the various districts they had already been allocated.

There is evidence to suggest that something of a similar nature took place in the wake of Plautius's invasion of Britain in AD 43. In the preceding years, the tribes situated in the south and south-east of the island had already been cultivated to such good effect by the Romans that, due to the divisions they had created, several princes and princelings had fled to seek their protection. These included Verica, the elderly ruler of the Regni and brother of Tincommius of the Atrebates, and Adminius, the exiled ruler of north-east Kent and younger brother of Togodumnus and Caratacus. There were thus, at the time of the landings, already several British refugees on the continent seeking to return home and re-establish themselves within their community, under Roman patronage. They would have been sufficient in number to form a government in exile. Among them, there was one Cogidubnus, a powerful and ambitious man, an aristocrat, supposedly of British origins and a protegé of Claudius. He had been brought up by the Romans from a very early age and, it may perhaps be judged, had been specifically groomed for this particular moment. Significantly, Tacitus referred to him in his *Annals* as 'an instrument of domination' and 'an example of the long established Roman custom of employing even kings to make others slaves'.[39]

The momentum generated by Plautius's landings at Richborough quickly resulted in the fall of Colchester. This success would then inevitably have been followed by the rapid redeployment of the legions as they consolidated their gains and prepared for further advance. A move of this nature would have required a relaxation of their grip on the territories of the tribes they had defeated in the decisive Medway battle, namely, the Regni, in whose territory lay Chichester, the Atrebates, with their capital at Silchester, and the Belgae, based at Winchester, and would have left the stage open for Cogidubnus to move in and take over their responsibilities. Initially, he would have had the support of the Roman garrison and administrative commander at Richborough, probably Cnaeus Sentius. Ultimately, so it would now appear, he undertook full control, aided by re-organized tribal armies, and was rewarded for his loyalty by a generous grant of 'certain *civitates*'.

Agricola, *Legatus Praetorius* in Britain, AD 78–84, extended these civilian-orientated policies still further during his governorship. According to Tacitus:

He gave private encouragement and official assistance to the building of temples, public squares and good houses. He praised the energetic and scolded the slack; and competition for honour proved as effective as compulsion. He educated the sons of the chiefs in the liberal arts and expressed a preference for British ability as compared with the trained skills of the Gauls. The result was that instead of loathing the Latin language they became eager to speak it effectively. In the same way, our national dress came into favour and the toga was everywhere to be seen. . . .[40]

Tacitus had no doubt about the purpose of what was happening. The unsuspecting Britons, he tells us, 'spoke of such novelties as civilisation, when in fact they were only a feature of their enslavement'.

In view of the procedure for the selection of Roman generals, with the seeming absence of any recognized military training academies to provide tactical instruction and set uniform standards for achievement, it is not surprising that their military qualities were frequently as varied as their personal characteristics. Many, such as Corbulo, placed an undue emphasis on discipline, which appears to have produced some battlefield success at the cost of disgruntled soldiery. Onasander saw fit to

Trajan's Column at Rome

counsel that 'a general should be alert to the psychology of an army, especially when things are going wrong'; and both Vegetius and Frontinus, in their handbooks, deemed it necessary to include similar chapters of advice, which suggests that such incidents were reasonably commonplace. One of these chapters dealt with 'quelling a mutiny of soldiers' and the other with ways of meeting 'the menace of treason and desertion'.[41] Julius Caesar, perhaps more than any, understood the handling of men, judging them 'by their fighting record, not by their moral or social position' and 'treating them all with equal severity – and equal indulgence'.[42]

Nevertheless, nobody can deny – and the Roman Empire stood as witness – that the system, however strange, produced men of high ability. The key to their achievement lay in the experience which contemporary military writers such as Pliny, Onasander and Frontinus constantly recommended newly promoted senior officers to seek. The renowned Gaius Marius, Cicero relates, 'acquired his military skill on active service and as a commander in wars'. But experience won under such circumstances can be a harsh schoolmaster unless there is a guiding hand. This could only have been provided by the senior centurions, probably the *primus pilus* of the First Cohort, many of whom in due course filled the important appointment of *praefectus castrorum*, camp prefect, and then found the way open to a procuratorship, a civil service staff appointment mainly concerned with financial matters. It is surely unlikely that the military talents of these men would have been then discarded: it is not improbable that they also functioned as staff planners and advisers, providing logistical advice as and when the situation required. A general, advised Onasander,

> should either choose a staff to participate in all his councils and share in his decisions, men who will accompany the army especially for this purpose, or summon as members of his council a selected group of the most respected commanders, since it is not safe that the opinions of one single man, on his sole judgement, should be adopted. . . . However, the general must neither be so undecided that he entirely distrusts himself, nor so obstinate as not to think that anyone could have a better idea than his own; for such a man, either because he listens to everyone and never to himself, is sure to meet with frequent misfortune. . . .[43]

CHAPTER TWO

Command and Control

Every operation requires a fixed time for its commencement and a period
and place for its execution. It also demands secrecy, recognised signals,
known persons by whom and through whom it is to be carried out and a
detailed operational plan.

Polybius, *The Rise of the Roman Empire* (*c*. 200–118 BC)[1]

In the twentieth century the demands of two world wars have escalated the
development of battlefield systems of communication with dramatic effect,
emphasizing their importance to victory. Nevertheless, despite the fact that we
now live in a greatly different age, heavily dependent upon advanced technology,
military thinking has changed but little since Onasander wrote his essay on
generalship. The simple principles of war remain undiminished in importance.
Equally, the arrangements made by a senior officer for the command and control
of his forces and the quick transmission of information and instructions to his
troops remain no less vital.

In step with this advance, as it has been extended and refined, the overall speed
of operations has been correspondingly enhanced. Today, orders may be
despatched to the front line and received by formations and units at all levels
almost as soon as they are issued by the commanding general. Thus, a junior non-
commissioned officer in the field, in charge of a half-section (that is to say, in
Roman terms, a half-*contubernium*, or four men), now possesses the ability not
only to remain in constant verbal contact with his superior officer but also to
speak to neighbouring sub-units. Soon, it is probable that every infantryman will
be equipped with a listening device, fitted within his helmet, so that he may be
kept fully aware of the events happening around him.

In the face of such progress, it is easy to forget that, up to the outbreak of the
Second World War, the Royal Corps of Signals still held, within its authorized
establishment, troops of mounted orderlies, or 'gallopers', for the delivery of
messages in the field; and that the British army, even as late as mid-1942, was
engaged in fighting a campaign on the North West Frontier of India equipped,
for communication purposes, largely with signal flags, heliographs and lamps. At
the same time, the remarkably effective practice of passing orders by hand signal
in the field and by bugle-call, both in the field and in barracks, was commonplace.
This latter instance, particularly, was a method well practised, by first the Greek
and then the Roman armies, more than two and a half thousand years ago and

The command group as recreated by the Ermin Street Guard

probably earlier. Asclepiodotus, a Greek philosopher who lived in the first century BC, a man with no military experience but an avid student of military theory, has described for us the manner in which they were employed.[2] Although he has been accused of a dry but admittedly orderly approach to his subject, it is possible to hear the voice of a twentieth-century soldier echoing the examples quoted by him (see Appendix 1). It should be the intention of every commander, he advised,

> to train the army to distinguish sharply the commands given sometimes by the voice, sometimes by visible signals and sometimes by the bugle. The most distinct commands are those given by the voice, but they may not carry at all times because of the clash of arms or heavy gusts of wind; less affected by uproar are the commands given by signals; but even these may be interfered with now and then by the sun's glare, thick fog and dust, or heavy rain. One cannot therefore find signals . . . suitable for every circumstance that arises, but now and then new signals must be found to meet the situation; but it is hardly likely that all the difficulties appear at the same time, so that a command will be indistinguishable both by bugle, voice and signal.

The bugle as a method of communication had its origins with the Etruscans, the leading bronze founders of the Mediterranean world before the coming of the

Celts. The trumpets they fashioned, and the methods they employed, were later adopted and adapted both by the ancient Greeks and the Romans. Regrettably, neither of these peoples have left us with any clear knowledge of the signal techniques they devised. Nevertheless, there are some slender signposts, firstly erected by Julius Pollux, a Greek scholar of the second century AD and then by Vegetius, an intellectual of the fourth century AD, whose popular textbook, *Epitoma rei militaris*, provides a valuable insight into Roman military practice.[3] The trumpet, or *tuba*, he wrote,

> sounds the charge and the retreat. The cornets are used only to regulate the motions of the colours; the trumpets serve when the soldiers are ordered out to any work without the colours; but in time of action, the trumpets and cornets sound together. . . .
>
> The ordinary guards and outposts are always mounted and relieved by the sound of the trumpet, which also directs the movements of the soldiers on working parties and on field days. The cornets sound whenever the colours are to be struck or planted. These rules must be punctually observed in all exercises and reviews so that the soldiers may be ready to obey them in action without hesitation according to the general's orders either to charge or halt, to pursue the enemy or to retire. For reason will convince us that what is necessary to be performed in the heat of action should constantly be practised in the leisure of peace.

Vegetius, in these paragraphs, lists four calls to be obeyed without hesitation – to charge, halt, pursue the enemy and to retire. From his wording it is possible to infer that a broader range of trumpet calls existed than he has defined. Plainly, whatever range of duties they may have covered, they had two distinct functions: one, to deal with routine administration; the other, broadly operational in nature.

Roman legions, unless on garrison duty, and with the possible exception of campaigns in Britain, rarely operated in isolation but were grouped in army formations. Thus, if their commander had wished urgently to signal an instruction to an individual legion in the field, this could have posed a problem, unless a drill had been contrived for the purpose. Imagine, for example, that an army of four legions was on the march and the commanding general wished to alert a particular legion to prepare for operations. How could its attention have been attracted by trumpet without alerting the whole column? The answer can only be that each legion possessed its own distinctive call, perhaps simply the blast of a musical note to identify its recipient. But what form did this take? Did it convey a musical message by a range of fanfares, each with its own especial meaning and, if so, what would these have been? Or did it simply sound a coded series of notes?

For these purposes, the Romans favoured four particular instruments: the *tuba*, the *bucina*, the *cornu* and the *lituus*. They were rarely employed for musical purposes but, more commonly, on military occasions and for ceremonial duty at civic and religious gatherings.

The *tuba* was an uncomplicated instrument, with a slightly conical shape over its entire length of about 4 feet. It was made entirely of bronze but was sometimes fitted

The cornicen *or horn blower*

with a horn mouthpiece. Without the prefacing call provided by the *cornu*, it was sounded mainly for routine duties. The *bucina* was very similar in size but, in its case, it was crafted with a narrow cylindrical bore, flaring out close to the bell. The *tuba*, readily identifiable by its characteristic sound, served a more important operational purpose. Homer, in his *Iliad*,[4] graphically described how the note of a similar, tuba-like instrument was recognizable across long distances of the battlefield:

> The loud trumpet's brazen mouth from far
> With shrilling clangour sounds th'alarm of war.

The physical effort required to play this instrument was considerable and demanded heavy lip pressure. For this reason, it was the habit of Roman trumpeters to blow with cheeks inflated. Sachs records that in some archaeological representations a chain is shown attached to the bell of the trumpet, presumably to enable the player to brace his lips more firmly against the mouthpiece; and that, in other instances, and for the same reason, the free hand is shown pressed against the back of the head.[5]

The main task of the *bucinator* was to announce the hours of the watch throughout the night and to sound all other necessary calls, as might any modern day orderly bugler, throughout his tour of duty. His role in this connection (almost entirely administrative although he does appear to have been employed to 'blow up' before battle), is emphasized in a 'morning report' papyrus of AD 239, listing the nine men on watch at the standards of *cohors XX Palmyrenorum*, day after day.[6] These included a centurion, three standard-bearers, a priest, a clerk to record the details of the watch, a *bucinator* and two others.

The *cornu* was slightly more melodious. It was made of horn and silver,[7] shaped like the letter G and gently tapered for the greater part of its outstretched length of roughly 11 feet. Horace speaks of its 'threatening rumble', but modern experiments with a facsimile are said to have produced 'a soft and yet voluminous sound'. Its partly circular shape was held together by a crosspiece which rested at an angle on the trumpeter's left shoulder. The tube curved over his head and the bell faced forward, in the manner of a French horn. It is frequently depicted in Roman sculpture, particularly on Trajan's Column. Militarily, the sounding of the *cornu* which, as we have seen, heralded the commander-in-chief's endorsement of whatever instruction was about to be conveyed, carried with it an implicit command for all soldiers to look towards their standards.

The *lituus*, 5 feet long, was a slender bronze tube which curved upwards at its end to form the bell, in the manner of the handle of a walking stick. In contemporary Roman literature its sound was described as *stridor*, a shriek.[8] Its appearance, however, rated better than this, for a surviving example, now in the Vatican Museum, has been described as 'an instrument of great elegance'. The *lituus* is judged to have been used mainly by the cavalry, but its employment is not well documented. It is, however, notable and significant that each of this variety of trumpets possessed its own distinctive sound.

Little is known of the scale of their distribution within a unit but lists of trumpeters of *legio III Augusta* in Lambaesis, which have been unearthed, show totals of 38 *tubicines* and 35 *cornicines*. Using these figures, and on the basis that preserved inscriptions make proportionately less mention of *bucinators* than other trumpeters, it has been estimated that there may have been some 20 of the latter per legion, an average of 2 per cohort.[9]

We have already noted the part played by the commander-in-chief's *cornu*, carried by his personal trumpeter, the *cornicen*. Since the duties of the two instruments were closely linked, he would doubtless also have had a *tuba* in his retinue, with its musician, the *tubicen*. The 'brazen mouth', or carrying range, of this latter instrument would have made it invaluable for passing instructions, over distance, to his formation commanders. Indeed, it is likely that he would have held groupings of both these trumpets, in the manner depicted on the Adamklissi monument,[10] two panels of which show three *cornicines* apiece (thus suggesting a total of six), each man blowing with all his might, so that they might be heard 'from afar', above the noise of battle. Legion commanders, and officers commanding reserve units, may also be expected to have employed both instruments in a similar manner, if not for the use of their formation or unit, then, essentially, for those occasions when they might have been on detached duty or for the purpose of relaying onwards their army commander's messages to neighbouring formations.

The simplest of signals are those which have been preplanned. Polybius[11] demonstrates this when he describes the procedure for breaking camp practised by the Romans:

As soon as the first signal is given, the men strike their tents and assemble their baggage, but no soldier may strike his tent or set it up until this has first been done for the tribunes and the consul. At the second signal they load the baggage on to the pack animals, and at the third the leading maniples must advance and set the whole camp in motion.

The military habits of the eternal soldier change but little, for they are sustained by simple, orderly solutions which withstand the passage of time. The Roman method of dismantling camp provides yet another case in point.

In 1944, towards the end of the Burma campaign, I was adjutant of a Punjabi battalion, encamped with 5th Indian Division on the Brahmaputra plain. We had been engaged on active operations for three years or more and were now being pulled out to return to the North West Frontier. The instructions for breaking camp, contained in the battalion's 'Standing Orders for War', were almost identical to those described by Polybius. We were due to march out at 0800 hours. At 0745 hours, the orderly bugler sounded the battalion call, followed by a G. This was the signal for baggage to be loaded on to the trucks, which stood at the end of every company line. At 0750 hours the bugler sounded a further G: guy ropes were now pulled up, pegs removed and bagged and a sepoy stood inside each tent, holding the centre pole upright. I was standing at the main gate, together with my commanding officer and the Jemadar adjutant, when the third G was sounded. We watched with pride as our camp came down, as if felled by a single stroke. Where, a moment ago, a hundred tents had flowered, providing a home for 600 men, there was now only a flattened field, upon which, once the tents had been bundled and loaded, stood a battalion ready to march. The sergeant of the guard of the British regiment encamped opposite us watched the whole proceeding, expressing his admiration with uninhibited military frankness.

In the face of such similarities, and our lack of knowledge of specific trumpet calls employed by the Roman army, the *Signals by Bugle Horn* practised in 1798 by the newly evolving light infantry are worthy of note,[12] for they demonstrate the potential of this method of communication. The detailed signals described in this handbook were initially listed in a training manual written by a German officer of the 60th Foot, Baron de Rottenburg, and published in that year at the behest of the Commander-in-Chief of the Army, HRH the Duke of York, in 'order that the officers of the army at large may imbibe that degree of military skill and information, which will enable them to discharge their duty to the satisfaction of their superiors, and their own honour, on the most trying occasions'.

There was a total of sixteen calls including several indicating the sighting of a variety of enemy forces, others instructing troops to carry out pre-rehearsed movements, and one for the assembly of officers. In addition to this, the number of calls was greatly increased by the additional sounding of up to three Gs: one, to denote the right of the line; two, to indicate the centre; and three, the left. For example, two Gs sounded before the *Extend*, required the line to extend outwards from the centre; one G sounded before the *Close*, required the line to close on the right flank. Calls were based upon three principles: they should never be resorted to, except when the voice could not reach; they should be as few and uncomplicated as

The range of instructions possible to be passed by bugle (or trumpet) was well revealed by Sir John Moore's Light Troops in 1798

possible; and no movement should ever be executed until the last sound of the bugle horn had died away. Naturally, the weight of firepower with which an army in 1798 was equipped required formations to be deployed over wider areas. Buglers, therefore, addressed smaller units than would have been the custom in Roman times and the instruments themselves had, musically, been greatly developed over the intervening centuries.

The task which confronted Roman trumpeters can best be assessed by considering the circumstances of an actual battle. In 48 BC, Caesar confronted Pompey at Old Pharsalus in northern Greece with 80 cohorts, or 22,000 men under command.[13] Frontinus narrates that

> Gnaeus Pompey [110 cohorts or 45,000 men] drew up three lines of battle, each one ten men deep, stationing on the wings and in the centre legions upon whose prowess he could most safely rely, and filling the spaces between these with raw recruits. On the right flank he placed six hundred horsemen, along the Enipeus river, which with its channel and deposits had made the locality impassable; the rest of the cavalry he stationed on the left, together with the auxiliary troops, that from this quarter he might envelop the troops of Caesar.[14]

Pompey (Cn Pompeius Magnus), a powerful Roman general of the 70s and 60s BC and opponent of Julius Caesar in the Civil War, 50–48 BC

Against these dispositions, Gaius Caesar also drew up a triple line, placing his legions in front and resting his left flank on marshes in order to avoid envelopment. . . .

Caesar stationed the Xth Legion on the right of his line, with the IXth on his extreme left and, since the latter legion had suffered heavy casualties in the Dyrrachium battles, he reinforced it with the VIIIth. He distributed his remaining five legions in between them. He was heavily outnumbered by his enemy and we may thus expect that his lines were no greater than six ranks deep. His cohorts were barely 275 strong, as opposed to an established strength of 500 and Pompey's strength of some 400.

He gave command of his right wing to his general, Publius Sulla, the centre to Domitius Calvinus and the left wing to Mark Antony. Caesar positioned himself, in this instance, behind Sulla on the right wing, from where he could watch the movements of his antagonist, Pompey. He rarely pinned himself to any particular position in the field but generally sought a point of observation from where he might follow the cut and thrust of battle and send help to wherever it might be needed. Caesar quickly observed that enemy cavalry were concentrating together on Pompey's left and, to counter this move, he withdrew six cohorts from his third line and posted them out of sight behind his right wing cavalry and infantry.

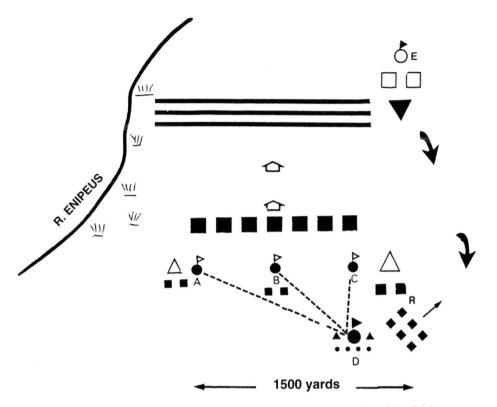

1500 yards

Notes: A. Left wing – commander, Mark Antony. B. Centre – commander, Domitius Calvinus. C. Right wing – commander, Sulla. D. Army commander, Julius Caesar, with supporting arms commanders, staff officers, trumpeters, gallopers etc. E. Enemy commander, Pompey. R. Right wing reserve, with concealed reserve of infantry to counter expected enemy cavalry charge.

Battle at Pharsalus, 48 BC (source: Caesar's War Commentaries, *ed. J. Warrington, III,*

This redeployment would have had no effect upon the width of his front of some 1,200 yards (1,500 yards if allowance is made for flanking troops) which, incidentally, if he had been at full strength, would have reached a distance of 1½ miles.

Caesar's positioning of himself during the Pharsalus battle is of interest. An army commander, according to Vegetius,[15] habitually took up his position in the set-piece battle, with his headquarters, on the right flank of the First Cohort of his right flank legion, and placed himself between this and his flanking cavalry. Customarily, he wore a scarlet cloak (as did Caesar) so that, wherever he might be dragged during the ebb and flow of the fighting, his whereabouts was clearly visible to the troops and, perhaps more importantly, to the junior formation commanders who looked to him for orders. Nearby, and to his rear, he held an élite reserve of horse and light infantry whose role was to manoeuvre into a position from which he could launch a crucial, wide flanking attack upon the right wing of his enemy. The logic behind this tactic was that the enemy held their shields on their left arms, thus exposing their right sides.

We may conjecture that the commander-in-chief's headquarters group was of considerable size. Apart from his personal escort, with standards, trumpeters and mounted orderlies, its numbers would have included mounted staff, specialist officers and liaison officers from his legions, together with others from the cavalry and reserve infantry. Only a selected few of these may be expected to have accompanied him when he chose to move around the battlefield, for too many would have been a hindrance. Mounted trumpeters, for obvious reasons, must have provided important members of this party.

The army's second-in-command was 'posted in the centre of the infantry to encourage and support them' and therefore, we may judge, he had a limited roving commission either side of his post. In case of need, he held a reserve 'of good and well-armed infantry', located clear, and thus to the rear, of the main body, ready to intervene whenever the situation might demand. Almost certainly, he would have been stationed, with his personal staff, standards and trumpeters around him, at the head of these reserves. His role, when the occasion arose, was to thrust through the ranks of infantry lined up in front of him and confront the enemy head-on.

The next officer in seniority, the third-in-command, likewise held in hand a reserve of cavalry and infantry and was posted to command and secure the left flank.

Each of these three men, as has been demonstrated, was stationed several hundred yards apart, in clear, predetermined locations, each with specific individual tasks and his own signal support but looking to his commander for overall guidance. It is thus of interest to compare their positioning, and the signalling requirements we have conjectured, with a similar disposition of commanders found in an action which took place during the crusade of Richard I and which has been recorded for us by Geoffrey de Vinsauf.[16] He relates that, in order to establish battlefield control of the allied force, 'it had been resolved by common consent that the sounding of six trumpets in three different parts of the army should be a signal for a charge', with variations for other phases of combat. In other words, the crusading army was seemingly employing the Roman system of battlefield communication by signals.

The scenario discussed above is not an extravagant view of the communications problem which would have confronted a Roman commander in the field. In the case of an army on the march, with baggage and a straggling animal train, it would no doubt have been greater. When an army was concentrated for defence, as during an incident in Caesar's campaign against the Helvetii in 58 BC, when he was driven to occupy a hill feature, it would have been less. The scale of the deployment of the enemy forces is also a very relevant factor. In 57 BC, when in conflict with the Belgae, Caesar estimated that the light of the enemy watchfires opposing him extended over a front of more than 8 miles. Whatever the eventuality, the solution lay in careful preplanning, an appreciation of the distances over which the trumpet calls were required to carry, the direction of the wind, the shape of the ground and a clear understanding of individual responsibilities within a command structure which, to modern military eyes, was not always as clear-cut as it might have been. Despite this, it proved remarkably effective.

We have already discussed in Chapter 1 the easy movement of top-ranking officers of the Roman army between civil and military posts during the course of their careers. In Republican times, commanders generally were consuls, supreme magistrates at Rome, who were given charge of the army on campaigns. In the imperial army, legion commanders were legates, ex-*praetores* who had in the past held military rank and were now appointed by the emperor to this elevated post. Each legate had a staff of six tribunes who, as we shall see, held a variety of appointments; their tasks were mainly administrative and they exercised no definite military command within the legion. The qualifications of consuls, legates and tribunes have already been well documented[17] and there is no need here to debate them further, except to add that the purpose of this strange mix of civil and military was, of course, designed to keep the hands of the soldiery away from dangerous meddling in political affairs.

Field Marshal Viscount Montgomery, notoriously intolerant of anything he considered to be potentially inefficient, has described the structure of the senior layer of command in the Roman army as 'a military nonsense'.[18] Julius Caesar seemingly held much the same view; he certainly displayed an undisguised mistrust of the worth of his tribunes. When his army, encamped at Besançon in Gaul, became unnerved by gossip about the courage, stature and the high military qualities of the German enemy soon to oppose them, he remarked that the unrest had begun 'with the military tribunes, the prefects of the auxiliary troops, and the men with little experience of war who had followed Caesar from Rome in order to cultivate his friendship'.[19] He appreciated the military risks inherent in nominating short-term politicos to command his legions and obtained authority to select and appoint his own legates. These were tough men with campaigning experience, excited by the opportunity to soldier with him and with no eye cast in the direction of Rome. It must be said, however, that while the early Republican system of appointing senior officers left much to be desired, it was greatly strengthened by the later reforms of Marius (104–102 BC) and Augustus (31 BC to AD 14). Due to these re-organizations, the Roman army achieved a peak of efficiency in the first and second centuries AD.

The mainstay of the Roman army was provided by the centurionate. These men, Polybius has told us,[20] were subjected to a meticulous selection procedure:

Romans look not so much for the daring or fire-eating type, but rather for men who are natural leaders and possess a stable and imperturbable temperament; not men who will open the battle and launch attacks, but those who will stand their ground even when worsted and hard-pressed and will die in defence of their posts.

In the event, they seem to have found veterans, intelligent, loyal, steadfast and tough, who were prepared to do both.

Customarily, centurions were hand-picked professional soldiers, promoted from the ranks after between fifteen and twenty years' service. There was also a fast-stream system of entry into the centurionate from men of selected property status, but the numbers involved were minimal. In modern terms, it is tempting to regard the centurion as a warrant officer platoon commander, a rank re-introduced in the British army prior to the Second World War but progressively abandoned later, as young commissioned officers became available. Clearly, the position of a centurion was more elevated than this, for a chosen few were regularly promoted to fill the appointment of *praefectus castrorum*, prefect of the camp in peace or war. In other words, the prefect of the camp commanded the modern equivalent of Rear Echelon, with responsibilities for its defence and a full range of other duties, more importantly including the administration of the sick, the maintenance of stores and weaponry, and the re-supply of forward units.[21] Occasionally, he was required to command troops in battle, a fact which underscored both his seniority and his recognized military ability.

The chief centurion of a legion was the *primus pilus*. He had the honour of commanding the first century of the First Cohort and had charge of the legionary eagle; he thus held a vital position in the chain of command, which, we may judge, would have enabled him to influence operational decisions. In the same manner, in Republican times, the senior centurion in each maniple had charge of the maniple standard and the senior centurion of the senior maniple commanded the cohort. In imperial days only vestiges of this arrangement remained for, by that time, centuries were recognized as individual units and the seniority of their respective commanders was strictly enforced.

Vegetius, in *Epitoma rei militaris*, provides a conflict of figures relating to the strength of the First Cohort but agrees, nevertheless, with the generally held opinion that, in the time of the Principate, it was twice the size of the other nine cohorts of a Roman legion. The reason for this differential has been widely debated and it has been speculated that the device may have been initiated to provide a home for the administrative staff and technicians of the legion.[22] This idea is not easily acceptable, for it would have been unusual to find specialists of this nature in the fighting line: their proper place would have been with the baggage train, under the hand of the *praefectus castrorum*.

The First Cohort, as with any other, was essentially a 'teeth' arm unit, which occupied the right of the line of a legion, traditionally the first target of an enemy attack. This flank was vulnerable since the soldiery bore their shields on their left arms, leaving the right side of their bodies unprotected. Additionally, the cohort would have accommodated within its ranks the legionary eagle and other images and, here, in its midst or close by, the legion commander would have stood with his command post and trumpeters. We may judge that the First Cohort of a legion, which had been granted the honour of being posted right of the line of an army in battle, had an even more important role, for it would have been linked to the commander-in-chief and was probably required to provide some of his needs, in the manner of a defence battalion with a modern divisional headquarters.

The standards of the legions had an important role to play in all this, and it is necessary here to consider their significance. To speak of a standard today is, for a layman, to speak of a distinctive banner, the royal standard, the colours of a regiment or, perhaps, the guidon of a cavalry regiment. The *signa* of the auxiliary,

Standard-bearer of XX Legion Valeria depicted by a member of the Ermin Street Guard

legionary and praetorian regiments of the Roman army bore no resemblance to these. The legionary standard, or *aquila*, in Republican times comprised a silver eagle mounted on a thick golden staff, the base of which was provided with a spike so that it might easily be plunged into the ground. Sometimes the staff was fitted with large projecting handles to enable it to be easily plucked out. The bird itself was traditionally shown with a golden thunderbolt gripped in its talons, its wings raised and its head cast forward, displaying its readiness for flight. On occasions, it was featured with its neck strongly bent to the left,[23] as if awaiting authority from the god, Jupiter, with whom it was closely associated, to speed ahead of the marching columns, to seek out and destroy their enemies and secure their advance. Not surprisingly, the Roman soldier regarded his legionary standard with considerable awe.

There is, of course, another reason why the eagle-standards of the legions would have been held in deep regard. In the manner of the colours of a British infantry regiment, surrounded by an aura of past achievements on historic battlefields, they symbolized their legion's valorous past and offered gallant promise for the future. Once consecrated, if they were damaged, however badly, they were not destroyed but repaired again and again, so that their 'life' might be preserved. The loss of an eagle-standard to the enemy, or in any other manner, was a shameful event. In 54 BC, the survivors of Sabinus's army, decimated by the Eburones, fell back to the base camp from which they had come. Lucius Petrosidius, the standard-bearer of the legion, seeing himself beset by a large crowd of Gauls, threw his eagle inside the rampart and died fighting heroically outside the camp. The rest had hard work to withstand the enemy's onslaught till nightfall; in the night, seeing all hope gone, every single man committed suicide. . . .[24]

When a Roman army was on the march, its standards were carried at the head of the legions (there was probably, as we shall see, also a military purpose in this). In camp, they were secured in a shrine of their own, while watch was kept over them as they stood, shaft planted in the ground, beside the altar. It is thus not surprising that they were superstitiously regarded as possessed of unusual powers. Germanicus,[25] so we are told by Tacitus, gained a decisive victory against the Cherusci on the Weser plain in AD 16, after having witnessed the 'splendid omen' of

eight eagles flying towards and into the forest. 'Forward,' he cried, 'follow the birds of Rome, the Roman army's protecting spirits!' The infantry attacked, and the cavalry, which had been sent ahead, charged the enemy's flank and rear.

The enemy host fled in the face of this inspired onslaught, suffering severe defeat, their bodies and weapons being scattered for 10 miles around. A further example of the veneration with which eagle-standards were regarded occurred in AD 41, when Furius Camillus Scribonianus, Governor of Dalmatia, declared civil war against Claudius and called upon the legions under his command to join him. They agreed to do so but the rebellion speedily collapsed when their 'standards resisted all attempts to pull them from the ground'.

In Caesar's day, the eagle was small enough, during one of his adventures, for him to have removed it and concealed it in his girdle.[26] In later years, the legionary standard was made entirely of gold, and the emblem was considerably larger. The staff which it surmounted frequently bore insignia, such as crowns or plates (*phalerae*), which recorded the battle honours and origins of the unit. Vegetius[27] informs us that the ancients

knowing the ranks were easily disordered in the confusion of action, divided the cohorts into centuries and gave each century an ensign inscribed with the number both of the cohort and century so that the men keeping it in sight might be prevented from separating from their comrades in the greatest *melees*. The centurions were distinguished by different crests upon their helmets to be more easily recognised by the soldiers of their respective centuries.

The standard of a maniple, or double-century, also comprised a staff, in this instance topped by an open hand with closed fingers outstretched upwards. It was decorated in vertical array by a wide range of devices representing crowns, half-moons and ships' prows, recording the prowess and origins of the unit in much the same manner as the eagle-standard spoke for the legion. The plates which adorned it, as Vegetius indicates, were probably engraved with the legionary number of the maniple and the number of its parent cohort. Polybius records that each maniple had two standard-bearers, selected from the ranks as being 'two of their bravest and most soldierly men'.[28] For this reason, it has been argued that each century of a maniple possessed its own standard but there is evidence to suggest that each maniple carried two standards: the first, already described, being held rather more for ceremonial duty; the second being a *vexillum*, a small banner of coloured linen, some 50 centimetres square, with a gold fringe on its lower edge and provided with a hem so that it could be affixed to a crossbar on the staff. A standard of this nature would have been much lighter to handle in the fore-front of a battle and, held high aloft, would patently have been easier to identify amid the hurly-burly of the fighting.

Cassius Dio, in his account of the crossing of the Euphrates by Crassus in 58 BC,[29] when the 'portents' were supposedly set against the Romans, provides us with interesting evidence that such an operational banner was carried at army commander level with the purpose, its size would suggest, of enabling his whereabouts to be quickly identified on the battlefield. Additionally, it may have been employed as a substitute for the eagle. Dio relates that the latter

> is found in all the enrolled legions, and it is never moved from the winter-quarters unless the whole army takes the field; one man carries it on a long shaft, which ends in a sharp spike so that it may be set firmly in the ground. Now one of these eagles was unwilling to join him in his passage of the Euphrates at that time, but stuck fast in the earth as if rooted there, until many took their places around it and pulled it out by force, so that it accompanied them quite reluctantly. But one of the large flags, that resemble sails, with purple letters upon them to distinguish the army and its commander-in-chief, was overturned . . . in a violent wind. Crassus had the others of equal length cut down so they might be shorter and hence steadier to carry. . . .

From the moment the signalled orders of the commander-in-chief to his legions had been transmitted, the responsibility for passing them onwards and downwards was assumed by sub-unit commanders. They achieved this by what Vegetius describes as the 'motions of the colours', that is to say, the coordinated movement of the various legionary standards, conveying such simple messages as 'halt', 'advance' and 'retreat'. This was common practice until the end of the nineteenth century, when a regiment's colours were still being used as a rallying point, or to indicate a general move into line, or control the rate of an advance or withdrawal. Colonel Galbraith of the 66th Foot, at Maiwand in 1880, attacked by a large army of Afghan tribesmen and holding aloft his regimental colour, rallied 190 officers and men to his side, all of different units, before falling mortally wounded. When he fell, it was snatched once more from the ground and raised high, so that others might see it and be attracted to it. So long as its colours flew, a regiment never died.

There were many Roman similarities to this behaviour, some of which have already been quoted above. In 55 BC, during Caesar's first invasion of Britain, the soldiers of the Xth Legion were hesitant about disembarking until the standard-bearer leapt ashore, holding his eagle aloft, and called upon his comrades to follow him. On another occasion, Caesar, after landing on the North African coast to confront

Labienus at Ruspina in 47 BC, observed that his infantry, which comprised some thirty cohorts arrayed in single line, were becoming disorganized as they ran forward to attack. They were, he noted,[30]

> exposing their flank as they advanced in pursuit of the cavalry too far from the standards, [and] were suffering casualties from the javelins of the nearest Numidians. . . . Accordingly, he had the order passed down the ranks that no soldier should advance more than four feet from the standards.

Thus, Caesar employed his standards to control the pace of his attack. Such a level of achievement could not have been attained unless standard-bearers had been trained to act in concert, to move at the same speed, to maintain a correct distance the one from the other and, we may judge, to dress by the right flank where their senior commander was located, with the First Cohort of his senior legion. By this means, the standards would have held together an unbroken front of advancing troops and would have maintained the line and direction of their assault. More than this, their use in this manner would have eradicated the fault of 'bunching', so often found in attacking infantry.

The fact that Caesar's order not to 'advance more than four feet from the standards' was passed verbally 'down the ranks' is also noteworthy, particularly since, as we have seen, the distances involved were not small. The attention attached by the Romans to this technique has been well underlined by Josephus.[31] In AD 65, as Governor of Galilee, he was preparing an army to resist an anticipated onslaught by Vespasian. He appreciated that his enemy's 'invincible might' was largely due to unhesitating obedience and practice in arms, the result of much training and great attention to detail. He determined to re-organize his army on the same model but recognized that the time available to him did not allow him the opportunity to reach a comparable standard of efficiency. For this reason, he made his mind up to concentrate on essentials. He compiled a brief list of training priorities which included instruction on 'how to pass on signals [and] how to sound the advance and the retreat'. The prominence he attached to the passage of signals is significant for, without doubt, it reflects the consideration given to this skill by the Romans themselves.

The value of pre-planning to simplify the performance of communications and, as a consequence, the tactical or administrative control of a force of whatever size, has already been mentioned. This principle is obliquely underlined in two accounts by Josephus of generals advancing to battle. He provides details of their order of march. In each case, trumpets and standards are grouped together at the head of the column, but his description of the order of march of Vespasian's army, as the latter set out from Ptolemia to invade Galilee, is the most complete and worthy of comment. Behind the vanguard, Josephus narrates,[32]

> rode Vespasian himself with the cream of his horse and foot and a body of spearmen. Next came the legionary cavalry; for each legion has its own troop of 120 horse. These were followed by the mules that carried the battering-rams and other artillery. After them came the generals, the prefects of the cohorts,

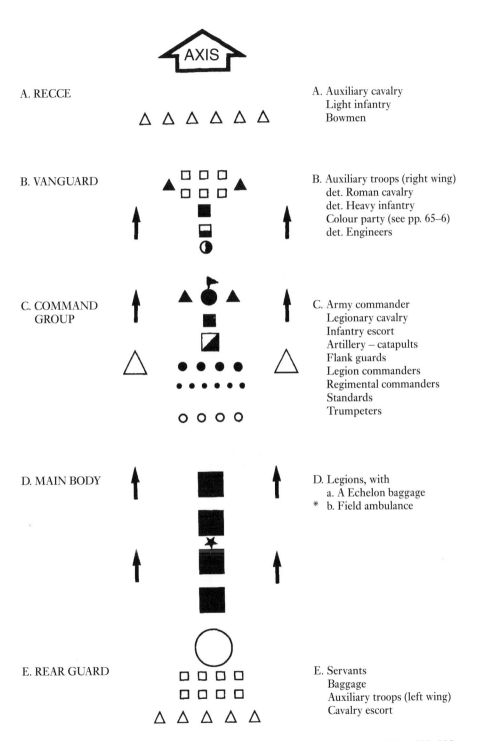

AXIS

A. RECCE

A. Auxiliary cavalry
   Light infantry
   Bowmen

B. VANGUARD

B. Auxiliary troops (right wing)
   det. Roman cavalry
   det. Heavy infantry
   Colour party (see pp. 65–6)
   det. Engineers

C. COMMAND
   GROUP

C. Army commander
   Legionary cavalry
   Infantry escort
   Artillery – catapults
   Flank guards
   Legion commanders
   Regimental commanders
   Standards
   Trumpeters

D. MAIN BODY

D. Legions, with
   a. A Echelon baggage
 * b. Field ambulance

E. REAR GUARD

E. Servants
   Baggage
   Auxiliary troops (left wing)
   Cavalry escort

Order of march of the Roman army, AD 70 (sources: Josephus, The Jewish War, *III, 110;
Polybius,* Rise of the Roman Empire, *VI, 335; Vegetius,* Epitoma rei Militaris, *III, 78)*

and the tribunes, with a bodyguard of picked troops, and behind them the standards surrounding the eagle which is at the head of every legion. . . . The sacred emblems were followed by the trumpeters, and in their wake came the main body, shoulder to shoulder, six men abreast. . . .

The presence of the generals, so far forward in the column, grouped and separated from their own formations, is significant. It is also notable that they were accompanied by trumpeters and marched in front of the standards 'surrounding the eagle which is at the head of every legion. . .'. It is thus conceivable that they had brought with them their own legionary eagles, standards and trumpeters. If so, this would not have been empty ceremonial, for the Roman army was an essentially practical organization. The eagle, standards and trumpeters formed a vital, functional part within a legion's operational headquarters and it is easy to regard them as inseparable from their commanding general. It is therefore probable that these senior officers, assembled together in attendance on Vespasian, were formed as an 'orders group', a practice strongly rehearsed as a British army battle drill in the opening months of the Second World War and one which remains operative to the present time.

This procedural drill was one by which officers commanding supporting arms, such as cavalry and artillery, and those commanding reserves or sub-units as yet uncommitted to the battle, either moved in proximity to their commander or assembled at a time and place designated by him, so as to be immediately available for a personal briefing whenever the situation might demand. It had many obvious advantages. It saved time and labour in despatching gallopers to call commanders forward; it enabled commanders, when being briefed, to view their allotted task through the eyes of their superior officer; it saved considerable time in assembly; and, if operated correctly, it enabled commanders, before departing to receive their orders, to send a preparatory warning to their units, setting matters in train against their return and yet again increasing the speed of operational movement. Standards and trumpets may be expected to have played their part in such a tactical deployment.

Thus, to sum up: the Roman army exercised tactical command of its troops and control of their movements by the use variously of trumpets, standards and, on occasion, by the passing of verbal messages through the ranks. The trumpets had two distinct functions: one, to deal with routine administration; the other, operational. Operational orders were always prefixed by the sounding of the *cornu*, thus imprinting the commander-in-chief's authority, and were then followed by the relevant call on the *tuba* and a consequent movement of the standards. Due to the mass of soldiers involved, battlefield areas were large and, for this reason or because of adverse winds or unsuitable ground, communications were not always easy to establish. Hence, it is likely that the volume of sound of the instruments was enhanced by employing groupings of them, probably at least six of each type. In the field, they would have operated to a network of relay 'stations', based on the headquarters of formations. It is not unlikely that each formation possessed its own identifiable 'call-sign'. We know little of the manner in which the trumpet calls were employed.

The simplest trumpet calls, as experience has almost invariably shown, are those where action has been pre-arranged. Indeed, it would appear that signals of this category provided the mainstay of the Roman communication system. A medley of calls are mentioned by Caesar in his histories. On one occasion, unable to contain the ardour of his troops in the assault, he claims he signalled them 'Good luck'; frequently he mentions signals to prepare for battle, to charge and to withdraw. Again, in North Africa, with thirty cohorts under command (roughly three legions), he 'gave orders for the line to be extended to its maximum length and for every other cohort to turn about, so that one was facing to the rear of the standards, while the next one faced to their front'.[33] Such complicated manoeuvres were almost certainly pre-rehearsed, if utter confusion were not to result, and, probably more often than otherwise, were executed by command of a trumpet. It is thus more than likely that a much larger range of trumpet calls existed than has been speculated above (see Appendix 2). The simplicity of the technique allowed scope for substantial enlargement.

In the above paragraphs we have discussed the importance attached by the Romans to efficient tactical communications, with the momentum and added control these offered to their military commanders in the field. We have not yet, however, mentioned the parallel strategic communications system which was to be found at government level and which allowed Rome control over the empire's client states and her armed forces in the field. Its prime task was to centralize control of defence and administration and to facilitate the collection of tribute from her dominions. Along an ever expanding network of roads, reaching to her furthest frontiers, this gave an edge to a policy of integrated diplomacy, supported by a broadly unobtrusive, outward-looking, military presence. Indeed, it has been argued that the decay and downfall of the old Republic was, in essence, brought about by the almost total absence of a proper, centrally coordinated communications policy, with the resulting dangerously loose control of ambitious, politically conscious officials.[34] Such communication service as then existed largely rested in private hands and, during the winter months, its operations were generally suspended.

When the emperor Augustus (31 BC to AD 14), ascended the imperial throne, he was quick to see the dangers presented by such laxness and at once set about establishing a national courier service, making progressive improvements to it as he gained experience from its operation. In the early days of his reign, so we are told by Suetonius,[35]

> he kept in close and immediate touch with provincial affairs by relays of runners strung out at short intervals along the highways; later, he organised a chariot service, based on posting-stations, which has proved the more satisfactory arrangement, because postboys can be cross-examined on the situation as well as delivering written messages.

The initial 'pony express' system, and later the chariot postal service, with missives being passed by postboys from hand to hand, enabled exceptionally long distances to be travelled in the course of a day. An example of what was possible is that of Tiberius who, upon the death of his brother, is said by Valerius Maximus[36] to have covered 200 miles in a day and a night; Plutarch[37] relates that Julius Caesar on one occasion travelled 100 miles a day for eight days in succession, driving in a hired *raeda*. Many historians are agreed[38] that a speed of 10 miles an hour, or 160 miles in 24 hours, would have been eminently achievable by the postal service had the requirement not developed for the courier to be cross-questioned on the news he was bringing. The effect of this was twofold. It became impossible for one individual to sustain such a rate of travel, over the distances involved, without adequate periods of rest: and the need emerged for the courier to be an informed staff officer of integrity, capable of making a sensible report. News of the mutiny of the IVth and XXIInd Legions in AD 69, for example, was carried a distance of 108 miles to Vitellius, commander of the Army of the Lower Rhine, by the standard-bearer of the IVth. A delay in transit was considered acceptable providing that someone with reliable background information delivered the despatch.

As the service developed, Augustus insisted that all despatches were signed, sealed and franked with the time of writing. This latter requirement was considered of the utmost importance so that a standard time in transit between places of origin and destinations might be developed for staff-planning purposes. A laurel attached to the despatch symbolized news of victory. A feather affixed to the spear of a messenger, indicating haste, was the insignia of disaster and carried with it an implicit instruction to 'clear the line' and to give the courier all possible assistance.

Procopius, the sixth-century Byzantine historian,[39] provides one of the rare statements defining the speed of travel of an imperial courier. It operated, he writes,

> according to the following system. As a day's journey for an active man they fixed eight 'stages', or sometimes fewer, but for a general rule not less than five. In every stage there were forty horses and a number of grooms in proportion. The couriers appointed for the work, by making use of relays of excellent horses . . . often covered in a single day, by this means, as great a distance as they would otherwise have covered in ten.

This is almost certainly an exaggeration. The yardstick of the postal service, of which Procopius provides us a clue, was that an active man should be able to cover an average distance of 50 miles a day, that is to say a journey of between five to eight 'stages' of roughly 8 miles, the number of stages being dependent upon the difficulty of the terrain to be traversed. Within every stage, forty horses were located at a *mutatio*, a posting-station, together with a proportionate number of grooms, from which relay teams might be selected. At every third stage a *mansio* was located, where night quarters might be obtained by travellers on the road. The distance between each *mansio* was a standard 25 miles.

The Romans made full use of river craft wherever suitably situated (see Chapter 6) but couriers were generally disinclined, if land alternatives presented themselves, to travel by sea because of the inconveniences and uncertainties involved. Ships' captains were reluctant to venture out in bad weather, when passages were uncomfortable and almost always dangerous; moreover, the absence of a compass often compelled sailors to follow the coastline, thus adding to the

Four-wheeled carriage, probably used for fast transportation

journey time. Many journeys, such as the 1,200 miles travelled to Britain by Claudius in AD 43, made use of all the elements of travel.[40] He was aware his presence would be required alongside Plautius when victory appeared imminent. A message would thus have been passed to him by the quickest means, probably a coded signal passed from hand to hand by relays of pre-positioned couriers. It may have taken some ten days to reach Rome. He is known to have set out at once. Sailing from Ostia, Suetonius tells us,

> Claudius was twice nearly wrecked off the Ligurian coast, and again near the Stoechades Islands, but made port safely at Massilia (Marseilles). In consequence he marched north through Gaul until reaching Gesoriacum (Boulogne); crossed the Channel from there; and was back in Rome six months later.

On his northward journey, hampered by the retinue which accompanied him, 'he marched north by road', making full use of pre-positioned animals, supplies, carriages and transport. On his return, it is likely that he made full use of the speed and comfort offered by the River Rhône, on its journey southward to the Mediterranean, through Lyons and the Roman river port at Arles.

A wide variety of vehicles were available for the use of travellers and couriers using the staging service. The most common were the *raeda* and the *cisium*. The former was a four-wheeled covered carriage, capable of fast movement and popular with groups of people with baggage. The *cisium* would have been ideal for courier work. It was a light cart, drawn by two horses, one in the shafts and the other, leading, on a trace, and capable of maintaining a steady 50 miles or so over 10 hours, with one or more changes of horses. The *cisium* was fitted with a single seat, broad enough to accommodate a driver and a passenger. During the late Roman Empire, the *carruca*, a luxurious travelling coach, was developed. It was fitted with a bed on

Two-wheeled cart, similar to some still used in Italy

which the traveller reclined during the day and slept at night. It is difficult to believe, however, that something similar was not available to Claudius on his march to Boulogne, northward from Marseilles.

The postal service envisaged by Augustus was an important instrument of healthy government, with signals and messages flowing strongly in each direction, to and from the extremities of the empire, along a secure and constantly maintained communications network. Procopius, on the other hand, has left us a description of it which emphasizes, rather, an inward, one-way flow, with hints of treachery and insurrection, more in keeping with the collapse of an empire. The system was the brain-child, he wrote,[41] of earlier emperors who

> in order to obtain information as quickly as possible regarding the movements of the enemy in any quarter, sedition or unforeseen accidents in individual cities, and the actions of the governors or other persons in all parts of the Empire, and also that the annual tributes might be sent up without danger or delay, had established a rapid service of public couriers throughout their dominions.

He was, of course, writing in the sixth century, having already glimpsed a vision of an empire in decline.

CHAPTER THREE

Supply Trains and Baggage

The main and principal point in war is to secure plenty of provisions and to weaken or destroy the enemy by famine. An exact calculation must therefore be made before the commencement of the war as to the number of the troops and the expenses thereto, so that the provinces may in plenty of time furnish the forage, corn and all other kinds of provisions demanded of them to be transported.

Vegetius, *Epitoma rei militaris*, iii, 71

However well an army may be motivated and led, whatever heights its standards of discipline and training may reach, unless its resources are adequate, available and properly managed, it will not achieve the victory it seeks. 'Time and opportunity may help to retrieve other misfortunes,' Vegetius reflected, 'but where forage and provisions have not been carefully provided, the evil is without remedy.'[1] This is not to say that there is no room for calculated administrative risk. There is probably no better example of the benefit of such, than the spectacular advance made by the British 21st Army Group which followed the Allied thrust across the Seine in September 1944, after a gruelling three months' fight to break out of its Normandy beachheads.

Montgomery, smarting under the undeserved reputation for slow movement he had gained during the battle of the 'hinge' at Caen, gave orders to his commanders that

any tendency to be sticky or cautious must be stamped on ruthlessly. . . . The proper tactics now are for strong armoured and mobile columns to bypass enemy centres of resistance and to push boldly ahead, creating alarm and despondency in enemy rear areas.[2]

Second Army's passage northwards, he emphasized, must be 'swift and relentless'. As a result, when British XXXth Corps under Horrocks reached the frontiers of Belgium, their advance (across ancient Gaul, incidentally) had been so rapid and penetrating that they were still dependent on supplies brought by road from Bayeux, 250 miles away. The Americans at Mons and Verdun were even further extended, over a distance of some 400 miles through Paris to Cherbourg, which, at that time, was the only major port in Allied hands. Along the axis of this latter route, the impressive 'Red Ball Express' delivered to United States forces a huge daily total of 7,000 tons of stores. Even so, this load amounted to barely two-thirds of what was needed to keep the American armies advancing. They were grinding to a halt through lack of petrol. Horrocks had similar logistical problems and might have been excused had he acted to seize one of the enemy-occupied Channel ports at Boulogne, Calais, Dunkirk or Zeebrugge. He did not allow himself to be tempted. Instead, he veered away from the coast to thrust directly and successfully for the greater prize of Antwerp, 70 miles distant. The city, with its harbours and strategically important sluice gates, fell into his hands intact.

The advantages were immediate and greatly beneficial. It was an operation of which Julius Caesar would have approved, for so many of his campaigning successes were similarly based on audacious planning and speed of movement, to a degree that experienced military historians have sometimes looked askance at his planning ability. Major General J.F.C. Fuller,[3] whose strong views on the Roman general as a soldier we have already noted, has left us in no doubt of his opinion that, because of this failing, Caesar's armies were inadequately fed. Had it been otherwise, he has argued, why should it have been necessary for Caesar to mention his supply problems to his reader at every turn?

In Gaul, at least, the answer may lie partly in the fact that, when he needed them most to be successful, the crops failed. The harvest in 54 BC was woefully poor on account of drought; two years later, for the same reason, it was little better. On the other hand, although the failure of the harvests may have contributed to Caesar's problems, the reason is more probably to be discovered in the strategy employed by his opponents. The Roman general, frequently deep in hostile territory, was fighting campaigns against a numerous enemy who saw great advantage in disrupting his opponent's supply lines and denying him sources of local food. Caesar records a clear instance of this policy in his *de Bello Gallico*, during the closing stages of the Gallic rebellion of 52 BC. Prior to the last great battle at Alesia, about 30 miles north-west of Dijon, the leader of his enemy, the doughty and gallant Vercingetorix, carefully spelt out to his cavalry officers the lines on which he wished the forthcoming operation to be conducted:[4]

We must strive by every means to prevent the Romans from obtaining forage and supplies. This will be easy, since we are strong in cavalry and the season is in our favour. There is no grass to cut; so the enemy will be forced to send out parties to get hay from the barns, and our cavalry can go out every day and see that not a single one of them returns alive. What is more, when our lives are at stake, we must be prepared to sacrifice our private possessions. Along the enemy's line of march we must burn all the villages and farms within the radius that their foragers can cover. We ourselves have plenty of supplies, because we can rely upon the resources of the people in whose territory the campaign is conducted; but the Romans will either succumb to starvation or have to expose themselves to serious risk by going far from their camp in search of food.

These, of course, were not the precise words used by Vercingetorix: in the custom of many ancient writers of the day, they were probably put into his mouth by Caesar and represented the military dilemma by which he was then confronted. It was Caesar's problem that his enemies, operating from the strength of interior lines, exploited a vigorous scorched-earth policy, making maximum use of their superior numbers of cavalry to deny him supplies, and constantly threatened his baggage trains. The loss of the baggage, with its valuable contents, if it had occurred, would have dealt him an unpleasant blow. It was his task to ensure that this did not happen.

However much care may be devoted to its defence, an army on the march is a vulnerable entity. Today, with the protection of fighter aircraft overhead, with mechanized troop carriers, speedy bulk-carrying road transport and all the advantages of air supply, important reserves of *materiel* and men may be retained in safe areas, distant from the immediate dangers of the battlefield, until required to be called forward.

Such an arrangement was rarely feasible during Caesar's Gallic campaigning, when control of local supplies was his ambition but often beyond his grasp. Of necessity, he was compelled to seek help from uncertain allies to feed his troops in the field and, simultaneously, build up reserves of grain to satisfy the demands of the coming winter season. He retained these reserves, together with any surplus baggage, within a nearby firm base, in towns such as Amiens, Nevers or Sens-sur-Saône, mostly riverine settlements it should be noted and generally located within Aeduan territory. He would then provide it with the protection of one or two of his weaker legions, in essence thus creating a rear headquarters. Now and again, according to the situation, he gave its command to a dependable general, such as Labienus, who regularly acted as his second-in-command. On other occasions, he employed a senior *quaestor* for this duty, an appointment broadly comparable in rank to that of quartermaster-general. Whoever he may have selected, it was invariably a man in whom he had wholehearted trust.

Two noteworthy examples of this tactic provide us with an idea of the wide variety of 'baggage' involved and also, despite the protection awarded to it, of its vulnerability. The first incident,[5] recorded in 54 BC, occurred when the Nervii launched a surprise and devastating attack upon Cicero's winter camp. Caesar determined, at once, to march to the assistance of his brother officer who, within a few years, was to be embroiled in a civil war, fighting alongside Pompey, against his commander-in-chief. Before departing from his Amiens headquarters, Caesar called forward Marcus Crassus, encamped nearby with his legion, and instructed him to take command, in his absence, of everything he was leaving behind, 'the heavy baggage, the hostages furnished by various tribes, the state papers and the whole of the grain that had been collected to last through the winter'.

The second example took place two years later, when the Aedui, until recently Rome's ally, raised the flag of rebellion and declared their allegiance to Vercingetorix. This happened at a moment when Caesar had already disposed of his heavy stores, with other encumbrances, and had placed them under military guard at Nevers, an Aeduan town situated in a strategic position on the River

Loire. The 'heavy baggage' on this occasion is listed as including all the hostages he held from the various Gallic states, as well as his stores of grain, public funds and archives, a large part of his personal baggage, with that of his troops, and a number of horses he had bought in Italy and Spain for use in the war. The Aedui took uncompromising advantage of Caesar's absence. They massacred the garrison, together with some Roman merchants, probably traders marching with the legions; they shared out the money and the horses; they carried away as much grain as they could transport and threw the remainder into the river; and they handed over the hostages to magistrates at Bibracte, an Aeduan settlement on nearby Mount Beuvray, 12 miles west of Autun.

Almost certainly, these lists of 'baggage' are substantially understated, for it would have been normal for many other items of men and *materiel*, not listed by Caesar, to have been found at a headquarters of this importance. These would have included ancillary troops, with numerous clerks, technicians and specialists, together with other items such as reserve tentage, weaponry, clothing and cavalry equipment: a field hospital, with medical staff and accompanying sick; probably a training ground, or *gyrus* for cavalry horses, with associated veterinary staff (*veterinarii*); engineering stores and bridging equipment; and artificers' workshops,

Trajan's 'artificers at work during battle'

in addition to those, or detachments of them, which may have been located forward, travelling with the main body of the field army.

Reserves of tentage and other associated stores not required on the line of march would have been substantial. Roman officers were uninhibited about the exercise of privilege; the tent of a centurion, in area 20 feet square, was twice the size of the *papilio* designed to house an infantry section of eight men. The tents of tribunes and others of comparative rank were taller structures, carried on box-like frames of poles and slats and paved with cut turf, and constructed to accommodate a dining table and couches. The marquee of a commanding general, occupying ground space 200 feet square, was likened by Josephus to a temple. Julius Caesar, always a man of character, impressed his guests by carrying around a mosaic floor in portable sections,[6] which he presumably used to embellish his tent in winter quarters.

Thus, many uncertainties surround the size and composition of a Roman baggage train. A prime example is the fluctuating ration situation, created by the success or otherwise of foraging expeditions, with its effect upon the transport requirement. How should one compensate for this? How many servants would have travelled with the train and how were they employed? How many sick? How many ambulance wagons? How many hostages, if any, with their attendants? How many tradesmen moved with the column, always ready to exchange money or barter for loot? How much loot, accumulated by officers and men, and what scale of transport should be allowed for it? And many other questions similar to these, all of which would affect our calculations. Now and again, in *de Bello Gallico* and

Oxen, as well as horses, were used for hauling transport carts carrying water and wine

other writings, there are lines which contain the hint of an answer to some of these points, but clear evidence remains elusive.

One such passage is to be discovered in Caesar's account of the fighting in 58 BC, a year which found him campaigning in eastern Belgium, north of Liège. He had separated his army into three divisions of three legions each and, commanding one of these himself, he despatched them on a widespread foray, probably a reconnaissance in force, combined with a search for grain, forage and loot. He gave orders for all to re-assemble within seven days at the old Roman camp at Atuatuca, the fortifications of which were still intact. He had selected it for this very reason and, here, he now deposited his heavy baggage. He provided the XIVth Legion to watch over it and placed Cicero in overall command, warning him not to risk leaving camp due to his limited strength. It proved an uneventful week, and the soldiery left behind were disgruntled at being confined within the fortification for apparently so little purpose. Then, when the return of the legions was expected within a matter of hours, Cicero released them. He was convinced, so we are told, that there was no good reason why they should remain cooped up any longer;[7] there was, of course, the added incentive that he was nearly out of food and forage:

> Accordingly he sent five cohorts to get corn from the nearest fields, which were separated from the camp by only a single hill. A number of sick men had been left behind by the legions: from these there went with the cohorts, as a separate detachment, some three hundred men who had recovered from illness during the week, and permission to accompany them was granted also to a large number of servants, who took out a great many of the animals that were being kept in the camp.

Some of the detailed facts we are seeking are concealed in these words. The 'number of sick', of whom by the end of the week some three hundred had recovered, makes it likely that, at the time of Caesar's departure, there was an overall total of some four to five hundred casualties in the camp, a figure which would suggest the presence of a field clearing station, with carts, wagons and animals for medical stores and ambulances. But of even greater interest is the mention of 'a large number of servants' who, 'with a great many animals', left the fortification to accompany the cohorts to nearby fields, doubtless seeking fodder. The number of servants, their origins and the manner of their employment, is a subject to which we return below, for it contains a considerable and largely unappreciated manpower commitment.

The vulnerability of a marching column increases in direct proportion to the size of its baggage train. If the latter is needlessly unwieldy, it makes extravagant demands upon defence resources and detracts from the strike power of the fighting troops. It is an intriguing comment that Caesar, although he frequently mentions the wheeled transport operated by the enemy, rarely writes of using any himself. It may be that, in his yearning for surprise, speed and mobility, he depended upon the pack mule, at least for his first line transport. If so, he would have held the same view as Philip of Macedonia, who forbade wagons to be used by his army.[8] Philip, as well as Alexander the Great, saw them as a brake upon his movement and a tempting dumping place for unauthorized baggage, thus adding to his administrative burden. Indeed, Alexander, in his great march across Iran and Afghanistan to India, ordered all carts and their surplus contents to be burnt, beginning with his own. However, this is not to say that Caesar would have behaved as radically as this, for his light-weight general duty carts were employed in many valuable ways and were, moreover, capable of moving at 4 m.p.h.,[9] a speed which would have more than competed with that of the average infantryman.[10]

The logistical needs of Caesar's army in Gaul were a direct reflection of its size and composition. It is therefore necessary, before we go further, to determine how large it might have been.

In 58 BC, in the weeks prior to his campaign against the Helvetii, Caesar hastily put together a force of six legions, of which three had been summoned from winter quarters at Aquilea, a town in Cisalpine Gaul, at the head of the Adriatic; two had been newly raised in Italy and one was already occupying a defensive position, under the ubiquitous Labienus, between Geneva and Jura. Within a short time he increased this number to eight and his infantry corps remained virtually unchanged at this level throughout his campaign, except for its closing months when he called together fourteen legions to give him the decisive victory which, by then, he so desperately sought. He regularly deployed two of his less experienced legions to safeguard his rear headquarters, with its supply base.[11]

Caesar's cavalry wing was rarely more than four to five thousand strong and

A Roman auxiliary cavalryman: note the absence of stirrup irons

was mainly raised from Provence, from his allies the Aedui and other minor tribes associated with them. Occasionally, he acquired the additional help of a few hundred high-quality German cavalrymen. In the manner of the Pathans on the North-West Frontier of India in more recent years in their wars with the British, they fought for him with as much ferocity as they occasionally fought against him.

Fuller,[12] who queried the adequacy of Caesar's supply arrangements, has also questioned why Caesar, throughout a campaign which lasted several years, felt compelled to requisition between four and five thousand Gallic horsemen from chieftains whose good faith he held under grave suspicion. The answer, as previous Roman commanders would have discovered, for since the days of Marius (d. 86 BC) cavalry had ceased to be recruited from Roman citizens, is almost certainly logistical. By raising cavalry support in this manner, he was saved the tasks of recruiting, training and providing equipment; the tribesmen provided their own horses and doubtless found their own remounts; and, during the winter months, being generally unrequired, they returned to their homes and were removed from the ration list. Nevertheless, as events proved on at least one occasion, they were liable to recall.

There was also a hidden bonus. Horses, particularly cavalry animals, were ridden hard during the campaigning season and, as is normal in war, where days of plenty intermingle with days of famine, we may expect they received scant rations and were in poor condition on their return home. By this means of raising

Cavalry scouts depicted by the Ermin Street Guard

cavalry, with its 'yeoman' flavour of recruitment, the responsibility of coming back next year with an animal of renewed fitness now rested with the owner of the horse, and the Roman *quaestor*, upon whom it might otherwise have devolved, was relieved of an onerous and expensive administrative task. The savings in men, money and *materiel* must have been considerable and it would not be surprising to learn that Caesar filled many of his other transport needs in a similar manner.

For maximum efficiency, Caesar's transport would have been divided into three operational echelons:

* A Echelon, containing first line transport such as wagons (if any), carts and pack animals supporting the army in the field.
* B Echelon, or second line transport, such as wagons, carts and pack animals (both of the latter as required) operating between rear headquarters and the army in the field, ferrying supplies and stores to forward areas and returning with wounded, salvaged weaponry etc., in otherwise empty wagons.
* C Echelon, or third line transport, mainly grain wagons, plying between rear headquarters and/or the field army. River transport may also have been found in this category (and occasionally with B Echelon).

First line transport requirements of a legion are imprecisely known but we can arrive, with a broad degree of accuracy, at a total of some 1,250 horses/mules per legion for non-comestible items. This calculation is based on a scale of one pack animal per section of eight men (*contubernium*),[13] carrying its tent, mill, kettle, with other items of kit and tools; one two-wheeled cart per century, drawn by two horses or mules, for the artillery piece (*carroballista*); another two-wheeled cart, also drawn by two animals, for each century, perhaps to carry the centurion's tent and luggage, but possibly to take unwanted equipment from the soldiery when fighting was about to commence. To these totals should be added a detachment of 120 Roman cavalry (the normal legionary complement) and some 250 animals to cover the demands of staff officers, the ambulance and other supporting services. For an army of six legions, this figure would multiply to 7,500 horses or mules.

In order to calculate the total of first line pack animals required for the carriage of grain, without taking account of the requirement for animal feed, we need to be told how much would have been carried on the man and how much would have moved with column reserve. Livy, in an account of the war against the Aequians,[14] describes how soldiers brought with them five days' 'bread ration'. Let us, therefore, take, for purpose of discussion, an arbitrary allocation of five days' rations carried on the man, with a further ten days' reserve carried by pack transport. This would have called for 15 lb of grain to be carried by each man, with an additional and, it must be said, an improbable 5,625 pack animals to carry the column reserve. A more feasible solution would have been for each man to carry ten days' rations (30 lb), and for a further two days' reserve to be carried by pack transport. If these latter rations were the first to be consumed, an important reserve of 1,250 pack animals (the equivalent of 112 wagons)[15] would thus have been created for the transport of 'windfall' grain stocks foraged from the surrounding countryside.

It will be evident that these figures are, as yet, incomplete; nevertheless, it is already apparent that baggage animals in this quantity, moving through potentially hostile territory and with precious cargoes, would have been very likely to scatter in an emergency unless they were tightly controlled (see Appendix 2, note (e)). The majority of their loads would have been specialized, frequently needing quick identification, and for them to be even temporarily lost amid several thousand animals would have been administratively intolerable. Moreover, if the army commander was looking for a speedy and disciplined advance, then they must have been led by hand. The task of a muleteer has been described by the joint authors of a splendidly humorous book, *Jungle, Jungle, Little Chindit*, published in 1944. Any soldier who served in the 1942–45 Burma Campaign will readily identify with its sentiments and vouch for its truth:[16]

The mule man, mule-leader or muleteer looks after one mule, its saddle and harness. He must feed it, water it, wash it, groom it, keep its outfit clean, see that its load, when on, is properly tied and balanced, prevent it from becoming galled, broken-winded or lost, haul it up when it goes rolling down the mountain side, run after it when it runs away and take care that in harbour it stands in a space carefully cleared of rustling leaves and does not stamp on the face of nearby sleepers. Apart from these little jobs, and a certain amount of marching and fighting and attending to his own personal needs, his time is his own. . . . He will find that his mule responds kindly to attention and that mules, especially when tired, are not necessarily stubborn and do not necessarily kick (at least not very hard).

But whose was the responsibility for this task? Was this the role of the servants? It will be recollected that Caesar, recounting the ambush set up by the Eburones at Atuatuca, remarked that servants authorized by Cicero to leave camp took 'a great many' animals with them, presumably to forage for fodder and grain. Vegetius, in his *Epitoma rei militaris*,[17] likewise associates servants with the task of handling 'baggage' animals. The ancients, he writes,

were very careful that the servants or followers of the army, if wounded or frightened by the noise of action, might not disorder the troops. . . . They ranged the baggage, therefore, in the same manner as the regular troops under particular ensigns. They selected from among the servants the most fit and experienced and gave them command of a number of other servants and boys, not exceeding two hundred, and their ensigns directed them where to assemble the baggage and the troops. . . .

Julius Caesar, on the other hand, has described an incident which occurred during his conquest of the Belgae in 57 BC,[18] when he was setting up a marching-camp under difficult conditions. The servants, he tells us, 'had gone out to plunder', deeming that all was safe to do so, when they were alerted to danger by 'shouting and din [which] arose from the drivers coming up with the baggage'.

From these words, and the remarks of Vegetius above, we may judge that servants and drivers alike were both involved with the task of animal handling, the former because of their duties as servants to the military, the latter in a more general manner, perhaps as drovers of groupings of animals. As far as the servants are concerned, we can look for an example of their employment to Philip of Macedonia, justly famed in ancient times for his strict logistical discipline. He not only forbade the use of wagons in the army, but restricted numbers of servants to a scale of one for every ten infantrymen and one for each cavalryman, in the latter case for the purpose of carrying his hand mill and other equipment. Presumably this freed the horseman for the important task of looking after his animal and for other duties. If we take this as a yardstick, therefore, it would seem reasonable to assume that each *contubernium* (eight men) was provided with a servant to look after the section mule, making a total of 600 servants for this purpose within a legion, regardless of the needs of other ancillary troops,[19] making an estimated total of some thousand servants per legion on the basis of one servant per animal. The drivers, as general duty handlers with no other specific role, in a modern army would probably have been allocated two pack animals per man,[20] but in this instance would probably have been expected to cope with many more (but see below and Chapter 4, pp. 75–7).

The final requirement in assessing the size of a baggage train is the difficult matter of the horse feed. In peaceful times, a horse or mule may be expected to consume some 20 to 24 lb of dry fodder a day, but this would have been an unlikely scale in the field where hard feed, under combat conditions, would have been difficult to find.[21] At the very least, the animal would have needed five hours' or more good grazing, depending upon its temperament, always assuming the grass was sufficiently lush. Moreover, with the large numbers involved, the area of grazing would have needed to be extensive. Without doubt, feeding their animals on operations must have presented Roman planners with a considerable problem and their answer to it, without adding considerably to an already high transport commitment, is not easy to identify. An inkling of a solution is revealed by Caesar when he tells of the administrative difficulties he overcame in his pursuit of the Helvetii in 58 BC.[22] Due to the cold weather, grain in the fields had not yet ripened and there was an insufficient supply of hay. The Aedui, who had undertaken to re-supply him, had failed to do so and, an added complication, his enemy had swung away from the river rendering 'the grain that he had brought up the Saône of little use' to him. It thus appears that Caesar's second and third line transport, suggested above, justifiably included river craft.

This is a very significant revelation for, if he were making use of river transport (and, from this evidence, he was) then many of his logistical problems would have been resolved, including, importantly, the delivery of grain and hay for those of his animals which, by nature of their duty, were pinned to the column on the march. Linking the column with such a river supply base could have provided a task for the 1,250 reserve 'ration' mules we visualized above. The cavalry, on the other hand, widely deployed in a protective screen around the army on the march, and penetrating deeper into the surrounding countryside than the transport animals would have found possible (they could have covered 40 miles in a day) would have had ample opportunity to forage for themselves.

Relief from a funeral monument found at Neumagen, in Germany, showing barrels of wine being transported in a rowing barge. The steersman is clapping his hands, beating time for the oarsmen

But what were the sources of Caesar's grain supply and how did it reach him? To find the answers to these questions we must return to the commencement of his campaign.

Rome, for some years before Caesar's invasion of Gaul, had established friendly relations with the tribes of Transalpine Gaul, particularly the Aedui, an important tribe, but one whose influence was beginning to wane. In 61 BC the Aedui were defeated in battle by their neighbours, the Sequani, and, in the ensuing peace negotiations, were persuaded to cede to their enemy the right, which until now they had enjoyed unquestioningly, of collecting tolls on the River Saône. They appealed to Rome, as a result of whose intervention their privileges were quickly restored and the friendship which already existed between the two peoples was thus strengthened. In 58 BC Caesar was already looking ambitiously in the direction of Gaul, when the great western emigration of the Helvetii in that year provided him with the opportunity he was seeking, for the Helvetii, having passed through the Sequani homeland, now invaded Aeduan territory. The Aedui, 'unable to protect themselves or their property . . . sent to ask Caesar for help, pleading that they had always been loyal to Rome and that it was not right to allow their land to be ravaged almost under the eyes of his army'.[23]

Caesar quickly disposed of the matter of the Helvetii and next marched to the aid of the Sequani, whose territory was suffering under occupation by Ariovistus, a German warlord with clear ambitions to extend his influence south of the Rhine. He was persuaded by Caesar to withdraw and the latter then turned to cast his eyes elsewhere. As their Roman ally's appetite for conquest increased and his demands for supplies grew heavier, the Aedui began to question whether it was not better to be under the heel of a fellow Gaul than that of a Roman conqueror. Caesar complained that the Aedui kept putting him off from day to day, saying that grain was being collected, was in transit, was on the point of arriving, and so forth. When he saw there was going to be no end to this procrastination, and the day on which the soldiers' rations were due was approaching, he summoned the numerous chiefs who were in the camp . . . [and] reprimanded them severely for failing to help him at such a critical moment, when the enemy was at hand and it was either to buy corn or to get it from the fields.[24]

Despite their evident doubts, the Aedui and the Sequani, particularly the former, appear to have remained Caesar's principal suppliers, although, during the ebb and flow of the war, there were others further afield, such as the Veneti, who were occasionally called upon to provide this levy. The Aedui and Sequani appear not only to have transported supplies to Roman rear bases, but also to have delivered direct to the army in the field. This becomes evident during Caesar's narrative of his encounter on the Alsace plain with Ariovistus. The two armies were encamped, confronting each other, when the German general emerged from his defences to march his army around Caesar's assembled legions, and take up position 2 miles further on, 'with the object of intercepting grain and other supplies that were being sent up from the Sequani and the Aedui'. Again, in 52 BC, during the opening weeks of the rebellion led by Vercingetorix,

Caesar advised the Aedui to forget their disputes and quarrels and allow nothing to distract them from the war they had on hand. They might look forward to receiving from him the rewards they deserved when the conquest of Gaul was completed. In the meantime, they must send him without delay their cavalry and ten thousand infantry to be distributed at various places for the protection of his convoys.[25]

We can only conjecture the extent to which the Aedui used river craft to supply Caesar's legions but the location of their territory, adjoining the Auvergne region and largely comprising present-day Burgundy, would have rendered them well sited to exploit the far-reaching waterborne transport system this offered to them. The *departements*, which today provide the boundaries of this fertile wine-growing district, read like a gazetteer of famous French rivers, with their tributaries. To the north lies Seine-et-Marne, Aube and Haute-Marne; to the east Haute-Saône, Jura and Ain; to the south Rhône, Loire and Allier; and to the west Cher and Loiret. Thus the Aeduan homeland was not only prosperous and fertile, it was also one of considerable strategic importance, because of its location as well as for the great many rivers which fanned out from it, flowing westward to the Channel and southward to the Mediterranean Sea. Their employment of the waters of the Saône has already been mentioned. It would have been strange indeed if this important facility had passed unnoticed by the astute Julius Caesar in his journey of conquest.[26]

The vulnerable and unwieldy nature of a baggage train is self-evident. Nevertheless, it must also be admitted that, being unaware of a clear method of

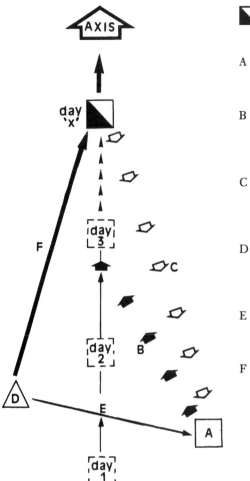

Field Army on the march

A   Rear HQ, frequently doubling as winter stores depot

B   Reinforcements, remounts, ordnance stores and weapon replacements moving forward to Field Army

C   Sick and wounded, with salvaged stores and weapons, returning to Rear HQ in empty transport wagons or rivercraft

D   Main supply source, either home base or tribal/client state

E   Winter rations being accumulated at Rear HQ during campaign season

F   'X' days rations being periodically delivered to Field Army direct from food supply source, probably under tribal escort

Supply technique employed by Caesar in Gaul, 58–51 BC

handling it, we tend rather to look at the great number of animals and stores which comprised its content and to ignore the discipline of organization which the Roman military command must have imposed upon it. Vegetius provides us with a hint of its shape when he wrote his line that the 'ancients ranged the baggage in the same manner as the regular troops under particular ensigns'. The latter, each in charge of a specific grouping, would have looked to the *quaestor* for their instructions. He, in his turn, would have received his orders from the commanding general. From this we may judge that, when transport was massed on the march or for active operations, legions and legionary sub-unit groupings would have been kept intact, even down to cohort level, if not below. By this means, the transport and baggage of any sub-unit could readily have been detached for duty with it should this, at any time, have proved necessary.

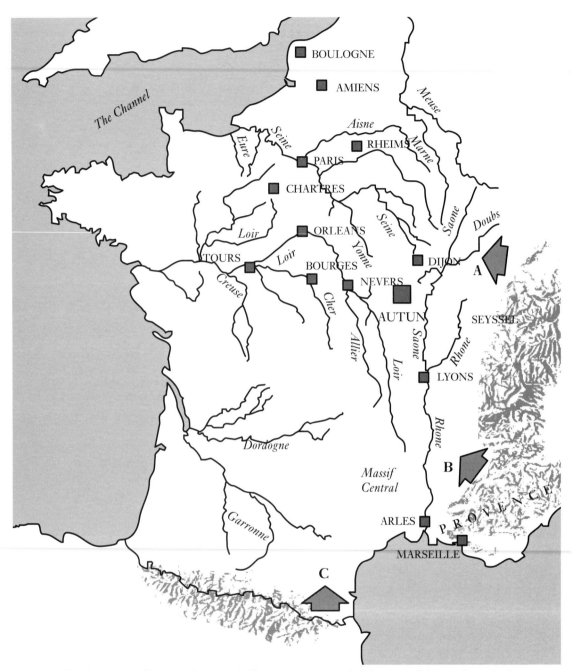

This sketch map illustrates the strategically important watershed location of Autun, the capital city of the Aedui, Caesar's allies and main food supply source. The arrows indicate the traditional invasion routes into Gaul. Caesar's legions entered Gaul broadly along the axis of arrow A

TABLE 1
BAGGAGE ON THE MARCH

		Pack Animals		Distance (a)	
		Legion	Army (b)	Legion	Army
REAR GUARD:					
!. Carts					
– artillery 60					
– centuries 60					
– sundry 30	Total 150	300 (c)	600	750	1,500
2. Ration reserve		125 (d)	1,250	625	3,125
3. General Duty		950	7,500	2,375	19,000 (e)
Total		1,375	9,350	2,875	23,625 (f)
MAIN BODY (b):					
4. Carts					
– artillery 60					
– centuries 60					
– sundry 30	Total 150	300 (c)	1,800	750	4,500
		1,675	11,150	3,625	28,125

NOTES: (a) Distance shown in yards: estimated 15 feet per animal, 30 feet per cart: animals and carts two abreast. (b) Based on an army of six legions with main body, two with rear guard. (c) Two animals per cart. (d) Estimated allocation of ration reserve. (e) GD transport for eight legions. (f) Rear Guard transport approximately 13.5 miles: Main Body transport 2.5 miles: servants/animal handlers included in space allowed for animals: overall transport 16 miles.

TABLE 2
FIELD ARMY'S GRAIN REQUIREMENT FOR ONE DAY (a)

	Numbers	Rations	Animals	Grain (b)
Personnel	37,500	3 lb		50
Cavalry				
– Gallic (c)		3.5 lb	4,000	6
– Roman (d)		3.5 lb	720	1
Reserve animals		3.5 lb	1,250 (e)	2
Baggage animals		3.5 lb	7,500 (e)	12
Servants	6,250	3 lb		8
Total	43,750	20 lb	13,470	79 tons

NOTES: (a) Cavalry wing 4,000, legionary troops 30,000, ancillary troops 3,500, Total 37,500. (b) To the nearest ton in each case. (c) animals only: see note (a). (d) But cavalry horses could well have been self-sufficient: see text p. 50. (e) Total baggage animals = 8,750.

Table 1, which is based on the baggage needs of an army of six legions, with ancillary and supporting troops, and consolidates the figures we have already discussed in the above paragraphs, reveals a conservative requirement of 8,750 transport animals. In these calculations some major assumptions have been made, namely, that the cavalry would have provided their own grain and forage; and that transport animals would either have found adequate grazing and foraged grain, or that feed would have been brought forward to them from the army's rear (perhaps riverine) supply base. Table 1 thus provides a minimum situation and reveals that the baggage element of an army of this size, with transport animals marching in pairs and carts moving singly, would have extended over a distance of some 12½ miles, a figure which compares reasonably with other notable instances. In the Boer War, for example, General Oliver's army of 6,000 men, together with its baggage train, is said to have extended on the march over a distance of 24 miles.[27]

It is thus not surprising, for this reason and because of the military value of the supplies they carried, that baggage trains provided such attractive targets for the enemy and were so keenly defended. A typical incident occurred in 52 BC, when Caesar was marching through the territory of the Lingones to the support of his provincial troops. Three divisions of cavalry under the Gallic leader Vercingetorix, who had been watching his progress carefully, descended upon his column. Of these, two threatened his flanks, while the third took up a position across his path to deny his vanguard further advance. Caesar split his cavalry up in a similar manner and

> ordered them to advance against the enemy. Simultaneous engagements took place all along the column, which halted and formed a hollow square with the baggage inside. If Caesar saw the cavalry in difficulties, he moved up some of the infantry and formed line of battle, which hindered the enemy's pursuit and encouraged the cavalry by assurance of support. . . .[28]

When we recognize the size of the baggage train, together with the distances involved, we can only admire the standards of training and the obvious military skills which permitted such a coordinated and controlled response.

CHAPTER FOUR

Marching-camp Techniques

The importance of [fortifying camps] appears not only from the danger to which troops are perpetually exposed who encamp without such precautions, but also from the distressful situation of an army which, after receiving a check in the field, finds itself without a retreat to which to retire and consequently at the mercy of the enemy.

Vegetius, *Epitoma rei militaris*

The ability to switch from the defensive to the offensive and back again is fundamental if flexibility is to be retained.

The British Military Doctrine[1]

Roman troops on campaign constructed a defended camp at their resting place each night, within which they accommodated, in a carefully detailed and pre-arranged manner, the headquarters, tented lines, animals, followers and baggage of whatever sized formation may have been concerned. Frontinus[2] claimed that they developed the idea after defeating Pyrrhus on the Arusian Plains (*c.* 275 BC), capturing his camp and noting its design. Today, a camp of this nature is referred to by historians as a Roman marching-camp.

Despite the numerous campaigns waged by the Romans on mainland Europe, the remains of only a few of the great number of marching-camp sites which, at one time, must have existed on the continent are still to be found; even those identifiable by crop marks are in scant supply. In Britain, however, particularly England and Scotland, the situation is vastly different. Due to the enthusiasm of eighteenth- and nineteenth-century amateur archaeologists, a survey of Roman camps was commenced at a very early date and, possibly encouraged by this, but certainly stimulated by aerial reconnaissance, the rate of discovery has accelerated in the past forty-five years. Almost three-quarters of the approximately four hundred sites which are known to exist have been recorded during that period.

The marching-camp was an instrument of aggression as much as of defence and it played an essential part, at least down to the third century, in Roman military thinking. It was specifically designed for operations deep in hostile territory. Its standard pattern of layout, which varied according to the size and nature of the forces it accommodated, was important for three reasons. Firstly, and primarily, it offered a secure base from which to continue the advance or, more specifically, the thrust towards conquest; secondly, it provided entrenchments upon which to retire in the event of receiving 'a check in the field'; and, thirdly, the daily construction of the marching-camps left in the wake of the army a series of fortified 'stepping-stones' by means of which the advance could be sustained. Clausewitz, in his day one of the greatest and most original writers on the subject of war, indirectly gave support to the technique. Even under the most favourable circumstances, he wrote,[3]

> and with greatest moral and physical superiority, the aggressor should foresee a possibility of great disaster. He therefore must organise on his lines of operation strong points to which he can retreat with a defeated army. Such are fortresses with fortified camps or simply fortified camps. . . . We must leave behind us a number of troops for the occupation of these strong points as well as the occupation of the most important cities and fortresses. Their number depends on how much we have to be afraid of invasions or of the attitude of the inhabitants.
>
> Napoleon always took great care with these measures for the protection of the rear of his army and, therefore, in his most audacious operations, risked less than was usually apparent.

The concept of the marching-camp fitted comfortably into this strategy, for even when the fortification served no immediate further operational purpose, it still lay available for re-occupation should the military situation require.[4] It was also invaluable in yet another sense. Its layout and construction were ideally contrived to provide a battle drill of operational and administrative behaviour which melded efficiently with the excellent Roman qualities of high military training and discipline.

Clausewitz, when advocating the merits of military theory, observed that it existed so that it should not be necessary to start afresh every time, sorting out the raw material on each occasion and ploughing through it. If theory could be formulated and implanted in the mind of a future commander, he argued, then it would always be ready to hand and in good order. The Romans, with their tactical employment of the marching-camps and other such operational devices, demonstrated that careful planning, with constant rehearsal in the field, leads likewise to a similar but, in this instance, practical end, with every man being aware of what is required of him at every moment. The situation, wrote Caesar, describing a near disaster which confronted him in 57 BC,

> was saved by two things: first, the knowledge and experience of the soldiers, whose training in earlier battles enabled them to decide for themselves what needed doing, without waiting to be told; secondly, . . . the generals did not wait for further orders but on their own responsibility took the measures they thought proper.[5]

Scene from Trajan's Column showing tents within a fortified enclosure

Major General J.F.C. Fuller (d. 1966), a fervent apostle of mobile tank warfare, and one whose preaching in this connection was fully justified by the events of the Second World War, regarded the Roman use of the marching-camp with less than enthusiasm. So completely did the spade dominate tactics, he once complained,[6] that the legions seldom accepted battle unless there was an entrenched camp close at hand; indeed, he continued, this occurred to such a degree that not a few Roman campaigns might be described as nothing more than mobile trench warfare. It was his conclusion that the lack of mobility induced by this practice rendered the legionary system unsuited against guerilla warfare. He was, of course, correct in thinking this and there were instances (for example, Viriathus in Spain in 146–140 BC and Scapula's campaign against the Silures in Wales, *c*. AD 50) when the Roman heavy infantry did not perform well in the face of this type of operation. Fuller saw the solution to their difficulties in the provision of a strong, well trained Roman cavalry wing, the many logistical problems for supporting which we examine in detail in these pages.

Undoubtedly, the tribal armies that confronted the Romans during their years of conquest possessed not only the crucial advantage of fighting a war on interior lines, but also a unique knowledge of the topography of their homelands, together with a considerable superiority in numbers. It is thus fair comment to wonder why, with these major benefits and an adaptable tribal command structure, the continental tribes did not turn whole-heartedly to guerilla warfare as a means of defeating their enemy, in the manner that Cassivellaunus used so successfully against Caesar in Britain in 54 BC.[7] The fact remains, however, that they failed to do so and, as a result, the legion remained an effective instrument of conquest. Was Fuller right in his judgment about the consequence of the Roman lack of cavalry? It is difficult to agree with his verdict, particularly when he himself has provided us with good reason to suggest otherwise, by his observation that

> a collateral factor which favoured the expansion of the empire was that, except in Parthia and to a lesser extent in Numidia, the legionaries were never, until toward the end of Rome's supremacy, called upon to face efficient cavalry.[8]

In these circumstances – rarely called upon to face guerilla war, never called upon, until the end of Rome's supremacy, to face efficient cavalry – there is little to indicate that the Roman system of war was incorrectly balanced. Indeed, it may be said that the strategy of the marching-camp, or mobile trench warfare as Fuller so aptly defined it, provided a stability in logistical and military terms which in other ways would have been difficult to contrive.

This, then, in broad terms, was the technique of the marching-camp; let us turn now to the practical application of the concept and its various uses, but particularly as a 'crash' defensive tactic to restore a deteriorating situation and as an instrument of attack.

Two comprehensive descriptions of the construction of marching-camps have been passed down to us, one written with great clarity by Polybius,[9] the other by Vegetius.[10] Both accounts contain valuable information and complement each other. Vegetius underlines the importance of selecting the location of the fortification with care. It should not be overlooked by high ground which might be exploited by an enemy; it should be 'topographically strong'; plenty of wood, forage and water should be accessible; and the 'dimensions of the camps must be determined by the number of troops and quantity of baggage' but, whatever size these may be, they should neatly fit within the perimeter provided for them. To be too small would hamper the defence; to be too large would be unwieldy.

The standard design of a marching-camp, according to Polybius, was in the shape of a square but it had, perforce, to conform to the demands of the ground and to the numbers accommodated. Rectangular layouts are frequently found but, whatever variations are discovered, the sides of the camp are almost invariably straight and the corner angles rounded. Vegetius, the accuracy of whose writings is sometimes queried, relates that

> the camp is formed square, round, triangular or oblong, according to the nature of the ground. For the form of a camp does not constitute its excellence. Those camps, however, are thought to be best where the length is one third more than the depth.[11]

Without doubt, in an emergency and on at least one occasion, Caesar took up a position on a hilltop, locating his baggage in the middle of his defences; but the adoption of circular defensive positions was not routine practice.

A portion of the experimental turf rampart reconstructed in 1966 at The Lunt, Baginton, Warwickshire

The outline of a marching-camp was delineated either by a rampart or a defensive ditch, generally the latter, with a rampart constructed from the spoil, thrown up on to its inside edge. This was then reinforced with sods of earth and strengthened by palisades. The palisades were either fashioned from locally foraged timber or from purpose-made stakes sometimes carried by the soldiery. Both Hyginus and Vegetius quote the dimensions of the ditch as being 5 feet wide and 3 feet deep and, remembering the problems of time and space involved, this would seem to be the maximum possible for a one-night marching-camp. Vegetius, in an unlikely passage, quotes other sizes of trench:

> After the ground is marked out by the proper officers, each century receives a certain number of feet to entrench. They then range their shields and baggage in a circle around their colours and, without other tools than their swords, open a trench nine, eleven or thirteen feet broad. Or, if they greatly apprehend the enemy, they enlarge it to seventeen feet. . . .

It may be that the soldiers cut the initial trace of the entrenchment with their swords, but it is not easy to imagine that thousands of tons of spoil could have been shifted without the use of proper entrenching tools and earth-shifting baskets. We will examine these quantities later, when investigating the time required for the construction of the fortification. According to Josephus,[12] each man was issued with a saw, axe, sickle, chain, rope, spade and basket for entrenching and other such work, although the evidence of Trajan's Column suggests that the last two were not personally carried by the soldiers: they could possibly have been loaded on the 'company' cart.

Polybius, rather more than Vegetius, spells out for us the drills by which the camps were erected:

> Whenever the army on the march draws near the place of encampment, one of the tribunes and those of the centurions who are in turn selected for this duty, go ahead to survey the whole area where the camp is to be placed. They begin by determining the spot where the consul's tent should be pitched . . . and on which side of this space to quarter the legions. Having decided this, they first measure out the area of the *praetorium*, next they draw the straight line along which the tents of the tribunes are set up and then the line parallel to this, which marks the starting point of the encampment area for the troops. . . . All this is done with little loss of time and the marking out is an easy task, since all distances are regulated and are familiar. They then proceed to plant flags . . . [marking out the camp].[13]

There is no difficulty, Vegetius rather obviously remarks, in carrying on the fortification of a camp when no enemy is in sight; but, he adds, in the event of the enemy being close, it was ancient practice that all the cavalry and half the infantry should be drawn up in order of battle, confronting the enemy, with the charge of covering the force working on the entrenchments. The frequently over-confident Julius Caesar on one occasion failed to take this precaution and, as a consequence, nearly paid dearly for his omission.

Roman heavy infantry on the march

The team responsible for the layout of a camp, known as a colour-party in modern military parlance, was mainly composed of ten men detached from each of the centuries of the army on the march. It would have been commanded by a senior tribune or centurion, nominated and briefed by the army commander himself or, possibly, in certain circumstances, by the *quaestor*. Under normal conditions, it moved with the vanguard and carried with it, apart from its own kit, the 'instruments for marking out the camp-site',[14] including a variety of coloured flags and pennants used to identify the various segments of the camp and thus at once attract the attention of incoming troops to their areas so that they might march straight to them without further ado. Since the layout was, in any event, uniform, they would already have had a good idea where to go.

This battle drill, practised by the Romans more than two millennia ago, emphasizes the unchanging nature of a soldier's trade and carries with it a vision of a task which confronted the 7/14th Punjabis with whom the author served in 1942. The battalion had been hastily moved across India, from North-West Frontier Province, to Dimapur, in Assam, with the task of providing cover for General Alexander's Burma Army as it withdrew across the border into the Naga Hills. The battalion was accompanied by its modest complement of sixty regimental mules. When it arrived at Manipur Road Junction, the rail station for Dimapur, it detrained in the teeth of the monsoon which had recently broken, and was then instructed to proceed to Kalemyo, on the Chindwin River. No motor transport was available but the battalion was to make the fullest use of its own pack animals, together with forty Animal Transport (AT) carts which were being provided to lift essential baggage. It was to set forth by route march with all speed. Kalemyo lay 345 miles distant and, since the roads were filled with refugees during daylight hours, movement was to be by night.

Each early afternoon, therefore, the battalion 'colour-party' assembled on the side of the Kohima–Imphal road to hitch a lift. It was armed with 'the instruments for marking out the camp-site', and it also carried with it such essential items as dixies and condensed milk and sugar for the making of hot, sweet tea with which to greet a tired and wet battalion when it arrived in the middle of the night. The flour (*atta*) and oil (*ghee*) for cooking was transported on the AT cart which accompanied each rifle company. The order of march varied daily, for the rear of the column inevitably arrived an hour or more after the leading rifle company was well established.

The task of the colour-party was to select, clear and peg out a camp-site and the layout, as far as the ground would permit, was the same on each occasion. Battalion headquarters, for ease of communication, always lay on the road: transport animals remained with their owners but were to be visited daily by the Animal Transport officer; the first rifle company to arrive at the turn-off point on the approach to the camp moved diagonally deep to the left, the second to the right, and so on. There, liaising with each other, they would dig their defensive positions and construct their two-man bivouacs from a combination of groundsheets and foliage. The problems of preparing food in the rain and in the dark were soon overcome and a drill for marshalling men, animals and transport carts in the jungle and in a different yet broadly identical marching-camp each night quickly emerged.

If our camp-sites on the Imphal road were largely administrative, the writings of ancient historians contain numerous accounts of the manner in which their Roman counterparts were tactically applied.

Tacitus quotes an instance where the concept was used as a means of crash defence in a crisis.[15] The year was AD 14 and Germanicus was in course of returning from a particularly bloody raid across the Rhine when he was ambushed in the Caesian forest by a composite force of German tribes. He was anticipating trouble and was advancing warily behind a screen of cavalry and light infantry, with his main body deployed with 'the first brigade (legion) in the centre, the twenty-first and the fifth on the left and right flanks respectively and the twentieth in the rear'. The remaining auxiliary infantry followed behind. It was an unwieldy formation to adopt in a wood and the enemy took full advantage of the disarray which appears to have followed his initial contact with them. They made a feint against his vanguard and then launched their full force against his rear, causing confusion among the light infantry. Germanicus responded by releasing the XXIst Legion against the enemy, which

by a single, passionate attack broke through the German army and drove it with heavy losses into open country. Simultaneously, the vanguard emerged from the woods and established a fortified camp. From then on, the journey was without incident. The troops settled into winter quarters, their morale improved. . . .

In this example, the XXIst Legion provided the essential protective cover behind which Germanicus's vanguard was enabled to commence its work.

On another occasion,[16] Caesar manipulated the size of his marching-camp in order to deceive the enemy as to his true strength. When encamped one night, he received information from Cicero that the Gauls were mustering to attack him. Next morning, he broke camp at first light and marched to meet them. He had advanced only 4 miles or so when he saw the Gallic host on the opposite side of a wide valley:

> He felt that he had no cause for anxiety and had better take his time. He therefore halted and made a fortified camp on the most advantageous site he could find. This camp would have been small in any case, since he had no more than 7,000 men and no heavy baggage; but he reduced its size still further by making the camp roads narrower than usual, so that his force would seem contemptibly small.

He then summoned his cavalry to pull back within its fortifications and instructed his soldiery to 'increase the height of the rampart all round and block up the gateways; in doing so, they were to run about as much as possible and pretend to be afraid'. Many of the barricades they erected in this manner were sham and

Scene from Trajan's Column showing legionaries engaged in fort construction. In the foreground the soldiers can be seen digging ditches and transporting the earth in wicker baskets

constructed so as to allow quick exit. As a result, when the enemy drew near with over-confidence, the garrison burst out with unexpected speed and put them to flight inflicting considerable loss of life.

Probably the most illuminating account of the marching-camp as an attacking weapon, although the operation came to near disaster, is to be found in Julius Caesar's *de Bello Gallico*[17] and it deserves detailed attention because of the wealth of guidance it provides, not all of it readily discernible.

The incident occurred in the year 57 BC when, after subduing the Belgae, Caesar had advanced to enter the Nervean homelands, east of the River Scheldt, in central Belgium. He was at the head of an army which comprised 4,000 cavalry and eight legions, together with supporting detachments of Numidian light infantry from Algeria, archers from Crete and slingers from the Balearics. He had met with no immediate resistance and, for this reason, had not yet adopted the tactical order of march he normally practised when moving through hostile territory, namely, with his legions closed up in column of march, under his hand, and with their baggage held back, concentrated under the eye of his rear guard commander. Instead, and undoubtedly because under normal conditions it was administratively easier and more efficient to do so, he was moving with each one of his legions followed closely by its particular baggage train of pack animals and two-horse carts.

Legionary transport, in these circumstances, was frequently burdened with articles of equipment not required at that moment by the soldiery and, since the latter themselves were generally heavily laden, this was helpful. Trajan's Column depicts legionaries marching at ease, carrying shields and javelins, but without helmets. The helmets are shown, together with cavalry shields, loaded on to pack animals and carts following behind the marching troops.[18] When action was about to be joined, these items of kit would have been recovered and exchanged for others of lesser importance in the coming battle, such as shield and helmet covers, for example; but the practice of transporting equipment in this manner, with the risk of the legion's baggage being reverted some distance away to the rear of the column, was uncertain and needed tight control. In 54 BC, when Sabinus's army on the march was ambushed by Gauls, the word was passed along the column for the baggage to be abandoned. The outcome was that 'men everywhere were leaving their units and running to the baggage to look for their most cherished possessions and pull them out, amid a hubbub of shouting and cries'.[19]

The need for soldiers approaching battle to be unencumbered is, indirectly, constantly emphasized by Caesar. In 53 BC,[20] during his operations on the Rhine and after sending the baggage of the entire army to Labienus's camp, he relates how he started out 'for the territory of the Menapii with five legions in *light marching order*'. In 52 BC,[21] while preparing for battle near Bourges with Vercingetorix, he tells us again how he 'ordered his men to *pile their packs* and get their arms ready'. And yet again,[22] in 57 BC he explains how the Gauls planned 'to attack them on the march, when they would be hampered by the presence of transport and dispirited by having to fight with *their packs on their backs*'. This is a subject to which we return below.

As a consequence of Caesar's decision to adopt this routine order of march, his legions would have been separated from one another by a distance of approximately 2½ miles or, in terms of time, a gap of roughly 45 minutes. They would thus have been unable to give their neighbouring formations immediate close support should they have been required to do so. This apparent chink in the Roman general's defensive armour was quickly identified by spies among the many Celtic hangers-on who had attached themselves to his army and they wasted little time in passing news of it to his enemy, the Nervii, already gathering to confront him. The latter saw their advantage at once and quickly made plans to launch an attack against his leading legion, with the purpose of isolating and destroying it.

Meantime, Caesar, who had already been on the march for three days, had learnt from enemy prisoners that the River Sambre lay barely 10 miles from his encampment and that the Nervii, together with their allies the Atrebates, from the neighbourhood of Arras, and the Viromandui, from the Upper Somme, were positioned on its far bank awaiting his arrival. Caesar does not tell us the strength of the enemy ranged against him but it is noteworthy that these three allied tribes had contributed a combined contingent of some seventy thousand men[23] to the large Belgic army he had defeated in battle near Rheims a week or so earlier. The Sambre, at the point where they were assembling, was no more than 3 feet deep and scouts reported enemy cavalry pickets, an arm which the Nervii did not possess in great quantity, posted along the open ground on the opposite side of the river.

There can be no doubt about Caesar's reaction on learning of the presence and obvious intentions of the Nervii and their allies: he welcomed their offer of battle and saw an opportunity to destroy them. His first measure to this end is therefore of interest, for it conveys to us the tactical importance he attached to the marching-camp in the build-up to an attack. He at once despatched a reconnaissance party with orders to discover a suitable camp-site and then pushed forward a cavalry screen, strongly supported by slingers and archers, to provide for their protection and establish contact with the opposition. Then, having set the process in train and, 'in accordance with his usual practice when approaching an enemy',[24] he placed himself at the head of his army and set forth, followed by six legions in close column of march. He was, in his words, unencumbered by heavy baggage which, we may presume, now came under the command of the rear guard, to be watched over by the two legions he had recently raised in Italy.

By this sensible reshuffle of his order of march, Caesar, unintentionally or otherwise, thwarted his enemy's ambition of catching him unprepared; but, at first sight, although events will show this not to be so, he does appear to have exchanged this for yet another problem by divorcing himself from his entrenching tools, unless these were either carried on the man or in 'company' carts retained for the purpose by the forward legions. From the evidence of Trajan's Column,[25] which shows leading troops lightly clad in fighting order and those following behind marching with full kit, then this latter scenario appears to be a possible solution, for they could not have been separated too far from their essential equipment.

Caesar's reconnaissance party had little trouble in finding a suitable location. It selected a high feature, overlooking the Sambre and crowned by a suitable area from where the ground sloped evenly down to the river. Opposite, on the far bank, rose a hill of similar proportions, its summit covered by a wide, heavily shaded wood from which, for a distance of some 300 yards, a stretch of open ground likewise descended a gentle gradient to the river, which separated these two landmarks. In these woods, and doubtless also on the reverse slope behind, stood the enemy host, arrayed for battle but silent and unseen, awaiting the signal to attack.

It was at this moment that Caesar chose to arrive on the scene, followed by his legions. He was in time to watch his cavalry screen, with its supporting light infantry, cross the Sambre, and drive back the enemy cavalry pickets posted along its banks. They then pressed forward up the hill and unsuccessfully began the task of probing the wood at its summit, but refrained from entering because of the uncertainties which lay within its dark interior. Meantime, Caesar's six legions had shed their equipment, stacked their arms and commenced the work of measuring and marking out the camp and constructing its fortifications. Even by his account, they appear to have been left so blatantly unprotected that we can only wonder whether he was guilty of sheer carelessness or supreme arrogance. Either way, he was about to be taught a lesson. Certainly, in later times, he rarely undertook a construction task, for whatever purpose, without first setting in place a strong outpost to protect his legions while they worked:

> The Gauls concealed in the woods . . . were waiting full of confidence. As soon as they caught sight of the head of the baggage train – the moment they had agreed upon for starting the battle – they suddenly dashed out in full force and swooped down on our cavalry, which they easily routed. Then they ran down to the river at such an incredible speed that almost at the same moment they seemed to be at the edge of the wood, in the water and already upon us.[26]

This lively description by Caesar could only have been written by somebody who had experienced the full shock of the assault. It savours of the surprise Zulu attack upon two battalions of the 24th Foot at Isandhlwana in 1879, when Lord Chelmsford, at the head of a 'punitive' expedition, crossed into their territory to apprehend their indomitable tribal chieftain, Cetshwayo. Information of his whereabouts was totally lacking, so Chelmsford, leaving the 24th Regiment to guard his stores and baggage, continued to march forward with his main body in an effort to establish contact.

As Chelmsford's column progressed on its way, the officer commanding the newly organized base despatched a number of mounted scouts, working in pairs, to reconnoitre the countryside surrounding his position. Two of these men noticed a native shepherd boy behaving in a suspicious manner and, as they rode in his direction, he disappeared out of sight, down a hillside, into a valley. Curious to know more, they cantered after him to the edge where they had last seen him. To their horror, the reason for the strangeness of his behaviour at once became apparent. The entire Zulu army of 20,000 men was squatting in the valley, sitting silently, by regiments and in serried ranks, awaiting orders to move. As soon as the scouts came into its vision, the great host rose, uttered a deafening war-cry and then set off in

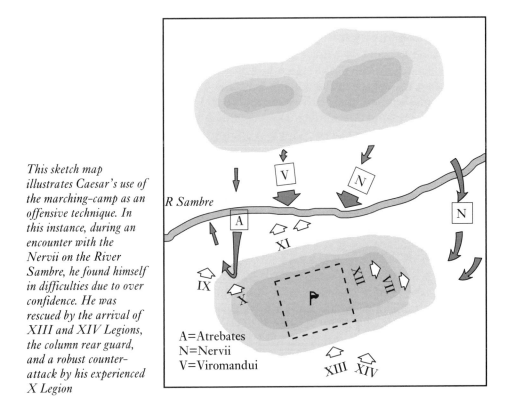

This sketch map illustrates Caesar's use of the marching-camp as an offensive technique. In this instance, during an encounter with the Nervii on the River Sambre, he found himself in difficulties due to over confidence. He was rescued by the arrival of XIII and XIV Legions, the column rear guard, and a robust counter-attack by his experienced X Legion

A=Atrebates
N=Nervii
V=Viromandui

their pursuit, in silence and with surprising speed. The scouts turned their horses and galloped, *ventre à terre*, to warn their comrades. The latter needed no telling: they had already been alerted by the thunderous noise of feet beating the ground, stirring a great cloud of dust, under which a black tide of warriors flowed towards them, deployed in the traditional Zulu 'buffalo horns' pattern of attack. The technique of this formation was that the 'forehead', comprising the main body of the assaulting *impi*, drove in frontally against the enemy, while the points of the horns carried out an enveloping movement around his flanks. As is now well known, the 24th Regiment, with their ammunition screwed down in boxes for which they had insufficient screwdrivers, were caught entirely unprepared and were annihilated in the engagement which followed.

The Nervii adopted a similar 'buffalo horn' formation as they burst from the woods with their allies to charge across the water and up the hill to Caesar's camp. Caesar's six legions hastily formed rank as best they could but were caught in considerable disarray. The Atrebates, taking the right horn of the attack, had the furthest distance to go and arrived on their objective 'breathless and exhausted with running'. They were also unfortunate to find themselves confronted by the experienced Labienus with the battle-hardened Xth Legion, in the company of the IXth. They were summarily thrown back by the Romans, who pursued them across the Sambre and up the slope to the woods from which they had come.

Here, they made a brief stand before being put to flight. The Viromandui, sharing the centre with a wing of the Nervii, fought their way into the Roman camp before being cast out by the VIIIth and XIth Legions and driven down to the river, where a fierce fight took place in which neither side gained the advantage. The Nervii, with their outflanking drive on the left, enjoyed the greatest success and were on the point of overwhelming the VIIth and XIIth Legions when Caesar arrived and ordered the two legions to combine forces and form a square. This restored confidence to these by now demoralized units and proved to be the turning point of the battle, for help was at hand:

> The two legions (XIIIth and XIVth) which had acted as a guard to the baggage at the rear of the column, having received news of the battle, had quickened their pace and now appeared on the hilltop, where the enemy could see them; and Labienus, who had captured the enemy's camp, and from the high ground on which it stood could see what was going on in ours, sent the Xth legion to the rescue.[27]

This welcome reinforcement restored the balance, so much so 'that even some of the Roman soldiers who had lain down, exhausted by wounds, got up and began to fight again, leaning on their shields'. One can almost hear the cheer which must have greeted the arrival of the Xth!

It is appropriate at this point to consider the factors of time and space which confronted Caesar when undertaking his march to the Sambre, which lay 10 miles away.[28] He had, so he tells us, sent his cavalry 'a little in advance', by which he probably means a distance of half a mile, and he then followed in their wake, marching at the head of six legions. In the event, it is unlikely that he used his entire cavalry wing of 4,500 horse for this purpose: it would have been prudent for him to have retained an element, perhaps 2,000 horse, for his right and left flank guards, with a further 1,000, as army reserve, moving close to his hand at the head of the column. None of these groupings need have moved *within* the column; they therefore play little part in our space calculations, other than to note that the reconnaissance cavalry, together with its attached archers and slingers, would probably have been deployed some 800 yards or more ahead of the main body.

The legionary infantry in this instance moved in close column and, according to Josephus,[29] customarily marched in ranks, six abreast, carrying their shields on their left arm and their javelins in their left hand. Almost certainly many of the soldiers were heavily loaded and it is thus unlikely that there could have been less than a space of 6 feet between the forward toe of one rank to the forward toe of the rank behind,[30] in other words, 3 feet between ranks. There is little more frustrating to an infantryman than to have the foot of a rear file catching his heel as he marches. Thus, a legion 5,000 strong would have occupied 1,667 yards in length, or, in the case of six legions, 10,000 yards (5.68 miles).

In addition, as has already been conjectured, we may expect that carts established with the legions, such as those with each century (total 60) and the *carroballistae* (total 60), with possible additions per legion for ambulance, engineer and other supporting arms (say 30), making an estimated 150 carts per legion or

900 carts with the main body, would also have moved with Caesar's fighting column. If these carts had moved two abreast and each cart required 30 feet of space, then they would have extended a further $450 \times 10 = 4,500$ yards (2.56 miles) or, when taken together with the marching troops, a combined total of 8.24 miles. More accurately, if space were allowed for demarcation gaps between cohorts and legions, this figure might be rounded up to 9 miles; but even this distance, if it were to be prevented from extending further, would have called for strict march discipline. The Romans were well aware of this necessity. Vegetius tells how both their cavalry and infantry were required to practise marching three times a month.[31] The infantry

> were obliged to march completely armed a distance of ten miles from the camp and return, in the most exact order and with the military step which they changed and quickened on some part of the march. . . . Both cavalry and infantry were ordered into difficult and broken terrain and to ascend or descend mountains to prepare them for all kinds of emergencies and familiarise them with the different manoeuvres that the various situations of a country may require.

In the face of the above calculations, if we take into account the ground consumed by the cavalry screen and the party reconnoitring for a camp-site, it is evident that the tail of Caesar's main body would barely have cleared camp by the time his forward elements were approaching the River Sambre. In effect, the heavy baggage, with its legionary escort, would not have moved out of its firm base until such time as the ground between the two fortifications had been secured. Should it so have happened that Caesar had been unable to achieve his objective, or his work preparing the fortifications had been threatened, then there would have been time for the *quaestor* or officer commanding the baggage train to be warned, turn about and re-occupy the whole or part of the fortified marching-camp he had just vacated. If, as is more likely, he chose to re-occupy only a part of it, then he would have needed to adjust the size of the camp to fit his numerical strength.

Caesar records an incident in 52 BC when he failed to take this precaution.[32] He was occupying a temporary camp in the Auvergne mountains, about 4 miles south of Clermont-Ferrand, when he received news that the Aedui were becoming disaffected. Without taking time to reduce the size of the camp for his rear party, he set forth in light marching order, with all his cavalry and four legions, to bring them under control. He left his heavy baggage behind in camp, together with two legions under the command of one of his generals, Gaius Fabius. Caesar dealt swiftly with the Aedui and turned for home. When he was well on his way, he was met by a galloper with the news that

> the enemy had assaulted the camp in full force, and, by continually sending in fresh troops to relieve their tired comrades, had exhausted our men who, on account of the size of the camp, had to remain hard at work on the rampart without relief. Showers of arrows and every other kind of missile had wounded many of the defenders. . . .

Clearly, in the battle on the Sambre, the Nervii had no intention of allowing Caesar's heavy baggage any such avenue of escape. They therefore refrained from attacking him until the head of his baggage train had come into view and, hence, his rear guard was firmly committed to the battlefield.

But let us return to the detail of Caesar's column on the march, for there are other factors of time and space to be considered.

If, as we have calculated, the main body of fighting troops was 9 miles long, then, marching at a generous 3 miles in the hour, the head of their column would have taken more than three hours to arrive at its destination and its tail would not have arrived until three hours later (see Table 3). In other words, a total in excess of six hours would have passed before the last of Caesar's six legions was firmly home or, looking at the timing through the eyes of those responsible for work on the fortifications, the leading legion would have been three hours in the camp before the last of the main body of infantry arrived and became available for work. The rear guard, with the baggage, would have been moving close behind the main body: but we may judge that a half hour would have yet remained before the Nervii, as the Roman commander narrated, 'caught sight of the head of the baggage train' entering the rear gate of the camp. It is a daunting thought that, even at this moment, with an estimated length for the rear guard of 23,625 yards or 13½ miles, some 3½ miles of column would still have been standing ready in its overnight base camp, waiting to move out.

Further, if we regard the army column as a whole, reaching, as it would have done, over a distance of 9 miles (main body) + 13½ miles (rear guard) = 22½ miles, and marching at 3 miles in the hour, then it is evident that Caesar's task of moving his entire force (in this case eight legions) from one camp to another would have taken 3 hours + 7½ hours = 10½ hours marching time, assuming that the two rear guard legions deployed themselves as flank guards to the baggage train they were protecting. Thus, if we add to the marching time a period of one hour for breakfast, packing and saddling-up in the morning, together with a further four to five hours during which to graze the animals upon arrival in the evening,[33] he clearly would have enjoyed a full day's work. Caesar tells us he selected a moment to commence these operations 'when forage began to be plentiful', presumably about mid-May since Gallic farmers knew little about the mixed blessings of fertilizers. In that month of the year and at the latitude of 51° at which he was operating, he might have expected to enjoy some 16 hours of daylight.

The amount of daylight, the fighting strength of the force and the size of its baggage train were factors that controlled the mobility of a Roman army and its rate of advance. If it had been possible for Caesar – and he was far from being alone in this – to make permanent use of river transport for supply purposes and thus reduce his dependency on pack animals, then his logistical problems might have been eased, but his room for manoeuvre would have been reduced. In comparison with his achievement in the Sambre episode,[34] the average distance between Agricola's camps in Scotland (10 to 12½ miles), during the campaign which led to his victory at Mons Graupius, are remarkably little different, even though, through the medium of the Roman navy's *Classis Britannica*, the latter may have received some provisioning by sea. In this respect, it is also notable that

TABLE 3
COLUMN ON THE MARCH
March timings

Data: a. March rate – 3 miles in an hour
b. Distance to Camp II – 10 miles
c. Overall length of Marching Column – 22.5 miles
d. Departure time – H hour

Serial No.	Time	Event	Remarks
1.	H hour	Recce Group departs Camp I	–
2.	+ 0 h 10 m	Vanguard departs Camp I	Followed by Command Group and Main Body
3.	+ 3 h 20 m	Recce Group arrives Camp II	–
4.	+ 3 h 30 m	Vanguard arrives Camp II	Followed by Command Group and head of Main Body
5.	+ 3 h 30 m	Camp layout commenced	Tail of Main Body departs Camp I
6.	+ 3 h 30 m	Head of Baggage train departs Camp I	
7.	+ 4 h	Protective Screen deployed	After arrival of first legion
8.	+ 4 h 30 m	Fortifications commenced	After arrival of second legion
9.	+ 6 h 30 m	Tail of Main Body arrives Camp II	–
10.	+ 7 h	Head of Baggage train arrives Camp II	Slightly slower march rate than Main Body
11.	+ 7 h 30 m	Fortifications complete	–
12.	+ 12 h	Tail of Baggage train arrives	Column complete at Camp II

(Source: Caesar, *de Bello Gallico*, II, 17–28)

Agricola's army of an estimated 5,000 cavalry and 16,000 infantry was considerably smaller in size than Caesar's eight legions in Gaul.

It has already been mentioned that two prime factors to be considered when selecting the site of a marching-camp, apart from its defensive qualities and its ability to be adapted to the Roman layout requirements, would have been the availability of water for man and beast, as well as an adequacy of grass for grazing and bedding. The very numbers concerned (in broad terms, in Caesar's case, 45,000 men and 16,000 animals) serve to emphasize the scale of the problem and underline the fact that the presence of a strong-flowing stream or river, providing easy access from the banks, would have been essential. This points, yet again, to the advantage of a riverine supply route. In the case of grazing, the imagination cannot grasp the confusion which would be created by turning such numbers of animals out to grass, even by day, unless tight control were exerted. Vegetius' comment, that 'the darkness of night, the necessity of sleep and the dispersion of horses at pasture afford opportunities of surprise'[35] is, almost certainly, not intended to suggest that animals were permitted to graze after dark but serves to understate the whole, operationally vital, problem of feeding the animals.

Today it may be expected that, on such an occasion, horses would graze on a scale of twelve to an acre; but modern animals are fussy eaters, picking out the succulent bits of grass and passing over the more unappetizing patches. The Roman cavalry horse and pack animal were less highly bred and, as a consequence, less particular in their eating habits. If, in their case, we allow a total of twenty grazing animals per acre, this poses a requirement of 800 acres (or 1¼ square miles) of reasonable quality grass, dependent, of course, upon the time of the year. The hay crop in Gaul before mid–April would have been scant and of poor nutritional value, demanding a yet wider grazing area. Indeed, the lack of an adequate supply of grass frequently caused a delayed start to a campaigning season. Thus, with this large area of pasture land to be watched over whenever the animals were put out to graze, the army commander was presented with a considerable security problem. If Vegetius tells us correctly, the burden of resolving it fell upon the cavalry:

> The cavalry furnish the grand guards at night and the outposts by day. They are relieved every morning and afternoon because of the fatigue imposed by this duty upon the men and horses. It is particularly incumbent upon the general to provide for the protection of the pastures and of the convoys of grain and other provisions either in camp or garrison, and to secure wood, water and forage against the incursions of the enemy.[36]

Purely to illustrate the scale of need, if a minimum stabling space of 12 feet × 3 feet were allowed for each of the horses/mules mentioned in the example above, and all the animals were stabled tightly together, each within this space, there would have been a total requirement of 64,000 square yards or 13.2 acres (5.35 hectares), without taking account of an unknown number of pack-transport reserves or remounts for the cavalry. Patently, it was administratively a formidably large but, in the military practice of the day, not unusual total of animals. In camp they would have been accommodated in the areas of the units responsible for them.[37] The pack animals provided for each of Caesar's 4,800 *contubernia*, for example, are thought to have stood in front of the tents of the 'sections' to which they were attached. The servants in whose charge they lay probably set down their beds in a corner of the section tent, keeping with them the saddlery and stores for which they were responsible. The sub-unit cart would probably have been parked, off the road but accessible for use, at the end of each line, which, in the case of the Roman infantry, housed a maniple or double century.

The cavalry equivalent of a century, a *turma*, comprised thirty-two troopers, and was commanded by a *decurion*. Their horses were probably tethered face to face, in

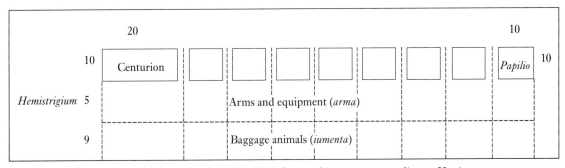

The arrangement of the century's tents within the marching-camp, according to Hyginus

the enduring military fashion, secured to a central picket line over a length of some 60 feet. This distance would have fronted four tents for the trooper and a double sized tent for the *decurion*. It is likely that a further tent would have been provided for servants, in which saddlery and spare stores could have been housed. The legionary, as opposed to auxiliary, cavalry were probably provided with a servant per man. The scale of provision of servants for auxiliaries is uncertain. They possibly rated, like the infantry, one for each eight men, together with a mule for tent and other camp equipment.

The scale of the old marching-camp at Rey Cross, lying between Scotch Corner and Carlisle on the windswept summit of the Stainmore Pass, permits us to consider a practical example. It is considered to have accommodated the ten cohorts of a legion,[38] together with a complement of auxiliaries, partly cavalry. It is thus a microcosm of Caesar's army and the 18–20 acres it occupies may, therefore, be fairly used to deduce the size of the marching-camp of eight legions set up by him on the Sambre, that is some 160 acres × 4,840 square yards (per acre) = 774,400 square yards. By taking the square root of this total, we see that his camp would have been half a mile, or 880 yards, square in size. From this we may further deduce that the defensive ditch of the camp, 5 feet wide and 3 feet deep, would have extended an overall distance of 4 × 880 yards = 3,520 yards (10,560 feet) and the spoil from it would have totalled 2241.4 cubic metres. Dependent upon the nature of the soil, one man could shift 0.4 to 0.7 cubic metres per hour, including a throw not exceeding two metres (see Appendix 3).

On this basis, the task would have taken 3,202 to 5,603 man-hours of work, depending upon the condition of the soil and, allowing one man for every 5 feet of working space, it would have required a labour force of some 2,112: more than this number would have caused overcrowding. Naturally, other fatigue parties would also have been involved, working on the ramparts and standing by to provide relief. Thus, presuming its line had already been pegged out by the advance party, the construction of the trench would have taken between 1.52 to 2.65 hours of work. In reality, we are probably talking of a period of 2¼ to 3½ hours' work after the arrival of the main body. Plainly, the task of digging would have been considerable and, however much the soldiery may have achieved with

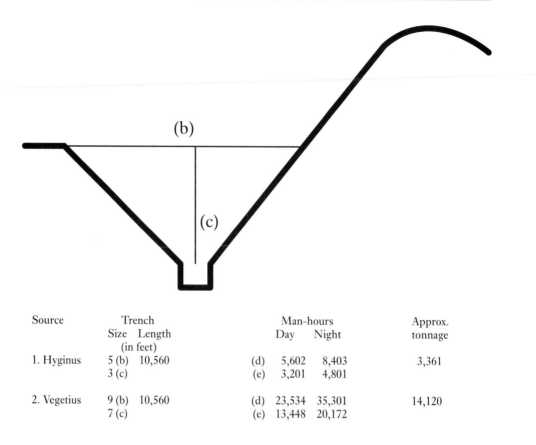

Source	Trench Size (in feet)	Length	Man-hours Day	Night	Approx. tonnage
1. Hyginus	5 (b) 3 (c)	10,560	(d) 5,602 (e) 3,201	8,403 4,801	3,361
2. Vegetius	9 (b) 7 (c)	10,560	(d) 23,534 (e) 13,448	35,301 20,172	14,120

Notes: a. Night-time work load, by light of full moon, calculated at two-thirds of daytime. b. Width of trench in feet. c. Depth of trench in feet. d. 2,241 cubic metres (.0283 cu. metres = 1 cu. foot) at 0.4 cubic metre per hour on difficult earth surface. e. 2,241 cubic metres at 0.7 cubic metres on easier ground. f. 9,413 cubic metres at 0.4 cubic metres per hour. g. 9,413 cubic metres at 0.7 cubic metres per hour.

Marching-camp defences (source: Royal Engineers Pocket Book, Labour Figures for Common Engineering Tasks, Table 112, p. 14)

their swords as Vegetius has suggested, it would have been imperative to carry the entrenching equipment and soil-shifting baskets well forward in the column, so that the exercise might be commenced and completed with all haste.

Equally, it is clear that before work could start a strong defensive screen would have had to be in position. In normal circumstances, the first legion to arrive would have been detailed for this duty, thus delaying the start of work until the arrival of the next in line. This probably explains the gamble Caesar took on the Sambre by failing to put a protective screen of infantry in place at the first opportunity.

The rampart of a marching-camp was constructed so as to be a distance of 200 feet from the lines of tents.[39] The space thus created had a multitude of uses.

Most importantly, it placed the tented accommodation out of range of any fire-arrows or javelins which might be fired or cast into the camp. It provided a highway by which the occupants of the camp might gain access to their quarters without committing the military sin of passing through another unit's lines. It was also employed as a parade-ground, a collecting point for plunder brought into the camp and for cattle rounded up for use by the commissariat. The plunder would have attracted traders like bees to a honeypot. At Atuatuca, it will be remembered,[40] the German cavalry attack on Cicero's camp overwhelmed the traders 'who had their tents at the foot of the rampart and left them no time to get away'. Here also, we would have found the *carroballistae* of the entire force, brigaded as one artillery whole, to add formidable strength to the defence of the ramparts.

The marching-camp, it has been said,[41] provided an important form of psychological security for Rome's troops but it could not keep a determined foe out of Europe: but to say this is not fully to recognize its concept. The marching-camp was an instrument of systematic attack and the highly trained and disciplined legions that provided its garrisons had little need of a psychological boost. The marching-camp technique, allied to their supreme confidence in themselves, furnished the legions with a formula for conquest which carried them to the furthest corners of the Mediterranean basin and beyond. Victory in war, Vegetius advised the emperor Valentinian,

> does not depend entirely upon numbers or mere courage; only discipline and skill will ensure it. We find that the Romans owed the conquest of the world to no other cause than continual military training, exact observance of discipline in their camps and unwearied cultivation of the other arts of war.[42]

As the Roman appetite for conquest waned, so the concept of the marching-camp was abandoned and the empire settled down to the defence of its frontiers. Unfortunately for Rome, she had no defence strategy of comparable genius to set in its place.

CHAPTER FIVE

Supporting Arms and Weaponry

And he [David] took his staff in his hand and chose him five smooth stones out of the brook and put them in a shepherd's bag which he had, even in a scrip; and his sling was in his hand; and he drew near to the Philistine.

I Samuel, 17: 40

But Mechanics, by means of one of its smallest branches – I mean, of course, the one dealing with what is called artillery construction – has surpassed argumentative training on this score and taught mankind how to live a tranquil life. With its aid, men will never be disturbed in time of peace by the onslaughts of enemies at home and abroad. . . .

Heron of Alexandria (second century)

In land warfare, terrain, at all levels of operations, is a critical factor, principally in the manner by which it provides cover for an assault, commands a position, presents obstacles to an enemy's advance or, alternatively, provides obstacles within which a defensive position may be adopted. Additionally, as we have discussed in earlier chapters, there is the importance of the administrative application of the terrain to military supply needs. A careful study of terrain and the areas of ground vital to the successful achievement of his military objectives forms part, therefore, of every commander's operational preparations and is a principle as old as warfare itself. Vegetius,[1] in his treatise on the art of war which he dedicated to his emperor, Valentinian II, made this point with clarity. Good generals, he advised,

are acutely aware that victory depends much upon the nature of the field of battle. When you intend to engage, endeavour to draw the chief advantage from your position. The highest ground is reckoned the best. Weapons thrown from a height strike with greater force; and the party above their antagonists can repulse and bear them down with greater impetuosity, whilst they who struggle with the ascent have both the ground and the enemy to contend with. . . . If you depend on your foot against the enemy's horse, you must choose a rough, unequal and mountainous situation.

Vegetius thus saw three advantages in the infantry axiom of 'going for the high ground': it impeded the enemy cavalry, it reduced the momentum of the enemy assault and it improved the weight of the available firepower, an important consideration, as much in attack as defence.

We do not need to remind ourselves, for many of the world's earliest archaeological discoveries are weapons, that man, habitually, is a quarrelsome animal, driven along this path as much by a determination to survive as by a natural aggression. Many historic finds, such as flint daggers, axe-heads attached to handles by thongs, spears of a wide variety, and bows with flint-headed arrows, the most ancient of which have lain concealed for 10,000 years and more, bear testimony to this fact. They also provide evidence of mankind's unceasing quest for improved 'firepower', from the moment that he instinctively cast the first stone or picked up a piece of flint to fashion as an arrow-head, until his manufacture of the devastating nuclear weapons which lie today in many of the world's arsenals. In August 1945, when atom bombs were dropped with devastating effect upon the Japanese cities of Hiroshima and Nagasaki, a war-weary world saw them as the ultimate weapon, which would guarantee peace for future generations. Heron of Alexandria, as the implications of the new torsion artillery weapon increasingly revealed themselves to his generation, was persuaded to take a similar view of this powerful new piece of artillery. With its aid, he wrote,

> men will never be disturbed in time of peace by the onslaughts of enemies at home and abroad, nor, when war is upon them, will they ever be disturbed. After peace has continued for a long time, one would expect more to follow when men concern themselves with the artillery section:[2] they will remain tranquil in their consciousness of security, whilst potential aggressors, observing their study of the subject, will not attack.

Heron must have been deeply disappointed by the subsequent history of events, just as we, in our time, have had our hopes and expectations violently dashed by a deeply troubled post-Cold War world, wracked with civil war and strife.

In modern practice, considerable firepower is brought to bear by the infantry itself, augmented, as the situation may demand, by artillery and other weapons of differing calibres and diverse means of propulsion. In Roman times, on the other hand, firepower, provided by the simplest of weaponry such as bows and arrows and slingstones, was concentrated in special units of light-armed troops to provide support for infantrymen, who themselves were each armed solely with a sword, perhaps a spear and a handful of javelins, and carried a shield for their protection. The javelins provided a form of unit firepower and were employed, both in defence and in the set-piece battle, to disrupt an enemy assault before it reached the crucial stage of hand-to-hand fighting. The general design of the javelin bore close resemblance to the carefully honed weapon used today for hunting and tribal warfare by the Karamajong and Turkhana peoples, whose territories adjoin each other in northern Uganda and Kenya, south of the Sudan border. I have seen these cast, with varying skill but without great difficulty, over distances ranging between 100 and 150 feet.

In each case, ancient or modern, the guiding principle for the use of firepower remains unchanged: concentration of fire is essential if maximum effect is to be obtained. By this means, according to the circumstance and whatever the range in relation to the stage of development of the weapon, an enemy's power of manoeuvre may be hampered, his forces neutralized and his will and ability to fight may be destroyed.

Initially, the three main infantry support weapons were the bow, the javelin and the sling, not necessarily in that order. The origin of the first two essentially belonged to Asia. The sling, shrewdly employed by David in his fight with the Philistine, Goliath, was widespread as a weapon, popular because of its simplicity, its lightness and its ease of manufacture. It comprised a piece of leather to house the missile, and two thongs, one of which was secured to the throwing hand and the other held, simultaneously, between the thumb and forefinger of the same hand. It was then cast, after a single twirl round the head, the missile being 'fired' at the moment that the second thong was released, its range being related to the angle of discharge, the length of the thongs and the amount of energy imparted by the thrower. David kept his supply of ammunition in a shepherd's bag, slung across his shoulders, thus keeping both hands free for the task of making his cast and then reloading. A slinger in a battle illustration on Trajan's Column, on the other hand, is shown carrying his reserve of stones in the folds of his cloak, draped over his left arm.[3] This appears a clumsy arrangement, which must have restricted the mobility of the soldier and slowed his rate of fire.

The use of the sling is widely believed to have been perfected in the Balearic Islands of Majorca and Minorca. Vegetius relates[4] that the inhabitants of these islands were taught the art of sling-stoning from a very early age, when, as children, they were not allowed food by their mothers till they had first made an accurate cast of a stone at a target. Islanders from Rhodes, on the other hand, also possessed a worthy reputation for their skill with the weapon, partly gained during the siege of Syracuse in the early third century BC. The development of leaden bullets as slingshot, shaped like acorns and known as *glandes*, has been attributed to these people.[5]

Lead missiles would have had many benefits, both logistical and military, for they would have been smaller than a stone, weight for weight, and thus larger quantities could have been carried both on the man and within the re-supply organization. Moreover, since they were fabricated, their availability would have saved time wasted in a search for the right size and shape of replacement stones, if indeed any were to be found at all on certain types of terrain. The provision of lead bullets introduced a logistical problem but this was probably no more taxing than that presented by the re-supply of stones, which generally were either rounded artificially or manufactured in baked clay to the required shape, weight and size. Livy underlined the need for the careful selection of missiles in his account of an encounter between Romans and Gauls in 189 BC:

The Gauls had insufficient protection from their shields, which were long, but not wide enough for the size of their bodies, and, besides that, were flat in surface. Furthermore, they had no other weapons than swords, which were of no service to them on this occasion, since the enemy did not engage them in close combat. The missiles they used were stones, but not of convenient size, since they had not collected them in advance, but every man took what came to hand in his agitated search; and they used them like men unused to the work, with neither the skill nor the strength to lend force to their impact.

All of which emphasizes the importance, well understood by generations of soldiers, of the dual values of victory, for this does not result solely in the defeat of the enemy but gains for the victor the retention of the battlefield, with its reward of a plethora of military salvage, whether comprised of sling-stone missiles in ancient days or armoured tanks in more modern times. A sensible commander, as we are reminded by Livy, seizes every opportunity to recoup such losses. When assault troops halted to gain breath, he tells us, during their ascent to attack an enemy fortification in the Galatian mountains, the legions 'made energetic use of the interval in collecting weapons all over the hills to ensure a sufficient supply of missiles'.[6]

During his early months under recruit training, every Roman soldier was taught the art of throwing stones, both with the hand and with the sling, the stone thrown by hand weighing about 1lb.[7] To this end, archers and slingers alike, the latter utilizing a device named by Vegetius as a *fustibalus*,[8] were required to set up aiming marks of bundles of twigs or straw and to strike them at a distance of 600 feet. A *fustibalus* is a rarely mentioned small-arm of olden times, defined by *Freund's Latin Dictionary*[9] as 'a sling-staff, an offensive weapon consisting of a staff with a sling attached'. The extra length and rigidity of a staff, fitted in this manner with a sling, would undoubtedly have provided considerably more distance than the range achieved by the solely hand-operated version, and one is driven to consider whether this was the purpose of the staff carried by David, mentioned in I Samuel 17:

40. . . . He took his staff in his hand and chose him five smooth stones out of the brook, and put them in a shepherd's bag that he had, even in a scrip; and his sling was in his hand; and he drew near to the Philistine.
41. And the Philistine came on and drew near unto David; and the man that bear the shield went before him. . . .
43. And the Philistine said unto David, Am I a dog, that thou comest to me with staves?

The role of the sling-staff contingent would have been similar to that of the archers, namely, to engage advancing enemy at long-range and break up the momentum of their advance. As the enemy drew near, the *fustibalatores* would have fallen back, through the ranks of the massed infantry, to assume a position at the head of the reserves. Conventional slingers, also, were sometimes used in this manner but, during the set-piece battle, they were normally posted, frequently intermingled with archers, on the left or right flanks of the main body as protection against cavalry attack. In an assault upon a fortified objective, their task would have been to provide covering fire for their own troops, by so directing it as to neutralize enemy counter-fire. In an advance, slingers were frequently employed as light infantry, probing ahead of the main body. Caesar, for example, when seeking out a Remi stronghold in 57 BC, records that he pushed his cavalry across the River Sambre, with slingers and archers, to engage and drive off the enemy's horsemen.[10]

The author[11] of *de Bello Africo* records a bizarre use of slingers against elephants during Caesar's operations at Ruspina against Labienus. These huge animals were generally employed to break into the main body of infantry, thus simplifying the work of the assaulting troops. The counter-stroke, by those under attack, was to bring the slingers forward and discourage the advance of the elephants by pounding them with slingshot. But, the chronicler explains rather ungenerously, the animals, for all their considerable battle training, were uncouth creatures, equally dangerous to both sides. The not unreasonable reaction of the elephants to this unwelcome attention was to turn aside and race back upon their own troops, carrying confusion into their ranks. Scipio, the senior cavalry general opposing Caesar in North Africa, undertook to stop this undesirable habit, but it proved a 'difficult and slow process' of hard, repetitive training. Nevertheless, it worked in this manner: Scipio drew up three lines to simulate a battle situation,[12]

> . . . one line of slingers, facing the elephants, to take the place of the enemy and to discharge small stones against the opposing front formed by the elephants; next he arranged the elephants in line, and behind them drew up his own line so that, when the enemy proceeded to sling their stones and the elephants in their consequent panic wheeled round upon their own side, his men should receive them with a volley of stones and so make them wheel around again . . . in the direction of the enemy. . . .

The years between the death of Alexander the Great (323 BC) until the ignominious defeat of Antiochus by the Romans at Magnesia (190 BC), constitute the prime period during which elephants played an important part in western warfare. Without doubt, they were used after this, for they were employed, among other occasions, by Marcius Philippus on operations in Macedonia in 169 BC, by both Caesar and Labienus in 46 BC in North Africa and by the emperor Claudius, who took a few with him from Gaul to Britain in AD 43. Their presence at this moment probably had more to do with the emperor's desire to impress the inhabitants with his power and importance than with any military purpose. Elephants, however, were never used again in the numbers which had been common in the early days of the Seleucid dynasty (312–64 BC), when Seleucus I defeated his rival, Antigonus, at the battle of Ipsus in 301 BC and was able to put 480 animals into the field.

Seleucus, once one of Alexander the Great's generals, had commanded the Macedonian infantry against King Porus of India in 326 BC, in battle on the Hydaspes river. Porus possessed a force of 200 elephants and was only defeated after an exhausting and bloody struggle. As a result of this experience, Seleucus at once determined that this was an arm of war to be obtained at almost any price and, later, in 305 BC, when his efforts to expand his Babylonian Empire to the Indus were halted by Candragupta on the eastern frontiers of Persia, he agreed territorial concessions in exchange for 500 elephants. Doubtless these were the animals that won him the day at Ipsus.

It thus happened that the animals used by the Macedonian Powers were of Indian stock and those employed by Carthage were African. The African elephant, the largest living land animal, stands on average 10 to 13 feet at the shoulder and weighs up to 8¼ tons; the Indian species is roughly 33 per cent smaller, reaching only to 10 feet at shoulder height and weighing some 5½ tons. Elephants have a voracious appetite and spend many hours eating. They may consume more than 225 kg of grasses and other vegetation in a day; unless the terrain was suitable, therefore, they could have been a logistical liability if employed in large numbers. Thus, the 500 animals employed by Seleucus would have required a daily diet of roughly 110 tons of fodder. In November 1944, during the Burma campaign, the Indian battalion with which I was serving was thrusting southwards up the Myittha Valley, with our forward patrols clearing the west bank of the Chindwin. During this probing period, we intercepted a valuable haul of 20 elephants, together with their handlers (mahouts), belonging to the Irrawady Steamship Company. They had been summoned to join the Japanese to assist with their transport problems. On arrival with us the animals were picketed around our position and, during the night, with their fore legs shackled by chains, they were allowed to forage in the jungle for fodder. Sleep did not come easily to us as they pushed their way through the undergrowth, snorting and rumbling, rattling their chains, and uprooting young trees in a quest for fodder. It is unlikely that the Seleucus at Ipsis permitted their large elephant corps a similar licence to feed in this dangerous, haphazard manner.

The elephant as a military weapon appears to have been encountered by the Romans first in Lucania, southern Italy, in war with King Pyrrhus of Epirus, when he twice defeated Roman legions in hard fought battles; but, although a novel military device, their use soon lost terror for experienced troops and the Romans, by opening up wide corridors in their ranks of infantry and so enabling the latter to isolate and encircle the animals, quickly learnt how to handle this form of attack. Scipio, once again, was the author of this tactic. He employed it for the first time in 202 BC, in a battle against Hannibal at Zama in North Africa. The front line of his infantry was, in the Roman custom, formed by maniples of *hastati*, which were habitually drawn up in battle with intervening gaps of similar dimensions between each maniple. Behind the *hastati*, the *principes* were arrayed, in a second line, not, on this occasion, covering the gaps between the front line maniples, which was the normal drill, but lined up behind the maniples in front. The *triarii* of the third line behaved in a similar manner. Scipio filled the intervals between the front line maniples with *velites*, lightly equipped skirmishers, who had instructions, in the event of an elephant assault, to conduct a fighting withdrawal down the open corridors thus formed behind them and, if overtaken, to filter away to left and right to seek shelter among the flanking heavy infantry. The victory achieved by the Romans at Zama provided them with a stepping-stone towards their final defeat of the Carthaginians.

The presence of these huge, ungainly animals in an army must inevitably have applied a brake to its mobility, not by their speed of march, it must be added, but by their sheer size; and the military benefits they brought would necessarily have had to be weighed against this limitation. This fact was clearly demonstrated in an incident experienced by Hannibal during the Second Punic War when, with a force of 50,000 infantry, 9,000 cavalry and 37 elephants he had surmounted the Pyrenees and was now marching through southern Gaul to Italy. Scipio, having learnt that his enemy was in course of crossing the River Rhône, set out on a forced march to intercept him. Hannibal, however, who had encountered a little local opposition, had by this time managed to get the bulk of his army to the left bank of the river, with the exception of his elephants and their guardians. He countered Scipio's move by despatching the whole of his cavalry force southwards to cover his movements and ordered his infantry to follow them in route march. Meantime he remained behind to supervise the passage of his animals.

He now constructed a series of solidly built rafts which, when lashed together, were 50 feet in overall width. The first pair of rafts rested wholly on dry land; others were then attached on the far side and fed into the waters of the river, until they projected a distance of some 200 feet. At this point, two more equally well constructed rafts to transport the elephants were firmly fastened to each other and placed in the river, but they were so connected to the main pontoon that the lashings could easily be cut. The whole pier was now piled up with quantities of earth until its surface had been brought up to the level of the bank and the elephants, which had previously resisted all efforts to get them afloat, were led along the earthen causeway, with two female animals leading the way:

> As soon as they were standing on the last rafts, the ropes holding these were cut, the boats took up the strain of the tow ropes and the rafts with the elephants standing on them were rapidly pulled away from the causeway. At this the animals panicked and at first turned round and began to move about in all directions but, as they were by then surrounded on all sides by the stream, their fear compelled them to stay quiet. In this way, and by continuing to attach fresh rafts to the end of the pontoon, they managed to get most of the animals over, but some became so terror-stricken that they leapt into the water when they were halfway across. The drivers of these were all drowned but the elephants were saved, because through the power and length of their trunks they were able to keep these above the surface and breathe through them, and also spout out any water which had entered their mouths. In this way most of them survived and crossed the river on their feet.[13]

It has been argued that the military role of the elephant in antiquity can be equated with that of the tank in the twentieth century.[14] Without doubt, it is possible to see the force of this suggestion as far as the earliest armoured vehicles are concerned, introduced in 1917 and used with such outstanding success at Cambrai as a device to break through the rain-sodden and blood-soaked German Hindenberg Line. Their dramatic arrival on the battlefield caused the enemy to scramble from their dugouts and shelters, in shocked amazement at their 'grotesque and terrifying' appearance.[15] The Roman soldiery, in their first encounters with elephants, behaved no differently.

A war elephant, surmounted by a combat tower, used by Hannibal in the Punic Wars. Elephants were often described as the tanks of ancient warfare

Scipio provided further grounds for comparison between animal and tank in an engagement with Caesar at Sidi Messaoud, midway between Ruspina and Leptis, when he arrayed his cavalry for battle, interspersed with elephants equipped with armour and towers,[16] the latter manned with archers. His worthy opponent at once recognized the manner in which the size and number of these animals 'gripped the minds of his soldiers' and appreciated the importance of having a similar strike force of his own. He promptly ordered a number of animals to be brought across from Italy, to enable his troops to familiarize themselves with this intimidating weapon and to train with them. Within a few weeks, he was threatening the town of Thapsus with his own army, supported by a contingent of sixty-four elephants similarly armed and caparisoned.

The elephant had three limited uses in ancient warfare: to act as a screen against enemy cavalry; to attack and penetrate the infantry mass; and to break into a fortified position; but, whenever employed in this last function it was generally unsuccessful. Moreover, when brought under fire, its behaviour, in large numbers, was unpredictable and frequently as dangerous to friend as to foe. Caesar witnessed evidence of this at Thapsus when, in a spontaneous assault on the enemy, his right wing, made up of massed slingers and archers, directed a rapid fire of missiles against the elephants covering Scipio's Moorish cavalry. The beasts, 'terrified by the whizzing sound of the slings and by the stones and leaden bullets directed against them, speedily wheeled round and trampled under foot the massed and serried ranks of their own supporting troops behind them. . .'.[17]

The Romans derived many of their infantry tactics, much of their weaponry and certainly a great deal of their knowledge of arrow-shooting and stone-shot artillery weapons from the Greeks. The latter, in their turn, had taken the Assyrian foot-soldier as a model upon which to base the Grecian army hoplite, their heavily armed spearman, who was destined to gain for himself a high reputation in military history. The Assyrians were also specialists in the art of siege warfare and their expertise in this was passed, through bitter experience, to Syria and Phoenicia and, ultimately to Carthage. From here, once again, military expertise found its way to Greece and thence to Rome. The Assyrian Empire, like all 'earth's proud empires', passed away but many of their peoples, in particular the Hamii, Ituraei and Damasceni, continued to provide mercenary soldiers to any who chose to buy their swords and many, in due course, served the Romans as auxiliaries alongside other specialist contingents provided by Rome's client states.

Tribal levies, possessing a wide variety of specialist skills missing from the Roman military arsenal, fought alongside legions in most theatres of operations and proved an invaluable complement to the Roman military establishment. They were categorized as auxiliaries. Evidence of the presence of Hamian archers has been discovered on both frontier walls in northern Britain.[18] Julius Caesar, as we have seen, was supported by Celtic cavalry, archers from Crete, slingers from the Balearic Islands, Numidians from Algeria and many others. The Numidians could boast proficiency in the use of both these supporting weapons. Vespasian (AD 69–79), during his wars against the Jews, employed Arabian archers and Syrian slingers. Probably the most colourful army of the era was brought together in North Africa by Labienus, when engaged in civil war against his erstwhile friend, Julius Caesar. Labienus's polygot force comprised 120 elephants, 1,600 Gallic and German cavalry, a further cavalry contingent of similar size commanded by Petreius, 8,000 Numidians who rode without bridles (a useful skill for mounted archers), a body of some 6,500 infantry recruited from half-castes, freedmen and slaves, and the customary contingents of provincial light infantry, composed of archers and slingers.[19]

The examples are countless. A segment of Trajan's Column, which features the *auxilia* in action, underlines the wide variety of such support troops.[20] They range from dismounted cavalrymen of obscure nationality, armed with long spears and carrying oval shields marked with a star and crescent, to a half naked club man, carrying a knobbed truncheon, a long slashing-sword and a shield for his protection. It is possible he came from the Aesti, a German tribe of whom Tacitus wrote that they seldom used 'weapons of iron, but clubs very often'.[21] Further to his right, a slinger is depicted in the act of casting a stone, while upon the opposite flank of the attacking column a company of archers is illustrated, pressing forward to the left. These men, depicted with high cheek bones and aquiline noses, appear to be from the Middle East, are possibly Syrians, and are shown wearing leather jerkins and voluminous skirts. They carry composite bows in their left hands and, on their backs, quivers of arrows, so positioned as to be conveniently reached by their free hand. The bows appear to be of the light but powerful 'Turkish' pattern,[22] a derivative of the Oriental composite bow, 3 ft 9 in in length when measured along its outer curve and 3 ft 2 in when fitted with a bowstring of 2 ft 11 in. The war arrow it discharged measured 2 ft 4½ in in length and required a draw weight of 118 lb to pull the bowstring back to its full capacity.

Composite bows were the outcome of necessity, for they originated from a time and place when the natural materials for bow-making were unobtainable. Their use appears to have been largely confined to such areas as modern-day Russia and China, from whence they found their way to India and the Middle East, the northern part of North America and the coastal districts of Greenland[23] – those areas which at one time endured the Ice Age. Bows constructed in this manner have been discovered in ancient Egyptian tombs.[24] Where it was available, the core of the composite bow was made of wood. On the belly side of the bow, that is to say the surface facing the archer, horn was glued; on its opposite side, sinew, taken from the neck tendon of either a stag or an ox, was affixed in a similar manner. Thus, when the bow was drawn, the sinew stretched. When the bowstring was released, the bow, pulled sharply by the sinew as it shortened to its normal length, snapped back to resume its original shape.

It can be imagined that stringing a powerful reflex weapon of such force presented problems to a man of average strength. Sir Ralph Payne-Gallwey, who made a lengthy study of Oriental bows, commented that he had heard of no one of

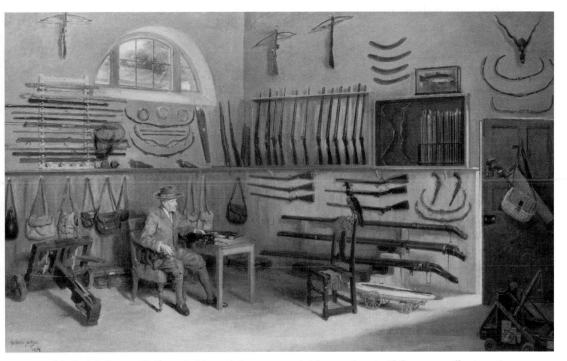

Sir Ralph Payne-Gallwey in his workshop surrounded by crossbows and Roman artillery weapons

his day who could string a Turkish bow unless by mechanical means, 'yet formerly the Turkish archer, unaided, could do so with ease', by bending it between his legs while stooping down to fit the string. He judged that the composite bow, without difficulty, would have been capable of driving a 1 oz war arrow a distance of 360 to 400 yards, well in excess of the performance of the European longbow with a comparable range of 230 to 250 yards. These distances are dwarfed, however, by those achieved by light target arrows shot from a Turkish-style weapon, where ranges in excess of 800 yards have been registered.[25]

The re-supply of arrows in battle was seemingly not considered important until the middle of the first century BC. The reason is not far to seek, for it lay in the very nature of battle itself, which was defensive and confrontational until, in the last resort, the swordsmen and spearmen were released for hand-to-hand fighting. Even Rome's wars of conquest have been described as 'mobile trench warfare'. Caesar, although he employed archers in his tactical armoury, rarely used them in the large numbers which became the custom in later years. In North Africa, at Ruspina, he mustered only 150 bowmen,[26] alongside thirty cohorts. Some weeks later, at Cercina, he received reinforcements from Italy which included the XIIIth and XIVth Legions, 800 Gallic cavalry and 1,000 slingers and archers,[27] and for many years a number in this latter range appears to have been about the norm. The practice was for both sides to fire their arrows away at each other, seeking, with their cavalry, to break their opponent's formation and achieve tactical advantage. The battlefield, therefore, was largely static and it would have been a perilous enterprise to wheel re-supply transport into the arena. The role of the archer, for this reason, was largely done once his quiver had been emptied.

The turning point came at the battle of Carrhae in 53 BC, when the Romans, in the person of Marcus Licinius Crassus, were taught a sharp lesson by the Parthians in the use of mobile firepower. It cost the Roman commander his life but it changed little else.

Crassus, a contemporary of Pompeius and Julius Caesar, had been seeking to gain for himself an equal military reputation and, to this end, he precipitated a war against a noble Parthian family, the Suren. He marched into Mesopotamia with, under his command, an unbalanced force of seven legions, about forty-four thousand men, supported by an inadequate number of cavalry commanded by his son, Publius. His objective was Seleucia on the Tigris and, as he crossed the Euphrates to thrust towards it, his troops, unacclimatized to desert warfare and inexperienced, were attacked and encircled at Carrhae by a Parthian force of 1,000 knights, with 10,000 mounted archers. Against all precedent, Sunenas, the enemy leader, had provided himself with unusually large reserves of arrows, carried by 1,000 camels, one camel load for every ten men. On the basis that a camel load weighed some 180 lb, this would have totalled roughly three thousand arrows per camel (at 1 oz per arrow) or 300 arrows per man. The camels offered a great advantage as transport animals since they could keep up, on the march, with the mounted bowmen.

When Crassus realized his danger, he organized his infantry into square formation and his men strove to protect themselves by covering both head and body with their shields against the unending shower of Parthian arrows, which the enemy replenished systematically by withdrawing sub-units from action. We are told that some thirty thousand Roman soldiers were killed by the missiles which rained upon them until nightfall. We can gain a rough idea of the size of the Parthian target, if we judge that each side of the Roman defensive square presented a front of 1,000 yards (45,000 men, arrayed nine deep, one yard frontal per man). It might have been larger but probably not smaller. The Parthians had no need to indulge in rapid fire. If they discharged their arrows at a rate of one per man per minute, releasing 10,000 at a time, they had a sufficient quantity of ammunition to last five hours. We may also assume that each bowman held a further ten to fifteen arrows in his quiver, probably designed in such a manner that they would not tangle on being withdrawn. This arrangement is clearly visible in the longbow quivers recovered from the Tudor ship, *Marie Rose*, and displayed in the museum at Portsmouth dockyard.

A tactic of the mounted archers of the Middle East, traditionally attributed to the Parthians but more probably initiated by the nomads of the steppes, was to pretend flight while firing back over the hindquarters of their mounts. This came to be known as a 'Parthian' shot, or, more commonly today, 'a parting shot'. Again, this was probably equally as much a device to escape unscathed, having exhausted their supply of arrows, as to entrap the enemy. One Roman general, Ventidius, is credited by Frontinus with being particularly successful in finding an answer to this swift, long-range attack.[28] He used to allow them to come within 500 paces and then, 'by a rapid advance, he came so near to them that, meeting them at close quarters, he escaped their arrows, which they shot from a distance'.

The defeat of Crassus at Carrhae dealt Roman prestige in the Middle East a stunning blow but, strangely, the technique which brought the victory and which introduced a mobile long-range weapon, with plentiful, almost unlimited, reserves of ammunition, was not yet adopted. By the time of the Jewish War of AD 67, however, when the trend had veered towards siege warfare, the importance attached to firepower is clearly recognizable in the forces deployed. The reinforcements which Titus brought from Greece to swell the army of his father, Vespasian, brought the total Roman expeditionary army to three legions, the Vth, Xth and XVth; 18 cohorts of infantry, totalling 18,000 men; and supporting levies amounting to roughly 5,000 cavalry and 11,000 archers, provided by local kings, Antiochus, Agrippa, Soaemes and Malchus of Arabia.[29] The number of bowmen in this instance, which included mounted men as well as foot soldiers, suggests that their value by now had been truly appreciated.

The role of the archer was multifarious. Julius Caesar, who seemingly used them but little in Gaul, employed them more frequently in North Africa, in one instance mingled with slingers to provide a protective screen against cavalry attacking his flanks; in another, spaced out among his mass of heavy infantry 'at definite points throughout the line, but chiefly on the wings'.[30] On another occasion he posted them with slingers in the course of a cavalry attack,[31] and again, in Gaul, while on the move he used them either with the vanguard of a column or as its flank guard.[32] Vespasian (AD 69–79) handled them more freely and in larger numbers. At Jotapata, he positioned his Arab bowmen and Syrian slingers, with his mini-catapults and supported by artillery, to withstand the Jewish onslaughts on his ranks.[33] At

Tarichaeae, he detached his archers to seize a flanking hill feature from which to give covering fire for his assault on the town.[34] During the siege of Jerusalem Titus deployed them effectively in street fighting, 'placing his bowmen at the ends of the streets and taking his own stand where the enemy were thickest'.[35]

Before completing this glance at the employment of the sling, the sling-staff and the bow in the role of supporting weapons, there is one other addendum which needs to be considered, namely, the rarely mentioned *amentum*. Ammianus Marcellinus refers to it obliquely when describing a battle with the Goths in AD 378. 'The Romans held the upper hand,' he tells us, 'since no bullet from the thong of a slinger, or any other missile when hurled, missed its mark.' The word *amentum* is usually taken to mean the thong by which a javelin, spear or arrow was given a whirling flight and propelled on its way by hand, with proportionately added momentum. The range is not stated but, in trained hands, we may guess it to have been as much as 200 ft.[36]

Distances covered by the range of small-arms weaponry employed by light and mounted infantry in Roman times may broadly be categorized as illustrated in Table 4. Inevitably, in their search for something that could reach out and disrupt, at a distance, the mass of enemy infantry before it reached close contact with them, soldiers demanded increasingly better performance from their weapons, both in range and in the nature of the projectiles they discharged. Originally, wrote Heron, the construction of these engines was developed from handbows. As men were compelled to project by this means a somewhat larger missile and one of greater range, they increased the size of the bows themselves and of their springs.[37]

TABLE 4

	Weapon	Distance (in yards)	Reference
a.	Sling	30–40	See fn 10, p. 157, but may be greater
b.	*Amentum*	65–70	A sling-arrow: see above
c.	Sling-staff	200	Vegetius, II, 15
d.	Longbow	230–50	Payne-Gallwey, *op. cit.*, Part VII, 20
e.	Comp. bow	360–400	*ibid.*

In this manner, just as the crossbow was born from the composite bow, the *gastraphetes* rapidly evolved, developed from the concept of the crossbow. The *gastraphetes* may be regarded as the first example of non-torsion artillery. In essence, the machine comprised a variety of parts which enabled a man to operate a bow of such power that, without them, he would have been utterly incapable of doing so. In the main, it comprised three elements. First, the bow, which provided the propulsive mechanism; second, the stock, to which the handbow was firmly

Auxiliary archers providing supporting fire in battle

fitted; and, third, a sliding part which could be moved freely, backwards and forwards on the stock, in a dovetailed groove. This part was also equipped with a shallow channel to accept the missile and a trigger mechanism to release it. The rear end of the stock was shaped concavely so as to permit an archer to press his body down upon it when drawing his bow, and thus derive added power. Vegetius provides clear evidence that the Romans employed the crossbow in their armoury. Crossbow archers, he explains, not entirely convincingly, for we have already seen light supporting weapons deployed in a variety of other ways, were normally sited in battle at the rear of the infantry:

> This was also the post of the archers who had helmets, cuirasses, swords, bows and arrows; of the slingers who threw stones with the common sling or with the *fustibalus*; and of the *tragularii* who annoyed the enemy with arrows from *manuballistae* [handbows] or *arcuballistae* [crossbows].[38]

In due course, the size and strength of the crossbow grew beyond the ability of man to operate it in the normal manner. It was then provided with a stock as a firm base, and with a winch mechanism to prepare the weapon for firing. The practice was for the archer to place the nose of the stock on the ground and, while holding the machine in a vertical position, to turn the winch and draw back the bowstring.

This machine provided the prototype of the original non-torsion *ballista*, which, in its turn, was developed into the more powerful torsion-motivated weapon. Marsden estimates that some *gastraphetes* were designed with a bow length of as much as 15 feet, capable of firing a shot of 40 lb in weight a distance of between 200 and 300 yards.[39]

Again, there was a quest for improved performance, the drive being provided by Greek engineers. They appreciated that, if the size of the missile were to be increased and the force of propulsion enhanced, the arms of the bow on the existing machine did not possess sufficient power to generate the energy required. The means by which they decided on the principle of torsion-propelled artillery remains obscure. They may perhaps have been driven to it from a consideration of the part played by animal sinew in the manufacture of a composite bow. However it happened, the spring of the bow was now replaced by two torsion operated lateral arms, which applied a much greater tension to the bowstring while maintaining, in most respects, the working shape of the non-torsion catapult. This, in essence, was the design of the Roman *ballista* and its counterpart, the cart-borne *carroballista*, the mechanical operation of which it is not proposed to discuss here in detail.[40]

Ballistae were manufactured in different sizes for use in differing military situations, the smallest, as we have seen, being not much larger than a heavy

A ballista *in action, depicted by the Ermin Street Guard. In this modern simulation, torsion is applied to the throwing arms by coiled rope. In ancient times it is likely that animal gut or horse-hair were used. On at least one occasion (n. 44), skeins of women's hair were utilized*

crossbow, although its performance in the field was much greater. It possessed arms of about 2 feet in length and was powered variously by skeins, about 4 inches in diameter, of sinew, cord, or horse hair. Indeed, the women of Carthage, in about 148 BC, are said to have sacrificed their hair for the purpose.[41] The largest variety of *ballista* was twice the size of the smallest, with arms between 3 to 4 feet in length, and was powered by skeins of sinew 6 to 8 inches in diameter. Payne-Gallwey experimented with these machines by constructing a small version in his workshops. He found it capable of projecting a stone ball, 1 lb in weight, a distance of 300 to 350 yards. He had little doubt that the large stone-throwing *ballistae* of the Greeks and Romans could cast a round stone, 6 to 8 lb in weight, a distance of 450 to 500 yards. These were often formed of heavy pebbles, enclosed in baked clay and designed to shatter on impact, so that the enemy could not retrieve and make use of them.[42] The logistical implications of this tactic, combined with the need to provide the machines with ammunition of a prescribed weight, size and quality, would have been considerable and would have presented substantial workshop and transport problems.

The production of a repeating catapult by Dionysius of Alexandria in the third century BC is surely worthy of note, if only for its inventiveness. Philon of Byzantium (*c.* 200 BC), who professed to have seen it, comments that its performance was unremarkable and that its range (200 yards) was less than that achieved by its more conventional counterpart.[43] He saw no reason to pursue its development. His main complaint appears to have been that its ability to shoot a large number of missiles rapidly at a given target was a disadvantage, for its drop shot had little spread, either laterally or longitudinally: it was, in other words, too accurate. It may be that he had a reluctance to accept innovation. A similar dissatisfaction was expressed when the Bren light machine gun was introduced during the 1930s as a replacement for the elderly Lewis gun; it subsequently served the British army with great efficiency throughout the Second World War and for many years afterwards.

The existence of a repeating catapult at such an early date gives obvious relevance to Payne-Gallwey's record of an ancient Chinese repeating crossbow,[44] capable of firing ten arrows within 15 seconds, particularly pertinent in view of the recognized flow of Oriental weapons to the Middle East during this period. With such a rate of fire, where 100 men could fill the air with 1,000 arrows in a remarkably short space of time, it was clearly a lethal weapon. Indeed, it was employed to good effect by the Chinese as late as the Sino–Japanese War of 1894–5. The last occasion it was used against the British was at the taking of the Taku Forts in 1860. There is, however, no evidence that this weapon played a part in Roman warfare although the possibility should clearly not be overlooked.

The *onager*, the large siege catapult employed by the Romans, was, in the same manner as the *ballista*, also constructed in varying sizes according to the military requirement. The machine, according to Ammianus Marcellinus,[45] was variously nicknamed *tormentum*, because the tortion provided by the sinew which powered it was produced by extreme twisting; or *onager*, because wild asses, when chased by

Sketch plan of a catapult for slinging stones, its arm being partly wound down

hunters, were said to kick back stones upon their pursuers, 'either crushing their breasts . . . or breaking the bones of their skulls and shattering them'.

Its frame possessed five main components:

a.   a solid wooden base, hewn out of oak, stoutly held together by cross-beams of equal strength, secured by mortise-tenon joints;

b.   a throwing-arm, which Ammianus defined as 'like the pole of a chariot', tapering in width to its top. Here it was fitted either with a throwing sling to hold a stone missile or a spoon-shaped receptacle for larger projectiles;

c.   a skein of elastic material to provide a spring. This was manufactured out of animal sinew, horse-hair or, on occasions, women's hair.[46] Payne-Gallwey records that when the arm of his machine was fully wound, it could not be moved 'even one inch' by three strong men armed with a rope;

d.   a winch mechanism, operated from the rear of the machine and employed to haul the throwing-arm down into a horizontal position. The cable on this device was fitted with a release lanyard;

e.   a heavy reinforced cross bar to stop the forward movement of the arm when it was released. This was padded with 'a great cushion of hair-cloth, stuffed with a fine chaff, and bound on with strong cords' so as to take the impact when the arm was released;

Ammianus defined this process in the following words:

A British (Durotriges) slingstone hoard uncovered at Maiden Castle, Dorset

Then, when there is a battle, a round stone is placed in the sling and four young men on each side turn back the bar with which the ropes are connected and bend the pole almost flat. Then finally the gunner, standing above, strikes out the pole-bolt which holds the fastening of the whole work, with a strong hammer, thereupon the pole is set free and, flying forward with a swift stroke and meeting the soft hair-cloth, hurls the stone, which will crush whatever it hits.

The longer the arm, the greater was the arc it described through the air and, all other things being equal, the further it projected its shot. Added power and increased range were also obtained for the weapon by fitting a sling to the head of the pole, in the same fashion that the performance of a sling was enhanced by being fitted to a sling-staff. When its release was triggered, the arm exploded upright, striking the crossbar with tremendous force and despatching the missile with added velocity. The throwing-arm was thus subjected to great strain and was no ordinary piece of wood: something specially designed was needed but the nature of its precise composition remains obscure. Payne-Gallwey suggests that the arm was manufactured from several spars of wood, glued and held together, with lengths of thick sinew fitted longitudinally, and bound round with broad strips of raw hide. He visualized that, by this means, it would have set as hard as metal.

An *onager* may be expected to have weighed, according to its stone or spear casting capacity, between 2 to 6 tons. It was therefore an unwieldy weapon which presented transportation difficulties. On occasions, it would have been stripped down, packed on to wagons and re-assembled when required for action. Sometimes it was fitted with wheels and directly pulled by teams of oxen or mules. Either way, it was slow-moving and consequently vulnerable. Cestius, commanding a Roman army at Jerusalem in AD 66 at the outbreak of the Jewish War, learnt this lesson to his cost. Finding himself surrounded, with the ground on all sides swarming with Jews, he gave orders for a night withdrawal. All animals were to be slaughtered, 'and even the wagon-horses, with the exception of those conveying the missiles and artillery'. The enemy pressed him hard, however, and compelled him to put on such a turn of speed 'that the soldiers in utter panic dumped the battering-rams and spear-throwers and most of the other engines'. These the Jews promptly seized and were soon operating against their original owners.[47]

The *onager* was a siege weapon and not one generally deployed in fluid operations. It possessed a considerable capability. Josephus[48] relates that the stones it cast 'were of the weight of a talent and were carried two or more *stades*': an *onager* could thus fire a half-cwt stone a distance of 400 to 500 yards. If we accept this statement, and Payne-Gallwey suggests that from the results of his experiments it is not unreasonable, then we must realize that this would not have been its effective range in siege warfare, when employed against high fortifications. A projectile flying through the air describes a parabola, and its range would have been foreshortened by the height of the defences, thus probably bringing the machine within range of enemy small arms.

Josephus's description of their performance at the siege of Jotapata is particularly vivid:

> The force of the spear-throwers was such that a single projectile ran through a row of men, and the momentum of the stones hurled by the 'engine' carried away battlements and knocked off corners of towers. There is in fact no body of men that cannot be laid low to the last rank by the impact of these huge stones. The effectiveness of the engine can be gathered by incidents of that night: one of the men standing near Josephus on the rampart got in the line of fire and had his head knocked off by a stone, his skull being flung like a pebble from a sling more than six hundred yards. . . . Even more terrifying than the actual engines and their missiles was the rushing sound and the final crash. There was a constant thudding of dead bodies as they were thrown one after another from the rampart. Within the town rose the terrible shrieks of the women. The whole strip of ground that encircled the battlefield ran with blood, and it was posssible to climb up the heap of corpses on the battlements. The din was made the more terrifying by the echoes from the mountains around. . . .

There is continuing debate about the manner in which these weapons were deployed. According to Vegetius,[49] there were ten *onagri* to each legion, a scale of one per cohort, and one *carroballista* per century, but it is militarily difficult to believe that they could have been usefully handled individually in this manner; the distribution provided by Vegetius may perhaps simply represent a legionary scale of entitlement. The principles of concentration of force and of firepower would by themselves have demanded that weapons of this category be 'brigaded', either by cohorts or, particularly in the case of *onagri*, by being grouped as legionary artillery. There are very few phases of war in which they could have been employed which would not have required some such organization.

There are numerous examples of this truth. Caesar, defending a hill against Belgic forces in 57 BC, dug himself in and concentrated his artillery 'at both ends of each trench, to prevent the enemy from using their numerical superiority to envelop his men from the flanks' .[50] In AD 14, Germanicus marshalled his artillery to cover his crossing of the Adrana river.[51] At the siege of Jotapata, mentioned above, Vespasian assembled 160 'engines for throwing stones and darts round about the city'. On the line of march, artillery, as positioned by Vespasian in the Jewish War and by Arrian in his campaign against the Alani in AD 134, moved *en bloc* behind the auxiliary cavalry and infantry cohorts, but in front of the legionary soldiers[52] and readily under the hand of the commanding general. Again, in the set-piece battle, as we have seen above, it was frequently mustered with the reserves, to the rear of the mass of infantry, or deployed to protect the flanks. Thus, in each phase of Roman war, in column of march, in defence, in set-piece battle, in siege warfare and in the assault, artillery weapons were grouped for operations, an entirely logical arrangement, since it is not easy to judge that a solitary *carroballista* could have offered much benefit to a century.

This leads us, therefore, to the question of the command structure and the administration of the artillery in earlier times. Even in the case of one legion, where ten *onagri* and sixty *carroballistae* were involved, the numbers concerned were considerable. In an army where two, three, four or even more legions were involved, the total of artillery would have been huge. There must, for this reason, have been some chain of command, some *principalis*, the equivalent of a commander, Royal Artillery, through whom the army commander could have passed his orders. The equally large administrative problems of attached artificers and workshops responsible for the maintenance of these weapons in the field would have been closely linked with this requirement. Again, the evidence for such a *principalis* is slight,[53] but it is not easy to believe that the commanding general could efficiently have passed his orders downwards to legions and cohorts in any other manner.

Finally, the numbers of men required to operate these weapons is very relevant. A *carroballista* would have required a junior commander, a gun-aimer, who probably did not have responsibility for loading the missile, one or two men on either flank of the weapon to turn the winch, one or two animal handlers, and perhaps two more men to re-supply ammunition, assuming that reserves of missiles were taken on to the field of battle, making a total of ten. It would also have been important for each artillery piece to have had some senior soldier responsible for its maintenance and knowledgeable of its frailties.

Vegetius[54] has suggested that a team of eleven men was required to operate and maintain each weapon and, although this figure is sometimes questioned, he may not be far wrong. In the case of an *onager*, particularly a large one firing heavy missiles, an even larger gun team would have been needed. The total number of artillerymen per legion, without taking artificers into account, would thus have been in the neighbourhood of 650, roughly of cohort strength. Clearly, many of these men would have been specialists and must have existed as such before the second and third centuries AD. It is strange, therefore, that, even in those late years, there are still only tenuous references to their existence (the *ballistarii*). The *Notitia Dignitatum* records a parade state of Tarrutenius Paternus (*c*. AD 150) in which the gunners are included among the *immunes* – men excused fatigues, guard duties and the like.

Thus, to sum up the true state of the disposition of the artillery weapons. Despite the clear statement by Vegetius that one *carroballista* was allocated to each century and one *onager* to each cohort, it would have been practical, for command and administrative reasons, for them to have been concentrated at unit and formation level, namely, the light weapons at cohort level and the heavy artillery at legionary headquarters. Operationally, everything points to the artillery having been handled in this manner. Apart from the military sense of the idea, it would greatly have assisted the training and allocation of specialist artillerymen and would have economized on the need for artificers and the use of workshops. It is notable that after *c*. AD 300, all recognized artillerymen (*ballistarii*) were designated to special artillery units. There is, however, no evidence to suggest that this is the way it happened at any earlier date, despite the logic of the arrangement.

CHAPTER SIX

Waterborne Operations

The war was pushed forward by land and sea; and infantry, cavalry and marines, often meeting in the same camp, would mess and make merry together.

Tacitus, *The Agricola*

'. . . and had not certain persons in their envy of [Caesar] . . . forced him to return here before the proper time, he would certainly have subdued all Britain together with the other islands which surround and all Germany to the Arctic Ocean, so that we should have had as our boundaries for the future, not land or people, but the air and the outer sea.'

Mark Antony in Dio's *Roman History*

The author of the above words about Caesar, Cassius Dio,[1] was a historian whose *Roman History* covered the years from the foundation of the city by Romulus up to his own times, the end of the third century AD. He thus wrote basking in the glow of his knowledge of imperial achievement, which enabled him to put a vision of the future into the mouth of Mark Antony, when recreating the latter's supposed speech to the Forum upon the assassination of Julius Caesar in 44 BC. Dio's phrasing hints at an early Roman ambition to extend their nation's influence to the very edges of a flat-earth world, where the land mass terminated, suspended in mid-air, and an endless ocean reached to the edges of a distant horizon. Whether or not Caesar nurtured such ideas, they certainly would not have been considered strange by Trajan, who visited the Persian Gulf in AD 116. After making a slow passage down the Tigris, and, 'when he had learnt its nature [the Persian Gulf] and had seen a ship sailing to India',[2] Trajan remarked that he would certainly have crossed over too, if he were still young; but he was destined never to see Rome again and he died in the following year.

Under Hadrian (AD 117–38), who presided over the heyday of imperial Rome, the northern frontier of the Roman world ran broadly along the axes of the Rhine and Danube rivers, with the exception that, east of Pannonia, for good defensive reasons, it deviated abruptly northwards to incorporate the Dacian salient, before resuming its course to the northern shores of the Black Sea, the Pontus Euxius. At the eastern extremity of the latter, the line now turned southwards, to pick a path through the fertile valley of the Euphrates river and reach a point north of Sura. Here, it turned again to head directly for the Red Sea, south of Eilat, in the

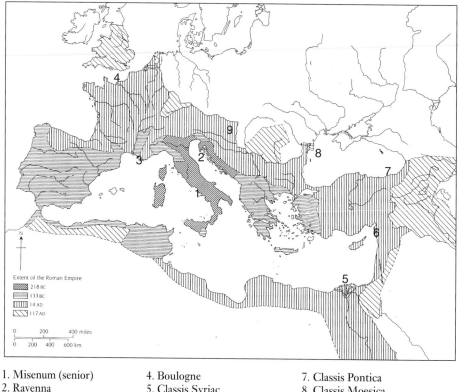

1. Misenum (senior)
2. Ravenna
3. Forum Julii (Fréjus)
4. Boulogne
5. Classis Syriac
6. Classis Alexandrina
7. Classis Pontica
8. Classis Moesica
9. Classis Pannonica

The growth of the Roman empire, showing principal naval ports (from The Oxford History of the Classical World*)*

Gulf of Aqabar. In broad terms, the Middle Eastern frontiers of the Roman Empire at this time encompassed the areas of modern-day Turkey, Syria, Israel and Jordan.[3] From the Gulf of Aqabar, the frontier proceeded westwards to include Egypt and the prosperous agricultural belt of North Africa's Mediterranean coastline, until its course was halted by the Atlantic Ocean. The western boundary of the empire now ran northwards, along Europe's western seaboard, to meet once more with the Rhine delta, embracing in its progress a large swathe of ancient Britain.

At the heart of the Roman Empire lay the Mediterranean Sea, the arrogantly named *Mare Nostrum*, Our Sea, which provided access, through the Pillars of Hercules,[4] to the inhospitable waters of the oceans which lay beyond. This area, together with the southern flank of Rome's African possessions and client states, where a sea of arid desert reached distantly towards an uneven skyline, provided to a considerable degree the trouble-free frontiers of 'air and ocean' pictured by Dio. Elsewhere, as we have seen, they were firmly delineated by the Rhine, the Danube, the shores of the Black Sea and, to a minor degree and at varying times, by the lines of the Euphrates and the Tigris.

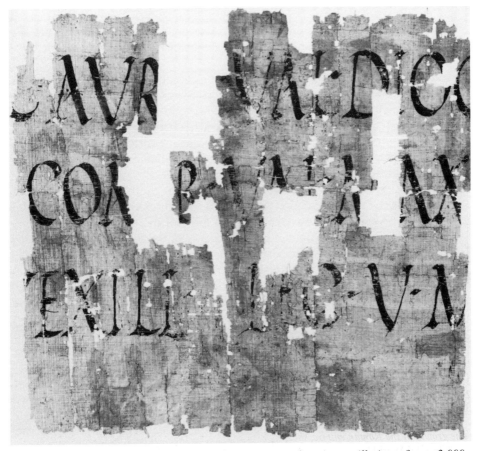

In the late empire Rome eked out its slim military resources by using vexillations of up to 2,000 men to supplement her frontier garrisons. This papyrus fragment from Egypt bears the names of Diocletian and Maximian in 'monumental' letters, and 'Vexillation of Leg. V. Macedonica'. *It provides a record of a mobilized detachment of this Danubian legion in Egypt, intended for a public notice or for carving an inscription on stone*

Rome could neither have won nor held her great empire had she not possessed a navy, trained and of sufficient size both to ensure her domination of the Mediterranean and Black Seas and to enable her to succour and communicate with her widely deployed armies in the field; although, in truth, the numbers of these were not great. 'Almost every nation under the sun bows down before the might of Rome', Josephus quotes Agrippa as saying *c.* AD 40, in a speech aimed at turning the Jews from the folly of war with such a formidable enemy;[5] and then, speaking particularly of North Africa and Asia Minor, he continued,

none of them [the nations] could resist Roman skill at arms. This third of the whole world, whose peoples could hardly be counted, bounded by the Atlantic and the Pillars of Hercules, and supporting the millions of Ethiopia as far as the Indian Ocean, is subdued in its entirety . . . and unlike you they take no offence when given orders, though only a single legion is quartered in their midst.

Reading these words, it is tempting to reflect upon the equally moderate forces deployed by Great Britain in the occupation of her empire, in particular the Indian sub-continent, whose population of 385 million people, comprising numerous castes and tribes, was peacefully governed by a highly skilled civil service, supported by 52,000 British regular soldiers, a further 135,000 troops of the Indian army, with an additional 45,000 men contributed by the Princely State Forces. The paramount responsibility of the military, apart from occasional duties in aid of the civil power, rested with the control of the North-West Frontier Province and the defence of that strategically vulnerable area in the event of exterior aggression. There was also a police force of modest strength, totalling 203,000 officers and men. Much of the governance of the sub-continent remained in the hands of Princely State rulers (client states, it might be argued), carefully and discreetly guided by British residents. As in the case of Rome, there was a major factor which rendered possible this 'light hand on the tiller' approach to government, namely, the benefits of *Pax Britannica* enjoyed by the governed and the sense of security they provided. There were, as well, other important influences, but they are not relevant to this chapter.

Parallel with the expansion of their empire, the British government, like the principate, directed its attention to the control of an increasing number of key strategic areas so that speedy reinforcement and the free flow of resources, along carefully planned and prepared lines of communication, might be guaranteed whenever an emergency demanded.

In the same manner, Rome's naval control of the Mediterranean formed a vital part of her strategy, although it must at once be said that, until the third century AD, her fleets were rarely confronted by opposition on the high seas. The execution of this policy rested in the hands of two senior squadrons, *classes praetoriae*, based individually at Ravenna and Misenum and charged with the task of guarding, respectively, the eastern and western seaboards of Italy. Of these two naval bases, Ravenna, built on stilts in what Strabo called 'the marshes', and lying in the north-eastern corner of Italy overlooking the northern extremity of the Adriatic Sea, was a large and busy city.[6] It was linked by canal to the mouth of the Primaro and to Spina. The harbour, frequented by the Roman navy and initiated by the emperor Augustus (31 BC to AD 14), was sited about 3 miles outside the town. It quickly emerged as an important centre, with detached flotillas at Aquiela, Ancona and Brindisi in Italy, another at Salonae (Split) in Dalmatia (Yugoslavia) and a further two in Greek waters.[7]

Misenum, a deep-water harbour established *c.* 22 BC, quickly became the foremost naval station in the empire. It stood at the end of the northern cape of the Bay of Naples, where its proximity to the emperor at Rome ensured its importance. The hinterland adjoining Misenum, according to Strabo, contained 'the most blest of all plains'; and the bay itself 'was . . . garnished by residences and plantations, which, since they intervene in unbroken succession, present the appearance of a single city'.[8] Many of these properties, with their fruitful, fertile lands, were the possessions of past and present imperial families.

In the fullness of time, a detachment of the Misene fleet was stationed at Ostia, at the mouth of the Tiber, with duties which appear to have included the transportation of the imperial family, officers and staff, the receipt of despatches and the task of carrying the emperor's orders to his commanders overseas. Indeed, it was from Ostia that Claudius, accompanied by his staff, an element of his Praetorian Guard and members of his family, had sailed to be present at the final conquest of Britain in AD 43. He descended the River Tiber by boat and, having twice been forced by storms to take shelter, then followed the coastline to Massilia (Marseilles) from where, 'advancing partly by land and partly along the rivers, he came to the ocean and crossed over to Britain'.[9]

The Misene fleet possessed subsidiary naval bases in Sicily, Sardinia and Corsica, together with another at Forum Julii (Frejus), in Narbonesis. Of these, the latter was probably the most important, by virtue of its valuable tactical location adjoining the mouth of the River Rhône and lying close to Marseilles, an important, well-fortified harbour, the possession of the people of a client state, the Massiliotes.[10] Tacitus records how Valerius Paulinus, in the first century AD, having seized the naval base at Forum Julii at a time of national crisis, despatched a flotilla of fast galleys 'to the Stoechades Islands which belonged to Marseilles'.[11] It is probable that a detachment from Frejus was also located at Arles, a Ligurian township situated at the point where the Rhône divides to form its estuary, north-west of Marseilles, with the task of establishing a military presence and ensuring the peaceful passage of river traffic to and from the north.

Ostia was an important port, particularly for the reception and storage of grain imported from overseas and destined for Rome. Strabo, nevertheless, describes it as harbourless. Silt carried down to the sea by the many mountain streams which feed the Tiber had, even then, created a bar across the estuary, forbidding access to large merchant ships. These were thus denied the opportunity of making their way upstream to the emporium at Rome, which lay 22 miles distant, and were compelled either to lighten their cargoes by partly off-loading into warehouses at Ostia, or to exchange cargoes off-shore, while anchored in what often proved to be troublesome tidal waters. Nor did rivercraft find the passage to Rome particularly easy. Laden barges plowing their way against the sometimes powerful waters of the Tiber almost invariably needed to be towed from the river bank by teams of buffalo; in other instances, horses were employed.[12] This factor should be noted, for it provides an answer to many of the military supply problems we have been considering and was common behaviour in ancient times, when men, rather than animals, were employed as the towing medium, and is still to be seen in many parts of the world today. Boats with a burden of 6 tons, provided with a strong towing team, could make 20 km a day upstream; downstream, as much as 30–35 km was possible.[13] The practice was further complemented by the fitting of inflated bladders to rivercraft to facilitate their movement through shallow waterways.[14]

The apparent lack of attention paid by early writers to the logistical problems of their times, particularly those affecting military operations, has often been a matter of frustrated remark by historians glancing at this period. Many of the

River scene with coracle and fishermen riding inflated pigskins. Relief from the Palace of Sennacherib (705–681 BC), now in the British Museum

ways and means of the ancients, such as those employed for the accumulation of reserves of foodstuffs, the evacuation of wounded (of whom there must have been many in the bloody and numerous campaigns of the era) and the forward provision of grain, remain obscure. It may be that the reason for this is to be found in the fact that the techniques employed were so glaringly obvious and so fully established in the public mind that they were deemed to be unremarkable. Strabo,[15] in a paragraph describing the river system of Gaul (about which more than average data are available, mainly due to the detail of Caesar's *de Bello Gallico*) makes it clear that he, at least, appreciated their potential in this regard. Some of the rivers flow down from the Alps, he wrote,

the others from the Cevennes mountains and the Pyrenees; and some of them are discharged into the ocean [*the English Channel*], the others into Our Sea. Further, the districts through which they flow are plains, for the most part, and hilly lands with navigable watercourses. The river beds are by nature so well situated with reference to one another that there is transportation from either sea into the other; for the cargoes are transported only a short distance by land, with an easy transit through plains, but most of the way they are carried on the rivers – on some into the interior, on others to the sea. The Rhône offers an advantage in this connection, for not only is it a stream of many tributaries . . .

but it also connects with Our Sea, which is better than the outer sea and traverses a country which is the most favoured of all in that part of the world.

Strabo[16] also describes how traffic was portaged for onward transhipment, either down the Garonne and the Dordogne (which share the same estuary), the broad waters of the River Loire or the River Seine, from whence it began 'its journey down to the ocean and to the Lexobi and the Caleti; and from these people it is less than a day's run to Britain'. Let us consider the direction and potential of these waterways in rather more detail.

The River Rhône rises from a glacier in south central Switzerland and, after entering Lake Geneva, continues on a zig-zag course through the Jura Mountains until it meets with its tributary, the Saône, at the city of Lyon. It then flows directly into the Mediterranean Sea and is the only significant river in Europe to do so. At suitable places along its course – and this was a feature which applied to most riverways of this scale in Gallic-Romano times – land and waterway routes interconnected to form transhipment points at which cargoes switched from river to land, or vice versa, to undertake the next stage of their journeys. Seyssel, for example, described by Chevallier as 'the outer harbour of Geneva on the open Rhône flowing down to the sea',[17] provided a vital nodal point of this nature and conveys a strong impression of the weight of traffic which then plied these routeways, penetrating to the heart of Europe. Seyssel lay at a point where two main lines of communication converged: one coming from the north from Germany and the Rhine, the other descending from the Great St Bernard and passing along the left banks of Lake Geneva and the Rhône. From it, it should be noted, for it puts its use in perspective, stone was later to be shipped downriver for use in the building of Lyon; to it, in another age, came amphorae from Italy and from Iberia.

The Saône, a tributary of the Rhône, is itself a substantial river which flows some 300 miles before melding with the waters of the main stream at Lyon. It rises near Epinal in south-west Lorraine, a watershed area which it shares with the Moselle, and, meandering southwards, passes through Chalons-sur-Saône, Tournus, Macon and Villefranche before joining with the River Doubs at Verdun-sur-le-Doubs, north of Lyons. It appears historically to have been a busy trading river, with many craft plying its waters. It will be recalled (Chapter 3 pp. 53–4) that the Aedui, in 60 BC, had lost a war with the Sequani over the payment of tolls on the Saône and had called upon Rome for military assistance to re-establish their 'rights'. The cause of the disagreement appears to have been rooted in a convoluted quarrel arising from Aeduan customs duties levied on exports of 'the finest of salted hog-meat', for which their neighbours had found an agreeable market in Italy.[18]

Traffic reaching the headwaters of the Saône was, in ancient times, confronted by a short overland portage between the Saône and the Moselle, ultimately connecting with the Rhine, whose waters in turn, flowing westwards through Coblenz, Cologne and Arnhem, provided access to the North Sea. A paragraph by Tacitus records how, during the reign of the emperor Nero (AD 54–68), Vetus had intended to link these two riverways but had been frustrated by local jealousies.[19] To keep the troops busy, wrote Tacitus, the imperial governor of Lower Germany, Pompeius Paulinus, finished the dam for controlling the Rhine, built 63 years previously by Nero Drusus. His colleague in Upper Germany, Lucius Antisus Vetus, planned to build a Saône-Moselle canal. Goods arriving from the Mediterranean up the Rhône and the Saône would thus pass via the Moselle into the Rhine, and so to the North Sea. Such a waterway, joining the western Mediterranean to the northern sea-board, would eliminate the difficulties of land transport. But the imperial governor of Gallia Belgica, Aelius Gracilis, jealously prevented [him] from bringing his army into the province he governed. . . .

Today, the vision of Lucius Antisus Vetus has surely been vindicated, for a thriving canal now exists between Metz and Coblenz, permitting passage of Rhine barges as large as 1,500 tons in capacity between the two rivers .

Nero Drusus, mentioned above by Tacitus, died in 9 BC.[20] During his service in Germania he constructed a canal which connected the Waal, a tributary of the Rhine, with the Ems, thus enabling rivercraft to avoid the hazards of the North Sea. Some sixty years later, his purpose was carried yet further forward by Corbulo who, for a similar reason of keeping 'the troops occupied', constructed a 23 mile long canal between the Meuse and the River Rhine. He was granted an honorary Triumph by Claudius in recognition of this work and others of the same nature, for he was renowned for his enterprise. Tacitus records that his exhausted troops secretly appealed to the emperor, begging that he should allocate honorary Triumphs to his generals *before* giving them command and thus restrain their energies!

The River Doubs, a tributary of the Saône, which in its upper reaches meanders through gorges and is partly torrent, cannot be omitted from this pattern of riverways. It follows a course of 267 miles, after rising near Mouthe in the Jura Mountains. Although today it has been canalized, in order to bypass otherwise difficult falls and rapids, it would not have been easily navigable in Roman times beyond a comparatively short distance from its mouth. Besançon, the largest town of the Sequani, may have fallen within this range, as might Belfort, an ancient town which occupies the Burgundy Gate and dominates the strategic passage way connecting the Rhine valley with the Paris basin and, consequently, the River Seine. It was at Besançon, where the Doubs forms an almost complete circle around the town, that Julius Caesar established his first winter base in 58 BC, after his brief and successful campaign against the Helvetii.

The number of vessels on this great network of riverine routeways, and available to the military for charter or requisition, would obviously have been considerable. For confirmation, we need look no further than an event in 52 BC, when Labienus[21] was despatched by Caesar, together with four legions, to seize Lutetia, a settlement of the Parisii situated on an island in the Seine. His arrival had been anticipated and, upon reaching the edge of the water opposite his objective, he discovered that all craft and other means which might have assisted his passage across had sensibly been removed. He therefore commenced to throw a causeway across the marsh separating him from the township, laying down a foundation of fascines (bundles of long sticks) and other materials, but the idea

Scene from Trajan's Column showing Roman infantry crossing a pontoon bridge. Each soldier carries his pack and other kit on a stick, in the fashion decreed by Marius

proved unworkable. Then, abandoning the project, he marched upriver to Metlosedum, the town of a neighbouring tribe, also standing on an island in the Seine, where he found an assembly of fifty boats. Floating these downstream, he lashed them together and formed a bridge which enabled him to get troops across the river and into his objective without further ado.

It is logistically significant that, throughout his campaigning in Gaul, Julius Caesar never strayed far from a network of a major river with its tributaries. His operations in 53 BC, for example, which ranged between Rheims, the capital of the Remi, Autun, the capital of the Aedui, and Lutetia, were plainly based on the facilities offered by the River Seine, with its major tributaries. Of these, he employed two for his purpose: the Yonne, which approaches Paris from the south, and the Marne, which, with its parent river, the Seine, rises on the Plateau de Langres, north of Dijon, and then sweeps in a great northerly curve to pass through Rheims, before joining the main stream, a few miles east of Paris. In the following year, Caesar based his activities upon the Loire and its tributary the Yeure, while still maintaining contact with his main grain providers, the Aedui. Their fertile territory in the Autun district was ideally located in a position of great influence, lying as it did at the heart of the French pattern of riverways. During this

A side view of Caesar's Bridge across the Rhine as depicted in the early eighteenth century by William Stukeley in his Itinerarium Curiosum

campaigning season, Caesar established a rear headquarters at Nevers, itself on the river, and carried his operations to Bourges and Orleans, before returning to Alise St Reine, 30 miles north-west of Dijon, to confront Vercingetorix at Alesia.

In due course, and with their customary thoroughness, the Romans provided a pattern of roadways to complement their river systems. One such road[22] which is significant, for it hints at a master plan which refuses to be intimidated by water obstacles of whatever size, was initiated by Claudius during his years as emperor. It extended from Chartres to the coast of the Cotentin peninsula where, on the other side of the Channel, it lay opposite the start of Vespasian's tactical road from Hamworthy to Bath, or, alternatively, the Isle of Wight and the estuary shared by the Rivers Stour and Avon. Of these two rivers Sean McGrail[23] has commented that their tributaries are wide-ranging and that, 'by their use and with a portage from the Wiltshire Wylye to the Somerset Frome, there is theoretical access to the Bristol Channel and the Mendip and Cotswold regions'. It is noteworthy that, as late as 1623, it was being visualized that 'the Avon might be made as navigable as the Thames' from Salisbury to the sea.[24] The justification for the proposition was that wood had to be carted to the city from distances of 18 to 20 miles, while 'a boat would carry as much as 20 wagons and 80 horses and such boats would bring up sea coal and send downstream corn, beer, bricks, stones, tiles and charcoal. . .'. Both these Roman options, it should be noted, pointed to Bath as their ultimate destination, linking with the Bristol Channel and the River Severn. Bath, situated on the Bristol Avon, could have been a key military administrative base and was the possible location of a military convalescent centre.[25]

If we return to Chartres, and extend Claudius's Roman road in exactly the opposite direction, we discover it runs to Lutetia, the settlement seized by Labienus a century earlier and the origin of modern-day Paris. Even at that moment in history, this was a commanding centre, with Roman roads radiating outwards to

Senlis, Meaux, Melun, Dreux and Chartres. Across the Seine, its fingers reached to an area bounded by the Meuse and the Escaut, the strategic importance of which, as a corridor to and from the Rhineland, has been periodically re-discovered over the centuries by successive generations of soldiers. This avenue led to the Roman garrison on the Upper Rhine, deployed on the empire's northern frontiers and covering the Danube Gap, the land bridge lying between the sources of the Rhine and the Danube. In support of these operations, particularly on the Lower Rhine and the river's tributary, the Ems, there existed the *classis Germanica*, a flotilla whose formation was dated by Tacitus to 6 BC.[26]

The Roman fortifications designed to close the Danube Gap were not set in place until the Antonine era, when a palisade was erected, covered by defensive positions much the same as those laid out by Hadrian along the Wall in northern Britain; but it was Augustus (31 BC to AD 14) who preoccupied himself for nearly twenty-five years in consolidating the Pannonian frontier (Northern Yugoslavia to the head of the Danube valley) and in pushing forward the Roman frontier to the Danube along the whole length of the river. It is likely that two Roman flotillas on the Danube, the *classes Pannonica* and *Moesica*, had their origins in his reign. Equally, it is probable that both the IXth Legion *Hispania*, moved from Pannonia for the invasion of Britain in AD 43, and Aulus Plautius, the regional governor of the province, were selected for this duty because of the specialist knowledge they had accumulated during riverine operations on the Danube in previous years. The line of the IXth Legion's advance, first along the line of the Thames to the Medway,[27] and then northwards up the east coast of Britain, while almost certainly working closely with the *classis Britannica*, would seem to bear this out. The ancient Roman canal linking the Wash, via the Witham, with the Trent at Torksey, may also be dated to this time, the middle of the first century AD.

Downstream from Pannonia, the responsibilities of the *classis Moesica*, apart from the security of the Danube delta, are deemed to have included patrolling the western shores of the Euxine (Black Sea), with the influence of the fleet extending as far south as Byzantium (Istanbul), and penetrating the Straits of Salonika.

During the reign of Vespasian (AD 69–79), the province of the Danube became increasingly a source of strength for Rome's eastern legions, providing both men and material for her army on the Armenian front. The supply line initially ran from the Danube estuary across the water to a port at Trapezus, on the south-eastern shore of the Black Sea. This was also the destination of supplies of grain, hides and fish provided for the same purpose by her ally, the client kingdom of the Bosphorus. Goods from here were transported by the *classis Pontica*, which also was charged with the task of subduing the many pirates who, at that time, were savagely exploiting merchants trading in those waters. Supplies landed at Trapezus were then conveyed over a difficult mountain road to Roman forces on the Euphrates and, at a later date, the Tigris. Trapezus, therefore, served a vital need, both as a port and as a naval base which, according to Josephus, in the first century accommodated a fleet of forty ships.[28]

By the end of the second century, the Pontus ports on the southern shores of the Black Sea had taken on a less critical military role, their logistical mantle having been assumed by the Levant, which, as a consequence, had been correspondingly enhanced in importance, as had the roles of the *classes Syriaca* and *Alexandrina*, jointly responsible for the naval security of the eastern Mediterranean coastline. This operational shift was achieved by the garrisoning of the Euphrates frontier in Cappadocia by Rome and by the extensive development of a system of military highways into Asia Minor. The expanding military district, of which Antioch had become the administrative centre, was now served by a fast-developing port at Seleucia, situated at the mouth of the Orontes, on the Mediterranean coast, north-east of Cyprus. Antioch also possessed the added logistical advantage of being historically linked to Palestine and Egypt by routes of high antiquity. The affect of this swing in the military balance was that the *classis Pontica*, while seemingly still maintaining a toe-hold in Trapezus, appears to have made greater use of Cyzicus, in the Straits of Salonika. The latter port, according to Strabo, at one time boasted 200 ship sheds and harbour facilities to match.[29]

It has already been remarked that the Roman navy held unchallenged seapower throughout its years of empire. There was no enemy of comparable size, nor with equivalent resources, to oppose it. It thus had small need either to train or equip for specialized set-piece battles on the high seas. Its purpose, rather, was to concentrate its efforts on fundamentally routine tasks such as anti-piracy control, and the provision of communications and transport facilities, at varying levels, for the imperial armies it served. Vessels used by the imperial navy included the *liburnian*, a fast, two-banked galley which took its design from local craft operated by the piratically minded inhabitants of the Dalmatian coast and offshore islands; and such other variations as the trireme, quadrireme, quinquereme, together with one 'six', the latter being shown as based at Misenum as the flagship of this, the senior squadron.[30] It was also, doubtless, heavily used by the imperial family.

A trireme was constructed with three banks of oars, but it does not follow that the larger categories increased in the same manner. Indeed, it is generally assumed that they did not do so and that a 'four', for example, had two banks of oars with two men per oar and a 'six' either three banks with two men per oar or, more likely, two banks with three men per oar. The numbers of these various categories within the navy is obscure but an archaeological study of ships' names on Roman navy graves at Misenum and Ravenna has provided the data for Table 5.[31] Thus, proportionately, trireme names discovered at both Misenum (48 per cent) and Ravenna (66 per cent) predominate, conveying the impression that this was the favoured vessel for both 'home fleets'. The size of the Misenum total, compared with that of its east-coast partner, underlines the high status awarded to the western Mediterranean squadron. The *liburnian* category, on the other hand, although not recorded here in any great number, appears to have been the workhorse of the provincial fleets. The *classis Alexandrina*, as one example, has been attested with nothing else.[32]

The emperor Augustus, frequently styled as the founder of the Roman navy, concentrated on the military virtues of speed and manoevrability when designing his ships. The need for these essential qualities had been impressed upon him in 31 BC, when he defeated Mark Antony in a naval battle at Actium. In the interests of both operational and administrative efficiency, he favoured a standardized fleet, limited both in numbers and in size differential. Vessels with these same qualities

TABLE 5

Archaeological study of ships' names on Roman Navy graves at Misenum and Ravenna

Grading	Misenum	Ravenna	Total
'Six'	1	–	1
'Fives'	1	2	3
'Fours'	9	7	16
'Threes'	52	22	74
Liburnians	13	2	15
Combined Total	76	33	109

were brought to Caesar's aid by Decimus Brutus in 56 BC, and turned an uncertain situation into a decisive victory over the Veneti on the Atlantic coast.

The Venetians, seemingly at the end of the campaigning season according to Caesar,[33] had seized some Roman soldiers sent out for grain and afterwards detained two envoys despatched by Crassus to demand their release. The purpose of the Gauls was to gain the release of their own hostages held by the Romans. When the news reached the Roman commander he was well on his way to Italy; he tells us that he at once foresaw the need for further warships and issued instructions for these to be constructed on the Loire (probably on its upper reaches, at Roanne, west of Lyon) and for the local recruitment of captains and seamen. They were then sailed down the river, to the estuary. These ships, however, proved inadequate for the task and he decided he must wait for his fleet 'to be assembled and brought up'. Directly they hove in sight, some two hundred and twenty enemy ships sailed out of harbour to confront them and neither the commander of the fleet, Brutus, 'nor the military tribunes and centurions in charge of the individual ships could decide what to do or what tactics to adopt'. Finally, they attacked and brought down the enemy's sails with grappling poles; after that, Caesar grudgingly remarks, 'it was a soldier's battle in which the Romans proved superior, especially since it was fought under the eyes of Caesar and the whole army. . .'.

Dio, however, tells a different story. Caesar, he relates,

constructed in the interior the kind of boats which he heard were of advantage for the tides of the ocean, and conveyed them down the river Liger [Loire], but in doing so used up almost the entire summer to no purpose. For their cities, established in strong positions, were inaccessible and the oceans surging around practically all of them rendered an infantry attack out of the question, and a naval attack equally so in the midst of the ebb and flow of the tide. Consequently Caesar was in despair until Decimus Brutus came to him with swift ships from the Mediterranean. . . . For these boats had been built rather light in the interests of speed, after the manner of our naval construction, whereas those of the barbarians surpassed them very greatly both in size and construction.[34]

The Venetian ships were fitted with both sail and oars, and were designed to be sufficiently heavy to compete with the high seas prevailing on the Atlantic coast. They could maintain their manoeuvrability and mobility providing there was a wind. When this fell, however, their weight was such that they could no longer 'be propelled as they had been with the oars and, because their of great bulk, stopped motionless'. Brutus chose this moment to attack, in a manner graphically described by Dio, which underscores the wisdom of Augustus's choice of design two or three decades later:

> . . . falling upon them, he caused them many serious injuries with impunity, delivering both broadside and rear attacks, now ramming one of them, now backing water, in whatever way and as often as he liked, sometimes with many vessels against one and again with equal numbers opposed, occasionally even approaching safely with a few against many. . . . If he found himself inferior anywhere, he very easily retired, so that the advantage rested with him in any case. For the barbarians did not use archery and had not provided themselves beforehand with stones, not expecting to have need of them. . . .

The Roman navy, both before and after its reconstruction by Augustus, largely functioned as a supporting arm of the army. Every crew was treated as a century of the Roman army, commanded by a centurion, the rank and file including not only the oarsmen, but also marines, archers, catapult operators and other specialists. Indeed, Casson[35] judges that the naval hierarchy was probably charged with nothing more than the operation and maintenance of the ship, while the army took care of everything else, including shore administration and responsibility for the fighting component.

This method of behaviour was particularly evident in riverine operations, where a fine line existed between the requisitioned rivercraft employed on the Rhône by Caesar for multifarious military purposes and the *lusoriae*, the small light galleys which, by the fourth century AD, had been adopted as the standard unit for use on such major rivers as the Rhine and the Danube. Neither would have held more than a handful of men for their own defence and, when operating in hostile territory, would have needed land-based protection. An account of Julian's operation on the Euphrates in AD 363, narrated by Ammianus Marcellinus,[36] clearly recognizes this fact when he tells us that 'the fleet, although the river along which it went winds with many a bend, was not permitted to lag behind or get ahead' of the army. Again, when Julian is compelled by circumstances to discuss the abandonment and destruction of the fleet,[37] he stressed the advantage 'that nearly 20,000 soldiers would not be employed in transporting and guiding the ships, as had been the case since the beginning of the campaign'. This appears an abnormally large number of men to devote to such a purpose but emphasizes the point that the need was recognized. It is possible to see these rivercraft as broadly the equivalent of those provided to the British Army by RASC/RCT Water Transport Companies in recent wars.

In Roman amphibious operations, the direct influence of the army in naval affairs is immediately visible. A classic example again involves the ubiquitous Caesar. In order to gather intelligence before setting forth on the invasion of Britain in 55 BC, he despatched a warship *under command of a soldier, Gaius Volusenus*, to make a general reconnaissance and then hasten back with his report. Volusenus, a military tribune, was Caesar's cavalry commander in later campaigns. In this, his first invasion across water, Caesar made three fundamental mistakes:

Firstly, he set fourth in two echelons, the infantry from Boulogne and the cavalry from Ambleteuse, six miles further north. Any sailor could have told him of the dangers of such a plan. The cavalry transports set sail too late and were carried back to the shore by the strength of the tide.

Secondly, he did not sail until about 25th August, proposing to stay three weeks. He therefore risked being trapped in Britain by the autumn equinoctial gales, a hazard of which Claudius, a century later, was seemingly well aware. It was, said Caesar, a matter about which Romans knew nothing, apparently ignoring the fact that Roman merchants had been trading across the Channel for many years and must have been aware of these dangers, as indeed should his ally and cavalry commander, Commius of the Atrebates.

Thirdly, he aimed to live off the land upon arrival but his enemies were equally determined that he should not be allowed to do so. This error was compounded by his inexperience of the vagaries of Channel weather for when several days of continuous storms blew up, wrecking many of his transports, his 'whole army was thrown into great consternation' and his administration was near collapse.

But to dwell on these failings unduly (from which, as ever, he extricated himself with skill) would be to deny the brilliant planning of the assault landing.

Caesar assembled for his 'reconnaissance' eighty transports, which he considered sufficient to convey two legions, together with an unstated number of 'warships, which he assigned to the *quaestor*, the generals and the officers of the auxiliary troops'. The latter vague description presumably also included a complement of auxiliary troops, such as archers and slingers, to operate with the mounted contingent when it arrived. Additionally, he possessed several scouting vessels[38] and eighteen further transports which, as we have seen, were marshalled separately, some miles away along the coast, and allotted to the cavalry. When Caesar returned to Britain in the following year, he came with an increased total of five legions and two thousand cavalry, transported by more than eight hundred ships. It is thus not unreasonable, on this first landing, to judge that with two legions, supporting troops and weapons, he brought with him some two hundred and fifty vessels.

He set sail at midnight. It was conventional practice, and had been for many years, that every ship should carry lights at night to identify itself when travelling in company: flagships carried lights on the stern.[39] As early as 204 BC Scipio had ruled, for his expedition against Carthage, that 'warships were to carry one light each, transports two, and the flagship would be marked at night by carrying three'. It was customary for the commander-in-chief to lead the way. In 48 BC, while campaigning in North Africa, Caesar set forth by sea 'instructing the rest of the captains to steer . . . by the lantern of his ship'.[40] Each sailing ship and warship towed astern at least one ship's boat, and these were to prove invaluable assets during the assault landing. Landfall was made at about nine o'clock but, as may be imagined, the fleet straggled far behind their leader and Caesar was compelled to ride at anchor until three o'clock in the afternoon to await their arrival. He took advantage of this enforced interval to assemble

> the generals and military tribunes and, telling them what he had learned from Volusenus, explained his plans. He warned them that the exigencies of warfare, and particularly of naval operations, in which things moved rapidly and the situation is constantly changing, required the instant execution of every order. On dismissing the officers he found that both wind and tidal current were in his favour. He therefore gave the signal for weighing anchor and, after proceeding about seven miles, ran his ships aground on an evenly sloping beach, free from obstacles.[41]

The above quotation is important, not so much for what is said but for what is left unsaid. Caesar was rightly and obviously using his flagship as a command ship for the operation but his account of these events in *de Bello Gallico* does not make it clear whether, when he assembled his 'generals and military tribunes', these officers were already members of his shipboard party or had been summoned from nearby vessels. The first alternative is more probably correct. One matter is, however, absolutely certain: they could not have been travelling with their regiments and formations, for these were yet to take six hours to assemble. Thus, it appears that his commanding generals and senior staff were sensibly moving alongside him, in the modern manner, and using the same 'orders group' procedure later practised by Vespasian when advancing in column of march.

A further piece of knowledge we are denied by Caesar is the manner in which his scattered task force was re-assembled after arrival, parallel with the shore and positioned in echelons as they would have needed to be, ready for the assault on the beaches. In this instance, with a mere 250 ships participating, the problem would not have been of the same magnitude as in the following year when eight hundred vessels and more were involved, nor as in the Claudian invasion of AD 43, when some thousand took part. It would, however, have been very necessary, after the problems encountered during the approach of his task force to its objective, for the commander-in-chief to re-form his regiments into their assault formations before going ashore. Moreover, this essential task could only have been achieved with speed and efficiency if the whole manoeuvre had been pre-planned. Vessels and groupings of vessels would have needed to carry identifying marks, probably coloured pennants, and carefully rehearsed signal procedures would have had to be in position.

A great variety of signalling methods was available. Diodorus[42] records how, in 307 BC, Demetrius used a burnished shield as a heliograph to order the fleet into action and the message 'was flashed by each ship to the next'. The Athenians in 410 BC hoisted a purple flag for going into action,[43] thus hinting that other flags, or other hues and dimensions, might have conveyed a wide variety of meanings. Dain[44] confirms this latter point and reveals that for general signalling a type of semaphore was used, for which the instructions were to

> signal with the flag by holding it upright, dipping it from right to left and then shifting it back again to right or left, waving it, raising it, lowering it, removing it from sight, changing it, switching it around by orienting the head now in one direction and now another, or using flags of different shapes and colours as was the practice amongst the ancients.

It was also commonplace for ships to fly flags to indicate their country of origin, or at least to identify the fleet to which they belonged. At the siege of Marseilles in 49 BC, Caesar relates[45] how the flagship of Decimus Brutus was identified and attacked by a couple of enemy triremes because it was 'conspicuous by its ensign'. Many Roman coins feature shipping flying different shapes and sizes of flag. An issue made at Side displays a small rectangular flag attached to a horizontal bar. Roman imperial coins issued by Trajan and Severus show a similar flag flown by what is taken to be the imperial flagship.[46] It might be the commander-in-chief's personal banner. Several ships are illustrated displaying two or three such banners, but one or two of these could be related to the formations or units being transported in them. Regimental and sub-unit standards, probably displayed upon the poop deck on such occasions, would have played little part in these naval activities but would have come into prominence during the landing operation, as beach 'assembly points', for example. It is to this phase of the assault that we now turn.

When Caesar made landfall off the coast of Britain, he found the 'enemy' already awaiting his arrival, posted on the cliff tops and ready to deluge the shore with javelins and other missiles. They had seemingly been alerted to their danger by tribal intelligence received from the continent. When he ultimately moved off after the arrival of his main body, to seek a more secure landing place, his opponents despatched their cavalry and chariots to anticipate his movements. Their infantry followed close behind, while maintaining visual contact with his fleet. By this means, as the first Roman ships approached the shoreline, the Britons were already in position to give them a rough welcome. Caesar's account of what happened next fully describes the grave difficulties which confronted him:

> The size of the Roman ships made it impossible to run them aground except in fairly deep water; and soldiers, unfamiliar with the ground, with their hands full, and weighed down by the heavy burden of their arms, had at the same time to jump down from the ships, get a footing in the waves and fight the enemy, who, standing on dry land or advancing only a short way into the water, fought

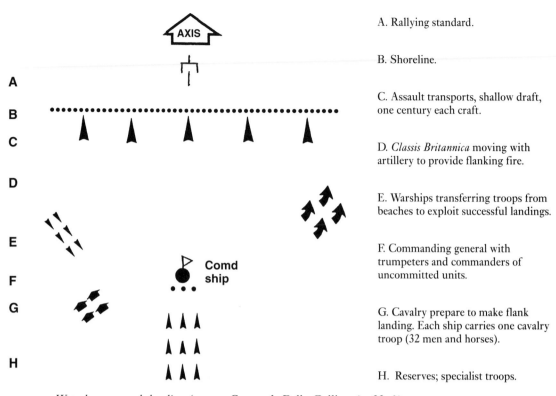

A. Rallying standard.

B. Shoreline.

C. Assault transports, shallow draft, one century each craft.

D. *Classis Britannica* moving with artillery to provide flanking fire.

E. Warships transferring troops from beaches to exploit successful landings.

F. Commanding general with trumpeters and commanders of uncommitted units.

G. Cavalry prepare to make flank landing. Each ship carries one cavalry troop (32 men and horses).

H. Reserves; specialist troops.

Waterborne assault landing (source: Caesar, de Bello Gallico, *iv, 23–6)*

with all their limbs unencumbered and on perfectly familiar ground, boldly hurling their javelins and galloping their horses, which were trained for this kind of work. . . . These perils frightened our soldiers, who were quite unaccustomed to battles of this kind, with the result that they did not show the same alacrity and enthusiasm as they did in battles on dry land.[47]

Caesar, from his command ship anchored offshore and, we may imagine, surrounded by a cluster of vessels which, apart from his staff, would have included reserve troops, auxiliaries, supporting arms, light galleys and ships' boats (the latter being a general purpose boat, also acting the part of signals 'galloper'), was concerned by this lack of movement. He was seeking a quick success. The sun, on 25 August, would have set at about seven o'clock and last light would have occurred about an hour later. Time was not a factor to be ignored. He reacted at once, ordering his warships to move to the flank of the assault beach and run ashore, taking the auxiliaries with them. From this stable position they were now enabled to direct fire from slingshot, archers and artillery on to the exposed flank of his British enemy, who, rendered uncertain by this unexpected new danger, paused momentarily to consider what they should do about it.

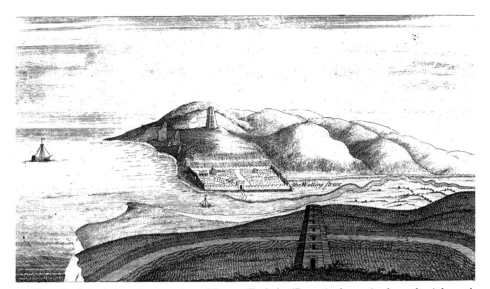

William Stukeley's imaginative view of Roman Dubris *(Dover), drawn in the early eighteenth century*

There now occurred a much quoted incident: the standard-bearer of the Xth Legion, one of Caesar's favoured formations, took advantage of this break in the fighting and, 'after praying to the gods that his action might bring good luck to the legion, cried in a loud voice: "Jump down, comrades, unless you want to surrender our eagle to the enemy. I, at any rate, mean to do my duty to my country and my general." ' His comrades, inspired by his bravery, at once poured off the ship to join him on the beach, and their example quickly spread to neighbouring landing craft. But this was not the end of the difficulties of the Roman task force.

Much of the great success of the Roman soldier on the battlefield lay in his knowledge of close formation fighting: the concept of the battle drill involved, the training of the soldiers, the interlocking of their shields, the nature of their equipment and the design of their short stabbing broadswords, all had their part to play in the technique. As the men now struggled ashore out of the water, wet and isolated, bereft of any formation, the Britons, with their traditional long, slashing swords, inflicted heavy casualties among them: but we are not told how many. The legionaries, pressed hard by the enemy, did not find it easy, in the general mêlée, to get a foothold on the beach, nor keep their ranks. They fought their way to any standard they could find and assembled around it and, ultimately, some semblance of order began to emerge. Caesar, in his command ship, was watching these events carefully. He now gave orders for all light galleys and ships' boats to be loaded with reserve troops and he deployed these shrewdly, with the purpose of exploiting areas of success where he could see them and bolstering any sector which might appear in danger of defeat.

In due course, as the legions fought their way out of the water and formed their battle lines, their heavy infantry gained enough space to mount a charge. The Britons withdrew in the face of this onslaught and, as they retreated, Caesar was

The Roman pharos *(lighthouse) at Dover*

driven to regret the absence of the cavalry which had failed to arrive, for he had no means of pursuing his enemy and sealing his victory.

There are questions to be answered, arising from Caesar's account of this expedition. The first concerns the use of warships to provide artillery fire and the scale of issue of weapons to each vessel. It would have been sensible, if it were planned to use them in this manner, for gunships to be prepared, equipped with twenty or thirty weapons, so that they might deliver concentrated fire. This would have economized on the numbers of vessels employed and, militarily, would have been more effective. We can only conjecture whether or not it happened in this way. Caesar's account of his North African campaign against Labienus in 46 BC certainly conveys the impression that warships carried more than one of these *carroballistae*, when he relates that, in order to improve his defences at Ruspina, 'he brought missiles and artillery from the ships into the camp'.[48] Warships, in later years certainly, and possibly even at this early date, carried many means of destruction. During the reign of the emperor Constantine, a particular type of galley, known as the *dromon*, was fitted with siphon-like flamethrowers, and could frequently boast more than one to a ship. These weapons proved to be devastatingly lethal. Each comprised a copper-lined tube of wood, fitted on its inboard end to an air pump, into which a substance known as 'Greek fire' was poured. When the pump was activated, the contraption squirted forth a stream of fire over its target. It was also common practice for naval vessels to carry a catapult as armament. This was employed to throw baskets of red-hot coals or jars of flaming pitch at an enemy craft.

Secondly, we are left to wonder what happened to Caesar's badly wounded, of whom there must have been quite a number. We may hazard a guess that ambulance ships formed part of his command group and that, while walking wounded would have been treated ashore, within their regiments, severe cases would have been repatriated to Boulogne with all speed. A *medicus* (ship's doctor) formed part of the crew of most warships of the imperial Roman navy.

Finally, in his detail of the landing in 55 BC, Caesar makes no mention of transport animals, except to say that 'he had come without most of his heavy baggage'. This implies that he did bring *some* heavy baggage and that, therefore, he must have had the means of carrying it, together with any grain he might have been able to forage, once ashore. It would thus seem that Caesar's task force contained a Q Echelon of supply ships. These administrative vessels may well have formed part of his command group and, during the assault phase, would probably have been anchored to the rear, but out of range of the busy command ship, with its reserves and supporting arms and vessels.

Model of a Roman grain ship

Seaborne landings of this nature, in the face of organized opposition, were rarely undertaken by the Roman army and it is this fact which makes the detail of Caesar's planning so remarkable, especially when compared with modern practice. It refutes the claim of the military historian, Major General J.F.C. Fuller, that the Roman general's 'two invasions of Britain were amateurish in the extreme'.[49] There were, of course, administrative failures in the conduct of his operation, partly due to over-optimism, partly because of excessive faith in the influence of his Celtic friend, Commius, the Atrebatan. But the successes and failures of Caesar's two invasions of Britain must surely have laid down military guidelines for future expeditions: there can be little doubt they would have been carefully noted and followed by the Claudian army a century or so later.

In earlier chapters we have already noted Fuller's view – somewhat harsh we have suggested[50] – of aspects of Caesar's command ability, provoked largely by his seeming lack of a wagon train and an organized commissariat. Fuller felt this latter omission to be the most serious of the Roman's deficiencies because it led to undue reliance upon his nation's allies 'to provide the vehicles needed to supply' him. But it would appear from this comment that he did not appreciate the presence of the waterborne option. Indeed, in the light of Caesar's skilful employment of the riverine routeways of Gaul, with his rear headquarters more often than not located in river-based tribal capitals, it is not easy to agree that such a commissariat did not exist. Clearly, he was not the originator of the concept of river supply, it dated to ancient times, but in Gaul he appears to have adopted and adapted it to good effect and, in doing so, to have been fortunate (or was it not entirely fortuitous?) that his chief ally and provider of grain, the Aedui, occupied the main watershed area of his targeted conquest.

In later years, the practice of using riverine military supply routes was developed to an extraordinary extent by the Romans. Ammianus Marcellinus[51] has recorded one occasion which occurred in AD 363, when Julianus Augustus was campaigning in Mesopotamia along the line of the Euphrates:

> While [the emperor] was giving audience his fleet arrived, equal to that of the mighty King Xerxes, under the command of the tribune Constantianus and Count Lucillianus; and the broad Euphrates was almost too narrow for it, consisting as it did of a thousand cargo-carriers of varied construction, and bringing an abundance of supplies, weapons and also siege-engines; there were beside fifty warships and an equal number which were needed for making bridges.

Marcellinus's detailed account of this occasion emphasizes a scale of operational planning of considerable ability.

CHAPTER SEVEN

Siege Warfare

For here lofty embankments were being raised, there others were filling up the deep ditches; elsewhere long passages were being constructed in the bowels of the earth, and those in charge of the artillery were setting up their hurling engines, soon to break out with deadly roar.

Ammianus Marcellinus xxiv, 4

The stronghold is a *machan* overlooking a kid tied up to entice the Japanese tiger.

Major General Orde Wingate[1]

A siege, in its most simple terms, is the investment of a fortified place by an encamped force with the purpose of either seizing it or compelling its surrender. There are thus three elements to a siege, of which the first is a fortified place, which may be a town, castle, port, hillfort or some other such feature from which a siege might be repelled, its location being carefully selected with an eye to water supply, ground, communications, tactical importance and defensibility, dependent upon the nature of the operation. In addition, there are the besieged and the besieger, these two components being mentioned individually because, although their presence is obvious, their motivation and purpose is necessarily different. A siege generally arises from the spontaneous action of those under attack, who may see it either as a means of warding off a stronger, better prepared enemy or, alternatively, as an integrant part of a premeditated system of offensive defence.

A classic example of this latter tactic was the system of burghal hidage[2] originated and adopted by Alfred the Great (AD 849–99) to frustrate the ravages of Viking raiders in southern England. His scheme was based on the creation of thirty *burhs*, each chosen for its prime tactical position and each situated within 20 miles of the other, thus enabling the local population, in time of war, to withdraw within its walls, leaving behind no stocks of food and destroying any standing crops which might bring comfort to the enemy. A specific number of hides (a taxable area of land often about 120 acres in size) were assigned to each *burh*, the occupants of each hide being required to provide one man to fight upon the ramparts in the event of an attack, the total defence force being calculated on the basis of one man to every five yards of rampart. A further man, contributed by each hide, was additionally required to march with the *fyrd*,[3] whenever it might be called out. Each *burh* stood ready to move to the support of its neighbour should the need arise.

A more modern example of offensive defence of this nature is to be found in the 'stronghold' concept devised during the 1941–5 Burma campaign by Major-General Orde Wingate, commander of the famous Chindit long-range penetration columns. He saw the 'stronghold', a firmly held and fortified administrative base, as a '*machan* overlooking a kid tied up to entice the Japanese tiger'. Its ideal situation was 'the centre of a circle of 30 miles radius consisting of closely wooded and very broken country, only passable to pack transport owing to great natural obstacles'. Ideally, it should have a 'neighbouring friendly village or two and an inexhaustible and uncontaminatable supply of water'. Wingate visualized his strongholds creating such situations that his enemy would inevitably be drawn towards them, into battlefields of his own choosing, in difficult terrain, where their forces would be worn down and their lines of communication open to harassment by his mobile fighting columns.

It is possible to get a glimpse of some such tactic in the defensive operation conducted in 52 BC by the brave but unfortunate Gallic leader, Vercingetorix, prior to the siege and capture of Avaricum (Bourges) by Julius Caesar and again at Alesia.[4] The vision fades, however, almost as soon as it emerges for, despite setting in place arrangements which might have made his victory possible, the young Gaul failed to carry them to fruition.

Vercingetorix was heading a rebellion against Roman rule. Caesar's *de Bello Gallico* does not provide us with a detail of the strength of the army his young opponent had gathered around him, beyond stating that he had won support for his cause in districts as far apart as Sens, Paris, Poitiers, Cahors, Tours, Evreux, Limoges, Angers and the whole Atlantic seaboard and that, armed with this power, he had ordered each of the allied states to furnish a specified number of troops without delay, together with a fixed quota of weapons, paying particular attention to cavalry needs.[5] Clearly, the numbers thus accumulated were considerable. In his campaign of 58 BC, Caesar estimated the strength of the Helvetian army then confronting him as numbering 92,000.[6] It is unlikely that Vercingetorix's army numbered less than this, on an estimated basis of 10,000 men donated by each of the tribes marching with him. On the other hand, a scratch force of this nature would not have possessed the disciplined military skills of the Roman legions opposing it, a fact of which both commanders would have been well aware.

Vercingetorix opened his campaign by summoning tribal leaders to a council of war, to gain their approval of his operational plan, which combined a scorched-earth policy with a design for defence. He outlined to them its background, which was directed towards denying any form of sustenance to the Roman legions. Supplies were to be centrally stored in defended areas where they would not fall into enemy hands. Fields were to be cleared of grain and fodder; nothing was to be left standing. All villages and farms along Caesar's line of march, wherever his foragers might conceivably reach, were to be burnt to the ground. 'When our lives are at stake,' he instructed his followers, 'we must be prepared to sacrifice our private possessions.' As an additional measure, the 'scorched earth' thus created was to be heavily patrolled by cavalry, of which he possessed large numbers and the Romans comparatively few, to ensure that not a single enemy foraging party, if any did emerge from their columns, might return alive to base.

Next, Vercingetorix turned his attention to the physical defence of his area. All towns, 'except those rendered impregnable by natural and artificial defences', were to be burnt. If this were not done, he warned,

> they may serve as refuges for shirkers among our own numbers, and give the enemy the chance of looting the stores of provisions and other property they contain. You may think these measures harsh and cruel, but you must admit it would be a still harsher fate to have your wives and children carried off into slavery and be killed yourselves, which is what will happen if you are conquered.[7]

These drastic plans were unanimously approved by the tribal elders, with one exception. The Bituriges had not appreciated that their town of Avaricum, one of the finest in Gaul and the heart of their tribal defensive system, was destined to be destroyed. They now pleaded for it to be spared. It could easily be held, they said, because of its natural strength, 'for it was almost completely surrounded by an area of river and marsh, in which there was only one narrow opening'. Vercingetorix was at length prevailed upon to grant their plea, although he was at first totally opposed to doing so. He committed 10,000 infantry to its defence. The response of the Bituriges was total. Next day, the number of fires burning on the skyline revealed to Caesar that more than twenty of their towns had been set alight. The remaining cities, spared destruction, prepared themselves for the forthcoming Roman assault.

Thus far, so good; but beyond this point the Vercingetorix plan fell into disarray. This, almost certainly, was brought about by the speed of Caesar's movement. Vellaunodunum, a town of the Senones in central France, lying between Sens and Orleans, succumbed to his attack within three days. He had initially intended to bypass it but was wary of leaving such a fortification across his line of communication. He then moved with equal rapidity against Cenabum, a town of the neighbouring Carnutes, lying on the site of modern Orleans, and arrived outside its walls two days later, while the tribal leaders were still collecting troops for its defence. Caesar plundered and burnt the unhappy town without compunction and then crossed the Loire, into the territory of Bituriges, to lay siege to Noviodunum, some 18 miles north-west of Bourges. Its terrified citizens yielded to him without resistance and he at once turned to the task of subduing Avaricum.

The crossing of the Loire by Caesar, and his march on Avaricum, drew Vercingetorix towards him but the latter carefully avoided physical engagement. He followed the Romans 'by easy stages' and then encamped deep in a marshy forest area, 15 miles from the town, presumably hoping to entice his enemy into this unfamiliar ground. If this were so, he was unsuccessful, for Caesar opened his assault upon the city without delay.

A logical and popular tactic, frequently contemplated early in such an operation, might have been for Caesar to isolate the water supply to Avaricum. It was a ploy used by Alexander the Great at the siege of Babylon (143–142 BC), when he is said not only to have diverted the course of the Euphrates from the city but also to have penetrated its defences by following the line of the dried up river bed he had thus created.[8] Caesar used a similar tactic in 51 BC, during his war with another Gallic tribe, the Cadurci, when besieging Uxellodunum. In the instance of Avaricum, standing as it did in marshy country at the confluence of the Yevre and Auron rivers, it was well provided with a secure water supply and Caesar, if he had contemplated action along these lines, would have been disappointed. Instead, he concentrated his attack upon the city fortifications, employing classic siege procedure.

The walls of Avaricum were constructed in the Gallic style, with layers of stone alternated with heavy balks of timber, these being laid in parallel lines, mortised together, with the gaps thus created being filled with rubble. Caesar described the technique as well adapted for the defence of a town: 'The masonry protects it from fire, the timber from destruction by the battering-ram, which cannot either pierce or knock to pieces a structure braced internally by beams running generally to a length of 40 feet in one piece.[9] The whole circuit of the wall was topped by towers, furnished with fighting platforms and protected externally by dampened hides against attack by fire.

Caesar was a master of the art of siege warfare, which normally followed a recognized pattern of events. The first and obvious phase was to impose a blockade, with the purpose of starving the garrison into submission. The second phase provided a natural corollary to this; a line of entrenchments, known as a circumvallation, was dug around the objective, out of range of bow, sling or catapult shot, with the dual purpose of denying access to the enemy fortification and of providing to the army encamped outside its walls shelter from surprise attack from within. These encompassing entrenchments, seemingly found unnecessary by Caesar at Avaricum, frequently covered considerable distances: 9 kilometres in the case of Aemilianus Scipio at Numantia in Spain,[10] and as much as 17 kilometres by Caesar at Durazzo, during his Illyrian campaign against Pompey.[11] The besieged at that time constructed '24 hill forts on a 14 mile circuit, within which they could safely go out to forage'.[12] The third phase of a siege comprised the development of a further line of entrenchments (a contravallation) which faced away from the place under attack and protected the rear of the besieging army, with its stores and workshops, from possible attack from outside. Simultaneously preparations for the assault were pressed forward, their purpose and magnitude being dependent upon the scale of the obstacles to be overcome.

Because of the natural defences surrounding Avaricum, and perhaps because of a lack of Gallic firepower, the Romans appear to have had no outer ditch and rampart obstacles to overcome. In other circumstances, these might have been found. Caesar's first task, therefore, was to entrench himself in a location from where he might cover the narrow gap which provided access across the marshes to the city. He then began to build a ramp, some 330 feet wide, which he angled towards its battlements. At the same time, he set in position a line of mantlets to provide cover for the soldiery engaged in this construction work and erected two tall defensive towers from where covering fire might be delivered upon any enemy opposition directed at his working-parties, in particular the enemy superstructure of defensive turrets which lined the entire length of their wall.

His opponents countered every move he made. As his ramp approached and grew higher, providing his assault towers with greater height, ultimately reaching

A cavalryman running down a barbarian, from the first-century tombstone of Flavinus, signifer *in the* ala Petriana *from Corbridge, England*

80 feet, they responded by extending upwards the fire-platforms constructed within their wall turrets and frequently made sorties by day and night to set fire to his workings. When the Romans threw ropes, with scaling hooks, up on to the walls, the enemy made them fast to windlasses and wound them up, sometimes with their human cargo. When the Romans erected ladders they cast them down. When Caesar constructed underground galleries to enable his men to approach the walls unseen and without danger, they countermined them 'and prevented their continuation by throwing into them stakes sharpened and hardened in a fire, boiling pitch and very heavy stones'. They also undermined his 'terrace'. Caesar noted that the Gauls were expert at tunnelling 'due to experience gained in the extensive network of iron mines to be found in their country'.[13]

While all this was progressing, Vercingetorix, according to Caesar,

> having run out of forage, had moved nearer to Avaricum and had taken command in person of the cavalry and light-armed infantry who regularly fought amongst the cavalry, in order to ambush the place where he expected our men would go the next day to forage.[14]

Caesar quickly took advantage of the enemy leader's absence from his main encampment and slipped away from Avaricum at midnight to conduct a surprise assault upon it at dawn. They had been alerted and he found their army lined up on high ground, almost surrounded by marsh, awaiting his arrival. He wisely determined to withdraw and return his attention to the siege. The enemy, he explains, plainly not wishing to yield them any credit,

> held all the fords and thickets that bordered the marsh, determined, if the Romans tried to force a passage, to overpower them by running down to the attack while they were stuck fast in the mud. Awaiting us at such a short distance, they looked as if they were prepared to fight a battle on more or less equal terms; but their position was so much stronger than ours that this show of courage was clearly a mere pretence.[15]

Vercingetorix also abandoned his mission without success and returned to base to find the tribes angry at his absence at such a crucial moment and complaining that he had chosen a camp-site too close to the enemy for comfort. He managed to persuade them that his choice had been carefully considered and that his action had been in the general interest. Avaricum fell to Caesar a few days later.

What, then, went wrong? Vercingetorix had generated popular support for his rebellion among the tribes. They had provided him with a cavalry wing of considerable size, far in excess of that possessed by the Romans, and a substantial host of tribal infantry, natural irregular soldiers, with a close knowledge of the local terrain. His carefully planned and rigorously executed scorched-earth policy, watched over by intensive cavalry patrolling, had set the stage for success but, almost immediately, it was weakened by the speed of Caesar's advance. The Roman general, in his unceasing quest for surprise, rapidly overran the territory of the Senones and the Carnutes and then crossed the Loire into the land of the Bituriges. He seized, on

Vercingetorix surrenders to Caesar after defeat at the Battle of Alesia

his way, the towns of Vellaunodunum, Cenabum and Noviodunum, even, in the case of Cenabum, as troops were being moved in to provide its garrison.

The capture and subsequent plunder of these places would have helped fill his supply depot with food, at least for some time, thus partially counteracting Vercingetorix's scorched-earth policy, but a chance still remained that it might succeed. The Gaul had wisely avoided close contact with the highly professional Roman army. His task now was to bring Caesar's rolling advance to a halt. His only hope of doing this would have been to put a substantial garrison into Avaricum, bring about a long siege, force Caesar into entrenchments, both circumvallation and contravallation, and then, by dint of vigorous patrolling and local diplomacy, deny him supplies while keeping him fully occupied, both to his front and rear. In short, to bring the Romans themselves under siege. Vercingetorix, by his initial reluctance to put troops into Avaricum, and then only to provide a minimum number, revealed a sad lack of appreciation of these possibilities.

It has already been remarked that events at Avaricum followed the natural course of any place under siege, that is to say, everything depended upon the degree of success of the assault on the walls. Traditionally, this could have been carried out in three ways, or combination of ways: by using heavy, iron-shod battering-rams to breach them, by employing scaling ladders and towers to surmount them and by employing sappers to undermine them.

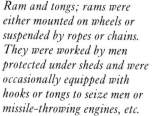

Ram and tongs; rams were either mounted on wheels or suspended by ropes or chains. They were worked by men protected under sheds and were occasionally equipped with hooks or tongs to seize men or missile-throwing engines, etc.

A battering-ram was either mounted on wheels or suspended by ropes or chains but, either way, it was provided with overhead cover to give protection against missile and blazing pitch attacks directed at it and its handlers by the besieged enemy on the battlements above. Occasionally, the latter brought up a swing-beam, fitted with a grapnel and operated by a counter-weight, which they lowered in an effort to disrupt the operation and seize the siege engines being deployed against them. Livy relates, with a nice touch of humour,[16] how a similar device was used in 214 BC by Archimedes, to help repel a seaborne assault on Syracuse. The grapnel was lowered on to a vessel's bows, the beam of which was then raised sharply out of the water by shifting the counter-weight: the result 'was to stand the ship, so to speak, on her tail, bows in air. Then the whole contraption was suddenly let go and the ship, falling smash as it were from the wall to the water, to the great alarm of the crew, was more or less swamped.'

Some Roman battering-rams are said to have been 100 feet long and to have required 200 men or so to manhandle them.[17] A tree large enough to provide a ram of this length would have probably come from the softwood family and we may judge the beam would have weighed 4–5 tons. On Trajan's Column, Dacians are shown using a ram in this manner against a Roman fort. According to Josephus, the ram was sometimes supported at its point of balance by ropes passing over another balk of timber, itself resting on stout posts fixed into the ground on either side. It was then operated by 'a great number of men' who, with 'a gigantic united heave' swung it repeatedly backwards and forwards, continuously inflicting shocks to the wall with its projecting iron head.[18] One mark of the engine, which later came into general use, took the form of a frame on wheels, in which the ram, suspended from a horizontal beam, was moved up to the walls. The whole contraption was sheltered by a wooden roof covered, as a protection against fire, with clay or damp hides and was nicknamed a 'tortoise' or *testudo*. These machines were not simply deployed at ground level: some varieties, such as those depicted on the Arch of Septimius Severus, were fitted with two or more stories so that the most vulnerable parts of a fortification, high up on a wall, might be attacked.

The task of the ram's head, from which the battering-ram derived its name, was to shatter the wall by the shock of its impact. Another variety of the weapon, known as the *terebra*, the 'borer', and described by Vitruvius, was fitted with a sharp point and was used for making holes in a wall. A further device was a hook attached to the end of a swinging battering-ram: it was used to pull down stones from the top of a wall once it had started to crumble.

Penetrating a wall by means of a battering-ram was necessarily a lengthy operation. The wall of the city of Jerusalem,[19] 15 feet thick and 30 feet high, was 'built of bonded stones 30 feet long and 15 broad, so that it would have been very difficult to undermine with iron tools or shake with engines'. The besieged thus frequently had time for counter-attack and this took two or more popular forms, either undermining the platform upon which the battering-ram was located, or dropping incendiary devices upon it from aloft or by sorties from the sally-port, aimed at its destruction. In the first instance, the technique was to tunnel under the ram, conserving the space thus created with timber props, while filling it with oil-soaked brushwood. The stake-props and brush wood were then set alight, as the miners hastily withdrew to safety. If all went well, the siege engine fell into the blazing hole as the supporting timbers collapsed, consumed by fire.

The ancient Greeks, and following them the Romans, gave considerable thought to the matter of incendiarism as a weapon in this type of operation. Aeneas the Tactician includes much advice in his treatise on *The Defence of Fortified Positions*. If a fire were to be effective, he advises, it has to be inextinguishable. He therefore recommends a formula made of pitch, sulphur, tow and granulated frankincense, the whole to be mixed in sacks of pine sawdust and kept available to be ignited and cast down upon the siege engines of the enemy as the situation demanded:[20] alternatively, he suggests that faggots covered with the lighted mixture should be lowered by rope on to the target below or 'hurled at the approaching engines'. In another paragraph[21] he advises that pestles should be prepared (large weighted darts, some 5 feet in length), covered with the mixture, and kept ready to 'be dropped upon the [enemy] engine as it is being pushed up [and] fashioned so as to stick into it'; and when mining, or counter-mining, dry brush should be retained in the tunnels created, ready to be ignited should the enemy succeed in breaking through.

Flaming missiles, such as arrows, javelins and sometimes shot fired by siege-engines, were frequently employed in the assault by the besieging troops. Fire extinguishing arrangements and other means of countering the fire were, therefore, important:

If the enemy tries to set anything on fire with a powerful incendiary equipment you must put out the fire with vinegar, for then it cannot easily be ignited again, or rather it should be smeared beforehand with birdlime (*a sticky material smeared on trees to trap birds*), for this does not catch fire. Those who put out the fire from places above it must have a protection for the face, so that they will be less annoyed when the flame darts toward them. . . .

If there were any wooden towers, or if a part of the wall is of wood, covers of felt or raw hide must be provided to protect the parapet so that they cannot be ignited by the enemy. If the gate is set on fire you must bring up wood and throw it on to make as large a fire as possible, until a trench can be dug inside and a counter-defence be quickly built. . . .[22]

Sorties by those under siege, directed at setting fire to the engines of war, were no less dramatic. Josephus has left us with a graphic description of one such event, led by three Jewish soldiers, which took place during the siege of Jerusalem in AD 70:

They dashed out as if towards friends, not massed enemies; they neither hesitated nor shrank back, but charged through the centre of the foe and set the artillery on fire. Pelted with missiles and thrust at with swords on every side, they refused to withdraw from their perilous situation until the engines were ablaze. . . . The Romans tugged at the battering-rams while the wicker covers blazed; the Jews, surrounded with the flames, pulled the other way and, seizing the red-hot iron, would not leave go of the rams. From these the fire spread to the platforms, outstripping the defenders. Meantime, the Romans were enveloped in flames and, despairing of saving their handiwork, began to withdraw to their camps.[23]

Whatever tactic was selected as the means of assault upon a fortification, it called for considerable courage from the participants and generally resulted in a high proportion of casualties. Livy,[24] writing of an incident during Scipio's siege of New Carthage in 210 BC, has equally vividly portrayed the dangers which confronted escalating parties armed with ladders. In the defence of the city, he wrote,

neither men nor missiles were as effective as the walls themselves, for few ladders were long enough to reach the top, and the longer the ladders the less secure they were. The first man up would find himself unable to get over, others would be mounting behind him and the ladder would break under their weight. Sometimes the ladders stood the strain, but the height made the climbers giddy and they fell. When everywhere ladders were breaking and men falling, and success was bringing added keenness and courage to the enemy, the recall was sounded, and thus the besieged were given the hope of an immediate respite from trouble and strife. . . . But scarcely had the din and confusion of the first assault died down when Scipio ordered fresh troops to take over the ladders from their exhausted or wounded comrades and make yet another, more vigorous attempt. . . .

A siege. This sketch from Polybius *(ed. 1727 by Chevalier Follard) depicts both defenders and besiegers at work. Note, particularly, the chamber undermining the tower, with props in position and waiting to be set alight*

Sapping was a military tactic already widely practised by the end of the sixth century BC. The besieged employed it as a means of counter-attack. For the besieger it had three main purposes, namely, to bring combat engineers, or assault troops preparing to scale the walls, close up to their objective without exposing them to missile attack; to undermine the wall and cause its collapse; and to penetrate under the wall, deep into the heart of the fortification under siege. This latter action frequently stimulated a complex pattern of mining and counter-mining such as occurred under Marcus Fulvius, during the Roman siege of Ambracia, in 189 BC. His assault on the walls of the town had been repulsed by its defenders, who built new walls as fast as he destroyed them. He therefore determined, under cover of mantlets, to tunnel his way through and was making considerable headway until the townspeople became alerted by the steadily growing mound of spoil removed from his hitherto undetected workings. They immediately excavated a trench, inside the wall, across what they judged to be his line of advance. Then, occupying this, they placed their ears to the side of the trench and listened for the sound of digging. When, at length, they judged it was sufficiently close, they burst through upon the enemy miners, assailing them with pick and shovel. They were quickly joined by armed men and the intruders were thrown back to take refuge behind a hastily prepared barricade. A novel device was now employed to drive them from the tunnel:

They pierced a hole in the bottom of a cask for the insertion of a tube of moderate size, and made an iron pipe and an iron lid for the cask, the lid also being perforated in many places. They filled this cask with small feathers and placed it with its mouth towards the tunnel; and through the holes in the lid very long spears, called *sarissae*, jutted out to keep off the enemy. A small spark was introduced among the feathers and they kindled it by blowing with a smith's bellows applied to the end of the pipe. Then, when the whole tunnel was filled with a mass of smoke, and with smoke rendered more pungent by the reason of the foul stench of burning feathers, scarcely anyone could endure to remain inside it.[25]

On occasions, siege operations were highly complex, using every aspect of technique. Polybius records that Philip of Macedonia, at the siege of Echinus in 211 BC, planned a two-pronged attack on the town and constructed two towers for this purpose. In front of each he provided a shelter for the engineers engaged in tunnelling towards the walls and for the protection of those men working the battering-rams with which each tower was equipped. These forward shelters, in turn, were linked rearward with his main camp by roofed underground tunnels,

Shelter providing protection for soldiers during attack or mining operations. Note the spades being used in front

'so that neither those coming from the camp nor those leaving the works should be wounded by missiles from the town'.[26] They were also interconnected and accommodated 'three batteries of *ballistae*, of which one threw stones of a talent's weight [approximately 58 lb] and the others stones of half that weight'.

The two towers, giant contraptions which on other occasions are said to have been constructed as high as 150 feet, were slowly inched forward as the sappers beneath them levelled the surface of the ground to make their movement possible. On the first floor of these, two catapults were located, with 'water jars and other appliances for putting out fires'. The second floor was manned by archers, slingers and javelin throwers ready to take on any defenders on the walls who might intervene to stop the progress of the work. It was also customary to find a drawbridge at this level, ready to be lowered on to the wall, at an appropriate moment, when sufficiently close to launch an attack.

The time-scale required to make these preliminary preparations is noteworthy. Polybius relates that the work carried out, together, presumably, with the manufacture of the two great siege engines, was

> entirely completed within the course of a few days, as the country around us has an abundance of the materials required. For Echinus is situated on the Malian Gulf, facing south, opposite the territory of Thonium, and the land is rich in every kind of produce, so that nothing was lacking for Philip's purpose.[27]

The administrative, manpower and supply resources needed to complete this task 'in the course of a few days' would have been considerable, but an ability to work to such timing would have been essential to any commander entering upon a siege operation. Caesar's adversary, Vercingetorix, for example, would have been wise never to have lost sight of this fact, for here lay the Achilles heel of any besieging army. Wingate well expressed this concept when defining the purpose of his 'strongholds'. He saw them as well defended and provisioned sites, suitably located in relation to his main objective, and as an orbit around which columns of his brigades circulated, harrying the lines of communication of the Japanese who surrounded him. Such an outside force, as visualized by him, was essential if the defenders of a stronghold were to be able successfully to discourage a besieging army; or, alternatively, the strongholds had to be so well armed, fortified and provisioned that defeat was an impossibility. The introduction of the artillery weapon transformed the face of siege warfare.

The first siege in which ancient artillery is known to have participated occurred in 397 BC. The occasion was the assault on Motya, the Carthaginian island fortress located at the western end of Sicily, under command of Dionysius I of Syracuse. The island accommodated both an emporium and a colony. It lay in a sheltered lagoon and was at that time connected to the mainland by a 1,700 m causeway which, according to archaeological research in 1962,[28] had seemingly been breached by the Motyans, presumably in anticipation of the coming assault. Dionysius appears to have repaired the damage and constructed additional moles, possibly as platforms for his covering towers and siege-engines, which he used to

A fortified town under siege by catapults and ballistae *(Polybius, ed. 1727)*

drive the defenders off the walls. It was, in essence, an attack from the mainland, across a long reach of water and under cover of light artillery fire, to enable the landing party to get ashore. The tactic thereafter expanded relatively rapidly but its employment was more evident in assault than in defence. The later siege of Halicarnassus by Alexander the Great (334 BC), marked a further development in the employment of artillery as a supporting arm: here, for the first time, the presence of stone-throwing machines was recorded. Alexander, having forced a breach in the wall, came under attack from a sortie from within. He reacted vigorously: large stones were hurled by the engines he had mounted on his covering towers, 'bullets were showered in volleys' and his assailants fled back to the safety of the city, having, according to Arrian,[29] suffered heavy loss.

Ancient artillery weapons were capable of a wide range of performance and, as a consequence, were employed to fulfil a great variety of tasks. In defence, they provided covering fire for sorties by raiding parties and were frequently deployed in counter-battery roles. At Halicarnassus, non-torsion arrow-firers were carefully sited to 'volley straight ahead at the advance guard of the engines' as they were being moved by the enemy into position. Similarly, they were located to cover likely lines of enemy approach to the stronghold they were defending. They were also frequently positioned in casements, on the curtain walls of fortifications, so as to bring down enfilade fire on to the flanks of enemy escalades.

A classic early example of these various defensive techniques was demonstrated by Archimedes, the famous Greek mathematician and inventor, who played an important role in the defence of Syracuse against the Romans in 213 BC. His tactical thinking and carefully constructed fire plan delayed the capture of the city for many months. When at length it fell to Marcus Claudius Marcellus, in the late autumn of the following year, Archimedes was slain by a Roman soldier. He was described by Livy[30] as unrivalled in his knowledge of astronomy but as being even more remarkable as the inventor and constructor of types of artillery and military devices of all kinds, 'by the aid of which, as it were, he was able by one finger to frustrate the most laborious operations of the enemy'.

Archimedes' battle plan was uncomplicated:[31] it called for a keen knowledge of the artillery weapon and was almost entirely dependent upon the delivery of a high volume of concentrated and continuous firepower. The Romans opened their siege of Syracuse by an assault from the sea; they could equally well have conducted a land attack, as they were ultimately to do. The Archimedes plan encompassed both possibilities. As soon as the Roman landing force came into target range at about 400 yards, the estimated maximum range of the Greek heavy artillery, it was his intention, as it advanced, to keep it continuously under fire from the city walls, in the first place using catapults and stone-throwers, shortening his range by adjusting his elevation where necessary and, subsequently, by the use of smaller pieces of artillery. Heavy weapons were necessarily slower to fire, because of the weight of their missiles and the difficulties of handling them: light artillery produced a wider and more effective volume of anti-personnel fire, although it was clearly not so damaging when directed at shipping.

There was, however, a blind spot in these arrangements: the batteries of bolt-shooting and stone-throwing catapults accumulated by Archimedes, mainly sited on defensive fortifications 30 to 40 feet high, were unable sufficiently to depress the angle of their fire to engage the enemy closer than a distance of 60 yards or so. He resolved this difficulty in two ways: firstly and perhaps obviously, although it appeared to cause the Romans some surprise, he arranged for the casemates of the fortification to be pierced with large numbers of loopholes at the height of a man and, at each, he positioned archers with rows of so-called 'scorpions', a small catapult which discharged iron darts. These were sited so as to be able to engage the landing-craft as they arrived, with their scaling-ladders, beneath the curtain wall, while simultaneously enfilading the defensive line of fortifications. Secondly, he set in place on the battlements numerous swing-beam cranes, with stocks of heavy stones (some weighing as much as ten talents) and leaden ingots, to be dropped on to ships and troops below, as they gathered for the assault.

The Archimedes fire plan was remarkable, not so much for the careful detail which any competent commanding general of the day might perhaps have conceived, but for the scale of planning and administration which set it in place and for the degree of coordination and communication which made it operational. The Greek artillery command structure would have had to be such that it was brought under one hand. Careful targeting and fire control would have been important but flexibility would have had to be retained, so as to be in a position to decentralize should the need arise for rapid, independent operations. Much would have rested upon a good system of communication. Training and rehearsal would have been an essential requirement and adequate quantities of weaponry would have had to be pre-sited, together with dumps of missiles of every variety, from ten talent stones, to stone-shot, to bolts and ammunition generally. The quantities in each case would have been huge and may perhaps be judged from the volume of war material seized by Scipio at New Carthage a few years later, where Livy[32] lists '120 catapults of the largest sort, 281 smaller ones; 23 large, 52 smaller *ballistae*; countless "scorpions" large and small, and a great quantity of equipment and missiles' as having fallen into his hands.

There has been much vigorous debate over the correct siting of such artillery weapons in a defensive siege role. It is linked with three essential requirements: namely, the need for an effective method of controlling range adjustments; the vital necessity of providing counter-battery fire, aimed at neutralizing enemy artillery directed at the destruction of the battlement defences or endeavouring to breach the curtain walls with their heavy stone-throwing engines; and the need to bring fire to bear upon the vulnerable blind spots, already mentioned above, at the base of curtain walls.

The range of non-torsion weaponry could only have been varied by increasing or lowering the angle of elevation. In later years, with the introduction of torsion weaponry, it was feasible to vary range by altering the tension of the spring but this also had the effect of lessening the force of the strike-impact and thus reducing the effectiveness of the weapon. It was not, therefore, a solution likely to render itself attractive to artillerymen. The height and presence of the wall was a key factor, adding to the effective range of artillery should this be based upon its summit; reducing the range, should the weapon be sited, albeit securely, behind the wall, and resolving many problems, including coverage of the blind spot, if positioned to its front. Philon of Byzantium, who lived towards the end of the third century BC and claimed he derived his knowledge of artillery matters from artificers in the arsenals of Rhodes and Alexandria, favoured the forward location.[33] He advised that platforms should be constructed in front of curtain walls and outworks for

as many and as large engines as possible, some at surface level, others below ground level, so that there may be plenty of room for their operation, so that the detachments may not be hit, so that they may inflict casualties while themselves out of sight, and so that, when the enemy draws near, the aimers may not be handicapped by being unable to depress their engines.

The advantages of positioning artillery in this manner cannot be denied but it would necessarily have lain exposed and the possibility of losing vital weaponry to enemy attack would have been very real. Likewise, the ploy by Archimedes of positioning 'scorpion' catapults to fire through portholes in curtain walls, or even the suggestion that some machines might be sited within the walls themselves, could not under normal circumstances have been generally acceptable, for it surprised the Romans. The reason for this is probably that the wall would have been weakened by being adapted for this purpose and would, as a consequence, have been rendered vulnerable to battering-ram attack. Marsden, the author of authoritative works on Greek and Roman artillery,[34] is in no doubt that a fortification's defensive artillery was set up on the ordinary single rampart walk, as well as within the stalwart towers with which walls were provided from about the middle of the fourth century.

The use of siege artillery in an assault followed a broader pattern than defence, mainly because the besieger had greater room for manoeuvre. It was frequently found in a counter-battery as well as an anti-personnel role, where it repelled sorties and directed its fire at the defending garrison manning the battlements. On occasions heavy artillery, casting stone missiles of great weight, was used in an effort to breach the walls of a stronghold. At the siege of Jotapata, during the Galilean war, Josephus records that Vespasian fielded 160 artillery weapons, set them up in a ring and then ordered them to bombard the men on the wall in a 'synchronised barrage' of javelins, firebrands, showers of arrows and stones weighing nearly one hundredweight, 'whilst a host of Arab bowmen with all the javelin men and slingers let fly at the same time as the artillery'.[35] As at Syracuse, a barrage on this scale, synchronized with such a number and variety of weapons, must have called for a highly effective system of command and control: nor could it have been put into practical effect unless gun-crews had been well drilled in firing procedures.

Josephus, in his work *The Jewish War*, has provided us with many forceful descriptions of battle but probably none more lively than his account of the second phase of the assault by Titus upon the walls of Jerusalem. The Jews had captured a number of artillery weapons from the Romans when they had earlier chased Cestius out of Antonia. They had few men who understood how to operate them but were being instructed in their working by deserters and they were directing what fire they could generate at Roman engineers preparing a way for an assault with battering-rams. The legionary engines responding to this fire, wrote Josephus,

> were masterpieces of construction, but none were equal to those of the Tenth; their spear-throwers were more powerful and their stone-throwers bigger, so that they could repulse not only the sorties but also the fighters on the wall. The stone missiles weighed half a hundredweight and travelled four hundred yards or more; no one who got in their way, whether in the front line or far behind, remained standing. At first the Jews kept watch for the stone – it was white, so that not only was it heard whizzing through the air but its shining surface could easily be seen. Look-outs posted on the towers gave them warning every time a shot was fired from the engine and came hurtling towards them, by shouting 'Baby on the way!'. Those in its path at once scattered and fell prone, a precaution which resulted in the stone passing harmlessly through till it came to a stop. The Roman counter was to blacken the stone. As it could not then be seen so easily, they hit their target. . . .[36]

Under cover of this counter-battery fire the Romans moved forward their battering-rams, but were showered with missiles and firebrands, which set alight the lattice

*Titus, son of Vespasian, emperor of Rome (AD 79–81) and victor of the siege of Jerusalem,
AD 70*

shields under which they were sheltering. Vespasian's son, Titus, the leader of this storming party, then placed 'the cavalry and bowmen either side of the engines, beat off the fire-throwers, repulsed those who were throwing missiles from the towers and got the battering-rams into action. Yet the wall did not give way. . . .'

Jerusalem, standing high upon a plateau and built upon a hard limestone formation (which, one must imagine, would have made the battlefield completion of defensive earthworks a heavy, arduous task, although Roman military discipline was to prove otherwise), provided a formidable obstacle to Roman ambitions. It was bounded on the west and south by the precipitous scarp of the Hinnom and on the east by the equally steep slopes of the valley of the Kidron, both of which rendered impossible the working of enemy battering-rams and assault towers. The tactical options for Titus, when making his plans, were limited. Moreover, within its walls, the city possessed an asset invaluable to its defenders and not available to its besiegers – a plentiful and secure water supply, said to have been completed by Hezekiah[37] when Jerusalem was under threat of siege by King Sennacherib of Assyria in 701 BC. This precious supply was conveyed by tunnel from the bountiful spring at Gihon, outside the south-eastern wall, to the Pool of Siloam, a reservoir securely located in the heart of the Upper and Lower Cities.

Apart from the natural strength of the terrain which surrounded it, Jerusalem, the 'stronghold of Zion', had powerful man-made defences. Initially built as a Jebusite town, it had fallen to the Israelites about 1000 BC and, according to 1 Samuel 5: 6–10, although relatively small compared with the scale of its later development, it had subsequently been powerfully fortified by David. A part of the original Jebusite city wall, repaired and strengthened in those years and recently revealed by archaeological excavation, measured a doughty 27 feet wide.

In the intervening years between its capture by the Israelites and the arrival of the Romans, Jerusalem grew in size and expanded in the only direction open to it, across the plateau, northwards and to the west. At various stages of its development, further substantial additions to its defences were made. Firstly, a northern wall, which reached eastwards from Herod's Palace, by the Jaffa Gate, to the Temple, was built to embrace the Upper City. Later, a further, second wall, was added by Antipater, the father of Herod Agrippa I. This pursued a zig-zag course from the palace to the Antonia: it was given added strength by the provision of a large fortification, the Middle Tower, which guarded its gate and acted as the hinge of its defence. The Antonia had been Herod's earlier home before he provided himself with a grander residence. Finally, a third wall was constructed by Agrippa I, king of Judaea (AD 41–44) but he failed to finish it. He feared that the added strength he was giving to the city might be misconstrued by his Roman masters as a gesture of defiance. Thus, at the moment of Titus's arrival, a portion of it, the return wall lying between the octagonal tower of Psephinus and the western, Jaffa Gate, still stood incomplete. Apart from this, it was a magnificent structure, 15 feet wide and 40 feet tall.

The defenders of the city, if one accepts Josephus' assessment of their quality, were a strangely mixed bag of some 23,400 men who had imposed themselves upon a reluctant population. In the main they were private armies, thrown up during Vespasian's earlier operations in Galilee. They arrived piecemeal and quickly

PHASE I

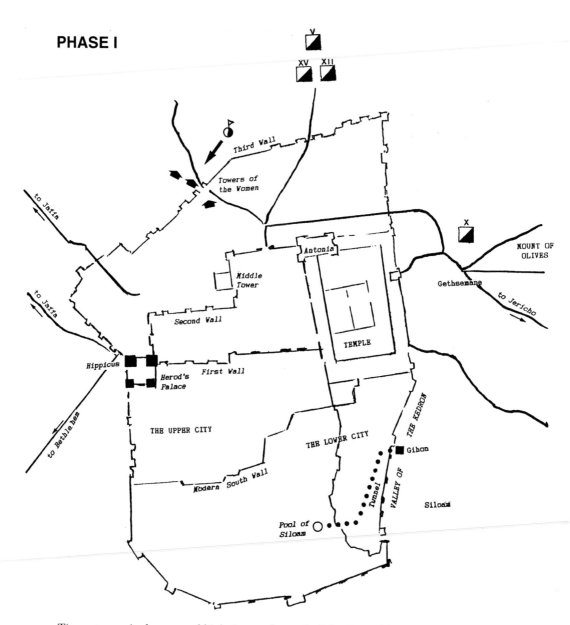

Titus, upon arrival, encamped his legions to the north of the city and deployed X Legion on the Mount of Olives, confronting its eastern walls. Meantime, he set forth to conduct a reconnaissance of the partially unfinished wall adjoining the Jaffa Gate. Here he was ambushed. Note the city's secure water supply flowing underground from Gihon to the Pool of Siloam

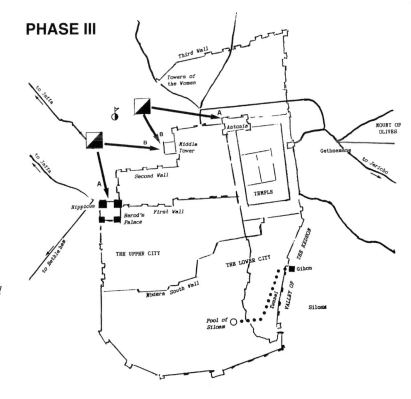

PHASE III

Titus opened the second phase of his siege of the city by grouping his army in two divisions and assaulting the wall running north-west from Herod's Palace. When this had been overcome, he directed his assault (Phase III, illustrated here), first, against the extremities of the second wall (arrows A) and then against the Middle Tower

divided themselves into two factions, treating each other with an uninhibited distrust which frequently erupted into open hostility. John of Gischala, leader of 6,000 Galileans and described by Josephus as a 'gangster and racketeer', occupied the Antonia and the Temple: here, he was joined by 2,400 Zealots, extreme patriots with a reputation for brutality, guided primarily by religious motives. The second faction was led by Simon bar Gioras, who occupied the City with its shops, magazines and foodstores. It comprised 10,000 Sicarii, fervent nationalists who lived by the dagger from which they derived their name, and 5,000 Idumaeans who had defected to his side during his recent invasion of their territory. During the siege warfare which was about to open, the two parties reconciled their differences and joined forces to great effect. During a lull in the fighting, however, they turned upon each other once again and destroyed a large part of their food resources in a senseless, fanatical encounter. According to Josephus, 'all the environs of the Temple were reduced to ashes, the city was converted into a desolate no-man's-land for their domestic warfare, and almost all the corn, which might have sufficed them for many years of siege, was burnt up'.[38]

These were the defences and the garrison which opposed Titus upon his arrival.

The Roman general had assembled an army of some 65,000 men. This was made up of four legions: the Vth from Emmaus; the Xth, of high reputation, had marched from Jericho; the XIIth, which was seeking to redeem its name after its recent ignominious defeat under Cestius Gallus; and the XVth, Titus's own

PHASE IV

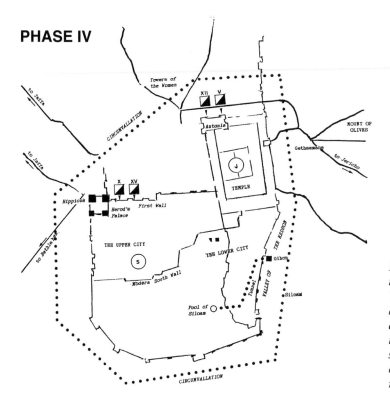

In this final phase Titus completed the destruction of the Second and Third walls and simultaneously assaulted the defences at the extremities of the First wall. Note the circumvallation with which he surrounded the city at this stage in order to contain the enemy within its walls and cut their supply lines

regiment which had come up from Alexandria, together with 1,000 men each from the IIIrd and XXIInd Legions, and a further 3,000 from the Euphrates garrisons. The balance of his force, twenty allied cohorts, eight regiments of cavalry, with a variety of auxiliaries armed with supporting weaponry, was furnished by Agrippa II and the rulers of neighbouring client kingdoms.

Titus was careful not to disclose his hand too soon. He approached Jerusalem from the north and camped in a depression 4 miles distant, north of Beit Hanina, invisible to look-outs posted high on the city's fortifications. From there, he set out on a reconnaissance with a bodyguard of some 600 men and, riding through the maze of vegetable gardens and partitioning walls which covered the ground on that side of the city and provided a source of food for it, he made his way directly towards the Damascus Gate. Here he turned right and headed in the direction of the octagonal tower of Psephinus but, as he passed the Towers of the Women, the Jews streamed out in considerable force and ambushed him. He managed to fight his way free. He now ordered his legions forward to new positions, the Xth to occupy the Mount of Olives, opposite the Golden Gate and the remainder to Mount Scopus; and, when they had completed the fortification of their camps, they were instructed to begin the task of levelling the ground between their position and the Jaffa Gate. He wanted no further surprises.

Titus would almost certainly have been aware of the unfinished state of the wall beside the Jaffa Gate when he rode forward to reconnoitre it. He quickly recognized its weakness and at once re-assembled his entire force, in two army groups, with battering-rams supported by spearmen, bowmen and slingers, to attack the reach between Herod's Palace and the Psephinus Tower. The Jewish defenders resisted stubbornly but found themselves unable to counter the fire which the Romans, in support of their battering-rams, brought to bear upon them from their 75 feet high assault towers. On their lofty perch, explained Josephus,

> these men were beyond the reach of Jewish weapons and there was no way to capture the towers . . . so they withdrew out of range, abandoning the attempts to hold off the assaults of the Romans, which by their incessant blows were little by little effecting their purpose. . . . Besides, through laziness and their habit of deciding wrongly, they thought it a waste of effort to defend this wall as there remained two more behind it. Most of them slacked off and retired: and when the Romans climbed through the breach made by Victor (the battering-ram) they all left their posts and ran helter-skelter to the second wall.[39]

This phase of the siege had taken Titus five days to complete. He now issued orders for the destruction of the outer wall (or Third Wall, as it is known), in its entirety from the Jaffa Gate to the north-eastern corner of the city. When this had been done, he commenced his attack upon the next line of defence, which now confronted him, the Second Wall.

Here, he determined to stretch the Jewish defences by launching his two army groups against it simultaneously, one to assault the western end of the wall, defended by Simon, adjoining Herod's Palace, and the other against its eastern extremity, the Antonia and the colonnade of the Temple occupied by John. He soon appreciated, however, that this tactic played to his enemy's advantage for, by dividing his forces in this manner he ensured that his troops got little rest, whereas the restricted width of the wall limited the numbers which the Jews needed to field at any one time. As a consequence, he now determined to concentrate his assault upon the Middle Tower, attacking in waves so that, while some of his legions were engaged in the arduous, dangerous work of fighting to penetrate the walls, others could be resting. He thus always had fresh formations to bring to the task. In this manner, after a sustained and bitter struggle, he broke through on 25 May,[40] fifteen days after his success in breaching the outer wall, but it was not until 4 June that he consolidated his hold upon it. He occupied the intervening days by holding a ceremonial pay parade, in the hope that this glimpse of Roman wealth and resources might persuade his enemy to yield. It did not.

Titus now embarked upon the final and, as it was to prove, the most lengthy and bloody stage of the siege, which was to endure until 26 September, when the last resistance within the city was overcome. First, he set about the systematic destruction of the newly breached Second Wall, with the exception of the reach on the extreme west, where it ran north and south. He retained this as a protective screen for his new camp and then set the Vth and XIIth Legions to work, facing the Antonia, building parallel ramps, 30 feet apart, upon which to site his assault towers. He gave a similar task to the Xth and XVth Legions, at the western extremity of the wall, north of the Upper City. These platforms were of vast size

Siege towers at Jerusalem, AD 70 (Polybius, *ed. 1727*)

and took seventeen days of intense labour to complete. As soon as they were finished, the great assault towers were moved forward to them in preparation for the next stage. The Romans, however, were unaware that John of Gischala had not been idle. As they laboured opposite the Antonia, so also had he been working hard, undermining their work with tunnels and caves, stuffing these with faggots daubed with pitch and bitumen, primed to be set alight. He chose his moment carefully before igniting them and then, as they turned to ashes in the heat of the flames they generated, the platforms fell with a thunderous crash into the cavity thus created:

> At once there was a dense cloud of smoke and dust as the flames were choked with debris; then when the mass of timber was burnt away a brilliant flame burnt through. This sudden blow filled the Romans with consternation, and the ingenuity of the Jews filled them with despondency; as they had felt sure that victory was imminent, the shock froze their hope of success even in the future. To fight the flames was useless, for even if they did put them out their platforms were already swallowed up.[41]

But worse was to come: two days later, Simon's forces emerged from behind their defences in a surprise raid upon the two platforms confronting his section of the wall. These they also set alight and doggedly refused to be driven away until the structures were well ablaze.

As a result of these counter-strokes, Titus was confronted by a crisis of resources. He had used his last remaining stocks of timber in the construction of the siege

Captured spoils from Jerusalem carried in Titus's triumphal procession, c. AD 81

platforms, and replacements were unavailable. The time, moreover, was approaching mid-summer and, in the desert sun, he was running short of water. Josephus makes no mention of Titus's administrative supply lines but the Roman had, by this time, already been positioned in front of Jerusalem for some five to six weeks. In this circumstance, he must already have been well into a programme of re-supply, hauling grain and water for men and animals from some distance away. The Jews, we may rest assured, would not have allowed these vital columns to move unscathed, for they appear to have had many means of penetrating under and over their city walls. Titus, himself aware of his enemy's self-created shortage of rations, now determined to seal off this traffic by constructing a circumvallation around Jerusalem, in a circular, 5 mile long fortification, strengthened at intervals by thirteen towers, each some 200 feet in circumference, between which his army constantly patrolled, night and day. In the end, before their surrender, the besieged were reduced to eating grass and the leather of their belts and sandals.

Titus's siege of Jerusalem provides a classic example of the art of siege warfares: the effectiveness of the countermining operations by the besieged, the importance to both sides of carefully planned administration and the need for plentiful resources. Particularly noteworthy, on the Roman side, is the manner in which the Roman general tightened his grip on his newly acquired territory at the successful end of each of his assault phases, before moving to the next, thus denying his enemy any opportunity of re-occupying their old defences by counter-attack. The strength of the great Roman war machine might have been unavailing, however, had it not been for the internecine fighting among their enemy that destroyed their stocks of food. Had this not happened, by their ingenious and heroic destruction of Titus's siege platforms, the Jews might have achieved a stunning victory.

Appendix 1

THE PEUTINGER MAP

This map – a road map of the Roman Empire – takes its name from the German map collector Conrad Peutinger (1465–1547). Peutinger received this map, a manuscript of the twelfth or thirteenth century, from Conrad Celtes, and copied only two sections of it. The section illustrated here (p. x) is based on the 1653 edition by Jan Janson.

It is conjectured that the Celtes manuscript was copied from an ancient map drawn around 365 CE. It describes the roads of the Roman Empire from Gaul in the west to India in the east. The map takes the form of a long, narrow parchment scroll (approximately 33 × 682 cm), divided into twelve sections. Section one, the extreme west, was lost. The Land of Israel appears in section eleven. There, as in the rest of the map, important settlements are noted, with distances between them marked in Roman miles.

Jerusalem is depicted by two buildings and the Mount of Olives. Above it appears the inscription: 'Formerly called Jerusalem (and today) Aelia Capitolina'. One of the roads leaving Jerusalem crosses the Negev Desert and ends at Eilat on the shores of the Red Sea. Among other sites mentioned on the map are the Jordan River, Tiberias, the Dead Sea, Jaffa, Ptolemaida ('Akko), Azoton (Ashdod) and Ascalon (Ashqelon).

In an attempt to accommodate the entire empire in a narrow scroll, the cartographer had to make the map narrow. To do so he reduced the areas of the sea to narrow strips. As a result, many lines running north to south are sketched in the map from right to left. The proper dimensions for east to west are largely maintained. The Peutinger Map probably served travellers to the Land of Israel, including pilgrims.

A story is told about the Roman road from Jerusalem to Eilat to the effect that, during the War of Independence in 1948, the Israeli High Command had a secret plan to conquer the Negev and Eilat. This plan was called 'Operation Fact'. Yigael Yadin, the chief of operations and an archaeologist by profession, knew of the Roman road leading from Jerusalem to Eilat – shown in the Peutinger Map – parts of which had been preserved under the desert sand.

The armoured column sent to conquer Eilat followed this route and reached the shores of the Red Sea. In doing so, they caught the enemy by surprise, for the Jordanians did not believe that the Israeli army would succeed in crossing the desert in the absence of a partly paved road.

Appendix 2

SIGNAL METHODS

I *Commands by Voice, Bugle and Signal*

The commands must be short and unambiguous. This would be attained if the particular command should precede the general, since the general are ambiguous. For example, we would not say, 'Face right!' but 'Right Face!', so that in their eagerness some may not make the turn to the right and others to the left when the order to turn has been given first, but that all may do the same thing together; nor do we say 'Face about right!' but 'Right about face!', nor 'Counter march, Laconian!' but 'Laconian, counter march!' and [passage missing]. . . .

Stand by to take up arms! Baggage men fall out! Silence in the ranks! and Attention! Take up arms! Shoulder arms! Take distance! Shoulder spear! Dress files! Dress ranks! Dress files by the file-leader! File-closer, dress file! Keep your original distance! Right Face! Forward march! Halt! Depth Double! As you were! Depth half! As you were! Length double! As you were! Laconian, counter march! As you were! Quarter turn! As you were! Right half turn! As you were!

These are in brief the principles of the tactician; they mean safety to those who follow them and danger to those who disobey.

Ascelepiodotus, Tactics, 11

II *Advanced Techniques*

There is no doubt that the Romans practised several advanced signalling methods, many of the more ingenious being inherited from the Greeks. Vegetius[1] describes a sophisticated semaphore system (another type of semaphore was employed by the Roman navy – see Chapter 6, pp. 115–17), operated from signal towers and equipped with wooden arms. Its range would necessarily have been minimal without the benefit of the telescope provided to the signal stations which, in the nineteenth century, linked naval dockyards on the south coast of England with the Admiralty building in Whitehall. These were sited, spaced every 7 or 8 miles, on suitable vantage points along the way, sometimes at the top of great buildings such as the Duke of York's headquarters in Chelsea: but if a message were to be recorded by the naked eye, as would have been the case in Roman times, the intervening distance would have needed to be much less.

Polybius has recorded two techniques, both of them highly ingenious.[2] The first he attributed to Aeneas, 'the author of the work on strategy'. It required the possession of two completely identical earthenware jars, each 3 cubits (or roughly 5 feet) in depth and 1 cubit (or 20 inches) wide, each drilled, low down, with apertures of similar size and then plugged; and each provided with a cork a little less in diameter than the mouth of the jar. A light rod, calibrated in equal sections of three finger-breadths, was driven through the exact centre of each cork so that, when the jars were ultimately filled with equal levels of water, they floated at the same height. The calibrations on the rods were marked, the one against the other, with carefully chosen and identical phrases, listed in an identical sequence. Thus, when both plugs were removed simultaneously and the water flowed out, the rods sank at an equal speed to an equal level.

The transmission of the message was simply achieved. The despatching signaller had first to display a lighted torch from his signal station and then wait until the distant recipient had raised another in response. When this had been done, and both were clearly visible, the despatcher lowered his torch, at which moment other signallers, at both the despatching and receiving ends, extracted the corks from their respective jars and allowed the water to escape until the message inscribed on the rod was level with the lip of the jar. At this moment, the despatcher's torch was again displayed and both corks were promptly replaced. If the signal drill had been carried out with dexterity and speed, then the rods should have fallen identical distances, enabling the message to be passed.

Polybius opined that this method was an improvement on the hilltop beacon, lit in accordance with a 'preconcerted code', but he argued that both methods had their obvious limitations, for

> . . . it is impossible to agree beforehand about things of which one cannot be aware before they happen. And this is the vital matter; for how can anyone consider how to render assistance if he does not know how many of the enemy have arrived, or where? And how can anyone be of good cheer or the reverse, or in fact think of it at all, if he does not understand how many ships or how much corn has arrived from the allies?

For these reasons, Polybius expressed his preference for a later method, 'devised by Cleoxenus and Democleitus and perfected by myself'. In this case, the alphabet was divided into five roughly equal parts and listed upon five 'tablets', numbered one to five. Each letter on each tablet was also allocated a number and these were arrayed in front of the despatching signaller, so that he might read them with ease. Under his command were two groups of transmitting signallers, each group stationed behind a screen, one on his left, the other on his right. Each team held at least six fire torches ready to hand. The purpose of the screens was to conceal their light when not in use.

When the despatcher wished to send a message, he raised two torches to attract the attention of the intended recipient who was required to respond by raising two torches in reply. Both sets of torches were then withdrawn. The message was now passed by spelling out the individual letters of each word, the number of torches exposed over the left-hand screen indicating the number of the tablet to be used, the number of torches over the right-hand screen indicating the number of the letter on the specified tablet. Those engaged in the work, stressed Polybius, 'must have proper practice so that, when it comes to putting it in action, they may communicate with each other without the possibility of a mistake'. In order to be certain the sentries did not waste time, or miss an incoming message, each signal station was required to plant a hollow tube, sighted on a fixed line and directed towards its neighbouring post.

What degree of efficiency could this system have achieved? Polybius, in an ambiguous phrase, states that the methods described by him were capable of despatching every kind of urgent message over 'distances of three, four or even more days' journey'. If one accepts a day's journey to be 20 miles then, at first sight, it appears he is mooting a single span of 100 miles or more, a clearly inconceivable range: more probably, he is suggesting the total distance across which a message could have been efficiently and economically relayed. On the Dacian frontier, for example, a system of Roman signal stations, watch towers and forts, all located about 6 miles apart, has been found between Bologa and Tehau.[3] These could all have played some part in a local signal network of this nature but, broadly, this still requires confirmation. Where, when and for what purpose such systems would have been employed are questions which still await answers.

1.   Vegetius, *Epitoma rei militaris*, pp. iii, 5.
2.   Polybius, *The Rise of the Roman Empire* (Penguin Classics, London, 1979), pp. x, 43–7.
3.   See Nicolae Gudea, 'The Defensive System of Roman Dacia', *Britannia* (1979), Vol 10.

Appendix 3

MARCHING-CAMP TECHNIQUES

Labour Figures for Common Engineering Tasks

Serial No.	Description	Unit	Output per man per hour	Notes
(*a*)	(*b*)	(*c*)	(*d*)	(*e*)
	Site clearance and demolition work			
1	Clearing bushes and scrub	m²	33	
2	Clearing dense undergrowth with saplings up to 100 mm diam.	m²	11.7	
	Earthwork			
1	Digging to depth not exceeding 1 m including loading into barrows	m³	0.4–0.7	(i) (ii)
2	Digging only, to depth not exceeding 1.5 m and throw not exceeding 2 m	m³	0.4–0.7	(i) (ii)
3	Shovelling loose soil, throw not exceeding 3 m	m³	1.1–1.5	(i) (ii)
4	Filling loose soil into sandbags	bag	20	(i) (iii)
5	Filling loose soil into barrows	m³	1.1–1.5	(i)
6	Filling wet mud into barrows	m³	1.3	(i)
7	Wheeling 25 m, depositing and returning empty	m³	2.5–3.0	(i) (iii)
8	Spreading soil in 150 mm layers	m³	1.5–2.0	(i) (ii)
9	Ramming soil in 150 mm layers	m²	1.5–2.0	(i) (ii)
10	Levelling and trimming slopes to profile	m²	8	

(i) Daylight rate. For night with no moon: x½. For night with full moon or artificial moonlight: × 2/3

(ii) Depends on nature of soil (chalk to sandy loam)

(iii) Each metre rise is equivalent to 6 m on level; maximum slope 1 in 8

Note: statistics provided by The Royal School of Military Engineering and are MOD copyright.

Appendix 4

SIEGE OF JERUSALEM, AD 70

Sequence of Main Events

4 May	Titus arrives with his army, encamps and then carries out reconnaissance of city walls
10 May	Siege opens
25 May	Romans overwhelm the Third (outer) Wall, raze the NW reach to the ground and occupy the New City.
16 June	Roman ramps (platforms) at Antonia undermined by John of Gischala
18 June	Simon destroys the platforms confronting his stretch of the wall
14 July	Titus renews assault on Antonia
24 July	Standard-bearer of the Vth Legion, with trumpeter, gains a foothold on the wall. Jewish defenders seek refuge in the Temple
29 Aug.	Temple falls and contents looted; defenders now pull back to Upper City
8 Sep.	Titus recoups timber stores from source 10 miles away and constructs two new platforms over next 18 days
18 Sep.	Jerusalem capitulates after 139 days of siege

Notes

Introduction

1. Major General J.F.C Fuller, *Julius Caesar, Man, Soldier and Tyrant* (London, 1965), pp. 315–6.
2. Chester Wilmot, *The Struggle for Europe* (London, 1952), p. 75, fn 2.
3. Field Marshal Sir William Slim, *Defeat into Victory* (London, 1956), pp. xxi, 485.
4. Julius Caesar, *de Bello Africo*, p. 8.
5. Josephus, *The Jewish War*, Ch. III, p. 109.
6. Vegetius, *Epitoma rei militaris*, I, p. 1.
7. John Peddie, *Invasion, The Roman Conquest of Britain* (Gloucester, 1987), Ch. III.
8. Field Marshal Viscount Montgomery, *Concise History of Warfare*, I, p. 19.
9. Onasander, *The General*, Ch. III.
10. Livy, pp. xxxi, 42.
11. *ibid*; xliv, 37.
12. Vegetius, *op. cit.*, II, 31.

Chapter One

1. Field Marshal Sir William Slim, *Defeat into Victory* (London, 1956), IX, p. 186.
2. Vegetius, *Epitoma rei militaris*, I, p. 12.
3. J.A. Froude, *Caesar, A Sketch* (London, 1886), p. 550.
4. Theodor Mommsen, *The History of Rome* (London, 1911), IV, p. 430.
5. Dr T. Rice Holmes, *Caesar's Conquest of Gaul* (Oxford, 1911), pp. xii, 42.
6. Professor H. Last, *Cambridge Ancient History* (Cambridge, 1932), IX, p. 705.
7. T. Dodge, *Caesar, Great Captains Series* (Boston, Mass. 1892), Vol. 11, p. 767.
8. *ibid.*, pp. 692–3.
9. J.F.C. Fuller, *Julius Caesar, Man, Soldier and Tyrant*, (London, 1965), p. 318.
10. In AD 44, Caesar's dictatorship, previously bestowed for only ten years, was declared perpetual, an act which almost certainly contributed to his assassination.
11. W.V. Harris, *War and Imperialism in Republican Rome*, 327–70 BC (Oxford, 1979), pp. 13–17.
12. Pliny, *Epistulae*, VIII, pp. 14, 4–5.
13. Cassius Dio, *The Roman History*, pp. lx, 19; the official line from Rome was that Plautius had been ordered to notify Claudius if and when his invasion force got into difficulties; that Plautius was stalled in his efforts to cross the Thames and sent for the emperor, who duly arrived and resolved his general's problems. However, Claudius could not have afforded to be associated with failure, and we may therefore judge that his victory was already assured when he sailed upriver – indeed, when he left Rome.
14. Cicero, *Ad Familiares*, XV.
15. Frontinus, *Stratagems,* IV, pp. vii, 5.
16. Tacitus, *The Agricola*, p. 20.
17. Velleius Paterculus, II, pp. lxvii, 6, 1.
18. Suetonius, *The Twelve Caesars*, 60.
19. Caesar, *de Bello Gallico*, IV, p. 14; VII, p. 56; VIII, p. 3.
20. Caesar, *de Bello Africo*, p. 26.
21. Fuller, *op. cit.*, p. 322.
22. Frontinus, *op. cit.*, IV, pp. 1, 7.
23. Velleius Paterculus, II, pp. 114, 1–2, as in R.W. Davies, 'The Roman Military Medical Service', *Saalburg Jahrbuch* (1970), p. 98, fn 110.
24. Tacitus, *Annals*, pp. 1, 69.
25. For a full account see Davies, *op. cit.*
26. *de Bello Gallico*, VI, p. 36.
27. Montgomery, *Concise History of Warfare* (London, 1972), pp. 1, 17.
28. *de Bello Gallico*, VI, p. 7.
29. Frontinus, *op. cit.*, II, p. viii.
30. Vegetius, *Epitoma rei militaris*, I, pp. 1, 9.
31. Tacitus, *op. cit.*, pp. xiii, 34.

32. Frontinus, *op. cit.*, IV, pp. 1, 1–46.
33. *ibid.*, IV, pp. i, 38.
34. Suetonius, *op. cit.*, pp. 1, 62.
35. *ibid.*, pp. 1, 68.
36. Frontinus, *op. cit.*, III, pp. xiv, 2.
37. Vegetius, *op. cit.*, III, p. 3.
38. Frontinus, *op. cit.*, IV, pp. iii, 14.
39. Tacitus, *op. cit.*, pp. xii, 29.
40. Tacitus, *The Agricola*, p. 21.
41. Frontinus, *op. cit.*, III, p. xvi; I, p. ix.
42. Suetonius, *op. cit.*, I, p. 65.
43. Onasander, *The General*, III.

Chapter Two

1. Polybius, *The Rise of the Roman Empire* (Penguin Classics, London, 1979), p. ix.
2. Asclepiodotus, *Tactics*, p. 10.
3. Vegetius, *Epitoma rei militaris*, p. ii.
4. Homer, *Iliad*, p. 18.
5. Curt Sachs, *The History of Musical Instruments* (London, 1940), p. 145.
6. Michael P. Speidel, *Eagle Bearer and Trumpeter* (Rheinisches Landesmuseum, Bonn, 1967), p. 154.
7. *ibid.*
8. Philip Bate, *The Trumpet and the Trombone* (London, 1978), pp. 5, 101–5.
9. Speidel, *op. cit.*, p. 161.
10. Sir Ian Richmond, *Trajan's Army on Trajan's Column* (British School at Rome London, 1982), p. 49 and pl. 20a.
11. Polybius, *op. cit.*, pp. vi, 40; and Josephus, *The Jewish War* (Penguin Classics, London, repr. 1985), pp. iii, 87.
12. *Regulations for the Exercise of Riflemen* (The War Office, London, 1801).
13. Caesar, *War Commentaries*, ed. John Warrington (London, repr. 1965), III, pp. 292–4.
14. Frontinus, *Strategems* (Loeb Classical Library, London, repr. 1980), pp. 292.
15. Vegetius, *op. cit.*, III, 'Proper Distances and Intervals'.
16. Dr H.G. Farmer, *The Rise and Development of Military Music* (London, 1912), pp. i, 10.
17. See, among others, Lawrence Keppie, *The Making of the Roman Army* (London, 1984) and Graham Webster, *The Roman Imperial Army* (London, 2nd edn. 1979).
18. Field Marshal Viscount Montgomery, *A Concise History of Warfare* (London, 1972), pp. iv, 53.
19. Caesar, *de Bello Gallico*, I, pp. 39, 2.
20. Polybius, *op. cit.*, pp. vi, 24.
21. Vegetius, *op. cit.*, I, Prefect of camp, p.16.
22. For example, G. Webster, *The Roman Army* (Chester, 1956), II; George C. Boon and Colin Williams, *Plan of Caerleon* (Cardiff, 1967), p. 6.
23. Speidel, *op. cit.*, p. 138.
24. Caesar, *op. cit.*, V, p. 37.
25. Tacitus, *The Annals of Imperial Rome* (Penguin Classics, Harmondsworth, 1981), II, p. 14.
26. As in Graham Webster, *The Roman Imperial Army* (London, 1979), pp. 3, 137 fn 2 (Florus, pp. iv, 12).
27. Vegetius, *op. cit.*, Centuries and Ensigns of the Foot, II, 50.
28. Polybius, *op. cit.*, pp. vi, 24.
29. Dio, *Roman History*, III, pp. xl, 18.
30. Caesar, *de Bello Africo*, p. 15.
31. Josephus, *The Jewish War* (Penguin Classics, Harmondsworth, 1987), II, p. 587.
32. *ibid.*, III, p. 111.
33. Caesar, *de Bello Africo*, 17.
34. A.M. Ramsay, The Speed of the Roman Imperial Post, *Journal of Roman Studies*, pp. 60–1.
35. Suetonius, *Augustus*, pp. 49–50.
36. As in Ramsay, *op. cit.*, p. 67.
37. Plutarch, *Julius*, p. 17.
38. *ibid.*, p. 68.
39. Procopius, *Anecdota*, p. 30.
40. Suetonius, *Claudius*, p. 17.
41. Procopius, *op. cit.*

Chapter Three

1. Vegetius, *Epitoma rei militaris*, pp. iii, 71.
2. Chester Wilmot, *The Struggle for Europe* (London, 1952), pp. xxiv, 470.
3. J.F.C. Fuller, *Julius Caesar, Man, Soldier and Tyrant* (London, 1965), pp. xiv, 316.
4. Caesar, *The Conquest of Gaul* (Penguin Classics, Harmondsworth, 1984), pp.vii, 14.
5. *ibid.*, pp. v, 45.
6. I.A. Richmond and J. McIntyre, 'Tents of the Roman army and leather from Birdoswald', *Transactions of the Cumberland and Westmorland Archaeological Society* (1934), p. 34.
7. *op. cit.*, pp. vi, 36–7.
8. Donald W. Engels, *Alexander the Great and the Logistics of the Macedonian Army* (Berkeley, 1978), pp. i, 15.
9. *ibid.*, pp. i, 15, fn 15.
10. Generally calculated at 3 to 3½ miles in the hour, including a ten minute rest period.

11. They were, of course, on call in case of emergency and this, as will be seen, carried its risks.
12. Fuller, *op. cit.*, pp. xiv, 317.
13. Sir Ian Richmond, *Trajan's Army on Trajan's Column* (London, 1982), pp. i, 12–13.
14. Livy, *The Early History of Rome*, pp. iii, 27.
15. On the basis that each wagon carries 2 tons.
16. Patrick Boyle and James Musgrave-Wood, *Jungle, Jungle, Little Chindit* (London, 1944) pp. 4, 22.
17. Vegetius, *op. cit.*, pp. iii, 79.
18. Caesar, *op. cit.*, ii, 24.
19. That is, one servant for each of the 'Roman' cavalry and none for the native cavalry; but one servant/animal handler per infantry section. See also Engels, *op. cit.*
20. The GD drivers would have been employed transporting 'bulk' supplies, e.g. grain reserves, under the direct control of the baggage master and with no loyalties in any other direction.
21. Ann Hyland, *Equus, The Horse in the Roman World* (London, 1990), pp. 6, 87–100.
22. Caesar, *op. cit.*, pp. i, 16.
23. *ibid.*, pp. i, 11.
24. *ibid.*, pp. i, 16.
25. *ibid.*, pp. vii, 34.
26. The transport opportunities offered by these and other French riverways are examined in some detail in Chapter 6, pp. 106–9.
27. T. Pakenham, *The Boer War* (London, 1979), pp. 379–80.
28. Caesar, *op. cit.*, pp. vii, 67.

Chapter Four

1. *Design for Military Operations – The British Military Doctrine* (prepared under the direction of the Chief of General Staff, 1989).
2. Frontinus, *Stratagems and Aqueducts*, ed. G.P. Gould (Loeb Classical Library, London, 1980), IV, pp. i, 14.
3. General Carl Von Clausewitz, *Principles of War* (London, 1943) 3, pp. iii, 47.
4. See, e.g., Caesar, *The Conquest of Gaul* (Penguin Classics, Harmondsworth, 1984) pp. vi, 32, where Caesar recounts the re-occupation of an old fortification.
5. *ibid.*, II, 20.
6. Major General J.F.C. Fuller, *Julius Caesar,*

Man, Soldier and Tyrant (London, 1965), pp. iv, 87.
7. Caesar, *op. cit.*, IV, pp. 86–7.
8. Fuller, *op. cit.*, IV, 76.
9. Polybius, *The Rise of the Roman Empire* (Penguin Classics, London, 1979), VI, pp. 27–34.
10. Vegetius, pp. iii, 82–3.
11. *ibid.*
12. Josephus, *The Jewish War* (Penguin Classics, London, repr. 1985), III, p. 87.
13. Polybius, *op. cit.*, VI, p. 41.
14. Josephus, *op. cit.*, III, p. 110.
15. Tacitus, *The Annals of Imperial Rome* (Penguin Classics, London, repr. 1981), I, p. 51.
16. Caesar, *op. cit.*, V, pp. 49, 5.
17. *ibid.*, II, pp. 17–27.
18. Sir Ian Richmond, *Trajan's Army on Trajan's Column* (London, 1982), pp. i, 11–13.
19. Caesar, *op. cit.*, V, p. 33.
20. *ibid.*, VI, p. 5.
21. *ibid.*, VII, p. 18.
22. *ibid.*, III, p. 24.
23. *ibid.*, II, p. 4.
24. *ibid.*, p. 19.
25. Richmond, *op. cit.*
26. Caesar, *op. cit.*, II, p. 19.
27. *ibid.*, p. 26.
28. *ibid.*, p. 16.
29. Josephus, *op. cit.*, III, p. 134.
30. I have confirmed this spacing with the regimental sergeant-major at the School of Infantry. The fact that the men were carrying shields and javelins should have made little difference.
31. Vegetius, *op. cit.*, I, p. 30.
32. Caesar, *op. cit.*, VII, pp. 40–1.
33. Ann Hyland, *Equus, The Horse in the Roman World* (London, 1990), pp. vi, 90.
34. David J. Breeze, 'The Logistics of Agricola's Final Campaign', *Talanta*, 16–19 (1987/8), pp. 7–22.
35. Vegetius, *op. cit.*, III, p. 82.
36. *ibid.*, p. 84.
37. Polybius, *op. cit.*, VI, pp. 28–35.
38. S.S. Frere and J.K.S. St Joseph, *Roman Britain from the Air* (Cambridge, 1983) pp. ii, 23–4.
39. Polybius, *op. cit.*, VI, p. 31; on the other hand, Hyginus, writing late in the second century, records the space as 60 feet.
40. Caesar, *op. cit.*, VI, p. 37.
41. Arthur Feller, *The Fall of the Roman Empire:*

The Military Explanation (London, 1986), pp. ii, 28.
42. Vegetius, *op. cit.*, I, p. 13.

Chapter Five

1. Vegetius, *Epitoma rei militaris*, III, p. 93.
2. We may judge that this refers to both light (*ballista*) and heavy (*onager*) artillery, but particularly the latter.
3. Sir Ian Richmond, *Trajan's Army on Trajan's Column* (London, 1982), pp. 2, 19, fn 22.
4. Vegetius, *op. cit.*, I, p. 23.
5. W.W. Tarn, *Hellenistic Military and Naval Developments* (Cambridge, 1930), I, p. 20.
6. Livy, *Rome and the Mediterranean*, pp. xxxviii, 21.
7. Vegetius, *op. cit.*, II, p. 58.
8. *ibid.*, pp. 52, 58.
9. C.T. Lewis and C. Short, *Freund's Latin Dictionary* (Oxford, 1879).
10. Caesar, *de Bello Gallico*, II, 7: I am indebted to my friend Colonel Charles Lane for the information that, when serving in the Oman, he witnessed Arabs knocking over small game with slingshot at ranges between 30 and 50 yards.
11. The authorship of the works which deal with Julius Caesar's Alexandrian, African and Spanish Wars is a matter of uncertainty. It is sometimes attributed to one Hirtius, a comparatively junior officer with limited access to the inner counsels of his commander-in-chief. Most scholars are inclined to accept that the true identity of the author remains obscure.
12. Caesar, *de Bello Africo*, 27.
13. Polybius, *The Rise of the Roman Empire* (Penguin Classics, London, 1979), III, pp. 42–7.
14. Major H.G. Eady, R.E., The Tank, *United Services Journal* (1926), p. 81.
15. Montgomery of Alamein, *A Concise History of Warfare* (1972), pp. 18, 291–2.
16. Caesar, *de Bello Africo*, p. 83.
17. *ibid.*, 83.
18. Richmond, *op. cit.*, pp. 2, 19, fn 22.
19. Caesar, *de Bello Africo*, p. 19.
20. Richmond, *op. cit.*, pp. 17–20, Plate 4.
21. Tacitus, *The Germania*, p. 45.
22. Sir Ralph Payne-Gallwey, *The Projectile-Throwing Engines of the Ancients* (London, 1907; repr. 1973); 'Treatise on the Turkish and other Oriental Bows'.
23. Robert Hardy, *Longbow* (Cambridge, 1976), pp. 14–21.
24. Payne-Gallwey, *op. cit.*, Introduction, p. vii.
25. *ibid.*
26. Caesar, *de Bello Africo*, pp. 12–14.
27. *ibid.*, p. 34.
28. Frontinus, *Stratagems*, II, ii, 5; this tactic by Ventidius would appear to confirm the range of a war arrow estimated by Payne-Gallwey (fn 22 above) as 360–400 yds.
29. Josephus, *The Jewish War*, III, p. 60.
30. Caesar, *de Bello Africo*, p. 60.
31. *ibid.*, p. 78.
32. Caesar, *de Bello Gallico*, II, p. 19.
33. Josephus, *op. cit.*, III, p. 220.
34. *ibid.*, III, p. 510.
35. *ibid.*, V, p. 370.
36. Ammianus Marcellinus, III, p. 15, 13; range estimated from distances achieved by Karamajong/Turkhana tribesmen (see p. 81).
37. Heron, *Bel W*, p. 75; Heron of Alexandria lived in the second half of the second century AD and was the author of an authoritative manual on contemporary artillery weapons.
38. Vegetius, *op. cit*, II, p. 15.
39. E.W. Marsden, *Greek and Roman Artillery, Historical Development* (Oxford, 1969), I, p. 15.
40. *ibid.*, and also in his work *Greek and Roman Artillery: Technical Treatises*, Marsden provides considerable detail. See also Payne-Gallwey, *op. cit.*, fn 22, above.
41. *ibid.*, III, p. 83.
42. Payne-Gallwey, *op. cit.*, Pt III, p. 25, fn 1.
43. Philon, *Bel*, 76, as in Marsden, *op. cit.*, IV, p. 94.
44. Payne-Gallwey, *The Crossbow* (London, 2nd edn., 1958), IX, pp. 44–5.
45. Ammianus Marcellinus, pp. xxiii, 4, 4–7.
46. Polybius records that in 250 BC Rhodes sent to Sinope ¾ ton of women's hair for her war with Mithridates (iv, 56, 3); and that in 225 Seleucus made a gift of several tons of hair to Rhodes (pp. v, 89, 9).
47. Josephus, *op. cit.*, II, p. 548.
48. *ibid*, V, p. vi.
49. Vegetius, *op. cit.*, II, p. 15.
50. Caesar, *de Bello Gallico*, II, p. 8.
51. Tacitus, *Annals*, I, p. 56.
52. Josephus, *op. cit.*, III, 112, and V, 36; also Arrian, *Alani*, p. 5.
53. Vegetius, *op. cit.*, II, p.15.
54. This is discussed in Marsden, *op. cit.*, pp. 8, 192–4.

Chapter Six

1. Dio's account of a speech by Mark Antony upon the murder of Julius Caesar: IV, pp. xliv, 43.
2. Dio, *Roman History*, pp. 28, 3.
3. Later, in the year 298, after a great victory by Galerius, a peace agreement with Persia advanced the border yet further, along a line from Singara, east of Sura, across the Tigris, to a position south of Lake Van; here it turned sharply westwards, once again to join the old boundary. This new arrangement benefited Rome for it rendered her eastern borders more secure but it was an agreement which lasted barely thirty years.
4. The Straits of Gibraltar.
5. Josephus, *The Jewish War*, II, p. 367.
6. Strabo, *The Geography*, II, pp. 5, 1, 6–7.
7. Tacitus, *Annals*, IV, p. 4.
8. Strabo, *op. cit.*, pp. 5, 4, 8–9.
9. Dio, *op. cit.*, VII, LX, p. 21.
10. Strabo, *op. cit.*, pp. 4, 1, 3–4.
11. Tacitus, *The Histories*, pp. 3, 43.
12. Raymond Chevallier, *Roman Roads* (London, 1989), I, p. 61.
13. Lionel Casson, *Ships and Seamanship in the Ancient World* (Princeton, 1971), pp. 2, 29, Appx 2.
14. Chevallier, *op. cit.*, III, p. 162.
15. Strabo, *op. cit.*, pp. 4, 1, 2.
16. *ibid.*, pp. 4, 1, 14.
17. Chevallier, *op. cit.*, pp. 3, 169.
18. Strabo, *op. cit.*, pp. 4, 3, 2.
19. Tacitus, *Annals*, XIII, p. 53.
20. *ibid.*, XI, p. 20.
21. Caesar, *de Bello Gallico*, I, p. 39.
22. Chevallier, *op. cit.*, pp. 3, 162.
23. Sean McGrail, 'Cross Channel Seamanship and Navigation in the Late First Millenium BC', *Oxford Journal of Archaeology*, pp. ii, 3 (1983).
24. *Wiltshire Archaeological Magazine*, XLVII.
25. John Wacher, *Roman Britain* (London, 1978), pp. 6, 179.
26. Tacitus, *Annals*, XII, p. 30.
27. John Peddie, *Invasion, The Roman Conquest of Britain* (Gloucester, 1987), pp. 4, 66–88.
28. Josephus, *op. cit.*, II, p. 367.
29. Strabo, *op. cit.*, XII, pp. 8, 11.
30. Casson, *op. cit.*, pp. 7, 141.
31. *ibid.*, fn 1.
32. *ibid.*, fn 2.
33. Caesar, *de Bello Gallico*, III, pp. 7–16.
34. Dio, *op. cit.*, pp. 50, 32.
35. Casson, *op. cit.*, 13, p. 313.
36. Ammianus Marcellinus, XXIV, pp. 1, 4.
37. *ibid.*, XXIV, p. 7.
38. Caesar, *de Bello Gallico*, IV, p. 26.
39. Casson, *op. cit.*, pp. 11, 248, fn 91.
40. Dio, pp. 49, 17, 2.
41. Caesar, *de Bello Gallico*, IV, p. 23.
42. Diodorus, pp. 20, 51, 1.
43. *ibid.*, pp. 13, 46, 3.
44. A. Dain, *Naumachia* (Paris, 1943), p. 30.
45. Caesar, *War Commentaries, The Civil War*, ed. John Warrington (London, 1965), II, p. 229.
46. John Paul Adams, *Logistics of the Roman Army* (Yale, 1976), II, p. 142.
47. Caesar, *de Bello Gallico*, IV, p. 24.
48. Caesar, *de Bello Africo*, p. 20.
49. J.F.C. Fuller, *Julius Caesar: Man, Soldier and Tyrant* (London, 1965), p. 316.
50. See Introduction and Chapter 3, pp. 43, 49.
51. Ammianus Marcellinus, XXIII, pp. 3, 9.

Chapter Seven

1. Michael, Calvert, *Prisoners of Hope* (London, 1952), p. 282; a *machan*, an Urdu word, is a tree-top platform used by big game hunters.
2. For further reading see F.M. Stenton, *Anglo-Saxon England* (Oxford, 1971); J. Peddie, *Alfred the Good Soldier* (Bath, 1989).
3. Calvert, *op. cit.*
4. Caesar, *de Bello Gallico*, pp. vii, 14–31; vii, 68–90.
5. *ibid.*, pp. vii, 4.
6. *ibid.*
7. *ibid.*, pp. vii, 14.
8. Frontinus, *Stratagems*, III, pp. vii, 4.
9. Caesar, *de Bello Gallico*, pp. vii, 23.
10. Appian, *Iberica*, p. 90.
11. Caesar's War Commentaries, *de Bello Civili*, pp. iii, 269.
12. *ibid.*, p. 270.
13. Caesar, *de Bello Gallico*, pp. vii, 22.
14. *ibid.*, pp. vii, 18.
15. *ibid.*, pp. vii, 19.
16. Livy, *The War with Hannibal* (Penguin Classics, Harmondsworth, 1965), pp. xxiv, 34.
17. Jacques Boudet (ed.), *The Ancient Art of Warfare* (London, 1966), Vol. I, Chart 8, p. 128.
18. Josephus, *The Jewish War*, III, pp. 204–32.

19. *ibid.*, pp. v, 162.
20. Aeneas the Tactician, *The Defence of Fortified Positions*, p. xxxv.
21. *ibid.*, p. xxxiii.
22. *ibid.*, p. xxxiv.
23. Josephus, *op. cit.*, pp. v, 472.
24. Livy, *op. cit.*, pp. xxvi, 45.
25. *ibid.*, pp. xxxviii, 7.
26. Polybius, The *Histories*, pp. ix, 41.
27. *ibid.*
28. See *Illustrated London News*, Archaeological Section 2150, 21 September 1963, p. 425: a brief account of the Leeds–London Universities Expedition to Motya in collaboration with the Mission Archaeologique Française.
29. Arrian, *Anabasis of Alexander I*, I, pp. xx–xxiii.
30. Livy, *op. cit.*, pp. xxiv, 34.
31. *ibid.*
32. *ibid.*, pp. xxvi, 47.
33. As in E.W. Marsden, *Greek and Roman Artillery, Historical Development* (Oxford, 1969), pp. vi, 117, which, for a full account of the working on ancient artillery weaponry, should be read with his *Greek and Roman Artillery, Technical Treatises* (Oxford, 1971).
34. *ibid.*
35. Josephus, *op. cit.*, pp. iii, 158–83.
36. *ibid.*, pp. v, 279.
37. 2 Chronicles 32:30: 'This same Hezekiah also stopped the upper watercourse of Gihon, and brought it straight down to the west side of the City of David.'
38. Josephus. *op. cit.*, pp. v, 25.
39. *ibid.*, pp. v, 302.
40. See Appendix 4 for chronological sequence of events.
41. Josephus, *op. cit.*, pp. v, 472.

Bibliography

PRIMARY SOURCES

Aeneas, *The defence of fortified positions*
Ammianus Marcellinus, *Rerum gestarum libri*
Appian, *Iberica*
Arrian, *Anabasis of Alexander I*
Asclepiodotus, *Tactics*
Caesar, *de Bello Alexandrino*
———, *de Bello Africo*
———, *de Bello Civili*
———, *de Bello Gallico*
———, *de Bello Hispaniensi*
Cassius Dio, *Historia Romana*
Cicero, *Ad Familiares*
Diodorus, *Bibliotheca historica*
Frontinus, *Strategemata*
Heron, *Belopoeica*
Homer, *Iliad*
Josephus, *The War of the Jews*
Livy, *History of Rome*
Onasander, *The General*
Philon, *Belopoecia*
Pliny the Younger, *Epistulae*
Plutarch, *Julius*
Polybius, *Rise of the Roman Empire*
Procopius, *Anecdota*
Strabo, *The Geography*
Suetonius, *Augustus*
———, *Julius Caesar*
———, *Claudius*
Tacitus, *Agricola*
———, *Annals*
———, *Germania*
———, *Histories*
Vegetius, *Epitoma rei militaris*
Velleius Paterculus, *Early Roman History*

Secondary Sources

Adams, John Paul. *Logistics of the Roman Army*, Yale, 1976.

Boudet, Jacques. *The Ancient Art of Warfare*, London, 1966.

Boyle, Patrick and J. Musgrave-Wood. *Jungle, Jungle, Little Chindit*, London, 1944.

Breeze, David. 'The Logistics of Agricola's Final Campaign', *Talanta*, 16–19, 1987–8.

Casson, Lionel. *Ships and Seamanship in the Ancient World*, Princeton, 1971.

Calvert, Michael. *Prisoners of Hope*, London, 1952.

Chevalier, Raymond. *Roman Roads*, London, 1989.

Von Clausevitz. *Principles of War* (repr.), London, 1943.

Eady, Major H.G. 'The Tank', *United Services Journal*, 1926.

Dain, A. *Naumachia*, Paris, 1943.

Davies, R.W. 'The Roman Military Medical Service', *Sonderdruck aus dem Saalburg-Jahrbuch*, 1970.

Dodge, Colonel T. 'Caesar', *Great Captains Series*, Boston, Mass., 1892.

Engels, Donald W. *Alexander the Great and the Logistics of the Macedonian Army*, Berkeley, 1978.

Farmer, Dr H.G. *The Rise and Development of Military Music*, London, 1912.

Feller, Arthur. *The Fall of the Roman Empire: The Military Explanation*, London, 1986.

Frere, S.S. and J.K.S. St Joseph. *Roman Britain from the Air*, Cambridge, 1983.

Fuller, Major General J.F.C. *Julius Caesar, Man, Soldier and Tyrant*, London, 1965.

Froude, J.A. *Caesar, A Sketch*, London, 1886.

Gudea, Nicolae. 'The Defensive System of Roman Dacia', *Britannia*, vol. 10, 1979.

Hardy, Robert. *Longbow*, Cambridge, 1976.

Harris, W.V. *War and Imperialism in Republican Rome, 327–70 BC*, Oxford, 1979.

Holmes, Dr T. Rice. *Caesar's Conquest of Gaul*, Oxford, 1911.

Hyland, Ann. *Equus, The Horse in the Roman World*, London, 1990.

Keppie, L. *The Making of the Roman Army*, London, 1984.

Last, Professor H. *Cambridge Ancient History*, Cambridge, 1932.

Lewis and Short, *Freund's Latin Dictionary*, Oxford, 1879.

McGrail, Sean. 'Cross Channel Seamanship and Navigation in the late First Millennium BC', *Oxford Journal of Archaeology*, 1983.

Marsden, E.W. *Greek and Roman Artillery, Historical Development*, Oxford, 1969.

——. *Greek and Roman Artillery, Technical Treatises*, Oxford, 1971.

Mommsen, Theodor. *The History of Rome*, London, 1911.

Montgomery, Field Marshal Viscount. *Concise History of Warfare*, London, 1968.

Pakenham, T. *The Boer War*, London, 1979.

Payne-Gallwey, Sir Ralph. *The Projectile Throwing Engines of the Ancients*, London, 1907.

——. *The Crossbow*, 2nd edn, London, 1958.

Peddie, John. *Alfred, The Good Soldier*, Bath, 1989.

——. *Invasion, The Roman Conquest of Britain*, Gloucester, 1987.

Richmond, Sir Ian. *Trajan's Army on Trajan's Column*, British School at Rome, London, 1982.

Richmond, I.A. and J. McIntyre. 'Tents of the Roman Army and Leather from Birdowald', *Transactions of the Cumberland and Westmoreland Archaeological Society*, 1934.

Sachs, Curt. *The History of Musical Instruments*, London, 1940.

Spiedel, M.P. *Eagle Bearer and Trumpeter*, Rheinisches Landesmuseum, Bonn, 1967.

Slim, Field Marshal Sir William. *Defeat into Victory*, London, 1956.

Stenton, F.M. *Anglo-Saxon England*, Oxford, 1971.

Tarn, W.W. *Hellenistic Military and Naval Developments*, Cambridge, 1930.

Wacher, John. *Roman Britain*, London, 1978.

Webster, Graham. *The Roman Imperial Army*, 2nd edn, London, 1979.

Wilmot, Chester. *The Struggle for Europe*, London, 1952.

Index